BARRON'S

SSAT®/ ISEE®

SECONDARY SCHOOL ADMISSION TEST/ INDEPENDENT SCHOOL ENTRANCE EXAM

3RD EDITION

Kathleen J. Elliott, M.A.
English Department Chair
Lexington Catholic High School
Lexington, Kentucky

Carmen Geraci, M.A.
English Teacher
Lexington Catholic High School
Lexington, Kentucky

David Ebner, Ph.D.
Former Mathematics Teacher
High School of Fashion Industries
New York, New York
New York University, New York, New York
Touro College, New York, New York

BARRON'S

All inquiries should be addressed to:
Barron's Educational Series, Inc.
250 Wireless Boulevard
Hauppauge, NY 11788
www.barronseduc.com

ISBN: 978-1-4380-0225-5

ISSN 2327–2392

PRINTED IN THE UNITED STATES OF AMERICA

9 8 7 6 5 4 3 2

10%
POST-CONSUMER
WASTE
Paper contains a minimum
of 10% post-consumer
waste (PCW). Paper used
in this book was derived
from certified, sustainable
forestlands.

Contents

3 Verbal Skills Review   133

4 Reading Comprehension Review   171

Introduction to the SSAT and ISEE Exams

CHAPTER 1

DOING IT RIGHT!

Welcome!

As you know, getting high scores on any exam involves preparation. This preparation breaks down into two categories. Naturally, you need to show mastery of intellectual abilities—like reading comprehension or use of basic mathematic equations. But nowadays, to succeed at testing requires more than merely knowing information; you also need to be savvy about test-taking skills—like pacing yourself or knowing when to guess.

Those disciplined enough to set aside time for these kinds of preparation are, logically, in the best position to test well on such exams as the Independent School Entrance Examination (ISEE) and the Secondary School Admission Test (SSAT); these tests evaluate your intellectual ability as well as your ability to take standardized exams. The bottom line is this: You should prepare, carefully and diligently, before taking the ISEE and the SSAT exams.

However, as well intentioned as your desire might be, time has a way of slipping away. Testing day rapidly approaches, accompanied by feelings of (let's face it) fear. Your pulse races, your hands grow clammy, and your thoughts endlessly cycle through nightmares of self-doubt. You approach the testing site feeling, deep down, that you just aren't ready.

We at Barron's have designed the book you hold in your hands to accommodate students, like you, who find themselves faced with the trial of standardized exams, students who may well have studied hard but are nervous. If you have had the foresight and the self-discipline to begin preparations for your high school placement exam well in advance, congratulations! Barron's *SSAT/ISEE* is designed to reinforce the skills you already possess with plenty of practice sections and thoroughly explained answer keys.

That being said, we at Barron's have designed the book you hold in your hands to accommodate students like you who may have let time slip away from them. If you have purchased this book hoping for last minute tips on acing the exam, rest assured! This book comes to you chock full of study tips, elimination strategies, and information about exam format—information sure to help you succeed. Moreover, our book offers numerous and varied practice selections designed to make you comfortable with testing format, requirements, and pacing.

Now, we know that you want to get right to work. However, we would like to take a minute to thank you for purchasing this book. We strongly believe that our preparation guide to the ISEE and SSAT exams is the best on the market, and we hope that, by the time you finish using our guide, you will feel the same way. We prepared our book to offer more information about the exam you are preparing to take, more opportunities for further practice, and more thoroughly researched answer key explanations than our competitors. We believe that you have in your hands the best tool for "doing it right." So—let's get started!

THE ISEE VERSUS THE SSAT: AN OVERVIEW

The ISEE and the SSAT are the main two entrance exams for *non-parochial* private high schools. By contrast, the COOP (Cooperative Admissions Exam), HSPT (High School Placement Test), and the TACHS (Test for Admission into Catholic High Schools) are the main two entrance exams for *parochial* private high schools.

You should be aware that the ISEE and the SSAT differ somewhat in their organization and in their order of testing. The SSAT, for example, allows a wider range of reading comprehension topics, whereas the ISEE limits its reading passages to science and history selections. The SSAT begins with an essay, whereas the ISEE ends with one; the ISEE gives you four options for every question, whereas the SSAT gives you five. The ISEE differs significantly from the SSAT regarding such issues as whether you should guess when taking the exam. Make sure to familiarize yourself with the specific information regarding the exam you will take. Check out our discussion of the testing formats of the ISEE (beginning on page 3) and the SSAT (beginning on page 7) later in this introduction you are now reading; we discuss the various sections of the exams, what they test, and how they test. We also provide practice tests (two for the SSAT—see page 235—and two for the ISEE—see page 355) for your use. Finally, if you have more questions regarding the ISEE and/or SSAT, you can contact the companies directly.

Independent School Entrance Examination
Educational Records Bureau
470 Park Avenue South
New York, NY 10016
www.erblearn.org (Web site)
(800) 446-0320
(212) 672-9800 (fax)
isee@erblearn.org (e-mail)

Secondary School Admission Test
SSAT BOARD
CN 5339
Princeton, NJ 08543
www.ssat.org (Web site)
(609) 683-4440
(609) 683-4507 (fax)
(800) 442-7728 (fax)
info@ssat.org (e-mail)

THE INDEPENDENT SCHOOL ENTRANCE EXAMINATION

The ISEE is a multiple-choice exam, offered by the Educational Records Bureau (ERB), designed to test what you have learned as well as how you learn. The exam is offered at upper, middle, and lower levels, based upon your current grade in school. Regardless of the level at which you take the exam, the ISEE consists of five testing sessions that last approximately 2 hours and 45 minutes distributed across a 3-hour testing period that also includes two scheduled, 5-minute breaks (one after the second, the other after the fourth testing period).

The ERB gives ISEE exams periodically beginning in November and continuing into May, in more than 30 cities across the country. Check out the ISEE application booklet or the Web site for more information on locations and dates of testing. Exam applicants should preregister for the ISEE by mail or online (for $98) or by phone or fax (for $118). Students who miss the registration deadline can sometimes register late or (very rarely) register on a walk-in basis. The ERB can make special arrangements to accommodate students who have documented testing-related disabilities for additional fees; furthermore, the ERB offers fee waivers for students with documented financial need. Contact the ERB directly for details (and fees) concerning any of these special registration and/or testing circumstances. Payment can come in the form of credit card (Visa, MasterCard, or American Express) or personal check made out to the Educational Records Bureau (mail-in only).

Despite a wide range of application options, applicants for the ISEE can take the exam only one time during a six-month period. You should only attempt this exam when seriously applying to your desired high school. Seven to ten business days after your testing date, your parents will receive a copy of your scores. You may send copies of your score reports to as many as six high schools you hope to attend (identified by the appropriate identification codes and numbers listed on the ISEE registration forms); you can also order up to six additional test reports for a surcharge. Contact the ERB directly regarding the cost of additional reports, as prices are subject to change.

It is your job to figure out which exam level you ought to take. Unless your school administrators tell you otherwise, you should determine which level exam to take using the following chart:

If you are currently in . . .	then you should take the . . .
4th or 5th grade	Lower Level exam
6th or 7th grade	Middle Level exam
8th grade or higher	Upper Level exam

TIP

For the most current information on test dates, fees, and registration, check the ISEE official web site: *www.erblearn.org*

Regardless of the level at which you are taking the ISEE, the format of the exam remains basically the same, as the following chart indicates.

ISEE: Approximately a 2¾ hour-long exam spread over an approximate 3-hour period. Administrators give two breaks.

Section	Upper Level	Middle Level	Lower Level
Verbal Reasoning (see Ch. 3)	40 questions/ 20 minutes	40 questions/ 20 minutes	34 questions/ 20 minutes
Quantitative Reasoning (Ch. 2)	37 questions/ 35 minutes	37 questions/ 35 minutes	38 questions/ 35 minutes
Break	5 minutes	5 minutes	5 minutes
Reading Comprehension (Ch. 4)	36 questions/ 35 minutes	36 questions/ 35 minutes	25 questions/ 25 minutes
Math Achievement (Ch. 2)	47 questions/ 40 minutes	47 questions/ 40 minutes	30 questions/ 30 minutes
Break	5 minutes	5 minutes	5 minutes
Essay (Ch. 5)	1 question 30 minutes	30 minutes	30 minutes

Please note that while this chart implies a particular order to the exam, the ERB reserves the right to vary the order in which a testing section occurs. The test could proceed from verbal to quantitative as easily as from verbal to reading comprehension.

The material in this particular prep book is geared toward students taking the Upper Level exam. However, if you plan to take the Lower or Middle Level exam, parts of this book will still be helpful. Even the study aids provided by the Educational Records Bureau (the people who create and administer the ISEE) and sent to Lower or Middle exam takers target the Upper Level exam rather than the Lower or Middle exams. Rest assured, the Lower, Middle, and Upper exams are identical in type of question, formatting of the exam, and test-taking strategy; what differs is the difficulty level of the questions. Indeed, if you, as a Lower or Middle Level exam taker can master the Upper Level exam, you're probably in better shape for your test than you would be had you only studied material specifically targeted for the lower or middle difficulty level.

The best way to study for the ISEE is to try out some sample questions, so be sure to check out the chapters that review the skills tested in each section (see chart above) as well as the practice tests that appear at the end of this prep book. However, we think that it is useful for you to have a general sense of how the test is put together. Before you try out either the sample questions or the practice exams, take a peek at the following information.

Sections of the Test

Using objective testing format (i.e., multiple choice), the ISEE evaluates four basic academic skills:

1. **Verbal Reasoning**
2. **Quantitative Reasoning**
3. **Reading Comprehension**
4. **Mathematics Achievement**

The tests on Verbal and Quantitative Reasoning all focus more on judging how well you process new information and detect patterns; by contrast, the Reading Comprehension and Math Achievement sections focus more on judging how well you remember skills learned in school (e.g., math formulas or grammar and syntax rules).

VERBAL REASONING The ISEE's Verbal Reasoning section focuses on testing two skills: your ability to identify and use synonyms and your ability to identify words in context. You will be asked to answer "choose the best definition" questions (that test your knowledge of synonyms) and "complete the sentence" questions (that test your knowledge of words in context). For specific advice on how to prep for this section, see Chapter 3.

QUANTITATIVE REASONING This section asks you to detect numerical patterns or to use various math skills you have learned in class to answer problems. These questions can range over a vast range of skills. (See Chapter 2.)

READING COMPREHENSION The Reading Comprehension portion of the ISEE tests your ability to read prose passages quickly and for detail. This part of the ISEE tests many skills through coordinated testing exercises. You will be given various reading passages and asked to identify writing elements such as the main idea of the passage or the definition of a word as used in the context of the reading selection. Test writers can also ask you to identify why an author is writing and what the author might write next, if the passage continued. (See Chapter 4.)

MATHEMATICS ACHIEVEMENT You will be asked to compute answers to math equations involving mixed numbers, fractions, decimals, percents, and integers; be sure to review the concepts in Chapter 2 to help clarify your understanding of these topics.

THE ESSAY While the ISEE uses primarily an objective means to test your ability to use various verbal and math skills, it also provides schools with a subjective means of judging your abilities. This subjective testing format comes in the shape of an essay that focuses on a limited, highly polemic (i.e., controversial) topic. In other words, you will be asked to compose an opinionated essay complete with supporting detail. You should know, however, that the Educational Records Bureau does not evaluate your writing; the ERB sends your unread essay, along with your test scores, to the school(s) of your choice to aid with student admission and classroom placement.

Study Tips

At this point you may be wondering how best to maximize your performance on the ISEE. Naturally, you should study, familiarize yourself with the structure and pacing of the exam, and practice taking some tests. Study the chapters that follow and, if you have time and interest, check out the free maiterial on the ISEE web site; you can download or print out their advice and test prep as well. However important studying the material is, you should also pay attention to how the test is laid out on the pages of the testing booklet; we have taken great pains to mimic as well as we could the visual layout of the exam, so as to ease your test-taking nerves. Finally, the ISEE strives for consistency across testing sessions; you will do well to study the following chart, which outlines the type of questions that appear on the ISEE and the frequency with which these types of questions appear. For example, someone taking the Reading Comprehension section of the Upper Level ISEE can expect to see somewhere between 6 and 8 questions that ask him or her to identify a Main Idea question, while someone taking the Lower Level ISEE might only expect to see somewhere between 4 and 7 such questions.

Type of Questions:	Lower Level	Middle Level	Upper Level
Main Idea	4–7	6–8	6–8
Supporting Idea (Fact)	9–10	10–11	8–10
Inference	10–12	11–12	11–15
Vocabulary (Word in Context)	4–6	5	4
Organization/Logic	2–3	3–4	5–7
Tone/Style/Figurative Language	1–4	1–3	1–2

The following hints might also be of some reassurance to you. First, if you're the type of person who likes to write as you think, know that you can write in the test booklet if you need space to figure out problems or make diagrams; however, you are not allowed to bring your own scratch paper, and only answers submitted on the answer form will be scored. Second, don't forget that machines tally up your score, and stray marks will confuse the computer and invalidate answers. Third, as you might expect, you can check your work on the section being tested until the proctor calls an end to the timed testing period. Fourth, ISEE questions are worth one point each, and the test only recognizes correct answers. Since the ISEE treats skipped and wrong answers equally, you should answer every question on this exam, even if you have no clue what the correct answer is. In this case, luck is on your side.

Finally, take the essay seriously. You might be tempted, now that you know that the ERB does not score your writing, to slack off on the writing portion of the exam. Resist the temptation. Not only does the essay help your desired school determine which study options you have, but the essay can be a deciding factor (either in your favor or against) if your scores on the remainder of the exam are less than stunning. To that end, you want to make your writing as easy to read as possible for the school administrators who will one day be reading your work; be sure to use a blue or black ink pen for the essay, which will cut down on smearing and illegibility, and if your cursive handwriting is hard to read, consider printing.

THE SECONDARY SCHOOL ADMISSION TEST

The SSAT is a multiple-choice exam, offered by the Secondary School Admission Test Board (SSATB), designed to test *what you have learned as well as how you learn.* The exam is offered at an Upper and Middle level, based upon your current grade in school. Regardless of the level at which you take the exam, the SSAT consists of five testing sessions that last approximately 2 hours and 35 minutes, distributed across a 3-hour testing period that also includes scheduled breaks.

TIP

Be sure to check the official SSAT web site for the most up-to-date information: *www.ssat.org*

The SSAT dates back to 1950 when the Secondary School Admission Test Board was first developed. The SSAT began as a way to provide a fair evaluation of student performance across schools. The current form of the SSAT operates according to a very flexible schedule, and its test time and location can be set by individual schools and (once per month during the school year and then once more in June), usually on a Saturday. To sign up for the test, check out the contact information on page 2; you may register online or via fax, phone, or mail using a downloaded registration form. If you have special needs—such as economic hardship or a learning disability—be sure to contact the SSAT Board. The organization offers a limited number of test fee waivers, and students with documented disabilities may apply for special testing conditions (like large print or Braille versions of the test and/or even extended testing times, up to an extra 50 minutes per section of the test).

As part of the registration process, you may select two schools to which you will have your score reports sent; you may add additional score reports or, conversely, cancel score reports for an additional fee. After you register, the SSAT Board will send you an Admission Ticket to confirm your testing date. If you find that you need to cancel or change a testing date, you may do so at a cost; call the SSAT Board directly or check out their Web site for the required fee, as prices are subject to change. About two weeks after you take the SSAT, you and the schools you select will receive copies of your SSAT Score Report; your scores will remain on active file for one academic year after you take the SSAT, in case you find you need to request more copies of your results.

It is your job to figure out which exam level you ought to take. Unless your school administrators tell you otherwise, you should determine which level exam to take using the following chart:

If you are currently in . . .	then you should take the . . .
5th, 6th, or 7th grade	Middle Level exam
8th grade or higher	Upper Level exam

Regardless of the level at which you are taking the SSAT, the format of the exam remains basically the same, as the following chart indicates:

SSAT: Approximately a 2½ hour-long exam spread over an approximate 3-hour period. Administrators give two scheduled breaks.

Section	Upper Level	Middle Level
Writing Sample (essay) (Ch. 5)	1 question/25 minutes	1 question/25 minutes
Break	5 minutes	5 minutes
Quantitative Skills (Ch. 5)	25 questions/30 minutes	25 questions/30 minutes
Reading Comprehension (Ch. 4)	40 questions/40 minutes	40 questions/40 minutes
Break	10 minutes	10 minutes
Verbal Skills (Ch. 3)	60 questions/30 minutes	60 questions/30 minutes
Quantitative Skills (Ch. 5)	25 questions/30 minutes	25 questions/30 minutes
Experimental Section	16 questions/15 minutes	16 questions/15 minutes
	Total test time: 3 hours, 5 minutes	

Note that while this chart implies a particular order, the SSAT Board reserves the right to vary the order in which the testing section takes place. The essay portion usually comes first in the testing process, but a quantitative testing section could follow the first break as easily as a reading comprehension section might. It would do you better when studying to know the type of testing and the range of knowledge tested rather than memorizing a particular order in which topics are tested. Also note that the SSAT has increased the amount of time students can use to take the test by 30% since its inception, allowing students taking the test to finish the SSAT within the scheduled testing time more comfortably.

The material in this particular prep book is geared toward students taking the Upper Level exam. However, if you are supposed to take the Middle Level exam, you can still use this book to prepare for the exam. Rest assured: the Middle and Upper exams are identical in type of questions, formatting of the exam, and test-taking strategy; what differs is the difficulty level of the questions. Indeed, if you, as a Middle Level exam taker can master the Upper Level exam, you're probably in better shape for your test than you would be had you only studied material specifically targeted for the Middle Level.

The best way to study for the SSAT is to try out some sample questions, so be sure to check out the chapters that review the skills tested in each section (see chart above) as well as the practice tests that appear at the end of this prep book. However, we think that it is useful for you to have a general sense of how the test is put together. Before you try out either the sample questions or the practice exams, take a peek at the following information.

Sections of the Test

The SSAT tests academic skills using four different testing sections:

1. **Writing Skills**
2. **Quantitative Skills** (broken up into two testing sections)
3. **Reading Comprehension Skills**
4. **Verbal Skills**

WRITING SKILLS The SSAT begins with a subjective method of examining your abilities: an essay. Note that the SSAT Board does not evaluate this essay, but sends it, unread, with your scores to the schools indicated during registration. The school(s) of your choice is (are) free to use this essay in whatever way seen fit (as a way of making final judgment on a potentially weak application or as a means of determining classroom placement once admission decisions have been finalized). For help on how to make your writing as strong as possible, see Chapter 5.

QUANTITATIVE SKILLS The first part of this section focuses on your ability to work with basic addition, subtraction, multiplication, and division; percents, fractions, and decimals; ordering of numbers (greater than and less than); ratio and proportion; positive and negative numbers; odd and even numbers; sequences; frequency; basic algebra and geometry; angle measurement; and graph interpretation. The second part of the exam tests your problem-solving skills and your ability to use previous knowledge of mathematic concepts to solve modern problems. This portion of the exam asks a wide range of questions. For further practice, see Chapter 2.

READING COMPREHENSION SKILLS This section attempts to judge how well you comprehend what you read and your ability to infer vocabulary meaning through reading. Typically you need to read six to eight reading passages; you can be sure you will be asked to infer the meanings of words based on their usage in the reading passages or to create a title capturing the main idea of the passage. While, naturally, you are called upon to use your reading skills, the emphasis is on showing that you understand what you read. For more practice, see Chapter 4.

VERBAL SKILLS This section focuses on two specific types of questions: (1) synonyms and (2) antonyms. These questions test your ability to identify words and their relationship to each other. The SSAT will also ask you to show off your vocabulary skills by asking you to make analogies between words. Clearly, then, you need a good vocabulary for acing this section, so for further practice, check out Chapter 3.

One last comment. The SSAT continually tries to maintain rigorous and appropriate tests. To this end, it often includes experimental sections, consisting of 16 questions. You may be asked to take this part. It is not scored, but your answers help shape future exams, so take these challenges seriously.

Helpful Tips

At this point you may be wondering how best to maximize your performance on the SSAT. Naturally, you should study, familiarize yourself with the structure and pacing of the exam, and practice taking some tests. However, the following hints might also be of some reassurance.

First, if you're the type of person who likes to write as you think, know that you can write in the test booklet if you need space to figure out problems or make diagrams; however, you are not allowed to bring your own scratch paper, and only answers submitted on the answer form will be scored. Second, don't forget that machines tally up your score, and stray marks will confuse the computer and invalidate answers. Third, as you might expect, you can check your work on the section being tested until the proctor calls an end to the timed testing period.

More strategically, you should know how the SSAT scores your answer. Correct SSAT questions are worth one point each; skipped answers receive no penalty yet no credit. The SSAT, however, penalizes incorrect answers by $1/4$ point. Given that you run a risk of losing points by giving wrong answers, you should not guess wildly. If you cannot rule out any of the five answer options as being absolutely wrong, then you should not hazard a guess at all. However, if you can rule out any answer option (and, the more options you can eliminate, the better), then you should make an educated guess.

How can you make educated guesses? First off, don't assume that the answer will be the option you know least about. Sometimes the correct answer is the most obvious one. That being said, don't automatically pick the answer that seems obvious. Use the training that you've been taught (or will have learned by the time you finish studying this book). Check out root stems, prefixes, and suffixes. Review your math, and don't forget to carry or round off as necessary. Revisit your answers, as time allows. As annoying (and repetitive) as it sounds, read the questions carefully, and be sure you know what the question is asking you. Use logic, and stay calm. And, last but not least, practice using test samples, drills, and practice exams—like the ones in this book. Familiarity with the format, the structure, the range of questions, and the timing deadlines can only serve to strengthen your performance on the actual test.

Finally, take the essay seriously. You might be tempted, now that you know that the SSATB does not score your writing, to slack off on the writing portion of the exam. Resist the temptation. Not only does the essay help your desired school determine which study options you have, but the essay can be a deciding factor (either in your favor or against) if your scores on the remainder of the exam are less than stunning. To that end, you want to make your writing as easy to read as possible for the school administrators who will one day be reading your work; be sure to use a blue or black ink pen for the essay, which will cut down on smearing and illegibility, and if your cursive handwriting is hard to read, consider printing.

COUNTDOWN

You may be frustrated if you plan to pick up the skills necessary to ace an exam like the ISEE or the SSAT and move on. Mastering these exams usually comes as the result of hard, consistent work rather than quick attempts to marshal one's wits.

Moreover, the usual method of gauging your progress is not available to you in this case; neither the ISEE nor the SSAT exam publishes test scores achieved on their exams. Therefore, unlike with other standardized tests, you cannot take a practice exam and expect to rank yourself against other entering high school students across the nation. We've said it before, and we'll say it again: Your best method for preparing yourself for the ISEE or the SSAT is simply a great deal of basic skills preparation.

After all, some skills simply get better through consistent use. Verbal ability is one such skill. The more you read, the more you encounter verbal skills tested on exams such as the ISEE and SSAT. Analytical ability is another such skill; making comparisons, detecting contrasts, and analyzing theme and main idea patterns—all of these skills grow sharper with use and are almost impossible to pick up and drop at need. Absolutely the best way to prepare for an exam—and necessarily reduce test anxiety—is to cultivate an appreciation for all things intellectual.

Study Strategies

Cultivating such an appreciation does not have to be tedious; find creative and fun ways to incorporate intellectual activity in your life. First . . . read! Read! READ! Both the ISEE and SSAT, for example, use reading passages that are from four to six paragraphs long; moreover, both use primarily an informative, newsy writing style. Select short passages from weekly news magazines or the topical parts of your local newspapers (e.g., the weekly "science" section or the daily "living and arts" sections), and accustom yourself to identifying the author's intent in writing, the main points of the passage, and the meaning of unfamiliar vocabulary.

Also try out the vocabulary-based puzzles commonly found in local newspapers; games like Scrabble or word jumbles are great for building familiarity with vocabulary while still having fun. And, don't forget about TV game shows like "Who Wants to Be a Millionaire" or "Wheel of Fortune" that offer vocabulary-based questions in addition to their more trivia-based questions. Incorporating tricky ways to study verbal skills, therefore, can be accomplished. For fun yet useful mathematics skills, try logic puzzles and lots of word problems, brain teasers, and number games.

Standardized test takers can also check the SSAT Web site (*www.ssat.org*). Among other informative details, this page offers an SSAT question of the day. You read and answer the question, and immediately a computer scores your answer. This is a quick and easy way to see whether you're getting the hang of the test. Because the Web site does not track whether you are actually registered for the SSAT exam, ISEE test takers can use this resource, too. A vocabulary test is a vocabulary test, no matter who writes it. Take practice opportunities when you can get them.

Probably the second best way to prepare for an exam is to allow yourself sufficient time to review specific details such as how the exam is designed and the topics covered by the exam. We suggest that you maximize your chance of success by following the suggestions made in our chart Acing the Exam: Option A; in this chart we outline a thorough but comfortably paced course of study.

Following Option A requires that you devote a month's preparation to your task. It may be that devoting four weeks of preparation to a project is simply not an affordable luxury for you. Relax; just because it is difficult to master an exam by cramming does not mean that it cannot be done. Acing the Exam: Option B, offers a more streamlined but more challenging "quick study" program. You will need to have both the time and the drive to really focus your studying energies; you will be working "on deadline." However, either Option A or Option B should assist you greatly in your quest for a high exam score.

Regardless of the time you have available for studying, remember: Any study is better than no study at all.

Acing the Exam with 1 Month to Go

4 WEEKS AND COUNTING . . .

- Reread the introduction for ISEE, pages 3–7; for SSAT, pages 7–10. These sections will give you a sense of the kinds of questions you face, and the strategy you should use.
- Take a practice exam and score yourself.
- Note particularly troublesome topics.
- Identify questions that most troubled you; use the answer key explanation section to help you pinpoint these questions.
- Study your weak areas.
- Be sure to work through all of the practice sessions.
- Read through the answer key explanations; we present them to help you understand the logic behind the question.
- *Hey, SSAT takers!* Check out the SSAT Question of the Day located at *www.ssat.org* on a daily basis—these are actual questions modeled on the test that you may use as a practice tool.
- Ask for help when you need it—your parents may know the answers and, if they don't, ask your teacher(s) at school. That's what they're there for!

3 WEEKS TO GO . . .

- Study the chapters that discuss topics that *least* troubled you.
- Be sure to work through all of the practice sessions.
- Read through the answer key explanations; we present them to help you understand the logic behind the question.
- Ask for help when you need it! (We really can't stress this advice enough.)

2 WEEKS LEFT . . .

- Go back and review once more the material that *really* troubled you.
- Retake your first practice exam, focusing on the questions you missed.

1 WEEK . . .

- Take a second practice exam and compare your results. You will see improvement, provided you have stuck to your program!
- Review any areas that remain weak.
- Read through the answer key explanations.
- Ask for help when you need it—especially from your teachers!

TIME OUT!

- Give yourself a break. Do not study. Do something relaxing, like watching a movie, reading for pleasure, eating out with friends.
- Make sure you get to bed at a reasonable hour; no amount of preparation can help if you are exhausted and nervous.

Acing the Exam with 1 Week to Go

7 DAYS

- Reread the introduction. For ISEE, pages 3–7; SSAT, pages 7–10. These sections will give you a sense of the kinds of questions you face, as well as a sense of the strategy you should use.
- Take a practice exam and score yourself.
- Note particularly troublesome topics.
- *Hey, SSAT takers!* Check out the SSAT Question of the Day located at *www.ssat.org* on a daily basis—these are actual questions modeled on the test that you may use as a practice tool.

6 DAYS

- Identify the types of questions that confused you most; use the answer key explanation section to help you identify these questions.
- Study the information regarding the topics that *most* troubled you.
- Be sure to work through all of the practice sessions.
- Read through the answer key explanations; we present them to help you understand the logic behind the question.

5 DAYS

- Study the chapters that discuss topics that *least* troubled you.
- Be sure to work through all of the practice sessions.
- Read through the answer key explanations; we present them to help you understand the logic behind the question.

4 DAYS

- Talk with your teacher(s) at school if you need help; they are your most efficient help resource.

3 DAYS

- Review any stubborn trouble spots; extra work can't hurt.

2 DAYS

- Take a second practice exam and compare your results. You will see improvement, provided you have stuck to your program!
- Review any areas that remain weak.
- Read through the answer key explanations.

TIME OUT!

- Give yourself a break. Do not study. Do something relaxing, like watching a movie, reading for pleasure, eating out with friends.
- Make sure you get to bed at a reasonable hour; no amount of preparation can help if you are exhausted and nervous.

REALITY CHECK

No matter your level of test preparation, you may experience test-taking anxieties prior to the exam. We offer in this section a series of anxiety-reducing tips that we hope will help you do your best on the exam. Some of the tips we promote require long-term practice before you can see results; however, all are good advice.

GET FIT

- People who exercise handle stress better than people who do not. Get in the habit of following a reasonable, sustainable exercise regimen.

GET REST

- Recent studies show that people, especially men, who do not get regular, adequate sleep run a greater risk of developing psychoses than those who do. Your brain and body need sleep; give them adequate rest.

GET PACKED

- Gather together all items you will need prior to testing day so that they are ready to bring on testing day. We suggest you bring the following: Admission Ticket, three or four No. 2 (or equivalent) lead pencils, an eraser, two black or blue ink pens, a sweater or light jacket (in case of a cold room).

  Do NOT bring any of the following: books, papers, calculators, beepers, phones, or watches with activated alarm functions.

GET FED

- Taking tests on an empty stomach—or fueled by the empty carbohydrates in a donut or candy bar—is a sure-fire mistake. Your body needs a constant source of energy—not the roller coaster ride such foods contain. At the very least, drink a big glass of milk.

GET THERE

- Make sure you know where your testing site is and how long it takes to get there. Arrive at your testing site between 15 and 30 minutes early. Late arrivals will not be admitted.

GET PSYCHED!

- Remind yourself that you are prepared for your exam. Relax. Breathe. Concentrate.

GET FOCUSED

- Follow the directions exactly as they are asked. Record your answers clearly and accurately, filling in the circles on the answer grid completely. Erase any changes completely (or else the answering machine may score your erasures as answers). Pace yourself. If in doubt, guess strategically.

CONCLUSION

You have now finished the introductory section of this study guide. As a review, see the table of questions that follows. You should have a sense of your task and a sense of how you will master it. You are now ready to begin your study session, probably by taking your first practice exam.

Take a deep breath and plunge in. You'll be great!

Good luck!

Summary of SSAT and ISEE

	SSAT	ISEE
Type of exam	Multiple choice	Multiple choice
Where may I obtain information regarding the exam?	Secondary School Admissions Testing Board, CN 5339, Princeton, NJ 08543 Phone: (609) 683-4440 Fax: (800) 442-SSAT (7728) Fax: (609) 683-4507 E-mail: *info@ssat.org* *www.ssat.org*	Educational Records Bureau 220 East 42nd Street New York, NY 10017 Phone: (212) 672-9800 (800) 446-0320 (customer service) (800) 989-3721 x 312 (special testing circumstances) Fax: (212) 672-9800 E-mail: *isee@erblearn.org*
What are the different levels of the exam and for which grades are they offered?	Middle Level: Given in grades 5–7 for admission to grades 6–8. Upper Level: Given in grades 8–11 for admission to grades 9–12.	Lower Level: Given in grades 4–5 for admission to grades 5–6. Middle Level: Given in grades 6–7 for admission to grades 7–8. Upper Level: Given in grades 8–11 for admission to grades 9–12.
How can I register for the exam and what are the costs?	Call (609) 683-4440 for form and register by mail or register online at *www.ssat. org*. For Americans and Canadians, the cost varies from $80 for the elementary level test to $116 for the middle and upper level tests.	Register by mail or online for $98 or by phone at (800) 446-0320 for $118.

Summary of SSAT and ISEE (continued)

	SSAT	ISEE
Is there a late registration?	Yes	Yes
Are walk-ins permitted?	Yes	No
Should I guess?	There's a penalty for guessing, but if you're able to eliminate one or two choices, it pays to guess.	Yes
May I use a calculator?	No	No
What is the format of the exam?	One essay; the remaining questions are multiple choice.	One essay; the remaining questions are multiple choice.
Is there any passing grade on the exam?	No. Each school has its own standards for admission.	No. Each school has its own standards for admission.
How can I prepare for the exam?	Review the verbal and math sections of this book. Use a timer when you take the practice exams.	Review the verbal and math sections of this book. Use a timer when you take the practice exams.
What does the score report detail?	Scaled scores Percentile ranks Estimated national percentile ranks Predicted 12th grade SAT score	Scaled scores Percentiles Stanines
Is there an essay and, if so, is it graded?	One ungraded essay.	One ungraded essay.
Which subjects are tested?	Reading, Mathematics, Verbal Skills, and Writing	Reading, Mathematics, Verbal Skills, and Writing
What are the different parts of the exam?	Essay—25 minutes Quantitative 1 (Math)—25 questions, 30 minutes Quantitative 2 (Math)—25 questions, 30 minutes Verbal—60 questions (Synonyms, 30 questions and Analogies, 30 questions), 30 minutes Reading Comprehension—40 questions, 40 minutes	For the Upper Level Exam Essay—30 minutes Verbal Reasoning—40 questions, 20 minutes Quantitative Reasoning—37 questions, 35 minutes Reading Comprehension—36 questions, 35 minutes Math Achievement—47 questions, 40 minutes
Is the exam the same every year?	No. The exam changes to some extent. However, this book can prepare you for the exam.	No. The exam changes to some extent. However, this book can prepare you for the exam.
May I take the test privately?	No	You may register with an educational consultant and take the test privately for an additional fee. Check the Web site *www.erblearn.org*.

Mathematics Review

CHAPTER 2

INTRODUCTION

The following topics are included in this mathematics review section:

Integers	Pythagorean theorem
Fractions	Circles
Decimals	Volumes
Percents	Measurements
Algebra	Graphs and tables
Plane geometry	Word problems
Polygons	Statistics

The order of these subjects corresponds, wherever possible, to the development of mathematics. For example, to solve algebra problems, we have to be familiar with integers, fractions, decimals, and percents. And the same holds true for topics further down the list.

If you paid attention in class, you should be familiar with all of these problem areas. On the other hand, if you were dozing off or you need a brush-up, this section is just for you.

All of the problems have been thoroughly dissected in the solution areas, where the same format is presented throughout: statement of the problem, analysis, work, and answer.

To achieve the best results, copy the solutions to the sample problems presented in the text onto your own paper. The exercises following each section should then be a "piece of cake." Selected answer explanations for the exercises appear beginning on page 107.

INTEGERS

Natural and Whole Numbers

The first numbers developed by primitive peoples were the **natural** or **counting numbers**:

$$1, 2, 3, 4, 5, \ldots.$$

It's usually more useful to describe a collection of similar items by using "set" notation. In the preceding example, the set of natural or counting numbers may be indicated by {1, 2, 3, 4, 5, . . .}.

A zero was later added to introduce the set of **whole numbers**: {0, 1, 2, 3, 4, 5 . . .}.

This set may be represented on the number line:

In our number system, the **place** of the digit determines its value. For example, let's take a close look at the following whole number.

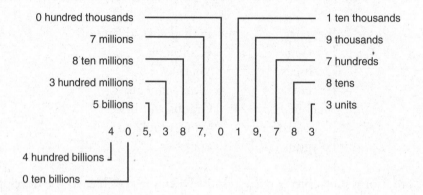

Altogether, the number reads four hundred five billion, three hundred eighty-seven million, nineteen thousand, seven hundred eighty-three.

Example 1

Change 456,372 into words.

ANSWER

Four hundred fifty-six thousand, three hundred seventy-two.

Example 2

Change "Thirty-six billion, four hundred seventy-nine million, five hundred eighteen thousand, four hundred twenty-six" into numerals.

ANSWER

36,479,518,426.

EXERCISES

1. What does the digit 4 represent in the number 456,695,098?
   (A) hundreds   (B) thousands   (C) ten thousands   (D) hundred millions

2. Change 304,473 into words.
   (A) thirty thousand, four hundred seventy-three
   (B) three hundred four thousand, four hundred seventy-three
   (C) thirty-four thousand, four hundred seventy-three
   (D) three thousand, four hundred seventy-three

3. Change "eight hundred fifty-three million, four hundred thirty-two thousand, five hundred sixty-four" into numerals.
   (A) 853,432,000   (B) 853,564   (C) 853,432,564   (D) 8,534,325,640

(see answers on page 105)

Comparing Integers

Negative integers (−1, −2, −3, . . .) were added to the whole numbers, so that we arrived at the set of **integers** (. . . , −3, −2, −1, 0, 1, 2, 3, . . .).

> The farther to the left on the number line, the smaller the number. For example, −2 is smaller than 0.

Example 1

Using the inequality symbol > (greater than), compare 3 and −8.

ANALYSIS

The integer on the right is the larger. If necessary, draw the number line.

WORK

3 > −8 (3 is greater than −8)

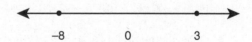

ANSWER

3 > −8

Example 2

Use the inequality symbol < (less than) to compare 6 and 0.

ANALYSIS

The integer on the left is the smaller.

WORK

0 < 6 (0 is less than 6)

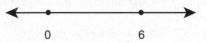

ANSWER

0 < 6

Example 3

Order the numbers 5, −1, and −2, from **smallest to largest**.

ANALYSIS

Draw the number line. The farther to the left, the smaller the number.

WORK

−2 < −1 < 5 (−2 is less than −1, which is less than 5)

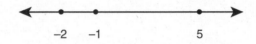

ANSWER

−2 < −1 < 5

EXERCISES

1. Use the inequality symbol > to compare 2, 0, and −2.
   (A) −2 > 2 > 0   (B) 2 > −2 > 0   (C) 0 > −2 > 2   (D) 2 > 0 > −2

2. Use the inequality symbol < to compare −5, 3, and −8.
   (A) −8 < −5 < 3   (B) −8 < 3 < −5   (C) 3 < −8 < −5   (D) −5 < −8 < 3

3. Order the numbers 6, −2, and 0 from largest to smallest.
   (A) 0 > −2 > 6   (B) 6 < −2 < 0   (C) 6 > −2 > 0   (D) 6 > 0 > −2

4. Order the numbers −3, 4, and −1 from smallest to largest.
   (A) −1 < 4 < −3   (B) −3 < −1 < 4   (C) −1 > 4 > −3   (D) 4 < −1 < −3

(see answers on page 105)

Exponents

Mathematicians have developed special shorthand notations. One of these very important notations is the exponential notation.

The following products are more conveniently indicated using exponents:

$$6 \cdot 6 = 6^2 \text{ (or 36)}$$
$$5 \cdot 5 \cdot 5 = 5^3 \text{ (or 125)}$$
$$3 \cdot 3 \cdot 3 \cdot 3 = 3^4 \text{ (or 81)}$$
$$a \cdot a = a^2$$
$$b \cdot b \cdot b \cdot b \cdot b = b^5$$

3 is the exponent.

Let's get technical: $4^3 = 64$ ◄——— The power is 64.

4 is the base.

Example 1

What does $5 \cdot 4^3$ simplify to?

ANALYSIS

Simplify 4^3 and then multiply by 5.

WORK

$$5 \cdot 4^3 = 5 \cdot 4 \cdot 4 \cdot 4 = 5 \cdot 64 = 320$$

ANSWER: 320

Any base raised to a zero exponent is equal to 1.

$$a^0 = 1$$

Example 2

Simplify $5^2 - 6 \cdot 3^0$.

ANALYSIS

Simplify each expression and then perform the operation.

WORK

$$5^2 - 6 \cdot 3^0$$
$$= 5 \cdot 5 - 6 \cdot 1$$
$$= 25 - 6$$
$$= 19$$

ANSWER

19

EXERCISES

1. Simplify $2 \cdot 4^3$.
   (A) 128   (B) 64   (C) 156   (D) 32

2. What does $5^2 \cdot 2^4$ simplify to?
   (A) 200   (B) 400   (C) 80   (D) 150

3. Simplify the following powers and then select the best answer.
   (a) 6^2 (b) 3^3 (c) 4^3
   (A) a < c and b > a   (B) c > b or a < b
   (C) a > b and b > c   (D) b > c or c < a

(see answers on page 105)

Order of Operations

Ordinarily, we perform arithmetic operations from **left to right**, with **multiplication and division preceding addition and subtraction**.

If there are parentheses in an expression, the operations inside the parentheses are performed first.

$$(7 + 5) \cdot 3 = (12) \cdot 3 = 36$$
$$480/6 - 3(4 + 6) = 80 - 3(10) = 80 - 30 = 50$$

Example

Simplify the expression $3 \cdot 4^2 - 48 \div 6 + 2(9 - 4)$.

ANALYSIS

Simplify the exponential expression as well as the expression in parentheses first. Then multiply and divide, working from left to right. Finally, add or subtract.

WORK

$$3 \cdot 4^2 - 48 \div 6 + 2(9 - 4)$$
$$= 3 \cdot 16 - (48 \div 6) + 2(5)$$
$$= 48 - 8 + 10$$
$$= 40 + 10$$
$$= 50$$

ANSWER

50

EXERCISES

1–4. Simplify the expressions.

1. $5^2 - 4 \cdot 3 + 28 \div 4$
   (A) 10   (B) 40   (C) 36   (D) 20

2. $64 - 3^3 + 6 \cdot 2$
   (A) 49   (B) 38   (C) 43   (D) 122

3. $5(-3) + (6 - 1)^2$
   (A) 15   (B) 40   (C) 10   (D) –10

4. $9^1 \cdot (-2)^3$
   (A) –27   (B) 36   (C) –72   (D) 27

(see answers on page 105)

Rounding Off Integers

Sometimes we want to get an approximation of a number. In these cases, we don't need an exact answer, so we "round off."

Aunt Rita is the cashier at a local restaurant. At the end of the week, she wants to round off the money in the till to the nearest ten dollars. If $6,384 is in the till, how much is that, **to the nearest $10**?

To round to any place value, look at the preceding place's value. If it is five or more, round up by one. On the other hand, if the preceding place value's digit is less than five, leave the original digit alone.

$$6 \quad 3 \quad 8 \quad 4$$
$$\uparrow$$

unit's place: $4 < 5$

$6,384 rounds off to $6,380

EXERCISES

1. Round off 456 to the nearest ten.
   (A) 450   (B) 400   (C) 500   (D) 460

2. Ronud off 5,678 to the nearest 100.
   (A) 6,000   (B) 5,600   (C) 5,700   (D) 5,800

3. Find the difference between 153 rounded off to the nearest hundred and 153 rounded off to the nearest ten.
   (A) 50   (B) 40   (C) 60   (D) 47

4. What is the sum of 783 rounded off to the nearest hundred and 437 rounded off to the nearest ten?
   (A) 1,240   (B) 1,140   (C) 2,350   (D) 1,400

(see answers on page 105)

Prime Numbers

A prime number is a counting number that can only be divided by 1 and itself without resulting in a remainder. The number 1 is excluded from the set of prime numbers.

Prime numbers less than 20: 2, 3, 5, 7, 11, 13, 17, 19.

Example 1

Is 48 a prime number?

ANALYSIS

If 48 can be divided by any number other than 1, it is not a prime number.

WORK

48 may be divided by 6:

$$48 \div 6 = 8$$

ANSWER

48 is not a prime number.

Example 2

Which of these numbers is prime?

(A) 17   (B) 18   (C) 22   (D) 35

ANALYSIS

A prime number cannot be divided by any number other than 1 and itself.

WORK

17 can be divided only by 1 and itself.

ANSWER

(A)

EXERCISES

1. What is the next prime number following 28?
   (A) 30   (B) 31   (C) 29   (D) 37

(continued)

2. List the prime numbers between 12 and 21.
   (A) 13, 15, 17   (B) 13, 17, 19   (C) 13, 17, 19, 21   (D) 13, 15, 17, 19

3. What are the prime numbers greater than 7 but less than or equal to 15?
   (A) 9, 11   (B) 9, 11, 13   (C) 9, 14   (D) 11, 13

(see answers on page 105)

Factors and Multiples

Factors are two or more numbers that, when multiplied together, result in another number called a product.

factors   product

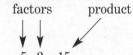

If we multiply 5 times 3, the result is 15: $5 \cdot 3 = 15$.

Prime factors are prime numbers that, when multiplied together, result in a product.

factors   prime factors

$$42 = 21 \cdot 2 = 7 \cdot 3 \cdot 2$$

Common factors are numbers that are factors of two or more numbers.

$\left. \begin{array}{l} 56 = 8 \cdot \underline{7} \\ 21 = 3 \cdot \underline{7} \end{array} \right\}$ The common factor of 56 and 21 is 7.

The *greatest common factor* of two numbers is the common factor with the largest value.

$\left. \begin{array}{l} 54 = \underline{18} \cdot 3 \\ 72 = \underline{18} \cdot 4 \end{array} \right\}$ The greatest common factor of 54 and 72 is 18.

A *multiple* of a particular number is the product of that number by other whole numbers.

$$0 \cdot 3 = 0 \qquad 4 \cdot 3 = 12 \qquad 7 \cdot 3 = 21$$
$$1 \cdot 3 = 3 \qquad 5 \cdot 3 = 15 \qquad 8 \cdot 3 = 24$$
$$2 \cdot 3 = 6 \qquad 6 \cdot 3 = 18 \qquad 9 \cdot 3 = 27$$

0, 3, 6, 9, 12, 15, 18, 21, 24, 27, . . . are all multiples of 3.

Example

Determine a common factor of 15 and 12.

ANALYSIS

Find the factors of each number and then find the common factor.

CHALLENGE QUESTION

Find the greatest common factor of 84 and 28. (See answer on page 105.)

WORK

$$15 = \underline{3} \cdot 5$$
$$12 = \underline{3} \cdot 4$$

ANSWER

3

EXERCISES

1. Find a common factor of 15 and 55.
   (A) 11   (B) 3   (C) 15   (D) 5

2. What is the greatest common factor of 48 and 54?
   (A) 8   (B) 3   (C) 6   (D) 9

3. 14, 21, 28, and 35 are all multiples of what number?
   (A) 3   (B) 5   (C) 2   (D) 7

4. What are the prime factors of 30?
   (A) 10, 3   (B) 3, 5, 2   (C) 15, 2   (D) 5, 6

(see answers on page 105)

FRACTIONS

numerator
↓

A fraction is a number in the form x/y where y is not 0 or 1 and x and y are whole numbers.

↑
denominator

Definitions	Examples
In a *proper fraction*, the numerator is less than the denominator.	$\dfrac{2}{5}, \dfrac{4}{9}, \dfrac{12}{45}$
In an *improper fraction*, the numerator is equal to or larger than the denominator.	$\dfrac{7}{4}, \dfrac{8}{3}, \dfrac{36}{5}, \dfrac{9}{9}$
A *mixed number* is a whole number with a proper fraction remainder.	$8\dfrac{5}{9}, 2\dfrac{3}{4}, 15\dfrac{7}{8}$
When we want the *reciprocal* of a fraction, we invert the fraction.	$\dfrac{5}{3}$ is the reciprocal of $\dfrac{3}{5}$
	$\dfrac{1}{7}$ is the reciprocal of 7 (or $\dfrac{7}{1}$)

Example

Match the items in the two columns:

A	**B**
1. $\dfrac{4}{3}$	(a) Proper fraction
2. $5\dfrac{2}{7}$	(b) Improper fraction
3. $\dfrac{8}{9}$	(c) Mixed number

ANSWER

1b, 2c, 3a

Comparing and Ordering Fractions

To compare fractions, change all denominators to the same common denominator.

Example

Compare $\dfrac{2}{3}$, $\dfrac{1}{2}$, and $\dfrac{3}{4}$ and then determine which of the following statements is true.

(A) $\dfrac{2}{3} > \dfrac{3}{4}$ (B) $\dfrac{1}{2} < \dfrac{3}{4}$ (C) $\dfrac{3}{4} < \dfrac{2}{3}$ (D) $\dfrac{2}{3} < \dfrac{1}{2}$

ANALYSIS

To compare, change all denominators to the same common denominator, 12.

WORK

$\dfrac{2}{3} = \dfrac{8}{12}$ With the same denominators, we can now compare fractions.

$\dfrac{1}{2} = \dfrac{6}{12}$

$\dfrac{3}{4} = \dfrac{9}{12}$

$\dfrac{6}{12} < \dfrac{9}{12}$

(B) $\dfrac{1}{2} < \dfrac{3}{4}$

ANSWER

(B)

Reducing Fractions

Example

Reduce 24/32 to its lowest terms.

ANALYSIS

Rewrite the numerator and the denominator as products of factors and then cancel the common factors.

WORK

$$\frac{24}{32} = \frac{\overset{1}{\cancel{8}} \times 3}{\underset{1}{\cancel{8}} \times 4} = \frac{3}{4}$$

ANSWER

$\dfrac{3}{4}$

> **TIP**
>
> When we reduce a fraction, we keep the numerator and denominator in the same ratio but with smaller numbers. To do this, we cancel like factors.

EXERCISES

Reduce the following fractions to their lowest terms.

1. 42/49
   (A) 6/7   (B) 5/7   (C) 4/9   (D) 6/9

2. 15/45
   (A) 5/9   (B) 5/15   (C) 1/3   (D) 3/9

3. 40/64
   (A) 1/2   (B) 5/8   (C) 20/32   (D) 7/8

(see answers on page 105)

Let's check whether 2/3 and 8/12 are equivalent.

We'll do that by multiplying 2/3 by 4/4 (= 1) and thus changing 2/3 to what we know for sure is an equivalent fraction.

$$\frac{2}{3} \times \frac{4}{4} = \frac{8}{12}$$

We can now clearly see that 2/3 and 8/12 are equivalent.

As a second example, let's determine whether 4/5 and 12/17 are equivalent.

Multiply 4/5 by 3/3 (=1).

$$\frac{4}{5} \times \frac{3}{3} \neq \frac{12}{17}$$

The two fractions 4/5 and 12/17 are not equivalent.

Changing Improper Fractions to Whole or Mixed Numbers

> **DEFINITION**
>
> An **improper fraction** is a fraction whose numerator is larger than its denominator.

Example 1

Change 14/7 to a whole number.

(A) 4   (B) 1   (C) $2\frac{1}{2}$ (D) 2

ANALYSIS

When converting improper fractions to whole or mixed numbers, divide the denominator into the numerator.

WORK

$$\frac{14}{7} = 2$$

ANSWER

(D)

Example 2

Change 25/6 to a mixed number.

ANALYSIS

Divide 25 by 6.

WORK

$$\frac{25}{6} = 4\frac{1}{6}$$

ANSWER

$4\frac{1}{6}$

EXERCISES

Change the following improper fractions to mixed numbers.

1. 32/7

(A) $4\frac{4}{7}$ (B) $3\frac{11}{7}$ (C) $5\frac{2}{7}$ (D) $4\frac{3}{7}$

2. 46/9

(A) 5   (B) $6\frac{1}{9}$ (C) $6\frac{2}{9}$ (D) $5\frac{1}{9}$

3. 54/8

(A) $6\frac{1}{8}$ (B) $7\frac{5}{8}$ (C) $6\frac{3}{4}$ (D) $6\frac{7}{8}$

(see answers on page 105)

Changing Mixed Numbers to Improper Fractions

Example

Change $3\frac{5}{8}$ to an improper fraction.

ANALYSIS

We want to reverse the previous process used to change an improper fraction to a mixed number so, to change $3\frac{5}{8}$ to an improper fraction, multiply 3 by 8 and add the numerator, 5. Then make this number the numerator and leave 8 the denominator.

WORK

$$3\frac{5}{8} = \frac{(3 \cdot 8) + 5}{8} = \frac{29}{8}$$

ANSWER

29/8

EXERCISES

Change the following mixed numbers to improper fractions.

1. $4\frac{3}{5}$

(A) 17/5   (B) 23/5   (C) 15/4   (D) 20/3

(continued)

2. $5\frac{2}{3}$

    (A) 19/3   (B) 17/3   (C) 13/2   (D) 11/3

(see answers on page 105)

Equivalent Fractions

Equivalent fractions are fractions that are equal in value.

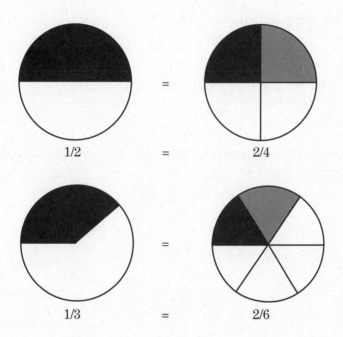

1/2	=	2/4
1/3	=	2/6

Let's change 3/5 to fifteenths.

In order to obtain an equivalent fraction with a 15 in the denominator, we multiply both numerator and denominator by 3 ($\frac{3}{3} = 1$).

$$\frac{3}{5} = \frac{3}{5} \times \frac{3}{3} = \frac{9}{15}$$

Example 1

Which of the following fractions is the equivalent of 5/7?

    (A) 12/17   (B) 9/14   (C) 10/18   (D) 10/14

ANALYSIS

First determine which of the denominators is a multiple of 7. Then multiply the numerator of our original fraction, 5/7, by the same multiple.

WORK

$$\frac{5}{7} \times \frac{2}{2} = \frac{10}{14}$$

ANSWER

(D)

Example 2

Are 4/9 and 12/15 equivalent fractions?

ANALYSIS

Reduce both fractions and then compare.

WORK

The numerator, 4, and the denominator, 9, have no common multiple, so we can't reduce the fraction.

$$\frac{4}{9}$$

On the other hand, we can reduce 12/15.

$$\frac{12}{15} = \frac{4}{5}$$

ANSWER

No

EXERCISES

1. Find the equivalent of 3/7.
   (A) 12/28   (B) 9/12   (C) 15/28   (D) 18/35
2. Is 7/8 equivalent to 21/24?

   Yes

(see answers on page 105)

Operations with Fractions

Example 1

Add 2/3 and 5/7.

ANALYSIS

Change both fractions to the common denominator, 21, and then add.

WORK

$$\frac{2}{3} = \frac{14}{21}$$

$$+\frac{5}{7} = \frac{15}{21}$$

$$\frac{29}{21} = 1\frac{8}{21}$$

ANSWER

$1\dfrac{8}{21}$

Example 2

Simplify

$$\frac{2 - \dfrac{2}{5}}{\dfrac{3}{4} + \dfrac{4}{5}}$$

ANALYSIS

Simplify the numerator and the denominator and then divide.

WORK

$$1\frac{5}{5}$$

$$\cancel{2}$$

$$-\frac{2}{5}$$

$$1\frac{3}{5} = \frac{8}{5}$$

$$\frac{3}{4} = \frac{15}{20}$$

$$+\frac{4}{5} = +\frac{16}{20}$$

$$\frac{31}{20}$$

$$\frac{8}{5} \div \frac{31}{20} = \frac{8}{\cancel{5}_{1}} \cdot \frac{\cancel{20}^{4}}{31} = \frac{32}{31} = 1\frac{1}{31}$$

ANSWER

$1\dfrac{1}{31}$

Example 3

Pedro bought a candy bar that weighed $3\frac{3}{4}$ ounces. If he ate $\frac{2}{3}$ of the bar, how many ounces did he eat?

ANALYSIS

Change $3\frac{3}{4}$ to an improper fraction and then multiply by $\frac{2}{3}$.

WORK

$$3\frac{3}{4} = \frac{15}{4}$$

$$\frac{\overset{5}{\cancel{15}}}{\underset{2}{\cancel{4}}} \cdot \frac{\overset{1}{\cancel{2}}}{\underset{1}{\cancel{3}}} = \frac{5}{2} = 2\frac{1}{2}$$

ANSWER

$2\frac{1}{2}$ ounces

Example 4

Simplify $\frac{4}{5} \div 2\frac{2}{5}$.

ANALYSIS

Change $2\frac{2}{5}$ to an improper fraction and invert. Then multiply $\frac{4}{5}$ by the result.

WORK

$$2\frac{2}{5} = \frac{12}{5}$$

$$\frac{4}{5} \div \frac{12}{5} = \frac{\overset{1}{\cancel{4}}}{\underset{1}{\cancel{5}}} \cdot \frac{\overset{1}{\cancel{5}}}{\underset{3}{\cancel{12}}} = \frac{1}{3}$$

ANSWER

$\frac{1}{3}$

EXERCISES

1. Find $\frac{3}{4}$ of $\frac{1}{2}$ of 240.

   (A) 80   (B) 60   (C) 110   (D) 90

2. Add $2\frac{2}{3}$, $3\frac{1}{4}$, and $\frac{5}{6}$.

   (A) $5\frac{1}{2}$ (B) $4\frac{3}{4}$ (C) $6\frac{3}{4}$ (D) $7\frac{2}{3}$

3. A beaker contains $12\frac{5}{8}$ ounces of alcohol. If $2\frac{3}{4}$ ounces is spilled out, how many ounces remain in the beaker?

   (A) $9\frac{7}{8}$ (B) $8\frac{5}{8}$ (C) $9\frac{5}{6}$ (D) $8\frac{1}{2}$

4. Simplify $\frac{5}{6} \div 2\frac{5}{12}$.

   (A) $\frac{12}{17}$ (B) $\frac{10}{29}$ (C) $\frac{11}{19}$ (D) $\frac{9}{16}$

5. Simplify

$$\frac{2 + \frac{3}{4}}{1\frac{1}{4} - \frac{3}{8}}$$

   (A) $2\frac{3}{5}$ (B) $3\frac{1}{7}$ (C) $3\frac{5}{9}$ (D) $4\frac{2}{5}$

(see answers on page 105)

CHALLENGE QUESTION

A large container is being filled with water at the rate of $2^3/_4$ gallons per minute. If the container leaks at the rate of 1/8 gallon per minute, how long would it take to fill a 14-gallon container?
(See answer on page 105.)

DECIMALS

Decimals are another form of fractions. The following list compares decimals with their equivalents in fraction format:

$$0.8 = 8/10$$
$$5.06 = 5 + 0/10 + 6/100$$
$$46.348 = 46 + 3/10 + 4/100 + 8/1{,}000$$
$$198.7039 = 198 + 7/10 + 0/100 + 3/1{,}000 + 9/10{,}000$$

Reading Decimals

Number	In Words
16.4	Sixteen and four tenths
234.05	Two hundred thirty-four and five hundredths
6.346	Six and three hundred forty-six thousandths
34.5078	Thirty-four and five thousand seventy-eight ten thousandths

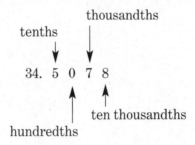

Example

What does the digit 4 represent in the number 563.047?

WORK

ANSWER

Hundredths

Comparing Decimals and Fractions

Example 1

Change $\dfrac{3}{8}$ to a decimal.

ANALYSIS

Divide 3 by 8.

WORK

$$
\begin{array}{r}
0.375 \\
8\overline{)3.000} \\
-24\mathrm{xx} \\
\hline
60 \\
-56 \\
\hline
40 \\
-40 \\
\hline
\end{array}
$$

ANSWER

0.375

Example 2

Change 0.68 to a fraction.

ANALYSIS

Rewrite 0.68 as a fraction and reduce to lowest terms.

WORK

$$0.68 = \frac{68}{100} = \frac{17}{25}$$

ANSWER

17/25

A repeating decimal is indicated by a line over the repeating digits.
For example,

$$0.5555\ldots = 0.\overline{5}$$
$$3.464646\ldots = 3.\overline{46}$$

EXERCISES

1. Which decimal is the equivalent of 5/8?
   (A) 0.655   (B) 0.700   (C) 0.625   (D) 0.850

2. Which fraction is the equivalent of 0.78?
   (A) 7/8   (B) 39/50   (C) 7/100   (D) 7/800

3. Which decimal is the closest equivalent of 2/3?
   (A) 0.6   (B) 0.66   (C) 0.666   (D) 0.676

(see answers on page 105)

Rounding Off Decimals

Example

Round off the product of 3.46 and 2.03 to the nearest tenth.

ANALYSIS

Multiply first. Then look at the hundredth's place. If it's 5 or more, round up. If not, drop all the digits beyond the tenth place.

WORK

$$
\begin{array}{r}
3.46 \\
\times \quad 2.03 \\
\hline
1038 \\
6920 \\
\hline
7.0238
\end{array}
$$

$$7.0238 \approx 7.0$$

hundredth's place

ANSWER

7.0

EXERCISES

1. Round off the sum of 25.06 and 67.43 to the nearest tenth.
   (A) 92.5   (B) 92.4   (C) 92.3   (D) 92.2

2. Round off the product of 8.53 and 0.9 to the nearest hundredth.
   (A) 7.6   (B) 7.681   (C) 7.67   (D) 7.68

(see answers on page 105)

Operations with Decimals

Example 1

Add 4.593, 23.08, and 476.

ANALYSIS

Line up the decimals by adding zeroes as placeholders and then add.

WORK

$$
\begin{array}{r}
4.593 \\
23.080 \\
+\ 476.000 \\
\hline
503.673
\end{array}
$$

ANSWER

503.673

Example 2

Stephanie weighed a beaker filled with liquid. If the beaker and the liquid weighed 15.478 grams and she spilled out 6.9 grams of liquid, how much do the beaker plus the liquid weigh now?

ANALYSIS

Line up the decimals and subtract.

WORK

$$
\begin{array}{r}
15.478 \\
-6.900 \\
\hline
8.578
\end{array}
$$

ANSWER

8.578

Example 3

Multiply 4.56 by 13.7 and round the answer off to the nearest tenth.

ANALYSIS

Add the number of decimal places in both numbers and then use the result to place the decimal in the answer.

WORK

$$
\begin{array}{r}
4.56 \\
\times\ 13.7 \\
\hline
3192 \\
1368\ \ \\
456\ \ \ \ \\
\hline
62.472 \approx 62.5
\end{array}
$$

ANSWER

62.5

Example 4

Divide 229.862 by 5.26.

ANALYSIS

$$\text{dividend} \rightarrow \frac{229.862}{5.26} = \text{Answer} \leftarrow \text{quotient}$$
$$\text{divisor} \rightarrow$$

Count the number of decimal places in the divisor. Move the decimal place in the dividend the corresponding number of places. Bring the decimal straight up into the quotient and then divide.

WORK

```
              43.7
5⟍26.)229⟍86.2
       210 4
        1946
        1578
         368 2
         368 2
```

CHECK

$$43.7 \cdot 5.26 = 229.862 ✓$$

ANSWER

43.7

EXERCISES

1. Add 84.29, 234.752, and 45.
   (A) 364.84   (B) 366.839   (C) 364.04   (D) 364.042

2. Jaime packed 12 scales. If each scale weighed 15.73 ounces, what was the total weight of all the scales?
   (A) 188.736 ounces   (B) 188 ounces   (C) 188.76 ounces   (D) 188.754 ounces

(continued)

3. Multiply 4.58 by 0.7 and round off to the nearest hundredth.
   (A) 3.206   (B) 3.23   (C) 3.208   (D) 3.21

4. Divide 2.0592 by 0.72 and round the answer to the nearest tenth.
   (A) 2.9   (B) 2.86   (C) 2.8   (D) 28.6

(see answers on page 105)

Scientific Notation

(i) $768 = 7.68 \times 100 = 7.68 \times 10^2$

(ii) $5.04 \times 10^4 = 5.04 \times 10 \times 10 \times 10 \times 10 = 5.04 \times 10{,}000 = 50{,}400$

(iii) $4.32 \times 10^{-2} = 4.32 \times 0.1 \times 0.1 = 0.0432$

> **DEFINITION**
>
> **Scientific notation** is a compact way of writing a number as the product of another number between 1 and 10 and a power of 10.

Example

Change 2.35×10^{-2} to its decimal equivalent.

ANALYSIS

$$10^{-1} = \frac{1}{10} \qquad 10^{-2} = \frac{1}{100} \qquad 10^{-3} = \frac{1}{1{,}000}$$

WORK

$$2.35 \times 10^{-2} = 2.35 \times \frac{1}{100} = \frac{2.35}{100} = 0.0235$$

ANSWER

0.0235

EXERCISES

1. Change 4.05×10^3 to a whole number.
   (A) 40.5   (B) 405   (C) 4,050   (D) 40,500

2. Change 6,941 to scientific notation.
   (A) 69.41×10^4 (B) 6.941×10^2 (C) 69.41×10^3 (D) 6.941×10^3

(see answers on page 105)

PERCENTS

Fractions, decimals, and percents are all different methods of indicating a part of a whole unit.

Changing Fractions and Whole Numbers to Percents

Example

Change 4/9 to a two-place percent.

ANALYSIS

Divide 9 into 4.000. Round off to two decimal places. Finally, when changing from a decimal to a percent, multiply by 100 or move the decimal over two places to the right.

WORK

$$
\begin{array}{r}
.444 \approx 0.44 = 44\% \\
9\overline{)4.000} \\
36xx \\
\overline{40} \\
36 \\
\overline{40} \\
36
\end{array}
$$

ANSWER

44%

EXERCISES

1. Change 6/7 to a two-place decimal.
   (A) 0.86   (B) 0.87   (C) 87%   (D) 0.89

2. Change 3/11 to a percent. Choose the best answer.
   (A) 28%   (B) 29%   (C) 0.27   (D) 27%

(see answers on page 105)

Changing Percents to Fractions

Example

Change 45% to a fraction and reduce to lowest terms.

WORK

$$45\% = \frac{45}{100} = \frac{9}{20}$$

ANSWER

9/20

EXERCISE

1. Change 68% to a fraction and reduce to lowest terms.
   (A) 17/25   (B) 68/100   (C) 4/50   (D) 19/100

(see answer on page 105)

Changing Decimals to Percents

Example

Change 2.33 to a percent.

ANALYSIS

To change from a decimal to a percent, multiply by 100 or move the decimal two places to the right.

WORK

$$2.33 = 2.33 \times 100 = 233\%$$

ANSWER

233%

EXERCISE

1. Change 68.5 to a percent.
   (A) 0.685%   (B) 6.85%   (C) 6,850%   (D) 68.5%

(see answer on page 105)

Changing Percents to Decimals

Example

Change 7.32% to a decimal.

ANALYSIS

To change from a percent to a decimal, divide by 100 or move the decimal two places to the left.

WORK

$$7.32\% = \frac{7.32}{100} = 0.0732$$

ANSWER

0.0732

EXERCISE

1. Change 46.3% to a decimal.
   (A) 463   (B) 4.63   (C) 46.3   (D) 0.463

(see answer on page 105)

Finding a Percent of a Number

Example

Find 7% of 430. Round off the answer to the nearest whole number.

ANALYSIS

Change 7% to a decimal and multiply.

WORK

$$7\% = 0.07$$
$$0.07 \times 430 = 30.1$$
$$30.1 \approx 30$$

ANSWER

30

Certain percentages easily convert to fractions:

$$12\frac{1}{2}\% = \frac{1}{8}$$

$$16\frac{2}{3}\% = \frac{1}{6}$$

$$33\frac{1}{3}\% = \frac{1}{3}$$

$$66\frac{2}{3}\% = \frac{2}{3}$$

Applications

Example

If there were 300 people at a dinner and nearly 39% ordered fish, approximately how many ordered fish?

    (A) 200   (B) 150   (C) 120   (D) 110

ANALYSIS

Change 39% to a decimal and multiply by 300. Then choose the closest answer.

WORK

$$39\% = 0.39$$
$$0.39 \times 300 = 117$$
$$117 \approx 120$$

ANSWER

(C)

EXERCISE

1. Out of a sample of 450 people, 8% were vegetarians. How many were not vegetarians?
    (A) 360   (B) 414   (C) 280   (D) 524

(see answer on page 105)

ALGEBRA

In the algebraic expression $a + 6$, a is the variable and 6 is the constant.

Example

Find the value of the expression $a + 6$ when $a = 8$.

ANALYSIS

Substitute 8 for a in the expression $a + 6$.

WORK

$$a = 8: \quad a + 6$$
$$= 8 + 6$$
$$= 14$$

ANSWER

14

> **DEFINITION**
>
> A **variable** is any letter or symbol used to represent a number and it derives its name from the fact that its value may change or vary.

> **DEFINITION**
>
> A **constant**, on the other hand, is a number and it derives its name from the fact that its value never changes.

Find the value of the following expressions when $b = 5$.

1. $4b - 7$

(A) 10   (B) 12   (C) 13   (D) 15

2. $2b^3 + 8$

(A) 198   (B) 212   (C) 286   (D) 258

(see answers on page 105)

Arithmetic Operations with Signed Numbers

RULES FOR ADDITION

(i) If the signs of the addends are the same, add the numbers and use that sign.

$$\begin{array}{r} (3) \\ +(+4) \\ \hline +7 \end{array} \qquad \begin{array}{r} (-2) \\ +(-4) \\ \hline -6 \end{array}$$

(ii) If the signs of the addends are different, subtract and use the sign of the larger.

$$\begin{array}{r} (+6) \\ + (-3) \\ \hline +3 \end{array} \qquad \begin{array}{r} (+2) \\ +(-4) \\ \hline -2 \end{array}$$

RULES FOR SUBTRACTION

Change the sign of the subtrahend (the second number) and use the rules of addition.

$$\begin{array}{r} +6 \\ - \\ -\oplus 2 \\ \hline +4 \end{array} \qquad \begin{array}{r} -7 \\ + \\ -\ominus 3 \\ \hline -4 \end{array} \qquad \begin{array}{r} +3 \\ + \\ -\ominus 4 \\ \hline +7 \end{array} \qquad \begin{array}{r} -2 \\ - \\ -\oplus 6 \\ \hline -8 \end{array}$$

RULES FOR MULTIPLICATION

(i) If the signs of the factors are the same, the product is positive.

$$(+3)(+4) = +12 \qquad (-2)(-9) = +18$$

(ii) If the signs of the factors are different, the product is negative.

$$(-4)(+6) = -24 \qquad (+7)(-3) = -21$$

RULES FOR DIVISION

(i) If the signs of the dividend and divisor are the same, the quotient is positive.

$$\frac{+8}{+2} = +4 \qquad \frac{-10}{-5} = +2$$

(ii) If the signs of the dividend and divisor are different, the quotient is negative.

$$\frac{+6}{-2} = -3 \qquad \frac{-9}{+3} = -3$$

Example 1

The average weight of a student on the soccer team is 159 pounds. Find Ruben's weight if the signed numbers represent pounds above (+) and below (−) the average weight.

Deviation from average weight	+11	−12	+15	−2	+4
Name	Jaime	Ruben	Clotilde	Oscar	Mary

ANALYSIS

Ruben is 12 pounds below the average weight, 159.

WORK

$$\begin{array}{r} +159 \\ -\ 12 \\ \hline 147 \end{array}$$

ANSWER

147

Example 2

Subtract

$$\begin{array}{r} (+34) \\ -(+89) \\ \hline \end{array}$$

ANALYSIS

Change the sign of the subtrahend and use the rules of addition.

WORK

$$\left.\begin{array}{r} + \ 34 \\ - \\ - \oplus 89 \\ \hline -55 \end{array}\right\} +34 - 89 = -55$$

ANSWER

−55

Example 3

Multiply: $(-3)(+4)(-2)(-4)$

ANALYSIS

Multiply the integers, and then count the number of negatives. An odd number of negatives will result in a negative answer, whereas an even number of negatives will result in a positive answer.

WORK

$$(-3)(+4)(-2)(-4)$$
$$= (-12)(+8) = -96$$

ANSWER

−96

Example 4

Divide −112 by −8.

ANALYSIS

When the signs of both the dividend and divisor are the same, the quotient is positive.

WORK

$$\frac{-112}{-8} = +14$$

ANSWER

+14

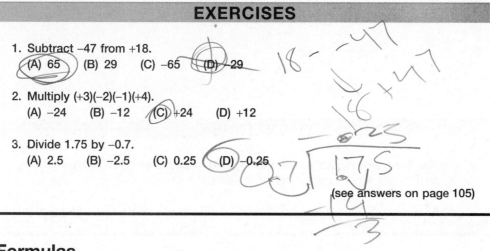

EXERCISES

1. Subtract –47 from +18.
   (A) 65   (B) 29   (C) –65   (D) –29

2. Multiply (+3)(–2)(–1)(+4).
   (A) –24   (B) –12   (C) +24   (D) +12

3. Divide 1.75 by –0.7.
   (A) 2.5   (B) –2.5   (C) 0.25   (D) –0.25

(see answers on page 105)

Formulas

A formula links together variables and constants in some sort of relationship. Given certain information, we can go on to find the value of an unknown quantity in the relationship.

In the United States and in English-speaking countries, temperature is generally measured on the Fahrenheit scale. The rest of the world measures heat in Celsius (or Centigrade). The Swedish astronomer Anders Celsius developed the Celsius scale. It actually makes more sense than the Fahrenheit scale because there are 100 degrees between the freezing point of water (measured at standard atmospheric pressure) at 0° Celsius and its boiling point at 100° Celsius. The German physicist Gabriel Fahrenheit devised the Fahrenheit scale in which the freezing point of water (also at standard atmospheric pressure) is 32° Fahrenheit and its boiling point is 212° Fahrenheit.

We frequently want to convert from one scale to another, so we need a convenient formula to help us with the conversion.

Example

The formula $C = (5/9)(F - 32)$ shows us the relationship between Celsius and Fahrenheit and allows us to change from one scale to another. Change 113° Fahrenheit to Celsius.

ANALYSIS

Let F = the Fahrenheit temperature.
Let C = the Celsius temperature.
We'll use the formula and simply substitute 113 for F.

WORK

$$C = (5/9)(F - 32)$$
$$F = 113: \quad C = (5/9)(113 - 32)$$
$$C = (5/9)(81)$$
$$C = 45$$

ANSWER

45° Celsius

EXERCISE

1. Use the formula C = (5/9)(F − 32) to change 104° Fahrenheit (F) to Celsius (C).
   (A) 36°C   (B) 40°C   (C) 45°C   (D) 81°C

(see answer on page 105)

Equations

Example

Find the value of x in the equation $5x + 12 = 47$.

ANALYSIS

Subtract 12 from both sides of the equation and then divide by 5.

WORK

$$5x + 12 = 47$$
$$\underline{-12 = -12}$$
$$5x = 35$$

$$\frac{5x}{5} = \frac{35}{5}$$

$$x = 7$$

ANSWER

7

CHALLENGE QUESTION
Find the value of the expression $\dfrac{6xy - 2z}{-4}$ when $x = -1$, $y = 3$, and $z = 5$.   (See answer on page 105.)

EXERCISE

1. Find the value of x in the equation $3x - 8 = 19$.
   (A) 8   (B) 9   (C) 6   (D) 7

(see answer on page 105)

Simplifying Exponential Expressions

Occasionally we can simplify exponential expressions. For example,

$$3^4 \cdot 3^6 = (3 \cdot 3 \cdot 3 \cdot 3)(3 \cdot 3 \cdot 3 \cdot 3 \cdot 3 \cdot 3) = 3 \cdot 3 \cdot 3 \cdot 3 \cdot 3 \cdot 3 \cdot 3 \cdot 3 \cdot 3 \cdot 3 = 3^{10}$$

We can see if we multiply powers with the same base, we simply add the exponents.

What happens when we divide powers with the same base?

$$\frac{7^8}{7^5} = \frac{7 \cdot 7 \cdot 7 \cdot \overset{1}{\cancel{7}} \cdot \overset{1}{\cancel{7}} \cdot \overset{1}{\cancel{7}} \cdot \overset{1}{\cancel{7}} \cdot \overset{1}{\cancel{7}}}{\underset{1 \cdot 1 \cdot 1 \cdot 1 \cdot 1}{\cancel{7} \cdot \cancel{7} \cdot \cancel{7} \cdot \cancel{7} \cdot \cancel{7}}} = 7^3$$

If we divide powers with the same base, we subtract exponents.

$$\frac{7^8}{7^5} = 7^{8-5} = 7^3$$

Let's see what happens when we divide a power by itself.

$$\frac{4^{35}}{4^{35}} = 4^{35-35} = 4^0$$

Any time a number is divided by itself, the quotient is 1, so

$$\frac{4^{35}}{4^{35}} = \boxed{4^0 = 1}$$

A base raised to a zero exponent simplifies to 1.

Example

Find the value of $\dfrac{8^7 \cdot 6^9 \cdot 5^0}{8^5 \cdot 6^8}$.

ANALYSIS

$5^0 = 1$. Whenever we divide powers with the same base, we subtract exponents.

WORK

$$\frac{8^7 \cdot 6^9 \cdot 5^0}{8^5 \cdot 6^8} = \frac{\overset{8^2}{\cancel{8^7}} \cdot \overset{6^1}{\cancel{6^9}} \cdot \overset{1}{\cancel{5^0}}}{\underset{1 \cdot 1}{\cancel{8^5} \cdot \cancel{6^8}}} = 8^2 \cdot 6^1 = 64 \cdot 6 = 384$$

EXERCISE

1. Simplify the following expression.

$$\frac{9^4 \cdot 6^3}{9^3 \cdot 6}$$

(A) 54   (B) 486   (C) 1,816   (D) 324

(see answer on page 105)

Roots and Radicals

Let's find the square root of 25.

$$\sqrt{25} = 5$$

or

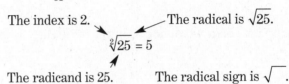

The index is 2.   The radical is $\sqrt{25}$.

$$\sqrt[2]{25} = 5$$

The radicand is 25.   The radical sign is $\sqrt{}$.

When no index appears, 2 is understood to be the index.

There are actually two square roots of 25:

$$(+5)(+5) = 25$$
$$(-5)(-5) = 25$$

We indicate a positive and a negative square root in the following manner:

$$\pm\sqrt{25} = \pm5$$

When we want the **positive square root** of a number, we call it the **principal square root**:

$$\sqrt{25} = +5$$

The negative square root is indicated by placing a negative sign in front of the radical:

$$-\sqrt{25} = -5$$

We can also find higher-level roots. For example, $\sqrt[3]{64}$ means the number that, when multiplied by itself three times, equals 64. Four times four times four equals sixty-four ($4 \times 4 \times 4 = 64$), so that $\sqrt[3]{64} = 4$.

Let's find $\sqrt[4]{81}$. Three times three times three times three equals eighty-one ($3 \times 3 \times 3 \times 3 = 81$), so that $\sqrt[4]{81} = 3$.

Simplifying Radicals

Example 1

Simplify $\sqrt{b^8}$.

ANALYSIS

We want to find a particular monomial that, when multiplied by itself, results in b^8.

WORK

$$\sqrt{b^8} = b^4$$

Check: $$b^4 \cdot b^4 = b^8$$

ANSWER

b^4

Example 2

Simplify $\sqrt{50}$.

ANALYSIS

Try to write 50 as the product of a square and another number and then simplify the result.

WORK

$$\sqrt{50} = \sqrt{25 \cdot 2} = \sqrt{25} \cdot \sqrt{2} = 5\sqrt{2}$$

ANSWER

$5\sqrt{2}$

Example 3

Simplify $\sqrt[3]{125x^9}$.

ANALYSIS

We want to find a term that, when multiplied by itself three times, equals $125x^9$.

WORK

$$\sqrt[3]{125x^9} = 5x^3$$

Check: $$(5x^3)(5x^3)(5x^3) = 125x^9$$

ANSWER

$5x^3$

EXERCISES

1. Simplify $\sqrt{c^{12}}$.
   (A) c^3 (B) c^6 (C) c^4 (D) $6c^2$

2. Simplify $\sqrt{98}$.
   (A) $6\sqrt{3}$ (B) $5\sqrt{3}$ (C) $4\sqrt{5}$ (D) $7\sqrt{2}$

(see answers on page 105)

Operations with Radicals

We can perform the basic arithmetic operations of addition, subtraction, multiplication, and division on radicals.

$$13\sqrt{7} - 4\sqrt{7} = 9\sqrt{7}$$
$$12\sqrt{6} - 17\sqrt{6} = -5\sqrt{6}$$
$$5\sqrt{b} \cdot 3\sqrt{c} = 15\sqrt{bc}$$

EXERCISES

Simplify the following radical expressions.

1. $5\sqrt{7} - 2\sqrt{7} + 6\sqrt{7}$
   (A) $11\sqrt{7}$ (B) $10\sqrt{7}$ (C) $13\sqrt{7}$ (D) $9\sqrt{7}$

2. $8\sqrt{2} \cdot 3\sqrt{2}$
   (A) $24\sqrt{2}$ (B) $48\sqrt{2}$ (C) 48 (D) 4

(see answers on page 105)

Inequalities

The following examples illustrate the inequality symbols.

Illustration	Translation
6 > 3	6 is greater than 3
9 < 12	9 is less than 12
–3 ≥ –4	–3 is greater than or equal to –4
0 ≤ 0	0 is less than or equal to 0

We read the expression $a > b$ as "a is greater than b." If we can't assign numbers to a and b, the truth of the statement can't be determined.

The expression 9 < 8 reads "9 is less than 8." It is obviously a false statement.

In the statement 4 > 8 or 3 < 5, only one condition has to be met because of "or." Four is not greater than eight. However, three is less than five, so that the entire statement 4 > 8 **or** 3 < 5 is true.

When we encounter a statement such as 5 < 7 and 2 > 3, both conditions have to be met because of "and." Five is less than seven. However, two is not greater than three, so that the entire statement 5 < 7 **and** 2 > 3 is false.

Example

Simplify the following powers and then select the correct answer.

(a) 5^2 (b) 2^5 (c) 2^3

(A) $a > b$ or $c > a$ (B) $c = a$ or $b < c$
(C) $c > b$ and $a = b$ (D) $b < a$ or $c < b$

ANALYSIS

Simplify each expression and then substitute.

WORK

(a) $5^2 = 5 \cdot 5 = 25$
(b) $2^5 = 2 \cdot 2 \cdot 2 \cdot 2 \cdot 2 = 32$
(c) $2^3 = 2 \cdot 2 \cdot 2 = 8$

(D) $b < a$ or $c < b$
    32 < 25 or 8 < 32 ✓

ANSWER

(D)

EXERCISE

1. Which of the following statements is true?
   (A) $4 < -5$ and $9 > 3$
   (B) $7 \geq -2$ and $6 < -5$
   (C) $12 \leq 19$ or $-5 > 0$
   (D) $-9 > -8$ or $7 < 0$

(see answer on page 105)

Operations with Monomials and Polynomials

Example 1

Simplify $+4t - 5t + 9t - 3t$.

ANALYSIS

Perform the additions and subtractions separately and then combine terms.

WORK

$$+4t + 9t = +13t$$
$$-5t - 3t = -8t$$
$$+13t - 8t = +5t$$

ANSWER

$+5t$

Example 2

Subtract $2a - 4$ from $-3a - 6$.

ANALYSIS

Change the signs of the subtrahend and then add.

WORK

$$
\begin{array}{ll}
-3a \quad -6 & \text{(minuend)} \\
\underline{-\,\oplus 2a \;\;\ominus 4} & \text{(subtrahend)} \\
-5a \quad -2 & \text{(difference)}
\end{array}
$$

ANSWER

$-5a - 2$

Example 3

Find the product of $4t^5$ and $-6t^3$.

ANALYSIS

Multiply the coefficients and add the exponents.

WORK

$$(4t^5) \cdot (-6t^3) = (4)(-6)(t^5)(t^3) = -24t^8$$

ANSWER

$-24t^8$

Example 4

Find the quotient of $24g^7 - 18g^5$ and $-6g^4$.

ANALYSIS

Divide the coefficients and subtract the exponents.

WORK

$$\frac{24g^7 - 18g^5}{-6g^4} = \frac{24g^7}{-6g^4} - \frac{18g^5}{-6g^4} = -4g^3 + 3g$$

ANSWER

$-4g^3 + 3g$

EXERCISES

1. Simplify $-3g - 4h + 8g - 3h$.
   (A) $4g + 7h$ (B) $-5g - 11h$ (C) $5g - 7h$ (D) $11g + 7h$

2. Subtract $8t - 4z$ from $-5t - 8z$.
   (A) $-13t - 4z$ (B) $13t + 4z$ (C) $-3t - 4z$ (D) $3t - 12z$

3. Find the product of $5a^3$ and $4a^7$.
   (A) $20a^{21}$ (B) $15a^{10}$ (C) $20a^{10}$ (D) $35a^{21}$

4. Find the quotient of $18r^6 - 12r^7$ and $-6r^5$.
   (A) $3r - 2r^2$ (B) $-3r - 2$ (C) $3r - 2r$ (D) $-3r + 2r^2$

(see answers on page 105)

Absolute Value

The absolute value of a number, *x*, is defined as its distance from zero or

$$|x| = \sqrt{x^2}$$

For example,

$$|-3| = \sqrt{(-3)^2} = \sqrt{9} = 3$$
$$|4| = \sqrt{4^2} = \sqrt{16} = 4$$

More practically, the absolute value of any number is its distance from the origin (disregard direction).

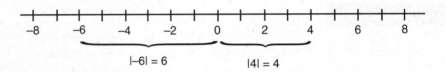

Example

Simplify 5|–6|.

ANALYSIS

Remove the absolute value sign and multiply by 5.

WORK

$$5|-6| = 5\,(6) = 30$$

ANSWER

30

EXERCISES

Simplify the following expressions:

1. 6|–4| + 4|7|
   (A) –24   (B) +4   (C) 52   (D) –4

2. 7|7| – 3|–2|
   (A) 55   (B) 45   (C) 27   (D) 43

(see answers on page 106)

Ratios and Proportions

The odds of a new business remaining open more than a year are 1 out of 3. What does this mean? It means that only 1/3 of all new enterprises will remain in business longer than a year, while 2/3 will close within the year.

1/3 is a ratio that also may be expressed as 1:3.

The ratio $a:b$ may be expressed as the fraction a/b.

The ratio 9:27 may be reduced:

$$\frac{9}{27} = \frac{1}{3}$$

a, b, c, and d are called the first, second, third, and fourth terms, respectively.

The two outer terms are called the extremes, while the two inner terms are called the means.

means
$$a : b = c : d$$
extremes

> **DEFINITION**
>
> If two ratios are equal, we have a proportion:
>
> $$\frac{a}{b} = \frac{c}{d}$$
>
> or
>
> $$a:b = c:d$$

Example 1

Do these ratios form a proportion?

$$\frac{4}{12} \overset{?}{=} \frac{5}{15} \quad \bigg| \quad \frac{3a^2}{7a} \overset{?}{=} \frac{6a}{14a^2}$$

$$\frac{1}{3} = \frac{1}{3} \quad \bigg| \quad \frac{3a}{7} = \frac{3}{7a}$$

Yes! | No

In a proportion, the product of the means equals the product of the extremes. In the proportion $a:b = c:d$, $bc = ad$.

Example 2

Find the fourth term in the proportion $2:7 = 12:x$.

ANALYSIS

The product of the means equals the product of the extremes.

WORK

$$2:7 = 12:x$$
$$2x = 84$$
$$x = 42$$

ANSWER

42

EXERCISE

1. Find the fourth term in the proportion $7:9 = 21:x$.
   (A) 21   (B) 18   (C) 27   (D) 36

(see answer on page 106)

Consecutive Integers

Consecutive integers are integers that follow one another:

$$1, 2, 3, \ldots$$
$$22, 23, 24, \ldots$$
$$75, 76, 77, \ldots$$
$$-4, -3, -2, \ldots$$

If we let x represent an integer, $x + 1$ represents the next consecutive integer, $x + 2$ the integer after that, and so forth:

$$x, x + 1, x + 2, \ldots$$

Consecutive even integers are even integers that follow one another:

$$2, 4, 6, \ldots$$
$$18, 20, 22, \ldots$$
$$62, 64, 66, \ldots$$
$$-8, -6, -4, \ldots$$

We have to add 2 to the first even integer to get to the next consecutive even integer:

$$8$$
$$8 + 2 = 10$$
$$10 + 2 = 12$$

If n represents the first even integer, $n + 2$ represents the next consecutive even integer, $n + 4$ the even integer after that, and so forth:

$$n, n + 2, n + 4, \ldots$$

If $n + 1$ represents the first even integer, $(n + 1) + 2$ and $(n + 1) + 4$ represent the next two consecutive even integers:

$$(n + 1), (n + 1) + 2, (n + 1) + 4, \ldots$$

Consecutive odd integers are odd integers that follow one another:

$$5, 7, 9, \ldots$$
$$13, 15, 17, \ldots$$
$$79, 81, 83, \ldots$$
$$-11, -9, -7, \ldots$$

Just as with even integers, we have to add 2 to the first odd integer in order to get to the next consecutive odd integer:

$$5$$
$$5 + 2 = 7$$
$$7 + 2 = 9$$

If $x - 4$ represents the first odd integer, $(x - 4) + 2$ represents the next consecutive odd integer, $(x - 4) + 4$ represents the odd integer after that, and so forth:

$$(x - 4), (x - 4) + 2, (x - 4) + 4, \ldots$$

Example 1

Find two consecutive integers whose sum is 71.

ANALYSIS

Let x = the first integer, and let $x + 1$ = the next consecutive integer. The sum is 71.

WORK

$$x + (x + 1) = 71$$
$$x + x + 1 = 71$$
$$2x + 1 = 71$$

Subtract 1: $\qquad 2x = 70$

Divide by 2: $\qquad x = 35$

$$x + 1 = 36$$

Check: $\qquad 35 + 36 = 71 \checkmark$

ANSWER

35, 36

Example 2

Find two consecutive even integers whose sum is 86.

ANALYSIS

Let x = the first even integer, and let $x + 2$ = the next consecutive even integer. The sum is 86.

WORK

$$x + (x + 2) = 86$$
$$2x + 2 = 86$$

Subtract 2: $\quad\quad\quad 2x = 84$

Divide by 2: $\quad\quad\quad x = 42$

$$x + 2 = 44$$
$$x + (x + 2) = 86$$

Check: $\quad\quad\quad 42 + 44 = 86 \checkmark$

ANSWER

42, 44

CHALLENGE QUESTION

The sum of the first and third of three consecutive odd integers is 14. Find the square of the second consecutive odd integer.

(See answer on page 106.)

EXERCISES

1. Find the largest of three consecutive integers whose sum is 231.
   (A) 79　(B) 83　(C) 80　(D) 78

2. What is the smaller of two consecutive even integers that add up to 70?
   (A) 32　(B) 36　(C) 34　(D) 38

3. Find the second of three consecutive odd integers whose sum is 141.
   (A) 45　(B) 47　(C) 51　(D) 49

(see answers on page 106)

PLANE GEOMETRY

Points

Points have no specific size or shape. Points are usually named with capital letters and are used to position objects and lines.

•　•　　　•
A　B　　　C

Lines

Lines, like points, have no specific width but they extend infinitely in opposite directions.

Line $\overleftrightarrow{AB}$ or $\overleftrightarrow{BA}$

INTERSECTING LINES

Lines $\overleftrightarrow{RS}$ and $\overleftrightarrow{TU}$ intersect at point V. Both lines are in the same plane.

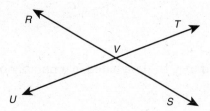

LINE SEGMENTS

Line segments, unlike lines, have a definite length and may be measured. Line segment $\overline{AB}$ names the segment while AB asks for the length of AB.

RAYS

Rays are parts of lines that extend from one endpoint indefinitely in one direction.

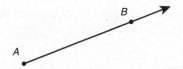

Ray AB or $\overrightarrow{AB}$

Planes

Planes are composed of an infinite set of points on a flat surface. Planes extend infinitely in all directions. The diagram below is only a section of the entire plane.

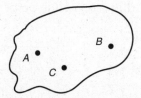

Plane ABC is indicated by three points on the plane. The three points are not located on the same line.

Angles

If two rays meet at the same point, they form an angle at the point of intersection, called the vertex.

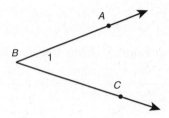

The angle thus formed may be designated in a number of different ways, all with the vertex in the middle:

(i) ∠*ABC*
(ii) ∠*CBA*
(iii) ∠1

EXERCISE

1. What is another name for ∠*DEF*?
    (A) ∠*D*   **(B)** ∠*DFE*   **(C)** ∠*E*   **(D)** ∠*FDE*

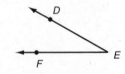

(see answer on page 106)

PROTRACTOR

A protractor is used to measure the number of degrees in an angle. In the diagram, for example, the protractor measures an angle of 29°.

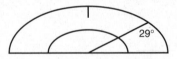

RIGHT ANGLES

Right angles measure 90°. In this case, *AB* is perpendicular to *BC*. Symbolically, *AB* ⊥ *BC*.

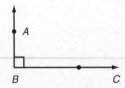

ACUTE ANGLES

Acute angles measure less than 90°.

OBTUSE ANGLES

Obtuse angles measure more than 90° but less than 180°.

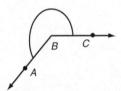

STRAIGHT ANGLES

Straight angles measure 180°. The two adjoining sides, *IH* and *IJ*, extend in opposite directions and form a straight line.

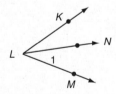

REFLEX ANGLES

Reflex angles measure more than 180° but less than 360°.

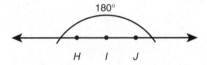

EXERCISES

1. What is another name for ∠1?
   (A) ∠L   (B) ∠NLM   (C) ∠KLN   (D) ∠NLK

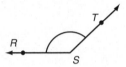

2. What sort of angle is illustrated here?
   (A) right   (B) acute   (C) obtuse   (D) reflex

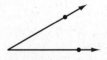

(see answers on page 106)

COMPLEMENTARY ANGLES

Two angles are complementary if their sum is 90°. In the diagram at the right, $m\angle a + m\angle b = 90°$.

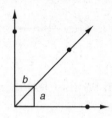

Example

Find the complement of 24°.

ANALYSIS

Complementary angles add up to 90°.

WORK

$$x + 24° = 90°$$
$$x = 90° - 24°$$
$$x = 66°$$

ANSWER

66°

SUPPLEMENTARY ANGLES

Supplementary angles are two angles that add up to 180°.

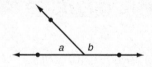

$$m\angle a + m\angle b = 180°$$

Example

Find the supplement of 47°.

ANALYSIS

Supplementary angles are two angles that add up to 180°.

WORK

$$x + 47° = 180°$$
$$x = 180° - 47°$$
$$x = 133°$$

ANSWER

133°

TIP

Remember, the letter "c" comes before the letter "s" and 90° comes before 180°.

EXERCISES

1. What is the complement of $(3x)$°?
   (A) $(180 - 3x)$°   (B) $(90 - 3x)$°   (C) $5x$°   (D) $(100 - 3x)$°

2. What is the supplement of $(9b)$°?
   (A) $(100 + 9b)$°   (B) $(180 - 9b)$°   (C) $(90 - 9b)$°   (D) $(100 - 9b)$°

(see answers on page 106)

ADJACENT ANGLES

If two angles share a common side as well as a common vertex but share no common interior points, they are known as adjacent angles. For example, angle *JKM* and angle *MKL* are adjacent angles because they share common side *KM* and common vertex *K*.

Example

Add the two adjacent angles.

WORK

$$\begin{array}{r} 32° \\ + 27° \\ \hline 59° \end{array}$$

ANSWER

59°

EXERCISE

1. Find the measure of ∠*a*.

   (A) 101°   (B) 47°   (C) 106°   (D) 53°

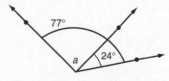

(see answer on page 106)

VERTICAL ANGLES

If two straight lines intersect, they form four angles. As we can clearly see, there are a number of adjacent angles:

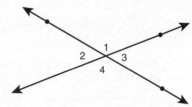

∠1 and ∠3 are adjacent angles
∠3 and ∠4 are adjacent angles
∠2 and ∠4 are adjacent angles
∠1 and ∠2 are adjacent angles

We also have two sets of angles that are opposite each other, called **vertical angles**, and their measures are equal:

$$m\angle 1 = m\angle 4 \quad \text{and} \quad m\angle 2 = m\angle 3$$

If the measures of two angles are equal, the angles are called congruent.

Example

Find the value of x.

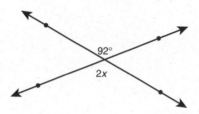

ANALYSIS

Because the angles represented by $2x$ and $92°$ are vertical angles, their measures are equal.

WORK

$$2x = 92°$$
$$x = 46°$$

ANSWER

$46°$

Perpendicular Lines

Perpendicular lines intersect in the same plane and form right angles (90°).

$AB \perp CD$

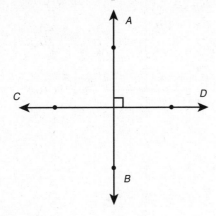

Coordinate Geometry

The simplest way to locate points on a plane (flat surface) is to use a graph.

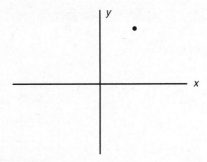

The horizontal axis is called the *x*-axis or abscissa.

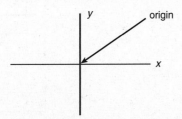

The vertical axis is called the *y*-axis or ordinate.

The point of intersection of the two major axes is called the **origin**.

The integers on the major axes locate points on the plane. For example, the ordered pair (4, 3) is located 4 units to the right and 3 units above the origin.

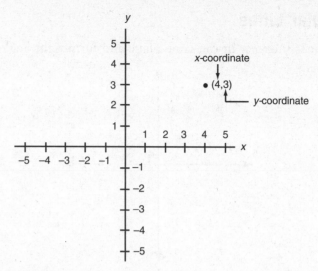

The first digit of the ordered pair indicates a move to the right (+) or left (−), and the second digit indicates a move up (+) or down (−).

EXERCISES

1. Name the coordinates of point *A*.
   (A) (−2, +3)
   (B) (−2, −2)
   (C) (2, −2)
   (D) (2, +2)

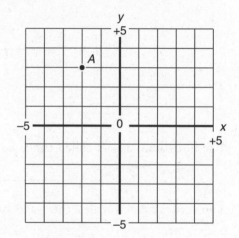

2. Which of the following points lies above the line *y* = 1 and to the left of the line *x* = −2?
   (A) *A*   (B) *B*   (C) *C*   (D) *D*

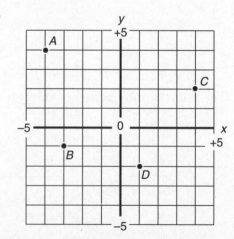

(see answers on page 106)

POLYGONS

A **polygon** is a plane (flat) figure totally enclosed by three or more straight line segments that share endpoints.

Name of polygon	Number of sides
Triangle	3
Quadrilateral	4
Pentagon	5
Hexagon	6
Heptagon	7
Octagon	8
Nonagon	9
Decagon	10

EXERCISES

1. What do we call a six-sided figure?
   (A) octagon   (B) pentagon   (C) hexagon   (D) decagon

2. What do we call an eight-sided figure?
   (A) heptagon   (B) triangle   (C) nonagon   (D) octagon

(see answers on page 106)

Angles in Polygons

RECTANGLES

A rectangle has four right angles. The sum of the measures of the angles of a rectangle is 360°.

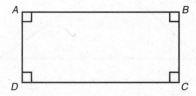

SQUARES

A square has four right angles and four equal sides. The sum of the measures of the angles of a square is 360°.

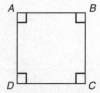

PARALLELOGRAMS

The sum of the measures of the angles of a parallelogram is 360°. Opposite angles are congruent:

$$\angle A \cong \angle C \text{ and } \angle B \cong \angle D$$

Two successive angles are supplementary:

$$m\angle A + m\angle B = 180°$$
$$m\angle C + m\angle D = 180°$$

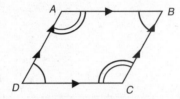

EXERCISES

1. What is the sum of the angles in a rectangle?
   (A) 180°   (B) 360°   (C) 270°   (D) 90°

2. In parallelogram *ABCD*, if the measure of angle *A* is 123°, find the measure of angle *B*
   (A) 123°   (B) 246°   (C) 57°   (D) 114°

(see answers on page 106)

TRIANGLES

Sum of the Angles in a Triangle

The measure of angle *A* + the measure of angle *B* + the measure of angle *C* = 180°.

$$m\angle A + m\angle B + m\angle C = 180°$$

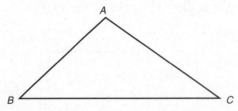

CHALLENGE QUESTION

In the isosceles triangle *ABC* on the right, the exterior angle at *C* measures 104°. Find the measure of angle *B*.

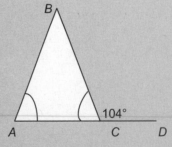

(See answer on page 106.)

Isosceles Triangle

In an isosceles triangle, the base angles are congruent and the sides opposite the base angles are of the same measure:

$$\angle B \cong \angle C$$
$$m(AB) = m(AC)$$

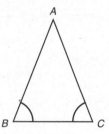

Equilateral Triangle

In an equilateral triangle, all the angles are congruent and all the sides are of the same measure.

$$\angle A \cong \angle B \cong \angle C$$
$$m(AB) = m(BC) = m(AC)$$

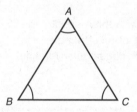

Right Triangle

In a right triangle, one angle is a right angle:

$$m\angle C = 90°$$

The other two angles are complementary:

$$m\angle A + m\angle B = 90°$$

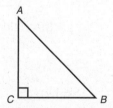

EXERCISE

1. Select the type of triangle whose base angles are congruent but whose vertex angle is different.

   (A) isosceles   (B) equilateral   (C) right

(see answer on page 106)

Types of Triangles, Classified by Angles

Acute

three acute angles

Right

one 90° angle

Obtuse

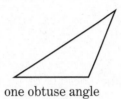

one obtuse angle

Equiangular

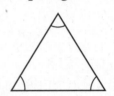

three angles of equal measure

EXERCISE

1. What do we call a triangle with three equal angles?
   (A) right triangle   (B) obtuse triangle
   (C) isosceles triangle   (D) equiangular triangle

(see answer on page 106)

Types of Triangles, Classified by Sides

Isosceles

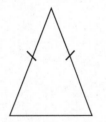

two sides of equal length

Equilateral

three sides of equal length

Scalene

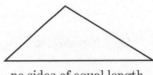

no sides of equal length

Perimeters

By definition, the perimeter (*P*) of a polygon is equal to the sum of its sides.

RECTANGLES

The perimeter of a rectangle is equal to the sum of its sides.

$$P = b + b + h + h = 2b + 2h$$

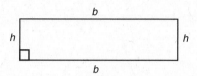

1. If the perimeter of a rectangle is 42″ and its width is 6″, find its length.
   (A) 8″   (B) 12″   (C) 14″   (D) 15″

(see answer on page 106)

SQUARES

The perimeter of a square is equal to the sum of its sides.

$$P = s + s + s + s = 4s$$

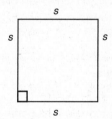

TRIANGLES

The perimeter of a triangle is equal to the sum of its sides.

$$P = a + b + c$$

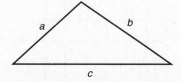

ISOSCELES TRIANGLES

In an isosceles triangle, two of the sides are equal.

$$P = a + a + b = 2a + b$$

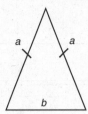

EQUILATERAL TRIANGLES

By definition, an equilateral triangle is constructed of three equal sides and the perimeter is the sum of those three sides.

$$P = s + s + s = 3s$$

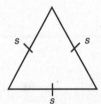

EXERCISES

1. If each of the congruent sides of an isosceles triangle is 11″ and the base is 4.6″, find the perimeter of the triangle.
   (A) 13.8″   (B) 37.6″   (C) 20.2″   (D) 26.6″

2. If the perimeter of an isosceles triangle is 45.9″ and one of the congruent sides is 8.6″, find the base of the triangle.
   (A) 37.3″   (B) 28.7″   (C) 35.6″   (D) 27.4″

3. Find one side of an equilateral triangle if its perimeter is 8.

   (A) $2\frac{2}{3}$ (B) $3\frac{1}{3}$ (C) 2.5   (D) $2\frac{3}{4}$

(see answers on page 106)

Areas of Polygons

RECTANGLES

The area (inside space of a rectangle) A, is determined by multiplying its base b by its height h.

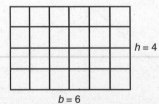

In the diagram, the base is 6, and the height is 4.

$$A = bh$$
$$A = 6 \cdot 4 = 24$$

SQUARES

All the sides of a square are equal, so, to find the area of a square, we multiply side *s* by side *s*.

In the diagram, both sides are 5.

$$A = s \cdot s = s^2$$
$$A = 5 \cdot 5 = 25$$

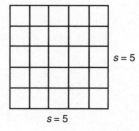

PARALLELOGRAMS

Area (*A*) = base (*b*) × height (*h*)

$$A = bh$$
$$A = 5 \cdot 4 = 20$$

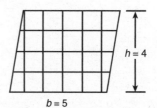

TRIANGLES

$$\text{Area}\,(A) = \left(\frac{1}{2}\right)\text{base}\,(b)\times\text{height}\,(h)$$

$$A = \left(\frac{1}{2}\right)bh$$

$$A = \left(\frac{1}{2}\right)(8\times 4) = \left(\frac{1}{2}\right)32$$

$$A = 16$$

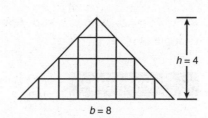

EXERCISES

1. The area of a rectangle is 54. If its length is 12, find its width.

   (A) 3   (B) 4   (C) $4\frac{1}{2}$ (D) $5\frac{1}{2}$

2. If the base of a parallelogram is 24.3 and its height is 8, find the area.
   (A) 194.4   (B) 188.6   (C) 203.8   (D) 200.6

3. If the area of a triangle is 36 square inches and its height is 8 inches, find its base.
   (A) 8 inches   (B) 9 inches   (C) 7 inches   (D) 12 inches

(see answers on page 106)

Pythagorean Theorem

The ancient Greek mathematician Pythagoras determined a relationship among the sides of a right triangle. He showed that if you erect squares on the sides of a right triangle, the sum of the areas of the two squares on the legs of the right triangle equals the area of the square erected on the hypotenuse of the right triangle.

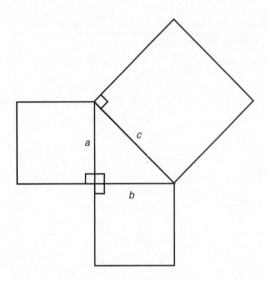

Pythagorean Theorem

$a^2 + b^2 = c^2$, where a and b are the legs and c is the hypotenuse of the right triangle.

Example

Find the hypotenuse of a right triangle whose two legs are 5 and 12.

ANALYSIS

Use the Pythagorean Theorem.

WORK

$a = 5$, $b = 12$:
$$a^2 + b^2 = c^2$$
$$5^2 + 12^2 = c^2$$
$$25 + 144 = c^2$$
$$169 = c^2$$

Take the square root of 169: $13 = c$

ANSWER

13

EXERCISE

1. Find the hypotenuse of a right triangle if its two legs are 6 and 8.
   (A) 5   (B) 12   (C) 9   (D) 10

(see answer on page 106)

CIRCLES

Radius and Diameter

This is circle *O*, with center *O*. *AB* is the diameter and *AO* and *BO* are the two radii. As you can see, the diameter, *AB*, is twice the size of the radius, *AO*.

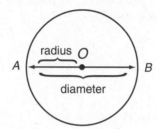

Circumference

The **circumference** is the perimeter of the circle. The circumference *C* is equal to the product of 2, π, and the radius *r*:

$$C = 2\pi r$$

Example

Find the circumference of a circle whose diameter is 6. Round the answer to the nearest tenth.

ANALYSIS

Use the formula $C = 2\pi r$, where C = circumference and $\pi = 3.14$. The radius is $\frac{1}{2}$ the length of the diameter.

WORK

$$r = \frac{1}{2} \cdot d = \frac{1}{2} \cdot 6 = 3$$
$$C = 2\pi r$$
$$\pi = 3.14, \ r = 3: \quad C = 2 \times 3.14 \times 3 = 18.84 \approx 18.8$$

ANSWER

18.8

> ### VOCABULARY
>
> The Latin root *cir-* or *circum-* means "around." (Think of a circle.) To *circumscribe* (scribe = write) something is to limit it, as if drawing a circle around it. *We circumscribed the scribe by locking him in a round room.*

EXERCISE

1. If the circumference of a circle is 31.4, find its radius. Use the formula $C = 2\pi r$, where C = circumference, π = 3.14, and r = radius.
   (A) 4   (B) 5   (C) 6   (D) 9

(see answer on page 106)

Area

$A = \pi r^2$, where π = 3.14 and r = the radius. In this case, r = 3, so

$$A = \pi r^2$$
$$A = (3.14)(3)^2 = 3.14\,(9)$$
$$A = 28.26$$

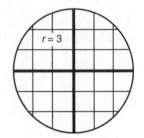

Example

If the area of a circle is 154 square inches, find its radius. Let π = 22/7.

ANALYSIS

Use the formula $A = \pi r^2$, where A = area and r = radius.

WORK

$$A = \pi r^2$$

A = 154, π = 22/7: $154 = \dfrac{22}{7}\,r^2$

Multiply by 7: $1{,}078 = 22r^2$
Divide by 22: $49 = r^2$
Find the square root of 49: $r = \pm\, 7$

ANSWER

7 inches

CHALLENGE QUESTION

Find the shaded area. Use the value π = 3.14 and round off to the nearest tenth.

9

7

$r = 3$

(See answer on page 106.)

EXERCISES

1. Find the area of a circle whose radius is 8. Use the formula $A = \pi r^2$, where A = area, $\pi = 3.14$, and r = radius. Round the answer to the nearest tenth.
   (A) 199.9   (B) 200   (C) 201.0   (D) 200.9

2. If the area of a circle is 12.56, find its radius. Use the formula $A = \pi r^2$, where A = area, $\pi = 3.14$, and r = radius.
   (A) 3   (B) 4   (C) 5   (D) 2

(see answers on page 106)

Central Angles

A central angle of a circle has its vertex at the center of the circle.

Example

If two central angles of a triangle are 40° and 80°, find the measure of the third central angle.

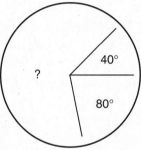

ANALYSIS

All of the central angles add up to 360°, so add up the two given angles and subtract the result from 360°.

WORK

$$x + 40 + 80 = 360$$
$$x + 120 = 360$$

Subtract 120: $$x = 240$$

ANSWER

240°

EXERCISE

1. If three central angles measure 65°, 87°, and 112°, find the measure of the fourth central angle.
   (A) 96°   (B) 104°   (C) 118°   (D) 76°

(see answer on page 106)

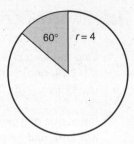

DEFINITION
A **sector** of a circle is an area of the circle determined by the intersection of two radii and the circumference of the circle.

Sectors

Example

If the radius of the circle at the right is 4 and the central angle is 60°, find the area of the shaded sector. To simplify matters, let $\pi = 3$.

ANALYSIS

• Find the area of the circle. Then determine the fraction of the entire circle the sector occupies.

WORK

Let A = area of the circle and r = radius.

$$A = \pi r^2$$

$\pi = 3$, $r = 4$:
$$A = (3)(4)^2$$
$$A = 3(16) = 48$$

TIP
A CENTRAL ANGLE limits an area of a circle in proportion to its ratio to 360°, the number of degrees in the entire circle.

There are 360° in the circle. 60° is 60/360 or $\frac{1}{6}$ of the circle.

$$\frac{1}{6} \times 48 = 8$$

ANSWER

8

EXERCISE

1. If a central angle measures 45° and the radius of its circle is 2, find the area of its sector. Let $\pi = 3$.
   (A) 2   (B) 1.5   (C) 3   (D) 2.5

(see answer on page 106)

VOLUMES

A great deal of present-day two- and three-dimensional geometry still depends upon the propositions developed by the Greek mathematician, Euclid. His most significant contribution to geometry is contained in his thirteen books of the *Elements*. Next to the Bible, the *Elements* is probably the most widely distributed and studied book in the world. The first four books cover plane geometry. The fifth and sixth include the theory of proportions and similarity, while books seven through nine discuss number theory—prime numbers, divisibility of integers, and so on.

Rectangular Solids

Volume = length × width × height
$$V = l \cdot w \cdot h$$

Example

If the length, width, and height of a box are, respectively, 8″, 7″, and 4.6″, find its volume, correct to the nearest cubic inch.

ANALYSIS

Multiply length, width, and height and then round off, correct to the nearest cubic inch.

WORK

$l = 8$, $w = 7$, $h = 4.6$:

$$V = l \cdot w \cdot h$$
$$V = (8)(7)(4.6) = 257.6 \approx 258$$

ANSWER

258 cubic inches

EXERCISES

1. Find the volume of a rectangular solid whose length is 6″, width is 8″, and height is 7″.
   (A) 56 cu in.   (B) 336 cu in.   (C) 288 cu in.   (D) 294 cu in.

2. We want to construct a box in the shape of a rectangular solid. If its volume is supposed to be 144 cubic inches, its length is 8″, and its width is 3″, find its height.
   (A) 4″   (B) 6″   (C) 9″   (D) 8″

(see answers on page 106)

Cubes

A cube is a rectangular solid whose sides are equal.
If we label each edge e, then the volume V is equal to
$e \cdot e \cdot e$, or $V = e^3$.

Example

Find the volume of a cube whose edge is 2.4 meters.

ANALYSIS

Just use the formula $V = e^3$ and substitute for e.

WORK

$e = 2.4$:

$$V = e^3$$
$$V = (2.4)^3 = (2.4)(2.4)(2.4) = 13.824$$

ANSWER

13.824 cubic meters

EXERCISES

1. Find the volume of a cube whose edge is 7 inches.
   (A) 49 cu in.   (B) 343 cu in.   (C) 98 cu in.   (D) 2,401 cu in.

2. If the volume of a cube is 216 cubic inches, find one edge.
   (A) 6″   (B) 8″   (C) 4″   (D) 12″

(see answers on page 106)

Right Circular Cylinders

Volume = area of base · height
Volume = π · square of the radius · height

$$V = \pi r^2 h$$

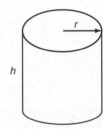

Example

Find the volume of a cylinder whose diameter is 8 feet and whose height is 5 feet. Let π = 3.

ANALYSIS

To find the radius, take $\dfrac{1}{2}$ of the diameter. Then just substitute the values into the formula.

WORK

$d = 8$: $r = \dfrac{1}{2}(d) = \dfrac{1}{2}(8) = 4$

 $V = \pi r^2 h$

$\pi = 3, r = 4, h = 5$: $V = (3)(4)^2(5)$

 $V = 3\,(16)(5)$

 $V = 240$

ANSWER

240 cubic feet

CHALLENGE QUESTION

A cylindrical shape is cut out of a cube. To the nearest tenth of an inch, find the volume in the shaded section.

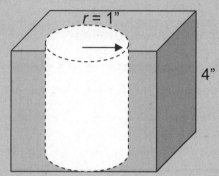

r = 1"

4"

(See answer on page 106.)

EXERCISE

1. Find the volume of a cylinder whose radius is 2 inches and whose height is 6 inches. Use the formula $V = \pi r^2 h$, where V = volume, π = 3, r = radius, and h = height.
   (A) 72 cu in.   (B) 36 cu in.   (C) 48 cu in.   (D) 40 cu in.

(see answer on page 106)

Cones

$\text{Volume} = \dfrac{1}{3} \cdot \text{area of the base} \cdot \text{height}$

$\text{Volume} = \dfrac{1}{3} \cdot \pi \cdot \text{the square of the radius} \cdot \text{height}$

$V = \dfrac{1}{3} \pi r^2 h$

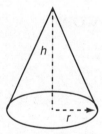

Example

Find the height of a cone when its radius is 2 millimeters and its volume is 20 cubic millimeters. Let $\pi = 3$.

ANALYSIS

Substitute the given values into the formula.

WORK

$$V = \dfrac{1}{3} \pi r^2 h$$

$V = 20$, $\pi = 3$, $r = 2$:

$$20 = \dfrac{1}{3} \cdot 3(2)^2 h$$
$$20 = 4h$$
$$5 = h$$

ANSWER

5 millimeters

EXERCISE

1. Find the volume of a cone whose radius is 1″ and whose height is 6″. Use the formula $V = \frac{1}{3}\pi r^2 h$, where V = volume, π = 3, r = radius, and h = height.

   (A) 12 cu in.   (B) 8 cu in.   (C) 6 cu in.   (D) 14 cu in.

(see answer on page 106)

Spheres

$\text{Volume} = \frac{4}{3} \cdot \pi \cdot \text{the cube of the radius}$

$V = \frac{4}{3}\pi r^3$

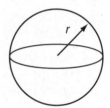

Example

Find the radius of a sphere whose volume is 256 cubic inches. Let $\pi = 3$.

WORK

$$V = \frac{4}{3}\pi r^3$$

$V = 256$, $\pi = 3$: $256 = \frac{4}{3}(3) r^3$

$256 = 4r^3$

Divide by 4: $64 = r^3$

Find the cube root of 64: $r = \pm 4$

ANSWER

4 inches

EXERCISE

1. Find the volume of a sphere whose radius is 2″. Use the formula $V = \frac{4}{3}\pi r^3$, where V = volume, π = 3, and r = radius.

   (A) 32 cu in.   (B) 48 cu in.   (C) 28 cu in.   (D) 16 cu in.

(see answer on page 106)

MEASUREMENTS

U.S. Weight Measures

$$1 \text{ pound} = 16 \text{ ounces}$$
$$1 \text{ ton} = 2,000 \text{ pounds}$$

Example

Change 128,000 ounces to tons.

ANALYSIS

There are 32,000 ounces in one ton. Divide 128,000 ounces by 32,000.

WORK

$$1 \text{ ton} = 2,000 \text{ pounds} = 16 \text{ ounces} \times 2,000 \text{ pounds} = 32,000 \text{ ounces}$$

$$\frac{128,000 \text{ ounces}}{32,000 \text{ ounces}} = 4 \text{ tons}$$

ANSWER

4 tons

EXERCISE

1. Change 46 tons to pounds.
   (A) 4,600 lb   (B) 46,000 lb   (C) 92,000 lb   (D) 9,200 lb

(see answer on page 106)

> **TIP**
>
> When converting from larger units to smaller ones, divide.
>
> When converting from smaller units to larger units, multiply.

U.S. Length Measures

The ancient Romans needed a uniform standard for measuring length. They decided to use the length of the foot of a soldier as this standard measure, the *foot*.

The Romans divided the foot into twelve sections, or *inches*. For longer distances, a mile was the distance marched by 1,000 steps of a Roman soldier, or 5,280 feet.

The natives accepted these measurements during the Roman occupation of Britain. In the twelfth century, the king's arm was accepted as a standard measure for a *yard*, or three feet.

1 foot = 12 inches
1 yard = 3 feet
1 yard = 3 feet × 12 inches (per foot) = 36 inches
1 mile = 5,280 feet

Example

Jesse can run 44,880 feet per hour. In terms of miles, what is his speed?

ANALYSIS

To change 44,880 feet to miles, divide by 5,280.

WORK

$$
\begin{array}{r}
8.5 \\
5{,}280\overline{)44{,}880.0} \\
42{,}240\,\text{x} \\
\hline
2\,6400 \\
2\,6400 \\
\hline
\end{array}
$$

ANSWER

8.5 miles

EXERCISES

1. How many feet are there in 4 miles?
   (A) 23,760 ft   (B) 21,120 ft   (C) 22,500 ft   (D) 20,000 ft

2. Change 216 inches to feet.
   (A) 12 ft   (B) 4 ft   (C) 21 ft   (D) 18 ft

3. How many feet are there in 13 yards?
   (A) 52 ft   (B) 65 ft   (C) 78 ft   (D) 39 ft

(see answers on page 106)

U.S. Liquid Measures

1 quart = 2 pints
1 gallon = 4 quarts

Example

How many pints are there in 16 gallons?

ANALYSIS

Change gallons to quarts; then change quarts to pints.

WORK

16 gallons = 16 × 4 quarts (per gallon) = 64 quarts
64 quarts = 64 × 2 pints (per quart) = 128 pints

ANSWER

128 pints

1. How many quarts are there in 9 gallons?
   (A) 27 qt   (B) 36 qt   (C) 4 qt   (D) 45 qt

2. Change 24 pints to quarts.
   (A) 8 qt   (B) 48 qt   (C) 12 qt   (D) 6 qt

(see answers on page 106)

Metric Length Measures

During the French Revolution, in the last decade of the eighteenth century, French scientists developed a standard unit of measurement, the **meter**. The meter is one ten-millionth of the distance between the North Pole and the Equator.

The system was so rational that most other countries—except the United States and Great Britain—adopted it.

1 meter = 100 centimeters
1 kilometer = 1,000 meters

Metric Weight Measures

1 kilogram = 1,000 grams

Changing Metric Measures and U.S. Measures

1 meter = 39.37 inches
1 kilometer = 0.62 mile
1 kilogram = 2.2 pounds
1 liter = 1.06 quarts
1 mile = 1.61 kilometers
1 pound = 0.45 kilograms

Example

Change 13 kilometers to miles.

ANALYSIS

One kilometer equals 0.62 mile, so just multiply 13 by 0.62.

WORK

$$
\begin{array}{r}
0.62 \\
\times 13 \\
\hline
186 \\
62 \\
\hline
8.06
\end{array}
$$

ANSWER

8.06 miles

EXERCISES

1. Change 12 miles to kilometers and round off to the nearest tenth of a kilometer. Let 1 kilometer = 0.62 mile.
   (A) 7.4 kilometers (B) 472.8 kilometers
   (C) 19.4 kilometers (D) 19.32 kilometers

2. How many pounds are the equivalent of 15.4 kilograms? Round off to the nearest whole pound. Let 1 kilogram = 2.2 pounds.
   (A) 34 lb (B) 31 lb (C) 16 lb (D) 45 lb

(see answers on page 106)

GRAPHS AND TABLES
Line Graphs

The average monthly prices for a gallon of regular gasoline are listed here.

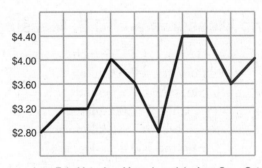

Jan Feb Mar Apr May Jun Jul Aug Sep Oct

Example

What is the difference in the average price per gallon of gasoline between the months of May and June?

ANALYSIS

Each horizontal line represents $0.40. Subtract the June price from the May price.

WORK

May price—June price: $3.60 − $2.80 = $0.80

ANSWER

$0.80

EXERCISE

1. Find the average price per gallon of gasoline for the months of February, March, and April and round off to the nearest cent.
   (A) $4.12   (B) $3.47   (C) $3.82   (D) $3.64

(see answer on page 106)

Circle Graphs

The circle graph shown here indicates how an average resident of Middletown spends time in a 24-hour day.

VOCABULARY

The Greek root *graph* (like the Latin scribe) means "to write" or "to draw." When you write your own name, you sign your autograph.
I was relieved to find out that geography class did not literally require me to draw a full-scale map of the earth. (That would have taken a lot of graphite!)

Example

Using the information in the chart, how much time is spent sleeping?

    (A) 7 hours, 12 minutes
    (B) 7 hours, 14 minutes
    (C) 7 hours, 34 minutes
    (D) 7 hours, 46 minutes

ANALYSIS

Multiply 24 hours by 30% and then change the decimal part of the answer to minutes.

WORK

$$0.30 \times 24 = 7.2 \text{ hours}$$

60 minutes = 1 hour: $\quad 0.2 \times 60 = 12 \text{ minutes}$

$$7.2 \text{ hours} = 7 \text{ hours, } 12 \text{ minutes}$$

ANSWER

7 hours, 12 minutes

EXERCISE

1. Use the circle graph in this section and determine, out of a 24-hour day, how much time the average resident of Middletown spends working.
   (A) 7 hours, 12 minutes (B) 8 hours, 24 minutes
   (C) 4 hours, 18 minutes (D) 9 hours, 8 minutes

(see answer on page 106)

Bar Graphs

A bar graph is simply another useful method of pictorially displaying some information.

Example

Using the information in the bar graph in this section, determine how much sales tax a person would save if she purchased a television set costing $450 in the state of New York rather than in the state of California.

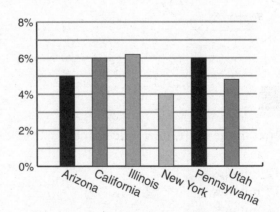

ANALYSIS

The state income tax in New York is 4% while it is 6% in California, resulting in a difference of 2%. Multiply $450 by 2% to find the difference in sales tax.

WORK

Change 2% to 0.02: $0.02 \times \$450 = \$9$

ANSWER

$9

EXERCISE

1. Review the following graph and then indicate approximately how many more people reside in Columbus than in Las Vegas.

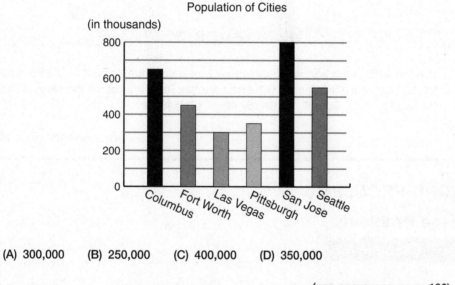

(A) 300,000   (B) 250,000   (C) 400,000   (D) 350,000

(see answer on page 106)

Tables

Banks usually change their interest rates monthly. The following table lists the **simple annual interest rates** offered by the indicated banks.

Bank	Annual Interest Rate
Homeland	3.0%
Nautica	2.0%
Bennington	1.0%
Kendale	3.0%

Example

Using the table, determine the interest earned on a deposit of $5,000 at the Kendale Bank for one month.

ANALYSIS

If we only want to determine the interest for one month, just divide the given simple annual interest rate by 12.

WORK

Kendale Bank's interest rate for one month = 0.03/12 = 0.0025
Actual interest for one month = 0.0025 × $5,000 = $12.50

ANSWER

$12.50

EXERCISE

1. Use the table in this section to determine how much more interest could be earned for the year on a deposit of $8,000 at the Nautica Bank than at the Bennington Bank.
   (A) $80.00   (B) $88.00   (C) $64.00   (D) $48.00

(see answer on page 106)

WORD PROBLEMS

Wage Problems

Example 1

Kendra is a programmer. She earns $26.50 per hour. How much does she earn in 16 hours?

ANALYSIS

Just multiply the wages per hour by the number of hours worked.

WORK

$$16 \times \$26.50 = \$424$$

ANSWER

$424

Example 2

Julio earns $12.54 per hour, while Shanequa earns $13.04 per hour. In 12 hours, how much more than Julio does Shanequa earn?

ANALYSIS

Multiply the wages per hour by the number of hours worked by each person. Then subtract Julio's total wages from Shanequa's total wages.

WORK

Shanequa's wages:	$12 \times \$13.04 =$	$\$156.48$
Julio's wages:	$- 12 \times \$12.54 =$	150.48
		$\$6.00$

ANSWER

$6

Example 3

Mildred earned $22.88 per hour and got paid $1\frac{1}{2}$ times that amount for overtime. If she worked 44 hours last week and any hours over 40 are considered overtime, how much did she get paid?

ANALYSIS

Multiply 40 hours by the amount she normally gets paid per hour, $22.88. She worked 4 hours overtime, so, for overtime pay, multiply 4 by $1\frac{1}{2}$ by $22.88. Then add the two results together.

WORK

Regular pay:	$40 \text{ hours} \times \$22.88 =$	$\$915.20$
Overtime pay:	$+ \ 4 \text{ hours} \times 1\frac{1}{2} \times \$22.88 =$	137.28
		$\$1,052.48$

ANSWER

$1,052.48

CHALLENGE QUESTION

A local supermarket employs ten workers and one manager. The manager's salary is $80,000 per year while the average worker earns $35,000 per year. If the workers receive an average wage increase of 10% while the manager gets a reduction of 10%, what is the total new annual budget for salaries?

(See answer on page 106.)

TIP

In the case where we have several investments, total the individual interest payments and set the sum equal to the entire interest received.

EXERCISES

1. Murray makes $12.74 per hour. How much does he earn in 38 hours?
   (A) $104.12 (B) $484.12 (C) $456.00 (D) $144.40

2. Hilda earns $14.36 per hour; her friend Janice gets paid $13.37 per hour. If they both work 39 hours, how much more money does Hilda earn?
   (A) $38.61 (B) $560.04 (C) $521.43 (D) $49.30

3. Jules gets paid $12.48 per hour for his first 40 hours of work per week. He gets paid $15.75 per hour for overtime, which is considered over 40 hours per week. How much does Jules make when he works 47 hours for the week?
   (A) $499.20 (B) $740.25 (C) $586.56 (D) $609.45

(see answers on page 106)

Investment Problems

Example

Malcolm has $10,000 to invest. If he invests some money at 4% per year simple interest and the rest at 3% per year simple interest and he derives an income of $385 for the year, how much should he invest at 4%?

ANALYSIS

Let x = the amount invested at 4%, and let $10,000 - x$ = the amount invested at 3%.

Investment	Percent Interest	Principal ($)	Interest = Percent × Principal ($)
Investment 1	4%	x	4%(x)
Investment 2	3%	$10,000 - x$	3%($10,000 - x$)

WORK

The interest from the two investments adds up to $385.

$$4\%(x) + 3\%(10,000 - x) = 385$$

Change to decimals:

$$0.04(x) + 0.03(10,000 - x) = 385$$

Multiply by 100:
$$4x + 3(10,000 - x) = 38,500$$
$$4x + 30,000 - 3x = 38,500$$
$$x + 30,000 = 38,500$$

Subtract 30,000:
$$x = 8,500$$

CHECK

$$0.04(x) + 0.03(10,000 - x) = 385$$

$x = 8,500$: $\quad 4(8,500) + 0.03(10,000 - 8,500) = 385$

$$340 + 0.03(1,500) = 385$$

$$340 + 45 = 385$$

$$385 = 385 \checkmark$$

ANSWER

$8,500

EXERCISE

1. Mrs. Jackson has $7,000 to invest. If she invests part at 6% simple annual interest and part at 8% simple annual interest, she will get an annual return of $520. How much should she invest at 8%?

    (A) $2,500   (B) $3,000   (C) $5,000   (D) $2,000

(see answer on page 107)

Age Problems

Example

Jack is twice as old as Lillian. Six years ago Jack was five times as old as Lillian was then. How old is Lillian now?

ANALYSIS

Let x = Lillian's age now
Let $2x$ = Jack's age now
Let $x - 6$ = Lillian's age 6 years ago
Let $2x - 6$ = Jack's age 6 years ago

WORK

Six years ago Jack was five times as old as Lillian was then.

$$2x - 6 = 5(x - 6)$$
$$2x - 6 = 5x - 30$$

Add 30: $\qquad 2x + 24 = 5x$

Subtract $2x$: $\qquad 24 = 3x$

Divide by 3: $\qquad 8 = x$

ANSWER

8 years old

EXERCISES

1. Jenny is now 18 and Carmen is 12. How many years ago was Jenny twice as old as Carmen?

   (A) 3 years ago   (B) 8 years ago   (C) 6 years ago   (D) 4 years ago

2. A father is now 28 years older than his son. Ten years ago the father was 15 times as old as his son. How old is the father now?

   (A) 40 years old   (B) 28 years old   (C) 36 years old   (D) 42 years old

(see answers on page 107)

Discounts and Price Increases

Example

If the city of Pottersville has 8,000 residents now and is projected to lose 8% of its population next year and another 5% the following year, what will be its population at the end of two years?

ANALYSIS

If Pottersville will lose 8% of its population, it will retain 92%, so take 92% of 8,000. Then, if it loses another 5% of its population, it will retain 95%, so take 95% of the 92% of 8,000.

WORK

$$0.92 \times 8,000 = 7,360$$
$$0.95 \times 7,360 = 6,992$$

ANSWER

6,992

EXERCISE

1. The price on a $200 suit was increased by 25%. The merchant was unable to sell the suit, so it was then discounted by 12%. What was the final selling price?

   (A) $225   (B) $220   (C) $240   (D) $210

(see answer on page 107)

Percentage Problems

Example 1

If a suit is reduced by $40 and this represents a 25% discount, what was the original price of the suit?

ANALYSIS

Let x = the original price, and set $40 equal to 25% of the original price x.

WORK

$$40 = 0.25x$$

Multiply by 100:

$$100 < 40 = 0.25x >$$
$$4,000 = 25x$$

Divide by 25:

$$160 = x$$
$$x = 160$$

ANSWER

$160

Example 2

What percent of 50 is 90?

ANALYSIS

Let $x =$ the unknown percent. "Of" indicates multiplication, so we have to multiply 50 by a percent in order to arrive at 90.

WORK

$$x \cdot 50 = 90$$

Divide by 50:

$$x = 90/50 = 1.8 = 180\%$$
$$x = 1.80$$

Change to percent:

$$x = 180\%$$

ANSWER

180%

Example 3

Tiesha works on a base salary of $525 per week plus a 6% commission on sales. If she sold $3,300 worth of items last week, how much was her total salary?

ANALYSIS

Find 6% of $3,300, and add to her base salary of $525.

WORK

$$0.06 \times \$3,300 = \$198$$
$$+\$525$$
$$\overline{\$723}$$

ANSWER

$723

EXERCISES

1. An auto dealer increases the price of a used car 15%. If the new price is $6,900, what was the original price of the car?
   (A) $5,000   (B) $6,200   (C) $5,900   (D) $6,000

2. Fifty is what percent of 20?
   (A) 250%   (B) 40%   (C) 25%   (D) 400%

3. Maria is a salesperson. She works on a base salary of $400 per week plus an 8% commission. If she sold $7,000 worth of pharmaceuticals last week, what was her salary?
   (A) $780   (B) $960   (C) $840   (D) $984

(see answers on page 107)

Distance Problems

Example

Glen drove a distance of 182 miles in $3\frac{1}{2}$ hours. What was his average rate of speed?

ANALYSIS

Use the distance formula $d = rt$, where d = distance, r = rate, and t = time.

WORK

$$d = rt$$

$d = 182, t = 3\frac{1}{2}:$ $\qquad$ $182 = r\left(3\frac{1}{2}\right)$

$$182 = \frac{7}{2}r$$

Multiply by $\frac{2}{7}$: $\qquad$ $\frac{2}{7} < 182 = \frac{7}{2}r >$

$$r = 52$$

ANSWER

52 mph

EXERCISE

1. Aristide is a train engineer. If the distance between two cities is 350.4 miles, and he wants to make the trip in 6 hours, what should his average rate of speed be?
   (A) 58.4 mph   (B) 62.6 mph   (C) 87.6 mph   (D) 43.8 mph

(see answer on page 107)

STATISTICS

Whenever we're presented with a lot of data, we usually have to sort it out. Statistics helps us make sense of the loads of data we're constantly receiving.

The Mean or Average

We are often interested in a typical product, consumer, voter, or the like. When we talk about "typical," we are looking for something representative of an entire group. We are talking about some sort of central tendency. We can measure central tendency in three ways:

1. The mean or average
2. The mode
3. The median

The mean or average is simply the sum of the various pieces of data divided by the number of data.

> **DEFINITION**
>
> The **mean** or **average** is simply the sum of the various pieces of data divided by the number of data.

Example

Julio is on the track team. He recorded the miles he ran each day for the past week: 5.9, 6, 3.7, 6.2, 4.5, 6.1, 3.8. To the nearest tenth of a mile, what was the mean number of miles he ran a day?

ANALYSIS

Add up all the miles and divide by 7, the number of days Julio ran.

WORK

$$\overline{x} = \frac{5.9+6+3.7+6.2+4.5+6.1+3.8}{7} = \frac{36.2}{7} = 5.17\ldots \approx 5.2$$

ANSWER

5.2

1. The Basic Cookware Company has a quality control program. On a weekly basis, inspectors check damages in their manufactured dishes. During the first six weeks of the program, inspectors found the following numbers of dishes damaged, by week: 23, 18, 34, 27, 26, 19.

If management wants to hold the mean number of damaged dishes per week to 24 for the first seven weeks, what is the maximum allowable number of damaged dishes during the seventh week?

(A) 21   (B) 24   (C) 18   (D) 25

(see answer on page 107)

DEFINITION

The **median** is the middle number in an ordered set of data.

The Median

Sometimes we're not interested in determining the mean. We want to find the middle number. The **median** is the middle number in an ordered set of data.

Example 1

Over the past week, Jose has slept the following numbers of hours per night: 9, 8, 9, 7, 6.5, 7.4, 6.3. Find the median.

ANALYSIS

To determine the median, list the numbers from smallest to largest and then select the middle number.

WORK

Median:

$$6.3, 6.5, 7, 7.4, 8, 9, 9$$

↑
middle number

ANSWER

7.4

Example 2

Find the median of the following numbers: 34, 56, 9, 67, 25, 49.

ANALYSIS

In this case, we have an even amount of numbers, so we'll first arrange the numbers in ascending order and then add the two middle numbers and divide by 2.

WORK

$$9 + 25 + \underline{34 + 49} + 56 + 67$$

$$\frac{34 + 49}{2} = \frac{83}{2} = 41.5$$

ANSWER

41.5

EXERCISE

1. Students in the physics class received the following grades on their last exam: 80, 75, 65, 92, 56, 79, 48, 58, 92, 85, 76, 68. Find the median.
   (A) 76   (B) 74.5   (C) 75.5   (D) 74

(see answer on page 107)

The Mode

The mode is the easiest measure in statistics.

Example

Mr. Vargas, the owner of Vargas's Shoe Store, has recorded the daily sales of shoes in his store for the past 12 days: 23, 18, 19, 12, 18, 16, 22, 12, 19, 15, 23, 19. Find the mode and the median and compare the two.

DEFINITION

The **mode** is the number that occurs most frequently in a given set of data. It's possible to have more than one mode.

ANALYSIS

List the numbers in ascending order. Find the number occurring most often as well as the middle number.

WORK

Mode: 12, 12, 15, 16, 18, 18, **19**, **19**, **19**, 22, 23, 23
    Nineteen occurs most often, so it's the mode.
Median: 12, 12, 15, 16, 18, 18, **19, 19, 19,** 22, 23, 23

$$\frac{18 + 19}{2} = \frac{37}{2} = 18.5$$

ANSWER

The mode is 19; the median 18.5.

1. Mr. Hiarnachy, the owner of Howie's Shoes, has recorded the daily sales of shoes for the past 12 days: 35, 19, 23, 32, 19, 28, 35, 31, 23, 18, 17, 19. Find the mode.
   (A) 35   (B) 23   (C) 22   (D) 19

(see answer on page 107)

Probability

Probability means the likelihood of a particular event occurring. Probability is a number between and including 0 and 1.

A probability of 0 means that the event will absolutely not occur.
A probability of 1 means that the event is certain to occur.

Probability is expressed as a percent or a ratio.

$P(\text{event}) = 25\% \text{ or } 1:4$

Example

A jar contains 6 blue marbles, 7 red marbles, and 2 white marbles. Without looking, find $P(\text{blue})$.

ANALYSIS

The probability of selecting a blue marble, $P(b)$, is equal to the number of blue marbles B out of the total number of marbles T.

WORK

$$P(b) = \frac{B}{T}$$

$B = 6$, $T = 15$:

$$P(b) = \frac{6}{15} = \frac{2}{5}$$

ANSWER

$\dfrac{2}{5}$

1. Out of a deck of 52 cards, what is the probability of selecting a king?
   (A) 1/13   (B) 1/4   (C) 2/13   (D) 3/52

(see answer on page 107)

ANSWERS TO MATHEMATICS REVIEW EXERCISES

Natural and Whole Numbers, p. 19
1. D 2. B 3. C

Comparing Integers, p. 20
1. D 2. A 3. D 4. B

Exponents, p. 22
1. A 2. B 3. B

Order of Operations, p. 23
1. D 2. A 3. C 4. C

Rounding Off Integers, p. 23
1. D 2. C 3. A 4. A

Prime Numbers, p. 24
1. C 2. B 3. D

Challenge Question, p. 26
28

Factors and Multiples, p. 26
1. D 2. C 3. D 4. B

Reducing Fractions, p. 28
1. A 2. C 3. B

Changing Improper Fractions to Whole or Mixed Numbers, p. 30
1. A 2. D 3. C

Changing Mixed Numbers to Improper Fractions, p. 30
1. B 2. B

Equivalent Fractions, p. 32
1. A 2. yes

Operations with Fractions, p. 35
1. D 2. C 3. A 4. B 5. B

Challenge Question, p. 35
5 1/3 minutes

Comparing Decimals and Fractions, p. 37
1. C 2. B 3. C

Rounding Off Decimals, p. 38
1 A 2. D

Operations with Decimals, p. 40
1. D 2. C 3. D 4. A

Scientific Notation, p. 41
1. C 2. D

Changing Fractions and Whole Numbers to Percents, p. 42
1. A 2. D

Changing Percents to Fractions, p. 43
1. A

Changing Decimals to Percents, p. 43
1. C

Changing Percents to Decimals, p. 44
1. D

Applications, p. 45
1. B

Algebra, p. 46
1. C 2. D

Arithmetic Operations with Signed Numbers, p. 49
1. A 2. C 3. B

Formulas, p. 50
1. B

Equations, p. 50
1. B

Challenge Question, p. 50
7

Simplifying Exponential Expressions, p. 52
1. D

Simplifying Radicals, p. 54
1. B 2. D

Operations with Radicals, p. 54
1. D 2. C

Inequalities, p. 56
1. C

Operations with Monomials and Polynomials, p. 57
1. C 2. A 3. C 4. D

Absolute Value, p. 58
1. C 2. D

Ratios and Proportions, p. 60
1. C

Challenge Question, p. 62
49

Consecutive Integers, p. 62
1. D 2. C 3. B

Angles, p. 64
1. C

Reflex Angles, p. 65
1. B 2. B

Complementary and Supplementary Angles, p. 67
1. B 2. B

Adjacent Angles, p. 67
1. D

Coordinare Geometry, p. 70
1. A 2. A

Polygons, p. 71
1. C 2. D

Parallelograms, p. 72
1. B 2. C

Challenge Question, p. 72
28°

Triangles, p. 73
1. A

Types of Triangles, Classified by Angles p. 74
1. D

Perimeters, p. 75
1. D

Equilateral and Isosceles Triangles, p. 76
1. D 2. B 3. A

Polygons, p. 77
1. C 2. A 3. B

Pythagorean Theorem, p. 79
1. D

Circumference, p. 80
1. B

Challenge Question, p. 80
34.7

Area, p. 81
1. C 2. D

Central Angles, p. 81
1. A

Sectors, p. 82
1. B

Rectangular Solids, p. 83
1. B 2. B

Cubes, p. 84
1. B 2. A

Right Circular Cylinders, p. 85
1. A

Challenge Question, p. 85
51.4 cu. in.

Cones, p. 86
1. C

Spheres, p. 86
1. A

U.S. Weight Measures, p. 87
1. C

U.S. Length Measures, p. 88
1. B 2. D 3. D

U.S. Liquid Measures, p. 89
1. B 2. C

Changing Metric Measures and U.S. Measures, p. 90
1. C 2. A

Line Graphs, p. 91
1. B

Circle Graphs, p. 92
1. B

Bar Graphs, p. 93
1. D

Tables, p. 94
1. A

Challenge Question, p. 95
$457,000

Wage Problems, p. 96
1. B 2. A 3. D

ANSWERS EXPLAINED TO SELECTED MATHEMATICS REVIEW EXERCISES

ORDER OF OPERATIONS, P. 23

4. ANALYSIS

Simplify each exponential expression and then multiply.

WORK

$$9^1 \cdot (-2)^3$$
$$= 9 \cdot (-2)(-2)(-2)$$
$$= 9 \cdot (-8)$$
$$= -72$$

ANSWER

(C)

PRIME NUMBERS, P. 25

3. ANALYSIS

A prime number is a counting number that can only be divided by 1 and itself without resulting in a remainder.

WORK

11 and 13 are greater than 7 but less than or equal to 15 and can only be divided by 1 and the numbers themselves.

ANSWER

(D)

FACTORS AND MULTIPLES, P. 26

4. ANALYSIS

Find the prime numbers that, when multiplied, result in a product of 30.

WORK

3, 5, and 2 are prime numbers.

$$3 \cdot 5 \cdot 2 = 30$$

ANSWER

(B)

EQUIVALENT FRACTIONS, P. 32

2. ANALYSIS

Change 7/8 to 24ths and then compare.

WORK

$$\frac{7}{8} = \frac{21}{24} \ \checkmark$$

ANSWER

Yes

OPERATIONS WITH FRACTIONS, P. 35

4. ANALYSIS

Change 2 5/12 to an improper fraction, invert, and multiply by 5/6.

WORK

$$\frac{5}{6} \div 2\frac{5}{12}$$

$$\frac{5}{6} \div \frac{29}{12}$$

$$\frac{5}{\cancel{6}_{1}} \div \frac{\cancel{12}^{2}}{29} = \frac{10}{29}$$

ANSWER

(B)

COMPARING DECIMALS AND FRACTIONS, P. 37

3. ANALYSIS

Which decimal is the closest equivalent of 2/3?

WORK

$$.666 = .666\frac{2}{3} = .666$$

$$
\begin{array}{r}
.6\,6\,6 \\
3\,\overline{)2.0\,0\,0} \\
1\ 8\mathrm{xx} \\
\overline{20} \\
1\,8 \\
\overline{20} \\
1\,8 \\
\overline{2}
\end{array}
$$

ANSWER

(C)

SCIENTIFIC NOTATION, P. 41

2. ANALYSIS

Scientific notation is a compact way of writing a number as the product of another number between 1 and 10 and a power of 10.

$$10^1 = 10$$
$$10^2 = 10 \times 10 = 100$$
$$10^3 = 10 \times 10 \times 10 = 1{,}000$$
$$10^4 = 10 \times 10 \times 10 \times 10 = 10{,}000$$

WORK

$$6{,}941 = 6.941 \times 1{,}000$$
$$= 6.941 \times 10^3$$

ANSWER

(D)

APPLICATIONS, P. 45

1. ANALYSIS

If 8% were vegetarians, 92% were not vegetarians. Change 92% to a decimal and multiply by 450.

WORK

$$
\begin{array}{r}
450 \\
\times .92 \\
\hline
900 \\
4050 \\
\hline
414.00
\end{array}
$$

ANSWER

(B)

ALGEBRA, P. 46

2. ANALYSIS

Substitute 5 for b in the expression $2b^3 + 8$.

WORK

$$
\begin{aligned}
& 2b^3 + 8 \\
= \ & 2(5)^3 + 8 \\
= \ & 2(5)(5)(5) + 8 \\
= \ & 2(125) + 8 \\
= \ & 250 + 8 \\
= \ & 258
\end{aligned}
$$

ANSWER

(D)

FORMULAS, P. 50

1. ANALYSIS

Substitute 104° for F in the given formula.

WORK

$$
C = \frac{5}{9}(F - 32)
$$

F = 104:

$$
C = \frac{5}{9}(104 - 32)
$$

$$
C = \frac{5}{\cancel{9}}(\cancel{72}^{\,8}) = 40
$$

ANSWER

(B)

SIMPLIFYING RADICALS, P. 54

2. ANALYSIS

We want to determine a term that, when multiplied by itself four times, results in $\sqrt{98}$.

WORK

$$\sqrt{98} = \sqrt{2 \cdot 49} = \sqrt{2}\,\sqrt{49} = 7\sqrt{2}$$

CHECK:

$$\left(7\sqrt{2}\right)\left(7\sqrt{2}\right) = 49\sqrt{4} = 49 \cdot 2 = 98$$

ANSWER

(D)

OPERATIONS WITH MONOMIALS AND POLYNOMIALS, P. 57

4. ANALYSIS

Division of polynomials proceeds in the same manner as regular division of whole numbers.

WORK

$$
\begin{array}{r}
-3r \;\; +2r^2 \\
-6r^5 \overline{)18r^6 - 12r^7} \\
- \\
\oplus 18r^6 \\
\hline
-12r^7 \\
+ \\
\ominus 12r^7
\end{array}
$$

ANSWER

(D)

CONSECUTIVE ODD INTEGERS, P. 62

3. ANALYSIS

Let x = the first odd integer
Let $x + 2$ = the second consecutive odd integer
Let $x + 4$ = the third consecutive odd integer

WORK

$$x + (x + 2) + (x + 4) = 141$$
$$x + x + 2 + x + 4 = 141$$
$$3x + 6 = 141$$

Subtract 6: $3x = 135$
Divide by 3: $x = 45$
The second consecutive odd
   Integer: $x + 2 = 47$

ANSWER

(B)

SUPPLEMENTARY ANGLES, P. 67

2. ANALYSIS

Supplementary angles add up to 180°.

WORK

$$180° - 9b° = (180 - 9b)°$$

ANSWER

(B)

PARALLELOGRAMS, P. 72

2. ANALYSIS

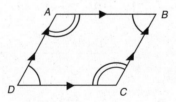

Two consecutive angles are supplementary: $m\angle A + m\angle B = 180°$

WORK

$$123° + m\angle B = 180°$$
Subtract 123°: $m\angle B = 180°$
$$m\angle B = 57°$$

ANSWER

(C)

EQUILATERAL TRIANGLES, P. 76

3. ANALYSIS

All the sides of an equilateral triangle are congruent, so, in order to find one side, just divide the perimeter, 8, by 3.

WORK

$$\frac{8}{3} = 2\frac{2}{3}$$

ANSWER

(A)

POLYGONS, P. 77

3. ANALYSIS

Use the formula for the area of a triangle, $A = \frac{1}{2}bh$, where A = area, b = base, and h = height.

WORK

$$A = \frac{1}{2}bh$$

$A = 36$, $h = 8$: $\qquad 36 = \frac{1}{2}b(8)$

$\qquad\qquad\qquad\qquad 36 = 4b$

Divide by 4: $\qquad\qquad b = 9$

ANSWER

(B)

AREA, P. 81

2. ANALYSIS

Use the formula for the area of a circle and substitute 12.56 for the area A and 3.14 for π.

WORK

$$A = \pi r^2$$

$A = 12.56$, $\pi = 3.14$: $\qquad 12.56 = 3.14r^2$

Divide by 3.14: $\qquad\qquad\qquad 4 = r^2$

Take the positive square root of 4: $\qquad r = 2$

ANSWER

(D)

SECTORS, P. 82

1. ANALYSIS

The full circle contains 360°, so, to determine the fraction of the circle the sector fills, reduce 45°/360°. Then multiply the result by the area of the circle.

WORK

$$\frac{45}{360} = \frac{1}{8}$$

To determine the area of the circle, use the formula $A = \pi r^2$, where A = area, π = 3, and $r = 2$.

$\pi = 3, r = 2$:

$$A = \pi r^2$$
$$A = 3(2)^2$$
$$A = 3(4)$$
$$A = 12$$
$$\frac{1}{8} \times 12 = 1.5$$

ANSWER

(B)

SPHERES, P. 86

1. ANALYSIS

Use the formula and substitute 2 for the radius and 3 for π.

WORK

$$V = \frac{4}{3}\pi r^3$$

$\pi = 3, r = 2$:

$$V = \frac{4}{\cancel{3}}(\cancel{3})(2)^3$$
$$V = 4(8)$$
$$V = 32$$

ANSWER

(A)

U.S. LIQUID MEASURES, P. 89

2. ANALYSIS

There are two pints to a quart, so, to change pints to quarts, divide pints by two.

WORK

$$\frac{24 \text{ pints}}{2 \text{ pints per quart}} = 12 \text{ quarts}$$

ANSWER

(C)

CHANGING METRIC MEASURES AND U.S. MEASURES, P. 90

2. ANALYSIS

One kilogram equals 2.2 pounds, so just multiply 15.4 kilograms by 2.2 and round off to the nearest whole pound.

WORK

$$
\begin{array}{r}
15.4 \\
\times\ 2.2 \\
\hline
3\ 08 \\
30\ 8 \\
\hline
33.88 \approx 34
\end{array}
$$

ANSWER

(A)

CIRCLE GRAPHS, P. 92

1. ANALYSIS

In order to determine what percent of each day is spent working, add up the given percents and subtract from 100%. Then multiply the answer by 24 hours.

WORK

$$15\% + 20\% + 30\% = 65\%$$
$$100\% - 65\% = 35\%$$

$$0.35 \times 24 \text{ hours} = 8.4 \text{ hours}$$

Change 0.4 of an hour to minutes:

$$0.4 \times 60 \text{ minutes in one hour} = 24 \text{ minutes}$$
$$8.4 \text{ hours} = 8 \text{ hours, 24 minutes}$$

ANSWER

(B)

TABLES, P. 94

1. ANALYSIS

The Nautica Bank is paying 2.0% annual interest, whereas the Bennington Bank is paying 1% interest. Change percents to decimals, multiply both by $8,000, and then determine the difference.

WORK

Nautica Bank:	$0.02 \times \$8,000 = \$160$
Bennington Bank:	$-0.01 \times \$8,000 = \ \ \$80$
	$\$80$

ANSWER

(A)

WAGE PROBLEMS, P. 96

3. ANALYSIS

Multiply $12.48 by 40 hours. Then multiply $15.75 by 7, the number of hours of overtime. Finally, add the two answers.

WORK

Nautica Bank:	$40 \times \$12.48 = \$499.20$
Bennington Bank:	$+ \ \ 7 \times \$15.75 = \$110.25$
	$\$609.45$

ANSWER

(D)

AGE PROBLEMS, P. 98

2. ANALYSIS

Let x = the son's age now and let $28 + x$ = the father's age now.
Let $x - 10$ = the son's age 10 years ago and let $(28 + x) - 10$ = the father's age 10 years ago.

WORK

Ten years ago the father was 15 times as old as his son.

$$(28 + x) - 10 = 15(x - 10)$$
$$28 + x - 10 = 15x - 150$$
$$18 + x = 15x - 150$$

Subtract x: $\qquad\qquad 18 = 14x - 150$

Add 150: $\qquad\qquad\quad 168 = 14x$

Divide by 14: $\qquad\qquad 12 = x$ (son's age now)

$$28 + x = 40 \text{ (father's age now)}$$

ANSWER

(A)

PERCENTAGE PROBLEMS, P. 100

3. ANALYSIS

Change 8% to a decimal and multiply by $7,000. Then add $400.

WORK

Commission: $\qquad 0.08 \times \$7,000 = \$560$

Base Salary: $\qquad\qquad\qquad\qquad + \$400$

Total: $\qquad\qquad\qquad\qquad\qquad \$960$

ANSWER

(B)

DISTANCE PROBLEMS, P. 101

1. ANALYSIS

Use the formula $d = rt$, where $d =$ distance, $r =$ rate, and $t =$ time.

WORK

$$d = rt$$

$d = 350.4$, $t = 6$: $\qquad 350.4 = r(6)$

Divide by 6: $\qquad\qquad 58.4 = r$

ANSWER

(A)

THE MEAN OR AVERAGE, P. 102

1. ANALYSIS

Let $x =$ the number of broken dishes during the seventh week. Add up all of the broken dishes for seven weeks and set the average equal to 24. The number of dishes broken during the seventh week must be less than or equal to the average.

WORK

$$\frac{23+18+34+27+26+19+x}{7} = 24$$

$$\frac{147+x}{7} = 24$$

Multiply by 7: $147 + x = 168$

Subtract 147: $x = 21$

ANSWER

(A)

THE MEDIAN, P. 103

1. ANALYSIS

The median is the middle number, so arrange the numbers in order and locate the middle number. If there is an even amount of numbers, find the average of the two middle numbers.

WORK

48, 56, 58, 65, 68, **75**, **76**, 79, 80, 85, 92, 92

Find the average of 75 and 76: $\dfrac{75+76}{2} = \dfrac{151}{2} = 75.5$

ANSWER

(C)

PROBABILITY, P. 104

1. ANALYSIS

There are four kings in a regular deck of cards.

WORK

$$\frac{4}{52} = \frac{1}{13}$$

ANSWER

(A)

Math Review Questions

1. Which of these numbers is the equivalent of 9^3?
   (A) 729
   (B) 512
   (C) 392
   (D) 649

2. Kelly weighs 119 pounds. Her brother, Hector, weighs 12 pounds more than Kelly while her sister, Jasmine, weighs 17 pounds less than Hector. Find their total weight.

   (A) 357 pounds
   (B) 364 pounds
   (C) 354 pounds
   (D) 350 pounds

3–4 The table below lists weights of a group of six persons.

Pounds	# of Persons
118	2
132	3
163	1

3. If we drop the two persons weighing 118 pounds, what is the average weight of the remaining persons, correct to the nearest tenth of a pound?

   (A) 154.6
   (B) 152.3
   (C) 141.4
   (D) 139.8

4. Find the average weight of all six persons, correct to the nearest pound.

   (A) 133
   (B) 143
   (C) 145
   (D) 139

5–6 **2,600 Cars Sold by Zany Dealers**

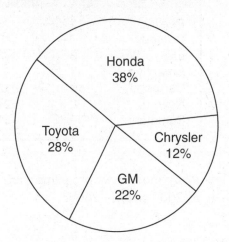

5. According to the chart, how many Chryslers did the dealership sell?

   (A) 298
   (B) 312
   (C) 324
   (D) 402

6. How many more Toyotas than GM cars did Zany Dealers sell?

   (A) 156
   (B) 312
   (C) 728
   (D) 208

Major Network Television Shows					
	2006	**2007**	**2008**	**2009**	**Summary**
Reality	2	3	12	14	31
Comedy	7	9	8	7	31
Law	3	6	7	5	21
Detective	7	7	6	10	30
Cartoons	10	12	12	16	50
News	20	24	15	15	74
Summary	49	61	60	67	237

7. How many more news programs were there in 2006 than in 2009?

(A) 6
(B) 7
(C) 5
(D) 4

8. In 2008, what percent of all television shows were detective stories?

(A) 25%
(B) 18%
(C) 30%
(D) 10%

9. Mario is on the track team. He ran the following number of miles each day for three meets: 5.9, 6, 3.7. What was the average number of miles he ran at a meet?

(A) 4.5
(B) 5.2
(C) 5.1
(D) 6.2

10. A cargo ship has a capacity of 4,000 tons. If it sails from Los Angeles to Singapore carrying 2/5 of its capacity and returns carrying 4/5 of its capacity, how many tons did it carry round-trip?

(A) 3,800 tons
(B) 4,600 tons
(C) 4,700 tons
(D) 4,800 tons

11. Carmen wants to paint a wall 12 feet high by 32 feet long. If 1 quart of paint covers 24 square feet of wall space, how many quarts of paint does she need to cover the entire wall?

(A) 16 quarts
(B) 14 quarts
(C) 15 quarts
(D) 13 quarts

12. The Maxim Movie Theater collected $1,314 yesterday. If the adults paid $1,050 and each child's admission was $5.50, how many children were admitted?

(A) 48
(B) 52
(C) 46
(D) 51

13. Emily works for 48 hours at the rate of $22 per hour for the first 40 hours and time-and-a-half for any hours above 40. What is her total salary?

(A) $1,144
(B) $1,250
(C) $1,380
(D) $1,360

14. Roger has a 0.250 batting average. If he went up to bat 240 times, how many times did he fail to get any hits? (A 0.250 batting average means that he got hits 0.250 times at bat.)

    (A) 170 times
    (B) 180 times
    (C) 190 times
    (D) 200 times

15. If $900 is to be divided equally among a group of people, how many persons are in the group?

    (A) 17
    (B) 19
    (C) 21
    (D) 15

16. Carter was on a diet. When he weighed himself at the start of his diet, he weighed 220 pounds. At the end of 6 months, Carter weighed 180 pounds. What fraction of his original weight did he lose?

    (A) 1/8
    (B) 4/13
    (C) 3/16
    (D) 2/11

17. A flat piece of metal weighs 2.4 grams per square centimeter. Find the weight of a 7-centimeter by 12-centimeter piece of metal.

    (A) 201.6 grams
    (B) 204.7 grams
    (C) 203.5 grams
    (D) 209.8 grams

18. Each of five cabbies drives an average of 453 miles a day. Six other cabbies each drives an average of 487 miles a day. How many miles do all eleven cabbies together drive per day?

    (A) 5,585 miles
    (B) 5,387 miles
    (C) 5,187 miles
    (D) 5,516 miles

19. Simplify $3(8.3 + 3.8) - 2(3.6 - 2.7)$.

    (A) 33
    (B) 32.4
    (C) 34.5
    (D) 36.8

20. Find the difference of 6.3 and $^1/_2$.

    (A) 6.1
    (B) 5 $^1/_4$
    (C) 5 $^3/_4$
    (D) 5.8

21. What is the difference of 4.11 and 3.26?

    (A) 0.97
    (B) 0.85
    (C) 0.92
    (D) 0.87

22. Find the product of $^3/_4$ and 2/5. Reduce to lowest terms.

    (A) 6/20
    (B) 5/8
    (C) 3/10
    (D) 4/9

23. Which of the following is a prime number?

    (A) 7 .
    (B) 9
    (C) 12
    (D) 15

24. Simplify $3(7 - 3)^2 - 4(6 + 2)$.

    (A) 18
    (B) 16
    (C) 17
    (D) 20

25. Without stopping, Maxine drives from Danbury to San Sebastian, a distance of 348 miles. If she leaves at 8 A.M. and arrives at 2 P.M., what was her average rate of speed?

    (A) 62 mph
    (B) 61 mph
    (C) 59 mph
    (D) 58 mph

26. Find the quotient of 1,296 and 27.

    (A) 43
    (B) 46
    (C) 43
    (D) 48

27. Change 5/8 to a decimal and round off to the nearest hundredth.

    (A) 0.63
    (B) 0.56
    (C) 0.64
    (D) 0.57

28. Which of the following numbers is a multiple of 7?

    (A) 56
    (B) 36
    (C) 48
    (D) 72

29. Add 3 3/4, 2 1/3, and 5 1/2.

    (A) 10 7/9
    (B) 10 5/9
    (C) 11 7/12
    (D) 9 7/11

30. Change 2.36 to a mixed number and reduce to lowest terms.

    (A) 2 36/100
    (B) 2 18/50
    (C) 2 3/8
    (D) 2 9/25

31. If points A (2, 2), B (4, 5), and C (6, 2) represent the vertices of a triangle, determine its area.

    (A) 12
    (B) 8
    (C) 6
    (D) 10

32. Use the formula $A = \pi r^2$ to determine the area, A, of a circle where $\pi = 3.14$ and r represents a radius of 6. Round to the nearest whole number.

    (A) 113
    (B) 109
    (C) 110
    (D) 108

33. On the real number line, if the distance between two numbers is 3.8, which of the following sets correctly represents the two numbers?

    (A) 4.7 and 11.3
    (B) 9.6 and 5.8
    (C) 12.4 and 6.5
    (D) 9.3 and 3.7

34. Henry receives a salary of $530 per week. José gets 30% more than Henry. If they both receive $70 per week raises, how much will José be earning?

    (A) $650
    (B) $458
    (C) $759
    (D) $568

35. The three-digit number $49x$ is divisible by 4 with no remainders. If the sum of the digits is divisible by 5 with no remainders, what is the number?

    (A) 492
    (B) 497
    (C) 493
    (D) 498

36. On the scale below the symbol ⊢⊣ represents 16 miles. If Jason drives at a speed of 64 miles per hour, how long will it take him to drive from city A to city B?

A  B

(A) 45 minutes
(B) 1 hour, 15 minutes
(C) 2 hours
(D) 1 hour, 30 minutes

37. Jessica weighs $x + 34$ pounds and Rhonda weighs 12 pounds less. If Jessica gains 5 pounds and Rhonda loses 2 pounds, what is the sum of their new weights?

(A) $2x + 59$
(B) $2x - 22$
(C) $x + 56$
(D) $3x - 8$

38. Each of the equal sides of an isosceles triangle is 7 and its base is 2 more than the base of an equilateral triangle. If the perimeters of the two triangles are equal, find a side of the equilateral triangle.

(A) 8
(B) 5
(C) 9
(D) 6

39. The areas of a rectangle and a square are equal. If one side of the square is twice the width of the rectangle and the length of the rectangle is 16, find the width of the rectangle.

(A) 6
(B) 10
(C) 4
(D) 8

40. In the accompanying triangle *ABC*, the lengths of *AC* and *BC* are 5 and 7 respectively. Find the length of the hypotenuse, *AB*, to the nearest tenth of an inch.

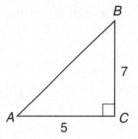

(A) 7.4
(B) 4.5
(C) 8.6
(D) 5.8

ANSWERS

1. ANALYSIS

Expand 9^3.

WORK

$$9^3 = 9 \times 9 \times 9 = 729$$

ANSWER

(A)

2. ANALYSIS

Let Kelly's weight = 119.
Let Hector's weight = 119 + 12 = 131.
Let Jasmine's weight = 131 − 17 = 114.

WORK

$$119 + 131 + 114 = 364$$

ANSWER

(B)

3. ANALYSIS

If we drop two persons, each weighing 118 pounds, we have left three persons, each weighing 132 pounds, and one person weighing 163 pounds. So, add 163 to the product of 3 and 132. Divide by 4 and round off to the nearest tenth of a pound.

WORK

$3 \times 132 = 396$

$+ \quad \underline{163}$

$\quad\quad 559$

$$139.75 \approx 139.8$$
$$4)\overline{559.00}$$
$$\underline{4\,xx\ xx}$$
$$15$$
$$\underline{12}$$
$$39$$
$$\underline{36}$$
$$30$$
$$\underline{28}$$
$$20$$
$$\underline{20}$$

ANSWER

(D)

4. ANALYSIS

Multiply 118 by 2 and 132 by 3. Get their sum, add 163, and divide by 6. Round off to the nearest whole number.

WORK

$2 \times 118 = 236$

$3 \times 132 = 396$

$+ \quad \underline{163}$

$\quad\quad 795$

$$132.5 \approx 133$$
$$6)\overline{795.0}$$
$$\underline{6\,xx\ xx}$$
$$19$$
$$\underline{18}$$
$$15$$
$$\underline{12}$$
$$30$$
$$\underline{30}$$

ANSWER

(A)

5. ANALYSIS

Change the percentage of Chrysler cars sold to a decimal and multiply by the total number of cars sold.

WORK

Chrysler: 12% = .12

$\quad\quad 2600$

$\quad\quad \underline{\times.12}$

$\quad\quad 520\,0$

$\quad\quad \underline{260\,0}$

$\quad\quad 312.00$

ANSWER

(B)

6. ANALYSIS

Change percentages to decimals, multiply by the total number of cars sold, and subtract.

WORK

Toyota 28% = .28

GM: 22% = .22

Toyota: 2600   GM: 2600

$\quad\quad \underline{\times.2\,8} \quad\quad\quad \underline{\times.2\,2}$

$\quad\quad 20800 \quad\quad\quad 5200$

$\quad\quad \underline{5200} \quad\quad\quad\; \underline{5200}$

$\quad\quad 728.00 \quad\quad\; 572.00$

Toyota: 728 cars sold

$- $ GM: 572 cars sold

$\quad\quad\quad\quad \underline{156}$

ANSWER

(A)

7. ANALYSIS

Subtract the number of news programs in 2009 from the news programs in 2006.

WORK

$$
\begin{array}{r}
\text{News programs in } 2006 = 20 \\
- \text{ News programs in } 2009 = 15 \\
\hline
5
\end{array}
$$

ANSWER

(C)

8. ANALYSIS

In 2008, there were 6 detective stories out of a total of 60 shows.

WORK

$$
\frac{6}{60} = \begin{array}{r} .10 \\ 60\overline{)6.00} \\ \underline{6\ 0\,x} \\ 0 \end{array} = 10\%
$$

ANSWER

(D)

9. ANALYSIS

Add up the figures and divide by 3.

WORK

$$
\begin{array}{r}
5.9 \\
6.0 \\
+\ 3.7 \\
\hline
15.6
\end{array}
\qquad
\begin{array}{r}
5.2 \\
3\overline{)15.6} \\
\underline{15\ \ x} \\
6 \\
\underline{6} \\
\end{array}
$$

ANSWER

(B)

10. ANALYSIS

For the weight carried from Los Angeles to Singapore, multiply 2/5 by 4,000. For the return weight, from Singapore back to Los Angeles, multiply 4/5 by 4,000. Then add the two results.

WORK

$$
\begin{array}{r}
\dfrac{2}{1\,\cancel{5}} \times \overset{800}{\cancel{4,000}} = 1,600 \\[2ex]
+\ \dfrac{4}{1\,\cancel{5}} \times \overset{800}{\cancel{4,000}} = 3,200 \\[1ex]
\hline
4,800 \text{ tons}
\end{array}
$$

ANSWER

(D)

11. ANALYSIS

First, find the area of the wall. Then divide by 24, the number of square feet 1 gallon of paint covers.

WORK

$$
\begin{array}{r}
3\,2 \\
\times 1\,2 \\
\hline
6\,4 \\
3\,2 \\
\hline
384
\end{array}
\qquad
\begin{array}{r}
16 \\
24\overline{)3\,8\,4} \\
\underline{2\,4\ x} \\
1\,4\,4 \\
\underline{1\,4\,4}
\end{array}
$$

ANSWER

(A)

12. ANALYSIS

Subtract the adult admissions from the total money collected. Then divide the result by $5.50, the price of a single child's admission.

WORK

$$
\begin{array}{r}
4\,8. \\
5\wedge50)\overline{264\wedge00.} \\
2200\text{x} \\
\hline
4400 \\
4400 \\
\hline
\end{array}
$$

$$
\begin{array}{r}
\$1314 \\
-\quad 1050 \\
\hline
\$\ 264
\end{array}
$$

ANSWER

(A)

13. ANALYSIS

Multiply 40 hours by \$22 per hour for Emily's regular wages. She worked 8 hours overtime, which is paid at one-and-a-half times \$22 per hour, so multiply 8 by 1.5 × \$22. Then add the two figures.

WORK

$$
\begin{array}{r}
\$22 \times 40 = \$880 \\
+\ \ 8 \times 1.5 \times \$22 = 12 \times \$22 = \$264 \\
\hline
\$1,144
\end{array}
$$

ANSWER

(A)

14. ANALYSIS

If Roger has a 0.250 batting average, that means he got hits 0.250 × 240 times. But he failed to get a hit 0.750 × 240 times (1.000 − 0.250 = 0.750).

WORK

$$
\begin{array}{r}
240 \\
\times\ 0.750 \\
\hline
12000 \\
1680\ \ \\
\hline
180.000
\end{array}
$$

ANSWER

(B)

15. ANALYSIS

Determine which number divides into 900 without a remainder that continues indefinitely.

WORK

$$
\begin{array}{r}
60 \\
15)\overline{900} \\
90\,\text{x} \\
\hline
\end{array}
$$

ANSWER

(D)

16. ANALYSIS

Find the difference in Carter's weight and then divide by 220, his original weight.

WORK

$$
220 - 180 = 40
$$

$$
\frac{40}{220} = \frac{2}{11}
$$

ANSWER

(D)

17. ANALYSIS

Find the area of the metal and then multiply by 2.4, the gram weight of 1 centimeter of metal.

WORK

7 × 12 = 84 square centimeters

$$
\begin{array}{r}
84 \text{ square centimeters} \\
\times\,2.4 \text{ grams per square centimeter} \\
\hline
336 \\
168\ \ \\
\hline
201.6 \text{ grams}
\end{array}
$$

ANSWER

(A)

18. ANALYSIS

Multiply 453 by 5 and 487 by 6 and add the two totals.

WORK

$$
\begin{array}{r} 453 \\ \times 5 \\ \hline 2265 \end{array} \qquad
\begin{array}{r} 487 \\ \times 6 \\ \hline 2922 \end{array} \qquad
\begin{array}{r} 2265 \\ +2922 \\ \hline 5187 \end{array}
$$

ANSWER

(C)

19. ANALYSIS

First, complete the work inside the parentheses. Then subtract the second term from the first one.

WORK

$$
3(8.3 + 3.8) - 2(3.6 - 2.7)
$$
$$
3(12.1) - 2(.9)
$$
$$
36.3 - 1.8
$$
$$
34.5
$$

ANSWER

(C)

20. ANALYSIS

Change $^1/_2$ to a decimal and subtract.

WORK

$$
\left(-\,^1/_2 =\right)\begin{array}{r} 6.3 \\ -.5 \\ \hline 5.8 \end{array}
$$

ANSWER

(D)

21. ANALYSIS

Subtract.

WORK

$$
\begin{array}{r} 4.11 \\ -3.26 \\ \hline 0.85 \end{array}
$$

ANSWER

(B)

22. ANALYSIS

Multiply numerators and denominators separately and then reduce.

WORK

$$
\frac{3}{4} \times \frac{2}{5} = \frac{6}{20} = \frac{3}{10}
$$

ANSWER

(C)

23. ANALYSIS

A prime number has no other factors than 1 and itself.

WORK

(A) $7 = 7 \times 1$
(B) $9 = 3 \times 3$
(C) $12 = 4 \times 3$
(D) $15 = 5 \times 3$

ANSWER

(A)

24. ANALYSIS

Complete the work in the parentheses first.

WORK

$$3(7-3)^2 - 4(6+2) = 3(4)^2 - 4(8)$$
$$= 3(16) - 32$$
$$= 48 - 32 = 16$$

ANSWER

(B)

25. ANALYSIS

Find the time between 8 A.M. and 2 P.M. and then divide that number into the distance.

WORK

$$\begin{array}{r} 2 \text{ P.M.} \\ -8 \text{ A.M.} \\ \hline 6 \text{ hours} \end{array}$$

$$\begin{array}{r} 58 \\ 6\overline{)348} \\ \underline{30\,x} \\ 48 \\ \underline{48} \end{array}$$

ANSWER

(D)

26. ANALYSIS

Divide 1,296 by 27.

WORK

$$\begin{array}{r} 48 \\ 27\overline{)1296} \\ \underline{108\,x} \\ 216 \\ \underline{216} \end{array}$$

ANSWER

(D)

27. ANALYSIS

Divide the denominator, 8, into the numerator, 5, and then round off to the nearest hundredth.

WORK

$$\begin{array}{r} .625 \\ 8\overline{)5.000} \\ \underline{48\,x\,x} \\ 20 \\ \underline{16} \\ 40 \\ \underline{40} \end{array}$$

To the nearest hundredth, $.625 \approx .63$

ANSWER

(A)

28. ANALYSIS

Find the product of 7 and some whole number that will result in one of the given numbers.

WORK

$$7 \times 8 = 56$$

ANSWER

(A)

29. ANALYSIS

Find a common denominator and then add.

WORK

$$\begin{array}{r} 3\dfrac{3}{4} = \dfrac{9}{12} \\[2mm] 2\dfrac{1}{3} = \dfrac{4}{12} \\[2mm] +\quad 5\dfrac{1}{2} = \dfrac{6}{12} \\ \hline 10 \quad \dfrac{19}{12} = 1\dfrac{7}{12} \\[2mm] 11 \quad \dfrac{7}{12} \end{array}$$

ANSWER

(C)

30. ANALYSIS

Let's first write 2.36 as a mixed number. Then we can reduce the fraction part.

WORK

$$2.36 = 2 \ 36/100 = 2 \ 9/25$$
(We divide the numerator and the denominator by 4.)

ANSWER

(D)

31. ANALYSIS

Locate the points on a graph and determine the base and height. Then use the formula $A = \dfrac{1}{2}bh$, where A = area of the triangle, b = the base, and h = the height.

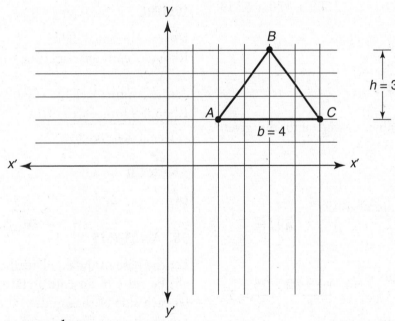

WORK

$$A = \frac{1}{2}bh$$

$b = 4, h = 3$:

$$A = \frac{1}{\cancel{2}_1}(\cancel{4}^2)(3) = 6$$

ANSWER

(C)

32. ANALYSIS

Substitute 3.14 for π and 6 for r and then round to the nearest whole number.

WORK

$$A = \pi r^2$$
$$A = 3.14(6)^2$$
$$A = 3.14 \ (36)$$
$$A = 113.04$$
$$A \approx 113$$

ANSWER

(A)

33. ANALYSIS

Subtract each set of numbers in order to find a difference of 8.6.

WORK

$$9.6 - 5.8 = 3.8$$

ANSWER

(B)

34. ANALYSIS

José is earning 30% more than Henry, or 10% of Henry's wage. Once we determine José's current wage, add $70.

WORK

Henry's wage: $530
José's wage:
$$130\% \times \$530 \text{ or } 1.30 \times \$530 = \$689$$
José's wage after a $70 raise:
$$\$689 + \$70 = \$759$$

ANSWER

(C)

35. ANALYSIS

Substitute the possible answers into the given information.

WORK

(A) The three digit number $49x$
is divisible by 4: $492 = \dfrac{123}{4}$

The sum of the digits is
divisible by 5: $\dfrac{4+9+2}{5} = \dfrac{15}{5} = 3$

ANSWER

(A)

Isosceles Triangle

36. ANALYSIS

To determine the number of miles between cities A and B, count the number of symbols and multiply by 12. Then divide the number of miles by 60 miles per hour, the speed of the car.

WORK

$$6 \times 16 = 96 \text{ miles}$$

$$\frac{96 \text{ miles}}{64 \text{ miles per hour}} = 1\frac{1}{2} = 1 \text{ hour, } 30 \text{ minutes}$$

ANSWER

(D)

37. ANALYSIS

List both current weights. Then list their new weights and add.

WORK

Jessica's current weight: $x + 34$
Rhonda's current weight: $(x + 34) - 12 = x + 22$

Jessica's future weight: $(x + 34) + 5 = x + 39$
Rhonda's future weight: $(x + 22) - 2 = x + 20$
_____
Total weight: $2x + 59$

ANSWER

(A)

38. ANALYSIS

Let the base of the equilateral triangle = x. Since all the sides of an equilateral triangle are equal, let each side of the equilateral triangle = x.
Let the base of the isosceles triangle = $x + 2$.

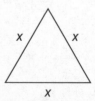

Equilateral Triangle

WORK

The perimeters are equal: $x + 2 + 7 + 7 = 3x$

$x + 16 = 3x$
Subtract x:
$16 = 2x$
Divide by 2:
$x = 8$

ANSWER

(A)

39. ANALYSIS

Let A_S = area of the square and let A_R = area of the rectangle.
Let x = the width of the rectangle and $2x$ = one side of the square. Since all sides of a square are equal, all of the sides are equal to $2x$.

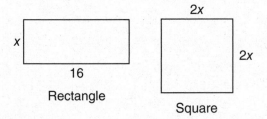

Rectangle   Square

WORK

$$A_S = A_R$$

The areas are equal: $4x^2 = 16x$
Divide by 4: $x^2 = 4x$
Divide by x: $x = 4$

(width of the rectangle)

ANSWER

(C)

40. ANALYSIS

Use the Pythagorean Theorem and let $a = 7$, $b = 5$.

WORK

$$a^2 + b^2 = c^2$$
$$(7)^2 + (5)^2 = c^2$$
$$49 + 25 = c^2$$
$$74 = c^2$$
$$c = \sqrt{74}$$
$$c \approx 8.60 \approx 8.6$$

ANSWER

(C)

Verbal Skills Review

CHAPTER 3

INTRODUCTION

The SSAT and ISEE test verbal skills through vocabulary. Both exams will require you to identify **synonyms**, words with similar meanings. The SSAT contains **analogies** (word relationships), while the ISEE asks you to **complete sentences**.

SSAT	ISEE
Time: 30 minutes	Time: 20 minutes
30 synonyms	20 synonyms
30 analogies	20 sentence completions

Before we discuss the **types** of questions, however, we'll need to review/examine/consider/recall our vocabulary. Don't skip over this section; it will help you on all parts of the verbal tests.

VOCABULARY

A strong vocabulary serves as an essential skill not only for the SSAT and ISEE, but for many of the other standardized tests (SAT, ACT, GRE, LMNOP, TTYL, LOL, ASAP, IMHO, and some very difficult blood tests) you will take in your academic career. Preparing for the vocabulary section may take the most effort, but the rewards

> **VOCABULARY**
>
> Throughout this book, we'll list vocabulary words worth knowing. Read the word, its definition, and a silly sentence. If you draw a picture of the sentence and write out the word in the margin, you'll remember the word more easily.

will be great—not only in improving your exam score but also in improving your studies in all other subjects in school. Moreover, a well-spoken person will win great respect in life.

Obviously, as your vocabulary grows richer, you will find it easier to solve the verbal portion of the test. Let's look at several strategies for vocabulary development. You should choose several of these to practice—at the same time! Language experts have found that overlapping several of these methods reinforces your knowledge and integrates information in different ways. The more ways you encounter a word, the more likely it will become a part of your everyday knowledge.

The best way to strengthen your vocabulary is to READ. Wow, how old-fashioned! Read what you enjoy. Some students love reading the sports section of the newspaper every day, and that's a great start. Branch out and read some sports magazines. Maybe you enjoy reading the comics section of the paper. You would enjoy checking out some of the many fascinating books on the history of comics.

PARENTS/TEACHERS

Building vocabulary will benefit your students in many ways. We make light of standardized tests in the text, but most of the ones your students will take in the coming years do include strong vocabulary components. More importantly, though, a rich vocabulary will help students academically throughout their school years and beyond.

STUDENTS

Reading is the best way to expand your vocabulary. Learning a foreign language can help, too.

Many students pride themselves on reading adult best-sellers. However, we should let you in on a secret: many of these books are actually written **below** your reading level! So if you like Stephen King, you should try Edgar Allan Poe, a horror writer with an incredibly large vocabulary. Perhaps you enjoyed reading young-adult mysteries like those about Nancy Drew or the Hardy Boys. Well, Agatha Christie novels and the Sherlock Holmes stories by Sir Arthur Conan Doyle contain just as much suspense.

To learn the most vocabulary from these books, you must promise to look up unfamiliar words in the dictionary. Any kind will do, but the best dictionary for you will provide **pronunciations** and **word histories** (etymologies).

Oh, it feels like such a chore to get the dictionary off the shelf and then open it up to search for the word. We're tempted to skip learning it.

Those of you with electronic readers can sometimes tap on an unfamiliar word to get the definition. Those of you reading the old-fashioned way have another solution: you should have a dictionary on your desk in front of you whenever you read or do homework. Furthermore, have it open **already**. This simple arrangement will improve your vocabulary immensely. It's not difficult to just flip a few pages and learn the word, its spelling, its pronunciation, its history (which can help you remember it and learn its root), and its various forms.

This brings us to one of the most interesting books of all: the dictionary itself. Don't laugh! Just skipping around in the dictionary is a fascinating way to learn, for every word contains a story. For instance, the day of the week Wednesday was named after the chief Norse god Odin. In Old English, or Anglo-Saxon, this god was called Woden. This is why *wodnesdæg* or Woden's Day or Wednesday is spelled with the letter *d.* (You've heard of the thunder god Thor? Which day is named after him? After the sun? The moon?)

The dictionary is one book that is not going to come out on video and DVD, so don't wait for the movie. Stop being so slothful /indolent /lazy /idle /lethargic; use the dictionary!

Vocabulary Memory Aids

We can easily read about a word, but remembering the information presents new challenges. One of the best ways to study and remember vocabulary words is by making flash cards. Again, if you have an electronic reader or a smart phone, you can download vocabulary applications; however, with flash cards, you can personalize the words with your own sentences and drawings. Keep a stack of flash cards handy, and write down any word that is new to you. Carry the cards with you so you can study them whenever you have a few minutes to spare—on the bus, before class, after lunch, or in study hall. You **should** carry them everywhere. You can even tape some cards inside of your locker, on your mirror, and on your dresser. Will it irritate your family to post vocabulary cards here and there throughout the house? Ah, perhaps that's an added benefit; just tell them it will help *them* in life, as well.

To make it even easier to remember, add some detail to the cards you carry around. Write the word on one side and the definition on the other side, of course. Then add a ridiculous picture to help you remember it. We learn visually, so don't be afraid to draw a crazy picture; the more outlandish you make it, the better you'll remember it.

Finally, write a sentence about the picture. A student once learned the word SPUTUM by writing the definition (saliva and mucous spit out of the mouth) on the back of the card and adding a simple picture of a sick person vomiting up some large Tums brand antacid tablets. The sentence he wrote was "The boy *spewed Tums* in his *sputum.*" It disgusted us, to be sure, but we never forgot the word.

Try some of these yourself. Draw pictures and compose sentences using the following words.

travesty—*a grotesque, mocking, or inferior imitation*
duplicitous—*deceitful; double-dealing*
panegyric—*a speech of high praise*
penultimate—*next to last*
spurious—*not genuine; not authentic*

Computers

If you use a computer and log onto the Internet, you have access to a myriad (many thousands) of reading sources. The next time you're working online, turn off your Instant Messaging, shut your Facebook, forfeit your games, and quit Twitter. Instead, read an article about something that interests you. If you have trouble getting started, go to a trivia site and get some ideas.

You can also painlessly improve your vocabulary by registering for one of the many organizations that will e-mail you a new word every day. Most of these include sentences, word histories, and interesting information about vocabulary. If you check your e-mail every day, learn the new word, and USE it several times that very day, the word will become part of your vocabulary.

Several sites also contain word games, such as vocabulary hangman. Do a web search for *SAT* or *ACT* and *hangman* or *vocabulary*, and you'll get many responses. Challenge the machine and you will emerge victorious!

Crossword Puzzles

Crossword puzzles provide another fun way to learn vocabulary. They especially help in preparing for vocabulary exams because the writers of these puzzles fill them with tricks in which a word can be used as different parts of speech. For instance, a crossword clue might simply read *test*. You have to read this two ways; it's either a noun (*a test*) or a verb (*to test*). You can fight the good fight, jump the high jump, and land on the land. Some words are pronounced differently and have different definitions. Is *desert* the hot, dry area (DEsert) or is it the verb meaning to leave or abandon (deSERT)? Both entrance exams contain words like this to test the flexibility of your thinking.

Be aware that if you do the crossword puzzle in the newspaper every day, the editors publish easy clues and puzzles on Monday. Then the puzzles get harder and harder every day. Don't try working your first puzzle on a Friday! By the way, some people think that using a dictionary while you work the crossword puzzle is cheating. We disagree; we call it LEARNING.

WORD HISTORIES

Knowing the roots of words can also greatly aid in figuring out definitions. You'll learn a lot of these in the dictionary (which, of course, you are using/utilizing/applying/employing/implementing), but we'll go over some common ones.

For instance, the root MOR (or MORT or MORS) means *death* in Latin. Take a few seconds to remember this. Got it? So if you're reading about some characters named Mordred, Morgan, Voldemort, and Professor Moriarty, and they live in a place called Mordor, you may safely assume **bad** news. Are your parents upset when they make their **mort**gage payments? Of course they are, because these house payments are named after a "death pledge." Dead bodies are kept in a **mort**uary. A **mort**ician prepares a body for a funeral. Something *im***mort**al cannot die.

Let's try a few more. Take a few minutes to memorize these.

sub—*under*
super—*over*
medi—*middle*
extra—*beyond*

sol—*sun*
luna—*moon*
terra—*earth (Latin)*
geo—*earth, ground (Greek)*
mar—*sea*

Practice

Using the roots you just memorized, define the following words. Use a note card to cover up the analysis (answers) on the next page until you try the words yourself.

1. sublunary
2. Mediterranean
3. subterranean
4. extraterrestrial
5. submarine

ANALYSIS

1. sublunary—*under the moon.* This refers to earthly things, perhaps worldly or mundane.
2. Mediterranean—*middle of the earth.* The people who named the Mediterranean Sea obviously thought they were the center of everything!
3. subterranean—*under the earth.* Your underground hideout is subterranean, Batman.
4. extraterrestrial—*beyond earth.* UFOs are often thought to originate beyond the limits of earth.
5. Well, how easy can these get? A *submarine* travels under the sea.

EATING

If you've ever studied dinosaurs, you're familiar with the root VOR, meaning *eat.* Since CARNE means *meat* (think of chili *con carne* or chili *with meat*), a CARNIVORE is a meat-eater. An HERBIVORE is a plant-eater. (Think of herbs, or plants.) If OMNI means *all* or *everything*, what is an OMNIVORE?

Well, people are omnivores. We eat pretty much everything, alas. Something with a huge appetite is ***voracious***. Take a minute to memorize that word. Write it on a notecard. Post it on the refrigerator.

BREATHING

Something else we do is breathe. The root ANIMA means *breath* or *spirit* or *soul.* An *animal*, of course, is a living, breathing creature. Someone *animated* is full of life. Animated cartoons move as if alive. Something ***in***animate is lifeless.

SPIR also means *breath* or *soul.* Your *spirit* lives. To *inspire* literally means *to breath into*, but we use it in its metaphorical sense, to arouse an *animated* or exalting influence.

CANT means *to sing.* We get the word *chant* from this root, as well as *cantor*, the leader of singing, and *incantation*, the chanting of spells.

DIC or DICT means *to speak.* When you *dictate*, you speak aloud. When you ***contra***dict, you speak against. Your *diction* is your choice of words. Need we mention the word *dictionary*?

LOCUT or LOQU also means *to speak* or *talk.* Someone who talks a lot is *loquacious*. Maybe you could post this word near the telephone.

SLEEPING

SOMNUS was the Roman god of sleep, so we have the words *somnolent* (sleepy, drowsy, or causing sleep), *somnambulist* (a sleepwalker), and ***in***somnia (an inability to sleep.) Put *somnolent* on a card to carry around or post it near your bed.

Practice

Bene means good or well.
Vale means goodbye or farewell.

1. What is a *benediction*?
2. What is a *valediction*?
3. What type of music is a *cantata*?
4. If *circum* means around, what might *circumlocution* mean?
5. What is *somniloquy*?

ANALYSIS

1. A *benediction* is a blessing (good speech, good words).
2. A *valediction* is a farewell speech. (A valedictorian delivers one.)
3. A *cantata* is sung. It's a musical work for voices.
4. *Circumlocution* means talking around, or using a lot of words to avoid saying something directly.
5. *Somniloquy* means talking in your sleep!

Studying the following lists of roots, prefixes, and suffixes can help you break down many words into understandable sections. For the following roots, can you write some words that use these as prefixes? For instance, for the root *uni*, you could write the word **unicycle**, the one-wheeled vehicle.

COUNTING

semi/hemi/demi—*half*
mono—*one*
uni—*one*
duo—*two*
bi—*two*
tri—*three*
quad/quat—*four*
quint—*five*
pent—*five*
sext—*six*
sept—*seven (September used to be the seventh month.)*
oct—*eight (October used to be the eighth month.)*
nov—*nine (You get the picture.)*
dec—*ten*
cent—*hundred*
mill—*thousand*
poly—*many*
proto—*first*

Okay, if the Latin root *ped* or *pod* means foot (think *pedal* or *pedestrian*), you should know the following words:

biped
quadruped
tripod
centipede

Note: The Greek root *ped* or *pedia* means child. So a *pediatrician* is a children's doctor; a *podiatrist* is a foot doctor.

FEAR

The root *phobia* means fear or dislike. The names of phobias interest some people. Surely you've heard of many of these:

acrophobia—*fear of heights*   photophobia—*fear of light*
brontophobia—*fear of thunder*   pyrophobia—*fear of fire*
pedophobia—*fear of children*   somniphobia—*fear of sleep*
philophobia—*fear of love*   sophophobia—*fear of learning*
phonophobia—*fear of sound*   triskaidekaphobia—*fear of the number 13*

. . . and the most ironically named one of all:

sesquipedalophobia—the fear of long words! (Dare we say multisyllabic words?)

STUDY

The root *logos* literally means *word* (see earlier root *locut/logo*), so a *monologue* is a speech for one person. Another form of this root is *ology*, which means the science or study of something.

archaeology—*study of ancient history*   geology—*study of the earth*
biology—*study of life*   graphology—*study of handwriting*
cosmology—*study of the universe*   psychology—*study of the mind*
etymology—*study of word origins*   seismology—*study of earthquakes*
genealogy—*study of family origins*   sociology—*study of society*

OPPOSITES

Take a look at these opposites. You've probably heard most of these; now you know how they work in words.

cide—*kill*
viv—*live, alive*   If you are full of life, you are *vivacious*. A *survivor* has lived
                     through something. To *revive* is to bring back to life.

micro—*small*   A *microscope* is an instrument you use to see small things.
macro—*large*

hyper—*over, above*
hypo—*under, beneath*

TIP

Learning Latin and Greek roots can help you troubleshoot unfamiliar words.

endo—*within*
exo—*out of, outside*

inter—*between*
intra—*within*

homo—*alike*
hetero—*different*

belli—*war*
pace—*peace*

pre—*before*
post—*after*

pro—*forward*
retro—*backward*

The following prefixes contain negative and positive feelings. There seem to be more negative roots. Hmmm. . . .

Negative
a/an—*not or without*
a/ab—*away or from*
anti—*against, opposite*
contra—*against*
dis—*apart, away*
dys—*bad, ill*
mal—*bad, ill*
mis—*hate*
in/im—*not*
non—*not*
un—*not*
e/ex—*out*
ob/op—*against*

Positive
bene—*good*
eu—*good*
philo—*love*
con/col/com/cor/co—*together, with*
syn/sym—*together, with*
pro—*forward*

Practice

After you've reviewed these lists a few times, learn the following roots:

auto—*self*
sophos—*wisdom*
biblio—*book*
bio—*life*
anthropos—*people*
morph—*form*
graph—*write, draw*
potens/potent—*power*

Now identify the following words. If you can't define them, divide them into their component roots. For instance, for number one, simply write out *biblio* and *phile*. Does that help you define the word? Use a note card to cover up the analysis/answers until you try the words yourself.

1. bibliophile
2. misanthrope
3. philosopher
4. anthropomorphic
5. autograph
6. autobiography
   (You might have to go back earlier in the chapter for the next two.)
7. postmortem
8. omnipotent

ANALYSIS

1. biblio + phile = *book lover*
2. mis + anthrope = *one who hates people*
3. philo + sopher = *lover of wisdom*
4. anthropo + morphic = *in the shape of man*
5. auto + graph = *self-write, your signature*
6. auto + bio + graphy = *your self-written story of your life*
7. post + mortem = *after death*
8. omni + potent = *all powerful*

FAMILY ROOTS

pater—*father*
mater—*mother*
frat—*brother*
sor—*sister*
gen—*birth* (Progeny means *children* or *offspring.*)

SENSES AND SUCH

vis/vid—*see*
tact/tangi—*touch*
audi—*hear*
son—*sound*
patho/pathy—*feelings, suffering*
corp—*body*
man—*hand*

LOCATION

ad—*to*
ante—*before*
circum—*around*
con/com—*together, with*
de—*from, down*
in/il/im—*in, into, on*
inter—*between*
intro—*within*
peri—*around, about*
re—*again, back*
se—*apart*
tele—*distant*
trans—*across, beyond*
super—*over, above*

Practice

If the root *port* means to carry, what do the following words mean? Use a note card to cover up the analysis/answers below until you try the words yourself.

1. transport
2. teleport
3. import
4. report
5. deport

ANALYSIS

1. transport—*to carry across*
2. teleport—*to carry a long distance*
3. import—*to carry in*
4. report—*to carry back*
5. deport—*to carry away from*

MORE MOVEMENT

tors/tort—*twist*
flect/flex—*bend*
fract/frag—*break*
rupt—*break, burst*
prehend/prehens—*seize, grasp*
ject—*throw*
vers/vert—*turn*
cur/curr/curs—*run*
grad—*step*

FAITH

deo/theo—*god*
cred—*believe*
fid—*faith, trust, loyalty*

AUTHORITY

archy—*rule*
vict/vinc—*conquer*
cracy—*government*
mand—*order, command*

> Did you know that Jupiter (deo-pater) is the father god?

> Now you know why dogs are named Fido. "I am faithful."

CON-CLUSION (TO CLOSE WITH)

Try combining and recombining these roots. You'll make up some new words and stumble onto some real ones you may not have heard yet!

WORD LIST

This list of commonly tested words will get you started. We've supplied **some** of the definitions; be sure to read your dictionary and write (and draw) your flashcards. Yes, this requires extra work. However, the actual *writing* of the definition will further impress this on your brain. You will more likely remember these words because of this extra step.

abate—

abet—to aid

abdicate—

abjure—to renounce, to give something up

abode—

accord—

acrid—

adamant—hard; stubborn

adept—

adjacent—

adjunct—

adroit—

advocate—

affable—

affliction—

agile—nimble, quick

akin—

allege—

allot—to distribute (not to be confused with *a lot*!)

aloof—distant or unsympathetic in attitude

allure—

ambiguous—

ameliorate—

amiss—

amorphous—without a shape

anarchy—

animosity—

antithesis—the opposite

apathy—

apathetic—

apex—

apocryphal—doubtful in authenticity

arbitrary—

ardor—passion (**ardent**—passionate)

articulate—(*v*) clear in speech; (*adj*) intelligible

aspire—

assess—

assimilate—

assuage—to make easier

astute—

atrocity—

audacious—

augment—

avert—

avid—

avuncular—helpful, friendly (like an uncle)

awry—

banal—

banter—

barter—

bellicose—warlike

belligerent—

benefactor—

benighted—

benign—good

bigot—

bizarre—

blatant—

bleak—

blithe—happy

boon—a gift

breach—(*n*) a break; (*v*) to break

brisk—vigorous, energetic

cache—

candid—

capacious—

capricious—

capsize—

cascade—

chaff—

chagrin—

chastise—

choleric—

circumlocution—talking in a roundabout way

citadel—

clad—

clarify—

> **TIP**
>
> When drawing your definitions, don't be afraid to use corny puns or ridiculous pictures. The more vivid the pictures and associations, the easier you will remember them.

coalesce—

cogent—

cogitate—

cognizant—

component—

concur—to agree

condone—

confiscate—

congeal—

connoisseur—

consensus—

console—to comfort

contiguous—

conventional—

copious—

cordial—

counsel—

counterfeit—

covet—

credulous—

crucial—

crusade—

culminate—

debilitating—

debunk—

debut—first appearance

deceptive—

decipher—

decree—

deface—

defer—

deficient—

deft—skillful

deplete—

deplore—

deploy—

deter—

dexterous—

dialect—

dilemma—

diminutive—small

dire—

discern—

discreet—

discrete—

disdain—

disgruntled—

dismal—

dispatch—

dispel—

disperse—

distraught—

distress—

docile—

doctrine—belief, creed; dogma

dormant—

dross—

dub—

dubious—

durable—

edible—

egress—an exit

elegy—

elite—

embargo—

embark—

encroach—

endeavor—

engender—

enigma—

enmity—

epoch—

equivocate—to lie by using ambiguous language

eradicate—

evoke—

excavate—

facile—easy; superficial

facilitate—

fallacy—

fastidious—

feign—to pretend

fission—

flagrant—

flustered—

foreboding—

forfeit—

formidable—

foster—

frugal—thrifty; not costly

fulsome—abundant; offensively insincere

fundamental—

> **TIP**
>
> The more work you put into looking up definitions, the more likely you will be to remember their meanings.

fusion—

garrulous—excessively talkative

gauche—

gaudy—

gaunt—thin, bony; emaciated

genial—

glut—

grapple—

gregarious—

grueling—

guile—

gullible—

haggard—

hamper—to hinder, to get in the way of, to interfere with

haughty—

haven—

heinous—

hew—to cut down

hybrid—

ignoble—not noble; common

illiterate—

immaculate—spotlessly clean; pure

impair—

impede—

implore—

imply—

inane—

incense—

incite—

incredulous—

indifferent—

indolent—

innate—

insipid—

insolent—

integrate—

invoke—

irascible—

irate—angry

ire—anger

jeer—

jest—

jocular—

jubilant—

juxtapose—

lament—

languish—

laud—

laudable—

lavish—

lax—

lexicon—

lithe—flexible, supple; graceful

lucid—

lucrative—

luminous—

malcontent—

meager—

meander—

mendicant—a beggar

mercenary—

merge—

meticulous—

mettle—

millennium—

mimic—

mirth—

modify—

mollify—

monotonous—

morose—

mundane—ordinary

muse—

nadir—the lowest point (opposite of *zenith*)

negligent—

neurotic—

nimble—

noisome—offensive; foul

nomadic—wandering, roaming

notorious—famous for something bad

obdurate—stubborn; hard-hearted

oblique—

obstreperous—noisily defiant

odious—offensive, repugnant

opulent—

ornate—

ostentatious—

ostracize—to exclude

ovation—

oration—

pact—an agreement

TIP

You can draw someone begging in ragged clothes. "Mend? I can't."

paragon—
parsimony—
partial—
partisan—
pathos—
pedantic—
perfidious—
peripatetic—walking
pernicious—extremely harmful
perturb—
petty—of small importance
pied—multicolored, patchwork
pious—
pique—anger
pivotal—
plausible—
plunder—
potent—powerful
precocious—
prim—excessively proper; prudish
principal—
prodigy—
profane—
profound—
prologue—
protean—
prudent—
pugnacious—inclined to fight, belligerent
pseudonym—
pungent—describing a sharp, acrid smell or taste
quench—
query—
rapacious—greedy; grasping
ratify—
ravenous—
raze—to demolish, to level to the ground
rebuke—
recalcitrant—
redoubtable—intimidating
regicide—
renounce—
renown—
rouse—
reprehensible—
reprimand—

repugnant—
robust—
rue—to feel regret
ruminate—to think, to turn over in your mind (literally, to chew cud)
sage—wise
sanguine—
serendipity—
serene—
servile—
shackle—
sham—
shrewd—
simulate—
smite—to strike, to hit
solace—
soporific—something that puts you to sleep
spontaneous—
sporadic—
squalid—
stamina—
stealthy—careful, quiet; sneaky; furtive
stint—
strident—
sublime—
subtle—
succumb—
susceptible—
sustain—
taciturn—untalkative
tact—
tedious—
tenacious—persistent, stubborn
tirade—
torpid—
toxic—
transient—
travail—hard work
trepidation—
truculent—fierce, ready to fight, pugnacious
turbulent—
unctuous—oily, slippery; having an insincere charm
ungainly—clumsy
unique—one of a kind
urban—

urbane—

usurp—to seize by force

utilitarian—

valor—

variegated—

veneer—

veracity—truthfulness

verbose—wordy

vex—to annoy

vilify—to abuse verbally; to malign

visage—a person's face

vivify—to bring to life; animate

vocation—an occupation; a calling

voracious—having great appetite; ravenous

wan—pale

wane—to decrease in size (along with *wax*, often used when describing the moon)

wary—cautious, on guard

wax—to increase in size

whim—

wince—

wrath—

yearn—

zeal—extreme devotion

zealot—

zenith—

zephyr—the west wind; a gentle breeze

SYNONYMS—SSAT AND ISEE

Both exams will ask you to identify words that have similar meanings—**synonyms**. Because you are acquiring a large, huge, voluminous, immense, massive, tremendous, enormous, capacious, colossal vocabulary, this will be easy/simple/undemanding.

Before we begin, find a note card; you'll need it for the practice exercises. (You've got plenty of them from practicing your vocabulary, right?) You're going to use a note card to **cover up the answer choices**. Here's a sample question:

SIMILAR most nearly means _____.

Use your note card, and cover up your answer choices! We don't want to see these yet. Now, **without looking at the answers**, fill in the blank above. How would you define the word *similar*? Perhaps you'd use the word *alike*. Now remove your card and look at the choices the test lists for you.

- (A) alike
- (B) merry
- (C) identical
- (D) different

Ah, your choice is there, so you can be confident that the correct answer is (A) *alike*. Something similar is not really identical; that choice is put there to lead you astray. Covering up the answers and guessing ahead of time can sometimes help you avoid confusion.

Great. Let's try some more easy ones:

EERIE most nearly means _____.

Remember to cover up the answer choices with your note card. What does *eerie* mean? Fill in the blank, and look at the answer choices.

- (A) drenched
- (B) noisy
- (C) unfamiliar
- (D) strange

Is it there? If you guessed *strange*, then you've solved this one: choice D. Choice C might have confused us if we had looked at the answers earlier. Something eerie might be unfamiliar, but that's not really the meaning of the word.

FAMISHED most nearly means _____.

- (A) agricultural
- (B) hungry
- (C) deprived
- (D) homeless

TIP

Use a notecard to cover up the answer choices for these practice sections. It's part of the learning strategy.

TIP

If you come up with your own response BEFORE you look at the answer choices, you can sometimes avoid a trick the test makers have planned for you.

TIP

Never choose an answer simply because you don't recognize the word.

The answer is B. Again, C might have confused us because someone famished is, indeed, deprived, but that's not the primary definition of this word.

IMMENSE most nearly means _____.

    (A) masculine
    (B) detailed
    (C) large
    (D) fulsome

The answer is C, of course, but you might have been tricked into choosing D. *Fulsome* sounds like a fancier word for *full*, but *fulsome* actually means *overdone* or *too much*.

This brings up a more difficult issue. What if you simply don't know the definition of the original word? Let's pretend you don't know the definition of the following:

DISSIDENT most nearly means _____.

    (A) loyal
    (B) weak
    (C) feeble
    (D) rebellious

If you don't know what the word *dissident* means, you can't guess ahead of time. You'll have to give up your note card and look at the choices. Are any of them similar?

Yes, *weak* and *feeble* are synonyms. Well, you know you can't mark *both* B and C as correct answers, so cross those two out. You're left with *loyal* and *rebellious*, words with opposite meanings. You can guess at this point, but give it just a bit more thought. Does the word *dissident* give you any kind of a feeling, positive or negative? Well, it's got the prefix *dis*; that doesn't sound very positive. *Rebellious* is our choice then, and it's correct.

Try a couple of more difficult ones. If you know them without looking, that's most helpful. If you don't know, use the elimination strategies above.

ACUMEN most nearly means _____.

    (A) dullness
    (B) intelligence
    (C) exactness
    (D) precision

Let's say you don't know the definition of *acumen*. Look at the answer choices. Can you eliminate any of them? *Exactness* and *precision* are synonyms, so they can't both be correct; eliminate them. That leaves *dullness* and *intelligence*. (The fact that they're opposites is a good sign we're on the right track.) You're odds are better now if you have to guess.

But think about it. *Acumen* sounds like the word *acute*. An acute angle has a narrow, sharp point. That's not dull. Choose B, *intelligence*, and you'll have the correct answer.

GARRULOUS most nearly means _____.

- (A) talkative
- (B) cheerful
- (C) silent
- (D) happy
- (E) angry

We can immediately eliminate choices B and D, as they mean the same thing. That leaves us with *talkative, silent,* and *angry*. This might be the best we can do, so we'll have to guess. Can you narrow it down even more?

It's more likely that it will be one of the pair of opposites—*talkative* or *silent*—so we'll choose one of those. Does the word *garrulous* sound noisy or quiet? It's just a guess, but if you think it's more noisy and choose (A) *talkative*, you'll be correct.

By the way, a synonym for *silent* is *taciturn*. Does that word sound quieter than *garrulous*?

Finally, let's try another experiment. What if the words looked like this?

BENE@$&*# most nearly means

- (A) diswhatchamacallit
- (B) rethingamajig
- (C) eudoohickey
- (D) contrathingamabob
- (E) antishutayoumouth

Luckily, you possess a vast knowledge of prefixes.

The positive prefix BENE- (Latin, *good*) can only match with EU (Greek, *good*). If you guess C, then, you have the best chance of being correct.

Practice

Try to cover up the answer choices and guess without looking. You can't use a note card during the actual exam, so now you can practice using your hand. We know; we made you get a note card. Use it as a bookmark.

1. DIALOGUE most nearly means _____.

    (A) verbiage
    (B) keypad
    (C) conversation
    (D) telephone
    (E) bilingual

2. ENVY

    (A) laziness
    (B) jealousy
    (C) greed
    (D) gluttony
    (E) generosity

3. DIMINUTIVE

    (A) faded
    (B) small
    (C) dark
    (D) dull
    (E) quick

4. PROLOGUE

    (A) protean
    (B) eloquence
    (C) introduction
    (D) sleep
    (E) professional

5. CORPULENT

    (A) weak
    (B) fat
    (C) sickly
    (D) thin
    (E) frail

ANALYSIS

1. **(C)** This one was probably easy enough for you to guess. Don't let the other choices having to do with words confuse you.
2. **(B)** Envy is jealousy, of course. Here you have two opposites (*greed* and *generosity*) that are both incorrect choices.
3. **(B)** *Diminutive* means *small*. It does not mean *dim*. Do you know the word *minute* (pronounce my-NUTE)? If not, make a note card.
4. **(C)** *Prologue* literally means *forward words*, so it is an introduction. It's the part of a story that you are told before the main plot begins. *Protean* has a different root. Named for the Greek god Proteus (who could change his shape at will), it means "able to take on many forms."
5. **(B)** The Latin root *corpus* means *body*. If you're corpulent, you've got a lot of body.

ANALOGIES—SSAT

The SSAT tests your ability to recognize relationships between words. These questions are called analogies. How can you do well on analogies? Of course, the best way is to **know** all of the words, so keep working on your vocabulary! Analogies seem difficult at first, but they are actually fairly easy to figure out.

The pattern of the analogy questions looks like this:

Word A is to Word B   as   Word C is to Word D.

This means that A relates to B in the same way that C relates to D.

Okay, now that you know that, you can forget it. The best way to learn analogies is to make your *own* sentence that includes the first pair of words. Try to make the sentence short, and try to use the word *means* or *is*, if possible. The relationship you're trying to build between these words should be clear, direct, and obvious.

For instance, let's say you get the following sentence.

Food is to pantry as clothes is to _____.

The sentence you create might be *Food goes into a pantry.*

Then, use the next word in your sentence:

Clothes go into a _____.

You may not even have to look at the choices. Fill in the logical word, *closet.* Then look at the choices to see if the word *closet* is there. If so, you've got the answer. If not, you'll need to create another sentence. Yours might not have been specific enough.

Oh, don't go crazy. You can overthink analogies and make them too complicated. *Food is edible and is kept cool and dark in a pantry; clothes are edible and they are kept cool and dark in a....* No, this is **too** specific.

> **TIP**
>
> Remember: analogies pinpoint the relationships between words.

Let's complicate matters. Let's take a look at some possible choices.

(A) closet
(B) hamper
(C) dryer
(D) store
(E) dressing room

Hmm. Clothes can go into all of these things. What's the relationship?

Well, let's create a new sentence that more specifically defines the relationship. *We put our food into a pantry until we need it.*

Do we put our clothes into the hamper, dryer, store, or dressing room until we wear them? No, we don't, so *closet* is still correct. We knew it all along.

Practice

Create sentences for the following pairs of words. Try to make the sentence as simple and logical as possible. As always, cover the answers.

1. piece, puzzle
2. grass, green
3. caterpillar, butterfly
4. practice, succeed

ANALYSIS

1. A piece is part of a puzzle.
2. Grass is green.
3. A caterpillar becomes a butterfly.
4. If you practice, you will succeed.

If you're stumped by an analogy, try this trick from the last section. Look at the choices. Are any of them synonymous? If so, they can't **both** be correct, so you can eliminate them! So even without looking at the analogy, can you eliminate any of the following choices? (Remember to look for **synonyms**.)

(A) error
(B) guilt
(C) mistake
(D) innocence
(E) culpability

An *error* and a *mistake* are the same, aren't they? We can eliminate A and C as choices because they can't both be the correct answer. This leaves us with *guilt*, *innocence*, and *culpability*. We've increased our chances of getting the right answer.

Note: If you see two **opposite** choices (such as *guilt* and *innocence*), one of these is very often the correct answer. (By the way, look up *culpability* if you don't know it.)

Still completely stumped by an analogy? This shouldn't happen too often because you now know so many vocabulary words and several tricks for solving the questions. However, as a final attempt, you can work backwards. You can make sentences with the answer words. If any of those make a very strong, logical connection, that *could* be the right answer!

[Unknown word] is to [another unknown word] as core is to _____.

    (A) apple
    (B) root
    (C) squirrel
    (D) leaves
    (E) autumn

The answer is **A**. The other relationships with *core* make no sense.

Practice

1. Freedom is to independence as purity is to _____.

    (A) error
    (B) guilt
    (C) mistake
    (D) innocence
    (E) culpability

2. Trust is to doubt as confess is to _____.

    (A) own
    (B) deny
    (C) admit
    (D) deter
    (E) defeat

> **VOCABULARY**
>
> **chaff**
> Something worthless or unnecessary is called *chaff*. Literally, chaff consists of the inedible husks of grains; the chaff is separated and discarded during threshing.

3. Empathy is to feeling as comprehension is to _____.

    (A) understanding
    (B) ignorance
    (C) malevolence
    (D) enmity
    (E) condescending

4. Ship is to sea as sprinter is to _____.

    (A) shore
    (B) wood
    (C) track
    (D) faucet
    (E) boat

5. Belligerent is to war as pacific is to _____.

    (A) ocean
    (B) peace
    (C) atlantic
    (D) baby
    (E) sea

ANALYSIS

1. **(D)** Freedom is a part of independence. Purity is a part of innocence. And, hey, we *told* you to look up *culpability*.
2. **(B)** *Trust* is used as a verb here. If you trust something, you **don't** *doubt* it. If you confess something, you **don't** *deny* it.
3. **(A)** Empathy is feeling. Comprehension is understanding.
4. **(C)** A ship sails on the sea; a sprinter runs on a track.
5. **(B)** Remember that *belli* is the root for war, and *pace* is the root for peace. Something belligerent is warlike; something pacific is peaceful.

More Analogies

Now that you've become proficient with simple analogies, prepare to encounter another twist. Although some of the analogy questions use the format described above, most of the analogies on the SSAT will look like this:

Apple is to Banana as _____.

    (A) Carrot is to Diamond
    (B) Elf is to Fairy
    (C) Grape is to Health
    (D) Illness is to Joy
    (E) Kid is to Little

The sentence has been divided differently, but your strategy remains exactly the same. Create a sentence using the first two words. In this case, it might be *Apples and bananas are both fruit.*

Now repeat the relationship in the sentence (that is, repeat the words "are both") with each pair of words. Do any of them make sense?

    (A) Carrots and diamonds *are both* _____.
    (B) Elves and fairies *are both* _____.
    (C) Grapes and health *are both* _____.
    (D) Illness and joy *are both* _____.
    (E) Kids and littles *are both* _____.

Can you fill in any of these blanks?

    (A) Carrots and diamonds *are both* _____?_____.
    (B) Elves and fairies *are both* **fantasy creatures**.
    (C) Grapes and health *are both* _____?_____.
    (D) Illness and joy *are both* _____?_____.
    (E) Kids and littles *are both* _____?_____.

The answer is **B**: Apples and Bananas *are both* **fruit**; Elves and Fairies *are both* **fantasy creatures**. Carrots and grapes are listed to fool you into making choices with plants in them. The **relationship** must be the same—**not** the words themselves.

Practice

Create sentences using the following pairs. Then write sentences *using your own pair* of words using the *same* relationship.

EXAMPLE

Parrot, bird

    A parrot *is a type of* **bird**.   A squirrel *is a type of* **mammal**.

  1. low, high
  2. chick, hen
  3. leg, table
  4. mug, drink
  5. companion, acquaintance

ANALYSIS

1. Low is the opposite of high.   _____ is the opposite of _____.

2. A chick is a young hen.   A _____ is a young _____.

3. A leg is part of a table.   A _____ is part of a _____.

4. You use a mug to drink.   You use a _____ to _____.
    (or A mug contains a drink.)   (A _____ contains a _____.)

5. A companion is closer/more   A _____ is closer/more intense/more
    intense/more important than   important than a _____.
    an acquaintance.

Practice

Try filling in some other relationships.

_____ means the same as _____.

_____ is the opposite of _____.

_____ means without _____.

_____ is a member of _____.

_____ uses _____.

_____ and _____ are part of the same thing.

_____ measures _____.

_____ lives in a _____.

_____ causes _____.

More Practice

1. Actor is to play as _____.

   (A) movie is to book
   (B) magazine is to program
   (C) poem is to character
   (D) musician is to symphony
   (E) text is to memorization

2. Mars is to Venus as _____.

   (A) Monday is to August
   (B) the moon is to night
   (C) winter is to cold
   (D) Mercury is to temperature
   (E) January is to March

3. Nickel is to quarter as _____.

   (A) dollar is to half-dollar
   (B) shrub is to tree
   (C) leaf is to green
   (D) change is to coins
   (E) whole is to fraction

4. Dog is to puppy as _____.

   (A) bush is to tree
   (B) beet is to root
   (C) tree is to sapling
   (D) petal is to flower
   (E) kitten is to fledgling

5. Bewilder is to confuse as _____.

   (A) variable is to constant
   (B) glee is to gloom
   (C) culpable is to guilty
   (D) dainty is to burly
   (E) recession is to depression

6. Useless is to need as _____.

   (A) protein is to nutrition
   (B) intrigue is to plot
   (C) durable is to strength
   (D) porous is to sponge
   (E) tacit is to sound

7. Quagmire is to swamp as _____.

   (A) apparel is to protection
   (B) chaos is to confusion
   (C) euphony is to cacophony
   (D) blunder is to pledge
   (E) veto is to pardon

8. Ballet is to dance as _____.

   (A) tap is to art
   (B) rap is to music
   (C) shoe is to slipper
   (D) position is to leap
   (E) performer is to ballerina

9. Forlorn is to cheerful as _____.

   (A) sweltering is to frigid
   (B) inept is to dormant
   (C) pacific is to serenity
   (D) hot is to inferno
   (E) swift is to antelope

10. Geologist is to rocks as _____.

   (A) botanist is to bones
   (B) biologist is to medicine
   (C) chemist is to glass
   (D) linguist is to butterflies
   (E) graphologist is to handwriting

ANALYSIS

1. (D) An actor performs in a play. A musician performs in a symphony.
2. (E) Mars and Venus are both planets. January and March are both months.
3. (B) A nickel is smaller currency/denomination than a quarter. A shrub is a smaller plant than a tree.
4. (C) A puppy is a young dog; a sapling is a young tree.
5. (C) We told you to look up culpable!
6. (E) Useless is without need. Tacit is without sound.
7. (B) A quagmire is a swamp; chaos is confusion.
8. (B) Ballet is a type of dance; rap is a type of music.
9. (A) Forlorn is the opposite of cheerful; sweltering is the opposite of frigid.
10. (E) A graphologist studies handwriting. By the way, a person who studies butterflies is a lepidopterologist. (*Pteron* is Greek for *wing*. Think of pterodactyls.)

Even More Analogies!

Some of the relationships on the SSAT are extremely tricky because they only relate if you look at the words *as words*. This means that in some cases you shouldn't think about what the words actually MEAN; look at how they're spelled or pronounced or where they fall alphabetically. The SSAT seems to have moved away from odd questions like the ones in this section, but you may still run across one or two of these, so it's worth considering.

Practice

Can you tell the relationships between these words?

1. Rue is to rude
2. Mime is to dime
3. Tired is to tried
4. Cough is to dough
5. Thyme is to time

ANALYSIS

1. These words have most of their letters in common, but one has added letters. Other examples are fiend and friend, and coma and comma.
2. *Mime* and *dime* rhyme.
3. *Tired* and *tried* contain the same letters in different order.
4. *Cough* and *dough* are spelled similarly, but they are pronounced differently.
5. *Thyme* and *time* are spelled differently, but they are pronounced the same.

Warning: On some occasions, the SSAT analogy tests can throw in some truly odd questions for which it is impossible to make a logical sentence. If you find yourself completely stumped by one of the analogies, you'll have to look for another type of relationship.

For instance, can you make a clear, logical sentence relating the following pair?

Cow is to orange as _____.

Huh? *"A cow is not really orange."* That is certainly **not** a strong relationship. *"I've never seen a cow eat an orange."* Oh, **so** much better! *"My cow's favorite color is orange."* Okay, it's not going to work.

At this point, either you've got to run around the room screaming or you've got to look at the answer choices. Let's look at the answer choices.

(A) horse is to avocado
(B) pulp is to navel
(C) milk is to juice
(D) calcium is to phosphorus
(E) vitamin is to mineral

The answer is **C**. Why? You've got to take the first word in the "analogy" and apply it to the first word in each of the choices: cow—horse, cow—pulp, cow—milk, cow—calcium, cow—vitamin. The strongest choice is C: Milk **comes from** a cow.

Now look at the second word in choice C and see if it relates to the second word of the analogy in the same way. Does juice **come from** an orange? Yes, it does, so that's definitely the correct response.

You will argue that the original pair is not really an analogy because they do not relate to each other at all. You will protest that this is unfair. You are absolutely correct. They are not analogous. They do not relate in the least. This is unfair. Life, as it turns out, is not fair. We may as well deal with it now.

Practice

1. Pots is to pans as _____.

   (A) skillet is to ham
   (B) plots is to lands
   (C) dishes is to silverware
   (D) kettle is to corn
   (E) stop is to snap

2. Fish is to automobile as _____.

   (A) boot is to camp
   (B) jeep is to military
   (C) tank is to garage
   (D) filet is to axle
   (E) bowl is to box

3. Stationery is to write as _____.

    (A) ambulatory is to left
    (B) stationary is to right
    (C) ceremony is to rite
    (D) unsatisfactory is to wrong
    (E) ring is to wring

ANALYSIS

1. **(E)** *Pots* spelled backwards is *stop*. *Pans* spelled backwards is *snap*.
2. **(C)** Fish can be kept in a tank; a car can be kept in a garage. This was extra tricky because a tank can be a receptacle for water or a military vehicle.
3. **(B)** *Stationery* and *stationary* are homophones; so are *write* and *right*. And these questions are so wrong. . . .

SENTENCE COMPLETION—ISEE

Before you begin this section of the book, go back to the previous section on analogies. Yes, we know that the ISEE does not contain analogies of the kind that appear on the SSAT. Bear with us. You don't have to study every word and every strategy of the section intently, but just get a general overview and make sure you **fill in the blanks** you find in the sentences. This skill will help you. We'll wait for you right here.

Got it? The ISEE will contain sentences with one or more blanks in them, and you must choose the words that best fit in these blanks. These are similar to analogy questions in that you must often look for relationships to find the correct answers. However, you might find these easier because the sentences have the clues built right in. It's called **context**.

For instance, the ISEE will give you a sentence such as this one:

Although the sentence may look as if many different words can fit into the blank, the construction of the sentence will point to a _____ answer.

The trick to figuring this out is simple. **Don't look at the answer choices—yet.** You might be tricked into using an answer that looks logical at first glance. No, no, no, you're on to their little game. What you will do is use your *own* word to fill in the blank. Here's how to figure it out.

1. The sentences are often in two or more parts, so look for clues in punctuation to separate them. Look for the **relationship** between the sections. Information may be *repeated* or *contrasted* or have a *positive/negative* or *cause-and-effect* connection. Often the connecting words are *signals*. For instance, each of the following words can give you a clue to the relationship between the parts of a sentence. Read carefully, though.

Similar	Contrasting	Cause/Effect
And	But	Once/now
Because	Although/though	Which
In fact	However	Resulting in
For example	In contrast to	
Colon (:)	Rather	
	Despite	
	Nevertheless	
	While	
	Yet	

2. Look for **clue words**. What words or phrases in the sentence are written to point to a correct answer? Underline them.

   For example, in the following sentence, we have separated the sentence into two parts and underlined signal and clue words.

   <u>Although</u> the sentence may look as if <u>many different words</u> can fit into the blank, the construction of the sentence will point to a _____ answer.

3. Fill in your **own** words into the blanks. It doesn't matter whether they're fancy or plain words. The words you choose will have a positive/negative/cause-effect/whatever connotation or relationship. Sometimes it's enough to know that it's a word that means something "good" or a word that means something "bad." Using your own simple words will help you cut through any tricky answers that simply look good.

   In the example, the word *although* tells us that the second half of the sentence will contain a contrasting word to the phrase "many different words." Perhaps you chose the word *single*.

4. *Then* look at the answer choices. Are yours there? Is anything synonymous? If so, that's the correct answer. Here are the choices for the example. Remember, the word we chose was *single*.
   (A) vague
   (B) variegated
   (C) sole
   (D) multitudinous

5. Do you want to double-check? Cut out the items that don't match. The choices you're given may include the *opposite* meaning words in order to fool you. Plug in the newly chosen word to *check* yourself. In the example, the correct choice is C.

More Sentence Completion

Oh, no! Some of these sentences contain **two** blanks!

During the tornado, we were _____ and moved to the basement, for many of these storms cause great _____.

Don't panic, my little cabbage. Just follow these steps.

1. Fill in **one** blank (just as we described earlier)—whatever comes more easily to you. Go ahead and fill in one of the blanks above. Let's say you looked at the first blank and chose the word *scared*.

2. Now look at the answer choices. Is your word **or a synonym** listed as the first word? It's important to include synonyms here.

   (A) terrified . . . damage
   (B) scared . . . jubilation
   (C) relieved . . . destruction
   (D) empathetic . . . inconvenience

Yes, your word is choice B—*scared*. Choice A—*terrified*—means the same thing. Choices C and D are not related to your choice, so you should **eliminate** them. Cross them out.

3. Now go back and follow the same steps for the second blank in the original sentence.

During the tornado, we were <u>scared/terrified</u> and moved to the basement, for many of these storms cause great _____.

Suppose you guessed the word *damage*. Is it a choice in answer A or B? Yes it is. The answer is choice A. Read it and see. This may seem more difficult, but it's not. It actually gives you two chances to eliminate wrong answers!

If you still have problems, eliminate pairs that don't have the same relationship between the words you chose. For instance, perhaps you chose two negative words or two contrasting words. Eliminate the choices that do not agree with you.

You can also start testing the remaining answers at this point. Again, always *check* yourself. These can be tricky.

> **TIP**
>
> Double blank problems are trickier. Be sure to double check your answers!

Practice

1. After several tries, the babysitter was finally able to _____ the crying baby.

   (A) pacify
   (B) verify
   (C) unify
   (D) identify

2. I didn't want to believe the story, but the wealth of details made it _____.

   (A) negligible
   (B) libel
   (C) intricate
   (D) plausible

3. Professor Plum was known for his _____ memory, yet he often could
   not _____ his own telephone number.

   (A) prodigious . . . consolidate
   (B) impressive . . . recall
   (C) erratic . . . dial
   (D) poor . . . remember

4. Spending time at my grandmother's house was a _____ event: We
   visited twice every _____, for summer and winter vacations.

   (A) semiannual . . . season
   (B) traditional . . . month
   (C) delightful . . . time
   (D) biannual . . . year

5. Of all the joys in life, I don't think there is anything more _____ than
   _____ with a puppy.

   (A) satisfying . . . snuggling
   (B) wretched . . . living
   (C) lovely . . . searching
   (D) conducive . . . running

ANSWERS

1. **(A)** The clue here is the word *crying*. The babysitter was finally able to stop
   the crying, so we're looking for the verb *calm*. *Pacify* is a synonym for
   calm.

2. **(D)** The word *but* tells us that we're looking for the opposite of "not believable" in the first half of the sentence. *Plausible* means *believable*.

3. **(B)** The word *yet* after the comma tells us that we are looking for contrast.
   For example, if we choose a negative word for the first blank, such as
   C (erratic) or D (poor), the second part of the sentence would have to
   disagree. These choices do not work. If we choose positive words, A
   (prodigious) or B (impressive), only B contrasts the second half of the
   sentence.

4. **(D)** If we visit every summer and winter, we visit *twice* a year. This is choice
   D. *Biannual* means twice a year. *Semiannual* (choice A) also means
   twice a year, but the second word in the pair doesn't fit.

5. **(A)** From the word *joys*, we know we are looking for positive terms.

Verbal Skills Review Questions

Synonyms—ISEE and SSAT

Directions: Choose the word that means the same or most nearly the same as the capitalized word.

1. IMPRUDENT

   (A) possessive
   (B) deadly
   (C) remote
   (D) unwise

2. GALLANT

   (A) awkward
   (B) clumsy
   (C) gracious
   (D) equine

3. QUERY

   (A) ask
   (B) excavate
   (C) align
   (D) meander

4. IMPULSIVE

   (A) sudden
   (B) incremental
   (C) premeditated
   (D) natural

5. ACRID

   (A) savory
   (B) bitter
   (C) false
   (D) luscious

6. MALADY

   (A) song
   (B) fuss
   (C) sickness
   (D) bastion
   (E) prayer

7. BARTER

   (A) argue
   (B) strike
   (C) flow
   (D) trade
   (E) fight

8. AVARICE

   (A) greed
   (B) keenness
   (C) detour
   (D) eulogy
   (E) domicile

9. HAUGHTY

   (A) arrogant
   (B) attractive
   (C) congested
   (D) suspicious
   (E) frivolous

10. NOISOME

   (A) loud
   (B) victorious
   (C) unrestrained
   (D) awkward
   (E) malodorous

Sentence Completion—ISEE

Directions: Fill in the word or words that best complete the following sentences.

11. Mickey seemed far more flexible, whereas Donald remained _____.

    (A) adamant
    (B) wishy-washy
    (C) pliant
    (D) tractable

12. My father is physically _____; in fact, he once pulled a fence post out of the ground with his bare hands.

    (A) obstinate
    (B) stodgy
    (C) powerful
    (D) infirm

13. Citrus fruits, such as _____, contain vitamin C, though juice manufacturers can also add calcium.

    (A) milk
    (B) oranges
    (C) apples
    (D) carrots

14. We have a _____ time putting Bella into her high chair because she thinks she's too _____ to sit in a baby seat.

    (A) hard . . . feminine
    (B) simple . . . facile
    (C) complicated . . . sympathetic
    (D) difficult . . . old

15. Before the _____ of the Internet, we _____ on the encyclopedia.

    (A) advent . . . relied
    (B) invention . . . wrote
    (C) loss . . . depended
    (D) convenience . . . carped

Analogies—SSAT

Directions: Select the answer choice that best completes the meaning of the following sentences.

16. Rudder is to boat as _____.

 (A) engine is to motor
 (B) president is to judiciary
 (C) rugby is to basketball
 (D) Nigeria is to Argentina
 (E) sleeve is to coat

17. Globe is to sphere as _____.

 (A) triangle is to pyramid
 (B) block is to cube
 (C) oval is to egg
 (D) earth is to orbit
 (E) circle is to gyroscope

18. Rival is to partner as _____.

 (A) opponent is to competitor
 (B) friend is to foe
 (C) enemy is to contestant
 (D) adversary is to antagonist
 (E) associate is to cohort

19. Gem is to sapphire as woodwind is to _____.

 (A) tuba
 (B) piano
 (C) clarinet
 (D) trumpet
 (E) timpani

20. Exercise is to fatigue as _____.

 (A) effort is to success
 (B) eating is to food
 (C) travel is to Rome
 (D) study is to book
 (E) money is to coins

ANSWERS

1. **(D)** Since *prudent* means wise and careful, *imprudent* must mean unwise.

2. **(C)** We associate gallantry with knights—brave, courteous, chivalrous. The closest match to this is gracious.

3. **(A)** To query is to ask. It shares the same root as the word *question*.

4. **(A)** Something done on impulse is done spontaneously or suddenly. This is the best match.

5. **(B)** Something acrid has a strong, unpleasant taste. Savory is the opposite.

6. **(C)** The root *mal* tells us that this will be a negative word. A malady is a disease or sickness.

7. **(D)** To barter is to trade. It might involve some argument, but that is not its primary meaning. [Besides, A (argue) and E (fight) cannot both be the answer.]

8. **(A)** Avarice means greed. Add this to your vocabulary list.

9. **(A)** *Haughty* and *high* share a root. If you are high and mighty, you are proud and arrogant.

10. **(E)** This is a tricky word that you should memorize. Noisome has nothing to do with noise. It means having an unpleasant smell. Therefore, the best choice for a synonym is malodorous, having a bad odor.

11. **(A)** The word *whereas* indicates we are looking for the opposite of *flexible*. *Adamant* is the only word that means stubborn, hard, or steadfast.

12. **(C)** This choice agrees with the fact that he can pull fence posts out of the ground.

13. **(B)** The phrase *such as* calls for an example of a citrus fruit. The rest of the sentence is meant to confuse you.

14. **(D)** Bella is too SOMETHING to sit in a baby seat, so we must be having a *hard* or *difficult* time putting her into a high chair. This leaves us with choices A and D. Of the two, D is the only one that makes sense.

15. **(A)** Before the coming of the Internet, we used the encyclopedia. A is the best choice.

16. **(E)** A rudder is part of a boat. A sleeve is part of a coat.

17. **(B)** A globe is in the shape of a sphere; a block is in the shape of a cube. Choice C is close, but it begins with the shape instead of the object.

18. **(B)** A rival is the opposite of a partner. Only choice B contains antonyms.

19. **(C)** A sapphire is a type of gem. A clarinet is a type of woodwind.

20. **(A)** Exercise can lead to fatigue; effort can lead to success! Good luck!

Reading Comprehension Review

CHAPTER 4

INTRODUCTION

Both the ISEE and the SSAT require you to demonstrate your ability to understand what you read. You can find examples of the kinds of texts you will be asked to read and interpret in this section as well as in the practice tests. However, the following chart gives you an idea of the kind of reading passages you will be asked to read, the number of questions you will be asked to answer, as well as the time period during which you must record those answers.

	ISEE	SSAT
Number of Passages	6	6–8
Length of Passages	4–6 paragraphs	4–6 paragraphs
Number of Questions	36 questions	40 questions
Time Allotted	35 minutes	40 minutes
Projected Rate of Answering	1 question/minute	1 question/minute
Type of Reading Passage	History Science Literature Contemporary Life	**Narrative** (stories, novels, essays) **Humanities** (art, poetry, biographies) **Social Studies** (history, sociology) **Science** (medicine, astronomy, chemistry, physics, psychology, etc.) **Argument** (editorials, opinion pieces)

You can count on the fact that reading passages on the ISEE/SSAT are not designed to be tricky or confusing in any way; you should feel confident that you can understand these passages. Reading carefully and focusing on *identifying the answers to the questions being asked* should allow you to complete this section of either exam with confidence.

Make sure you **read the passage from beginning to end** before looking at the questions. Reading correctly the first time saves you time reading the passage again. Often you will be tempted to guess at the answers without reading the passage, but you must answer the questions based on the information given in the passage, not on information you already have in your brain. **Read the questions and all the**

> **TIP**
>
> Read all the answer options before you select your answer. Answer the easiest questions first, then go back for the harder ones.

answers before trying to answer. Finally, **if in doubt, guess strategically**.

Making yourself aware of the types of reading comprehension questions the ISEE and SSAT **exams typically use** is also a good idea. The ISEE and the SSAT both use phrases that give clues as to the type of question you are answering. You can read some examples of the methods authors use to call your attention to the type of questions they ask in the following chart.

Main Idea Questions (finding the main idea)

Typically asks you to **find the main point** of the passage

Typically phrased in one of the following ways:
- The passage deals mainly with . . .
- The main idea of this selection may be expressed as . . .
- The title that best expresses the ideas of this passage is . . .
- The writer's main purpose is apparently . . .
- The best name for this story is . . .
- The best title for this passage is . . .

Supporting Idea Questions (distinguishing fact from opinion)

Typically asks you to **identify facts** in the reading passage

Typically phrased in a very direct, straightforward manner:
- When did the action described in this passage take place?
- Why did (so-and-so) do (such-and-such)?
- What is the setting of this reading passage?
- What did the protagonist of this passage *not* do?
- Which of the following statements is true, based on the reading?
- Which of the following questions is answered by the passage?

Inference Questions (drawing conclusions)

Typically asks you to **infer information from facts** given in the reading passage

Typically uses words that imply judgment or possibility:
- Why do you think that . . .
- What is most likely . . .
- Comparing the two paragraphs in this reading passage, we can say that . . .
- The author implies that . . .
- Based on the information in this passage, the reader can infer that . . .

Word-in-Context Questions
(figuring out meaning from context clues)

Typically wants you to **figure out meaning of words** from the context of other words in the sentence

Typically calls your attention to vocabulary and definitions:

- The word ____, as underlined and used in this passage, most nearly means . . .
- Which of the following gives an example of . . .
- Which of the following definitions most closely fits . . .
- Which of the following is an example of ____ . . .
- Which word can be substituted for ____ without changing the meaning of the sentence?

Organization/Logic Questions
(arranging grammatical concepts into a coherent whole)

Typically asks you to **identify the organization** of the passage

- Which of the following best illustrates the outline for this passage?
- The first paragraph consists primarily of a description of . . .
- To which of the following does the word ____ in line ____ refer?
- Which of the following best summarizes the primary purpose of paragraph two?
- Which of the following best describes the relation of the first paragraph to the passage as a whole?

Tone/Use of Figurative Language Questions
(the intonation of written words)

Typically asks you to **identify the mood** of the writer as s/he writes

- The author speaks of ____ with what kind of emotion?
- Which of the following best describes the author of the passage?
- The author's attitude is most likely . . .
- How does the author feel about ____?
- Which of the following emotions did the author most likely feel while writing this passage?

Each of the upcoming sections in this chapter, therefore, offers (1) **discussion of the types of** reading comprehension **questions**; (2) **discussion of useful strategy** for answering each type of question; and (3) **opportunities to practice** the skill under discussion. We strongly recommend that you work your way through all the review material before attempting the practice tests.

TIP

Check out the first and last lines of paragraphs; that's where authors usually put the sentences that express main ideas.

TYPES OF QUESTIONS

Main Idea Questions: Finding the Main Point of a Passage

Strategy

Finding the main point of a reading selection takes some practice, but you can rely on certain hints to help you. After all, authors *want* you to be able to identify their main point. To help you, they either begin or end their passages with a topic sentence that not only *introduces* their topic but also *summarizes* their main point in writing that passage.

Practice

Read the following selection and answer the questions that follow.

Shrek, the popular children's movie about an unlikely hero (Shrek the ogre) and an equally unlikely heroine (the lovely Princess Fiona), turns the traditional concept of the fairy tale on its head. Traditional fairy tales present
Line the reader with a passive, innocent, and weak heroine who requires rescuing
(5) by her <u>stalwart</u> hero. By contrast, *Shrek* offers a heroine who burps, eats like a horse, and, thanks to her knowledge of martial arts, actually saves her own rescuer at one point. One can only attribute this change in acceptable "heroine" characteristics to social changes affecting women in the United States since the 1950s.

The writer's main purpose in writing this passage is _____.

(A) to make the point that *Shrek* was a box office hit
(B) to make the point that traditional fairy tales have a passive heroine and a brave hero
(C) to make the point that changes in social expectations for women have redefined the roles fairy tale heroines can play
(D) to make the point that modern heroines are disgusting creatures who teach modern readers bad behavior

ANALYSIS

How did you do? The correct answer is **C**. Let's analyze the various answers.

Choice A argues that *Shrek* was a box office hit. Although this claim is true, the reading passage does not discuss box office returns at all. The only mention this reading passage makes of *Shrek*'s popularity is one brief descriptive word in the first sentence. One reference is not enough to apply to the whole passage. Therefore the correct answer is not A.

Choice B states that traditional fairy tales typically have a passive heroine and a strong hero; this is true. However, this comment comes as part of a chain of logical statements leading to a larger point. Remember that authors typically put their topic sentence at the beginning or end of reading passages; in this case, the author has put the topic sentence at the end of this passage.

Choice D emphasizes the reader's possible judgmental reaction to Princess Fiona's love of burping and violence. While one might be disgusted at these personal characteristics, nothing about the passage *necessarily* criticizes these "behavioral lessons." The final sentence, crucial to understanding the purpose of the passage, does not pass judgment on the "new heroine," but only makes a guess as to the *inspiration* of the character.

Choice C is the correct answer. This passage argues that fairy tales have changed over time to accommodate the tastes of modern audiences, no more and no less.

Word-in-Context Questions: Determining Hidden Meanings Through Detective Work

Strategy

The word-in-context question asks you to guess at definitions of words based on their context in the rest of the sentence. Having a big vocabulary helps, but logic and patience do too. After you read the passage, find the word you are being asked to define. Often this word will be brought to your attention in some way (for example, italicized, bolded, or underlined); look for context clues in the surrounding words to help you. Look in particular for synonyms, a definition, or an example.

| **Practice** |

The term **stalwart** *can be defined as* _____.

    (A) handsome
    (B) foolish
    (C) rash
    (D) brave

ANALYSIS

The correct answer is **D**. Did you get it? Let's analyze your options.

Choice A refers to a trait most fairy tale heroes have. However, nothing about the sentence indicates that this hero is necessarily handsome; also, if the reader knows that ogres are ugly, smelly, and misshapen, then one can infer that Shrek (referred to in the first sentence as both a hero and an ogre) is definitely not handsome.

Choice B might be a possibility, since many fairy tale heroes must perform foolish deeds to prove their bravery. However, the passage is setting up a contrast of the hero-heroine relationship in the traditional fairy tale. The wording of the sentence implies that the hero and the heroine are opposite in personality; typically one does not use the word *foolish* as an antonym for *weak*.

Choice C presents a tempting option. Often heroes in fairy tales are rash, taking dangerous chances in the course of their adventures. However, your job is to select

> **TIP**
>
> Be sure to read the sentence carefully; a word can change meaning drastically depending on context. Consider: it was *rash* of me to plunge heedlessly into the thicket, for now I have a *rash*.

the *most appropriate* answer, not just an *acceptable* answer. You should force yourself to read and consider all the possible answers rather than selecting the first possible answer that comes your way.

Choice D is the correct answer. The passage is setting up a contrast of the hero-heroine relationship in traditional fairy tales. The wording of the sentence implies that the hero and the heroine are opposite in personality; therefore, if the heroine is weak, then the hero must be the opposite: brave. A check in the dictionary proves that one definition for stalwart is indeed brave.

Supporting Idea Questions: Deceptively Simple

Strategy

What the ISEE refers to as "supporting idea" questions are really just questions that ask you to recall facts from the reading selection. These fact questions seem the easiest to handle, yet they often prove difficult. After all, you are only being asked to pinpoint fact-based statements and use this information in your answers. Too often, however, test takers skim these questions too quickly, hoping to make up time lost on other portions of the exam, and miss obvious answers. Often, too, authors use synonyms in their writing, nearly turning the fact question into a kind of word-in-context question. The bottom line? Don't rush, and pay attention to the actual question being asked of you.

> **TIP**
>
> When answering a Fact or Supporting Idea question, be sure to use the facts described in the passage to select your answer, *not* your own memory of outside learning.

Practice

Shrek rejects which traditional elements?

    (A) a weak heroine and her stalwart hero
    (B) an unlikely hero and heroine
    (C) a heroine who burps and knows karate
    (D) a passive heroine and an innocent hero

ANALYSIS

Hopefully this one was a piece of cake for you. The correct answer is **A**.

This question asks you to use backwards logic to get the answer. The passage describes details about *Shrek* that obviously do not fit with traditional fairy tales (burping, etc.); however, the question asks you to identify the elements of traditional fairy tales rather than restate the details that defy tradition. Choices B, C, and D all mention notable words and phrases from the reading passage and hope to catch you incorrectly associating these facts with the purpose of the reading passage. Only choice A relates a possible description of traditional fairy tale elements.

Although this sample question limited itself to questioning factual descriptions in this passage, not all fact questions are set up this way. Often factual questions can include data about science or mathematical topics; equally often, factual questions can require you to *use* the data discussed in the passages, for example, actually reading a series of historical dates and figuring out what century must be involved.

Inference Questions: Drawing Logical Conclusions from Written Statements

Strategy

Inference questions are by definition trickier and wider-ranging than the three types of questions we've discussed so far. Inference questions can ask you to detect a hidden meaning in the passage or use the information you read to infer unrevealed logical conclusions. Moreover, the question can require you to apply the logic of one passage to another, related situation.

The best way to approach an inference question is to make sure you understand the author's *purpose* in writing. After you understand the author's train of thought, you can then make educated guesses about what the author will say next. Don't allow yourself simply to restate information given in the passage; inference questions ask you to *go beyond* the superficial meaning of the sentences you read.

Practice

The author implies that _____ .

    (A) s/he likes fairy tales the way they used to be
    (B) s/he thinks the reader will like movies similar to *Shrek*
    (C) s/he thinks the movie *Shrek* is about an unlikely hero and an equally unlikely heroine
    (D) s/he approves of the change in traditional fairy tales

ANALYSIS

The correct answer is **D**. Ready for the breakdown?

Choice C can be eliminated more quickly than any of the others. Choice C merely restates a factual statement in the passage. Because inference questions ask you to draw inferences, mere restatement of fact is a direct warning. Choice B, on the other hand, is a bit more compelling because it clearly involves making an inference. Unfortunately, Choice B makes assumptions that are simply not appropriate to the question. At no point does the author imply that s/he has a clue as to the reader's taste in movies, much less try to match the reader's taste to other movies similar to *Shrek*.

Choice A is the most competitive answer on the list. Authors, unless they are writing editorials or critical reviews, usually strive to be unbiased in their writing; unbiased writing is respected in our culture. Choices A and D require the reader to attempt to figure out the author's approval or disapproval of a topic which the author is trying to discuss in a disinterested manner. Nevertheless, the author has left clues about her/his opinion on the "new" fairy tale. Words such as *passive* and *weak* have negative connotations, and the author associates these negative words with the traditional heroine; moreover, the author seems to approve of Fiona's martial arts skills ("thanks to her knowledge"). Together these details seem to suggest that the author approves of the changes in fairy tale lore; hence, the best answer for this inference question is D.

Organization and Logic Questions: Determining the Proper Order of a Passage

Strategy

Standardized tests strive to evaluate your understanding of writing techniques by asking you questions about how reading passages are organized. To answer organization and logic questions successfully, you need to know how to create coherent paragraphs. On a superficial level, you need to know your grammar—the types of sentences (declarative, interrogative, exclamatory), the rules for using pronouns, and other such grammatical rules. But you should also be familiar with topic (beginning) sentences, supporting (middle) sentences, and summation (concluding) sentences. Knowing what rhetorical questions look like can't hurt; after all, aren't they a powerful tool when used correctly? Being able to identify standard prose from other types of writing styles (like dialogue, scriptwriting, etc.) will help you, too. Moreover, you should know how writing moves from point to point, no matter how many paragraphs are used; that is, you should be able to recognize an introduction, proof, and a conclusion. In short, the better you are at writing (or grammar), the better you will perform on this type of question.

Practice

Which of the following best describes the organization of this passage?

    (A) the main idea followed by three examples that support it

    (B) the mention of a popular movie that eventually moves to a serious observation about gender relations

    (C) a rhetorical question followed by two possible answers

    (D) a dialogue that takes place between two people

ANALYSIS

The correct answer is **B**. Let's see why.

Break down the paragraph into types of sentences in the order that they are given.

Sentence one: Mention of a popular movie; statement that it is an unconventional story.

Sentence two: Description of a traditional story.

Sentence three: Description of the unconventional story in more detail.

Sentence four: Possible explanation for why the fairy tale is becoming more unconventional.

Now compare these notes to the possible answers. You can rule out choice A because sentences two through four do not work together to provide examples that apply to a single main idea. You can also rule out choice C because none of the four sentences is a question. You can also rule out choice D; nothing in the passage indicates a conversation—not topic, not question-and-answer format, not punctuation. The only correct answer is B.

Tone Questions: Identifying the Mood of the Writer

Strategy

Finally, standardized tests can ask you questions about the mood the writer is trying to evoke. You are trying to figure out how the writing makes you feel. Are you reading a letter to the editor by someone outraged at the high taxes they're paying? Then the mood of the piece is outraged. Is the passage laced with words that make you feel excited as it describes last night's football game? Then the mood is joyous at having won. Pay attention to context clues, descriptors, and punctuation. If the speaker is excited, s/he might sprinkle the text with exclamation points. If the reader is angry, s/he might use words that connote anger—or perhaps sarcasm. Take your time and listen to yourself as you read the passage; allow the words to evoke an emotional reaction inside you. And, don't forget that sometimes the tone of a piece can be toneless; often writers—like news reporters—strive for an unbiased, unemotional tone.

> **TIP**
>
> Writers use the terms *mood* and *tone* inter-changeably. Consider context clues like vocabulary and punctuation when dealing with mood questions.

Practice

Which of the following best describes the writer's tone in this passage?

- (A) bitter at having the fairy tales change over time
- (B) saddened at the thought of Princess Fiona marrying Shrek
- (C) excited at the new stories coming out
- (D) knowledgeable about a change in storytelling techniques

ANALYSIS

Did you pick **D**? We hope so.

After reading the passage, it should be pretty clear to you that choices A, B, and C are incorrect. The author does not use any emotionally loaded words that create a sense of anger, sadness, or excitement in the reader. Indeed, the tone of this piece is purposely toneless. (See? We warned you that might happen.) The author most likely wants to be taken seriously by professionals in the field of literature; s/he, therefore, strives for a knowledgeable, business-like, professional tone. Therefore, the answer is D.

Hopefully, this extended discussion of the types of questions you will find on the ISEE and the SSAT exams was useful to you. However, practice makes perfect, and in this section, we offer you more opportunities to practice.

Now, we think we should be honest with you. We wrote the preceding section on *Shrek* to make it easy and (hopefully) a little bit fun for you as you get used to the kinds of questions the ISEE and SSAT exams ask. However, the kind of reading comprehension questions you will be asked on the actual ISEE and SSAT exams will not discuss popular culture topics like movies, thrillers, or video games. You will most likely be faced with discussions of literature, social science, and history. Therefore, what follows are practice selections that are a bit more like what you can expect to find on the actual ISEE and SSAT.

Ready? Good luck!

Reading Comprehension Review Questions

Main Idea Questions

All of us have eaten, or seen, pretzels at some point in our lives. They come in all flavors and are even covered in yogurt or chocolate. But how many of us know that pretzels were originally associated with Easter? The
Line salty treat comes in an oval shape with a twisted portion in the middle.
(5) Legend says that the twisted middle parts were thought to resemble hands folded in prayer. Bakers made pretzels as a way of providing sacred treats for small children, constant reminders of the importance of religion.

1. *The writer's main purpose is apparently _____.*

   (A) to convince more of us to eat pretzels
   (B) to explain why pretzels were invented
   (C) to get Easter retailers interested in marketing pretzels
   (D) to show the danger of feeding pretzels to small children

TIP

Personal associations with words are okay for answering Main Idea or Word In Context questions. Did you ever watch Loony Tunes on TV when you were young?

The idea that people act crazy during certain phases of the moon is not a new one. The word "lunatic" has a long and, believe it or not, scientific history. People early on noticed the correlation between odd man-
Line nerisms and the full moon and created a word for the event. They chose
(5) the word "luny," a variation on *luna*, the Latin word for moon. Later generations chose to spell the word differently, changing the "u" to "oo." Today, scientists still note a significant rise in the occurrence of crazy behavior during the full moon phase. Traffic accidents increase; murder rates spike; even usually conventional people grow significantly more moody than
(10) normal. People still use the word "lunatic" or "loony" to describe these events.

2. *The writer's main purpose is apparently _____.*

   (A) to discuss the odd occurrences that take place during full moons
   (B) to explain how the word *lunatic* came into being
   (C) to argue that no scientific evidence exists to prove odd events take place during full moons
   (D) to chastise people for consistently misspelling the word *lunatic*

We still study the works of Ayn Rand, the author of many books, including *Anthem*, *Atlas Shrugged*, and *The Fountainhead*. A Russian immigrant, Rand saw firsthand flaws in communism. She later discussed these flaws in
Line such works as her play, *We the Living*. She became a staunch advocate of
(5) capitalism, holding on to its principles as desperately as she thrust away those of communism. She became best known for her misunderstood work *The Virtue of Selfishness*, in which she argues, not for selfishness as we know it, but for the ability to work for one's own goals, according to one's own standards—and the luxury of reveling in one's own self-won rewards. But

(10) the main reason we study Rand's works today is because of her influence on how people think about politics.

3. *The main idea of this selection may be expressed as _____.*

    (A) to give an overview of all the works written by Ayn Rand
    (B) to explain the principles of capitalism
    (C) to explain the influence of Rand's early family life on her writing
    (D) to explain the influence that communism had on Rand's writing

Word-in-Context Questions

It used to be that students were taught *not* to cheat. Cheaters were harshly disciplined for actions involving lying, cribbing notes for use on tests, sharing information about exams, and plagiarizing. School penalties for *Line* cheating might include extra homework assignments, detention, expulsion, *(5)* or even loss of scholarship money; parents reinforced these tactics by following up with such punishments as a loss of allowance, refusal to lend out the family car, or simply grounding.

Unfortunately, 21st century students either do not get the message or simply reject the message outright. Students surveyed recently not only clearly stated *(10)* their opinion that cheating is acceptable, but they also made the point that often cheating is necessary, <u>substantiating</u> this claim with a clearly outlined moral defense of the act.

> **TIP**
>
> Quiz yourself: what word do you see hidden in the term *substantiating*? Substance? Something solid?

4. *Which of the following definitions do you think best fits the word <u>substantiating</u> as used in the reading selection?*

    (A) undermining
    (B) backing up
    (C) refusing
    (D) calculating

Most people today find themselves infatuated with new technological advances, especially in the field of telecommunications. How many of us have not seen, for example, ads for cell phones, shameless <u>plugs</u> for low-cost *Line* wireless telephone payment plans, and combination coffee-and-cyberspace *(5)* cafes, places in which people can "jack in" while they drink their java. But consumers are not the only ones interested in high tech change—thieves are, too, and all the money you've spent to protect your files is moot if someone hacks your laptop at a wireless access point.

> **TIP**
>
> Knowing jargon and slang (and sometimes even knowing how-to text) can sometimes help with Word in Context questions.

5. *The word <u>plugs</u>, as underlined and used in this passage, most nearly means _____.*

    (A) an electrical triple-pronged device used for connecting an object that needs electricity to an electrical source
    (B) a collection of matter that blocks the forward progress of other matter through a structure, like a clog in a drain
    (C) a medical treatment used for treating baldness
    (D) an advertisement

Orson Scot Card's exciting science fiction novel *Ender's Game*, tells the story of Andrew Wiggins, also known as "<u>Ender</u>." He lives in an overpopulated society that strictly limits the number of children born to families *Line* to two. But, planet Earth has become the target of a vicious, territory-
(5)   hungry species known as the "Buggers." The Earth, desperately in search of a great military leader to help defend Earth, has given certain families permission to expand their families, hoping to birth a military messiah. Ender's family is one of these. Ender and others like him are selected to attend military school with the weight of the world's hopes and fears weighing on their
(10) shoulders.

6. *Which of the following definitions do you think fits the word* <u>Ender</u> *as used in the reading selection?*

   (A) a person who turns against his humanity to work for the "Buggers"
   (B) a person who was born last in a family
   (C) a person who was allowed to attend military school
   (D) a messiah who will end the intergalactic military conflict

Supporting Idea/Fact Questions

> **TIP**
>
> This article on skin regeneration illustrates well why you need to recall facts used in the passage rather than from outside reading. By the time you read this passage in this book, scientists might have discovered how to regrow skin using salamanders and this passage may be out of date. The answer key will still use the outmoded data to score your reading comprehension.

Although scientists have long used a patient's own skin cells to treat burn injuries, they have now discovered a way of *Line* evolving the technique to help people
(5)   recover from burns even more efficiently. These "living bandages" provide safe and efficient ways to heal previously difficult-to-treat wounds. The process is simple; doctors take a sample of cells from a patient
(10) and grow new cultures of these cells on specially made discs. They then take the discs and affix them to the injured area; the discs release the cells, prompting new layers of skin to grow in damaged areas. The innovation lies in the ability to grow new skin cells directly on the bandage, which is then applied directly to the wound, rather than the use of more roundabout
(15) methods of applying new skin cells to the damaged area.

7. *For what sort of injuries does the article state that doctors use this new grafting technique?*

   (A) diabetes
   (B) plastic surgery
   (C) severe burns
   (D) healing blisters on the feet

What began in Greece millennia ago came full circle; the 2004 Olympic games were held in Athens, paying tribute to the original event with a great

deal of pomp and circumstance. Athens was informed of this privilege back
Line in 1997, but despite a great push to provide the various facilities, Olympic
(5) officials nevertheless found themselves a bit pressed for time. Olympic officials planned, for example, to repair the main tennis court area and an
indoor basketball and gymnastics area; they also planned to install a 3,500-
seat cycling track. The projects barely got completed in time, a fact that
added significantly to critics' concern about security for the event.

8. *When did Greece find out it would be hosting the Olympic event?*

   (A) 2004
   (B) 1997
   (C) 3500
   (D) The article does not state

> **TIP**
>
> Rereading the passage, if you have time, is a big help in figuring out Supporting Idea questions.

The Harlem Renaissance, a literary outpouring beginning in the 1920s
and reaching into the 1940s, stands proudly as a time during which black
artists, authors, and musicians finally got the opportunity to show their
Line skills, and their pride, that grew out of their cultural heritage. Supported in
(5) part by the generosity of patrons like shipping heiress Nancy Cunard and
wealthy Carl van Vechten, people like James Weldon Johnson, Gwendolyn
Brooks, Langston Hughes, and Zora Neale Hurston got a chance to publish
their writing for a wide audience. Today we still study and appreciate the
efforts of these writers, both for the great works they produced and for the
(10) swaths they cut for visionaries that followed.

9. *Which of the following was a supporter of the art produced by the Harlem
   Renaissance?*

   (A) Zora Neale Hurston
   (B) James Weldon Johnson
   (C) Nancy Cunard
   (D) Langston Hughes

Inference Questions

Women, beginning with World War II, have worked to escape the traditional confines of house and home, only to find resentment and low wages
in the workplace. Females have managed to find new niches in which to
Line assert their authority and skill, including
(5) such places as the workplace and the
military. Women have also begun finding
homes in sports that have traditionally
been the stomping grounds for men only.
In recent PGA Tours, for example,
(10) women like Annika Sorenstam, Suzy
Whaley, and Michelle Wie—herself a

> **TIP**
>
> Make sure your logical inferences are indeed logical. The article on women in sports attempts to get the reader to infer that women often deserve more credit than they get, not that women only deserve credit when they achieve great things at age 14!

whopping 14 years old—have vied for top honors in golf and finished with quite respectable scores against their male counterparts. Although some sports may never lend a welcoming (or desired) hand to women (for example,
(15) football and other crushing contact sports), it's quite likely that men will have to make room for some challenging competition—and soon.

10. *What do you think that the author will discuss next?*

   (A) Nothing. The writing sample seems complete.
   (B) a history of women's activities since World War II
   (C) a discussion of the "new niches" women have found for themselves
   (D) an explanation of the last sentence, focusing on an especially gifted and challenging woman rising on the forefront of the more violent sports

     Jane Goodall, entranced by the *Tarzan* series, nourished a love of primates beginning at an early age. She saved her money and finally left England for East Africa at the young age of 26, along with her mother, Vanne; at the
Line time, British officials refused to allow a woman to explore and work in a
(5) jungle unattended. Finally allowed in the jungle, Goodall observed various fascinating facts about chimps. For example, she observed the chimps using twigs, stripped of their bark, as primitive "fishing rods," which they stuck into anthills to trap, and then eat, ants. Her life story is documented in the film *Jane Goodall's Wild Chimpanzees*.

11. *Based on the information in this passage, the reader can infer that _____.*

   (A) Jane read *Tarzan* because she loved primates
   (B) Jane took her mother along for her studies in Africa because of the British rules regulating women working on site in jungles
   (C) Jane has a pet chimp
   (D) Jane's mother named her Jane after the main female character in *Tarzan*

     Over the course of one month, John Doe (not his real name) ate all of his meals at fast food restaurants—from breakfast to lunch to dinner to snacks to beverages (including bottled water). Over the course of that single
Line month, Doe experienced extreme fatigue, increasingly persistent headaches,
(5) alarmingly high blood sugar rates, skyrocketing cholesterol counts, and—perhaps worst of all—a weight gain of 25 pounds. Despite the damage he did to his body, Doe remains satisfied with his experiment; he uses it as a real-life warning to people who consider eating at fast food restaurants a reasonable alternative to other nutritional sources.

12. *Which of the following would make the best title for this piece?*

   (A) Supersize Me!
   (B) Blaming the Victim
   (C) Let's Go Eat!
   (D) Unhealthy America

Organizational Questions

What would you like to be when you grow up? This is a question that people ask us from practically the first day of kindergarten. I say that asking this question is putting too much pressure on kids today. Now is the time
Line to be free, to be lazy, and, simply put, to be totally unaware of what we're
(5) going to be when we grow up.

13. *Which of the following best describes the opening sentence of this piece?*

    (A) statement
    (B) rhetorical question
    (C) interrogative sentence
    (D) fragment

First, we picked up all the chestnuts we could find off the ground. Then we stomped on them until their porcupine-like coating came off. Then we threw them in a big pot of boiling water. We boiled them for two hours;
Line then we let them cool. Finally, we cut the softened shells off, revealing the
(5) tan, wrinkled chestnut meat inside.

14. *Which of the following describes the outline used in writing this passage?*

    (A) a series of statements that give directions on how to get to the chestnut orchard
    (B) a series of questions that ask how to prepare chestnuts
    (C) a series of statements that give directions on how to prepare chestnuts
    (D) a series of questions that ask how to get rid of porcupines

If you think about it, you only have 80-odd years on this planet; whatever happens after death, you no longer get to experience things on earth. Realizing this fact might make you want to rethink how you are living your life.
Line Are you agonizing over negative feelings? If you are, you're creating stress
(5) for yourself that makes you inefficient, depresses you, and generally ruins your day. Are you putting up with people who drain you, emotionally and physically? Maybe it's time to distance yourself from them. It's time to make your decisions count.

15. *To what does the word "them" in line seven refer?*

    (A) negative feelings
    (B) this planet
    (C) your decisions
    (D) people who cause you stress

> **TIP**
>
> Normally It's not a good idea to use second person in your writing. This writer seems more interested in motivating someone than in practicing expository or analytical writing.

Tone Questions

TIP

Does the phrase "idiot box" connote a positive or negative mood? An idiot is a foolish or stupid person. This author clearly doesn't approve wholeheartedly of watching TV.

In October 2004, the FCC announced that by the year 2009 it would require that all TV stations broadcast using digital media; this meant that all TV stations would stop using analog media to disseminate their program-
Line ming. "So what," responded most consumers at the time. "What does that
(5) have to do with me?" Actually, however, the move from analog to digital posed a severe financial and technical burden on most consumers. The new purchase of a digital TV forced many Americans to purchase a set running anywhere from $700 to $999 (for the low-scale model), often in families who should have been paying bills with that cash. Those who didn't want
(10) to sink such resources into keeping in touch with the popular media had to lay hold of a clunky converter box that would allow older sets to capture and translate digital output. Before the "big switch" finally took place (after at least one deadline extension) most Americans did have to make some kind of compromise or go cold turkey on the idiot box.

16. *Which of the following best describes the author's attitude toward this topic?*

(A) afraid
(B) pleased
(C) disapproving
(D) jealous

Our department has been honored repeatedly in the past for our ability to provide high-quality classes in the field of political science. However, budget cuts and staff attrition over the past year have severely undermined
Line our previous successes. If you do not grant an increase in teaching positions
(5) and salary offerings, you will see our university self-destruct.

17. *How does the author feel about budget cuts?*

(A) S/he thinks they are necessary though hard to work around.
(B) S/he thinks they are a step in the right direction.
(C) S/he thinks they are bad because they are too small to make a difference.
(D) S/he thinks they are a big mistake.

In his "A Modest Proposal," Jonathan Swift outlines a proposal for a new economic plan for England; in particular he maintains that his plan will become "... a fair, cheap, and easy method of making [Irish] children
Line sound, useful members of the commonwealth." His plan appears quite
(5) good—until one discovers that Swift proposes these children become sound and useful members of the commonwealth by becoming England's new food source. Swift's plan makes no sense, unless one remembers that he himself was Irish and was repeatedly outraged by the English treatment of Irish citizens. Clearly, Swift's tongue was firmly in cheek when he wrote
(10) this satire.

18. *Which of the following emotions does the author suggest Swift felt while writing "A Modest Proposal"?*

    (A) anger
    (B) joy
    (C) fear
    (D) greed

> **TIP**
>
> Don't worry too much if identifying mood or tone is eluding you. The ISEE and the SSAT are far more interested in testing the other types of questions than testing for mood and tone. (But study anyway!)

A Mixed Bag

Using the theory that practice makes perfect, we offer you now even more opportunities to practice. This section offers several reading passages with questions related to each, much as the last section did. However, we modeled this series of practice questions more closely on the type of questions (and the format followed) on the actual ISEE/SSAT exams.[1] We suggest you work through these passages and questions without timing yourself; save testing under duress for the practice exams at the end of this book. Check your answers at the end of this chapter beginning on page 203. Good luck!

      In 2004, Americans alone spent nearly $1.9 billion on Easter candy—so much so that supermarkets had to double the shelf space they <u>allot</u> to Easter candy and holiday-related merchandise. Manufacturers produced as many
Line as sixty million chocolate Easter bunnies. And, if you take all the Easter jelly
(5) beans sold and lined them up end to end, they would circle the earth three times. In short, judging from the candy sales, people certainly seem to enjoy celebrating Easter.

      Interestingly, though, most people do not know the origin of Easter celebration practices. After all, most people consider Easter a religious holiday,
(10) a day devoted to the resurrection of Jesus Christ. What do Easter bunnies have to do with religion? Why do we associate chicks and eggs with church doctrine? Why do we color Easter eggs and arrange them carefully in Easter baskets? We're glad you asked.

      The Easter holiday dates back to a pagan holiday called Ostara, a holiday
(15) dedicated to the Anglo-Saxon goddess of spring and fertility. Over time, language changes changed the spelling (and pronunciation) from Ostara to Easter. Legend has it that Ostara, wanting to please some children, changed her pet bird into a rabbit; the rabbit then laid colored eggs for the children. The children wove birds' nests out of grass and put the colored eggs inside.
(20) Then, the children continued the ritual yearly, thinking that having colored eggs in the baskets brought good luck.

---

[1] *We need to stress two points at this time. First, we ask you to practice identifying the types of questions you are being asked; however, the ISEE and SSAT tests do not ask you to give this type of information during the actual exam. Second, the ISEE and SSAT do not ask many organizational or tone questions; therefore, we present you with proportionally fewer of these types of questions on this practice section.*

TIP

Review the chart printed at the beginning of the chapter if you need to remind yourself of the types of testing questions.

1. *The best title for this passage would be _____.*
   This question is a/an _____ question.

   (A) Here Comes Peter Cottontail!
   (B) What Does Easter Have to Do with Nests, Anyway?
   (C) The Evolution of Faberge Eggs
   (D) From Ostara to Easter: An Overview of Easter

2. *The author's use of the word **allot** implies that the word can be defined as ___.*
   This question is a/an _____ question.

   (A) few
   (B) many
   (C) devote
   (D) respond

3. *How much money did Americans spend on Easter last year?*
   This question is a/an _____ question.

   (A) sixty million dollars
   (B) one hundred thousand dollars
   (C) one point nine billion dollars
   (D) Nothing; Americans boycotted the event.

4. *Which of the following statements is implied by the passage?*
   This question is a/an _____ question.

   (A) People are wise not to investigate the reasons why they spend money.
   (B) Because people spent a lot of money on Easter, Easter is a popular holiday.
   (C) People will most likely spend a lot more money on Easter next year.
   (D) We have never before spent so much money on a holiday.

    Impressionism, an art form favored by artists such as Camille Pissarro, Pierre Auguste Renoir, and Mary Cassat, allowed artists a new form of self-expression. Based on the idea that art did not have to limit itself to mirror
Line images of real life or to boring pictures of stately historical topics, Impres-
(5) sionism allowed the imagination more influence. Consequently, Impressionism created enemies for itself almost immediately; indeed Impressionism got its name from a sarcastic comment made by French art critic Louis Leroy about how amateurish he considered the artistic style.

    Two very different painters, Claude Monet and Edgar Degas, in particu-
(10) lar favored Impressionism. Claude Monet (1840–1926) found great inspiration in nature, and he consistently used nature in his work. He frequently depicted the interplay of light and shadow in gardens (usually his own); just before his death, Monet completed perhaps his most famous piece, an enormous work of water lilies. Because of his use of nature, some argue, Monet's
(15) style is characterized by an ability to express the movement and the joy of life in still life format.

Edgar Degas (1834–1917), by contrast, preferred even more immediate —yet more fleeting—subjects: the swirling mass of humanity surrounding him. He drew inspiration from Japanese art forms and incorporated brilliant

(20) hues into his paintings of racetracks, dancers, and café frequenters. His interest in Japanese art also encouraged him to experiment with innovative, asymmetrical angles of observation. Degas' work <u>encapsulates</u> a distinctive, sympathetic interest in the struggles and defeats of women; perhaps the work that best shows Degas' sympathy for women is his work entitled *In a Café (The Absinthe Drinker)*.

5. *Which artist discussed in the passage died just before the end of World War I?* **This question is a/an _____ question.**

(A) Mary Cassat
(B) Claude Monet
(C) August Renoir
(D) Edgar Degas

6. *The author implies that _____.* **This question is a/an _____ question.**

(A) art created prior to Impressionism was far more realistic and conservative
(B) art created after Impressionism was far more realistic and conservative
(C) without the use of Japanese art forms, Impressionism would not have been created
(D) Monet only created one piece of art during his career

7. *The use of the word* <u>**encapsulates**</u>, *as used in this passage, is most likely defined by which of the following?* **This question is a/an _____ question.**

(A) denies
(B) leaves behind
(C) obscures
(D) shows

8. *This passage's main purpose is most likely _____.* **This question is a/an _____ question.**

(A) to convince the reader that Impressionist art is somewhat lacking in value
(B) to introduce some basic principles of Impressionism, as well as some famous examples of Impressionist art and artists, to the reader
(C) to make the point that Impressionist art is better than modern art
(D) to encourage the reader to investigate Japanese art forms

If you are like most Americans, you juggle quite a busy schedule. You probably face a full-time school schedule, an after-school job (or similarly

time-consuming leisure time activities), homework, and family obligations.
Line You also, like most Americans, must face a great deal of stress trying to get
(5) these tasks done. You may find yourself staying up late, drinking extra colas
or even coffee. Or maybe your nerves simply won't allow you to sleep—thus
allowing you time enough to meet your obligations.

You are not alone. Based on findings from recent studies, the average
American now sleeps only about seven hours a night, about an hour and a
(10) half less than people did a century ago. While this shift in lifestyle appears
to be more efficient—allowing us to get more done in less time—the long-
term <u>prognosis</u> is not good. In short, we are creating for ourselves a great
sleep debt that shows up in health care reports as well as highway accident
rates and on-the-job casualties.

(15) Going more than 24 hours without sleep simulates the effects of a couple
of stiff alcoholic drinks on the human system. Scientists place the blame on
modern lifestyles, which, more often than not, nowadays include too much
caffeine, smoking, alcohol consumption, lack of exercise, and irregular
hours. Whatever the cause, however, the long-term effects of sleep depriva-
(20) tion are even worse; unchecked, people suffering sleep loss face increased
risk of high blood pressure, heart failure, stroke, obesity, and diabetes.

9. *The word **prognosis** as it is used in the passage most closely means _____.*
   This question is a/an _____ question.

   (A) diagnosis
   (B) evaluation
   (C) prediction
   (D) argument

10. *The main point of this passage is that _____.*
    This question is a/an _____ question.

    (A) in the long run, allowing ourselves to function on less and less sleep will
        create serious health and social problems
    (B) scientists have traced the cause of diabetes to an unexpected source:
        extreme fatigue
    (C) school administrators should breathalyze students as a means of fighting
        fatigue in class
    (D) if you do not get enough sleep, you will necessarily have health and
        social problems

11. *How many hours of sleep, on average, did people once get routinely?*
    This question is a/an _____ question.

    (A) Seven
    (B) Seven and a half
    (C) Eight
    (D) Eight and a half

12. *Which of the following may we infer from this passage?*
    This question is a/an _____ question.

    (A) If you are sleeping fewer than six hours per night and drinking colas or caffeine throughout your day, you will be very efficient and productive.
    (B) If you are sleeping nine hours per night and drinking no caffeine-based beverages, you will be more productive than those who are getting less sleep.
    (C) If you are sleeping seven hours a night, but not drinking caffeine-based beverages, you will need other stimulants to keep you going.
    (D) If you are sleeping fewer than six and a half hours per night, drinking colas, and pushing yourself to be "efficient," you will exhaust your reserves and, most likely, create other problems for yourself in the process.

     Snakes are fascinating reptilian creatures, but they have long lived under a curse. After all, according to Christian belief, the devil took on a snake form to tempt humanity into sin. Even older texts than the *Bible* give the
Line snake a bad reputation. Take, for example, the *Epic of Gilgamesh*, in which
(5) Gilgamesh, the hero of the work, wins a flower that awards its bearer never-aging clothing. Unfortunately he loses it to the trickery of the serpent. The snake, moreover, enjoys a <u>dubious</u> reputation for being able to tantalize its victims, often by looking unfortunate creatures full in the eye and staring them down; Rudyard Kipling's "Rikki Tikki Tavi" pays tribute to this
(10) legend.

     Yet, the real-life snake is a fascinating creature, one deserving of more honor and compassion than such stories allow. The snake can accomplish amazing feats routinely. All snakes' jaws, for example, allow them to eat food much bigger than their heads. All snakes are born in eggs, but scientific
(15) study shows that some snakes actually wiggle free, from the egg sac, either exiting the mother's body through the mouth or directly through the skin. And the mother survives the process! Snakeskin rejuvenates easily (Gilgamesh's flower at work) as the snake increases in size. Indeed, the snake provides captivating entertainment—if only one has the courage to look him
(20) in the eye.

13. *Why do you think the author refers parenthetically to "Gilgamesh's flower at work"?*
    This question is a/an _____ question.

    (A) The phrase makes it clear that by using the flower, snakes can paralyze their victims.
    (B) The phrase states obviously that all of the author's details are fiction rather than nonfiction.
    (C) The phrase explains why a snake would want to steal Gilgamesh's flower of rejuvenation.
    (D) The phrase expands on the earlier, brief reference to the snake's actions in the Garden of Eden.

14. *The word **dubious** can be defined as _____.*
    This question is a/an _____ question.

    (A) stupid
    (B) untrustworthy
    (C) angry
    (D) doubtful

15. *The writer's main purpose for writing this passage is _____.*
    This question is a/an _____ question.

    (A) to discuss all of the ways authors have used snakes in their literature
    (B) to discuss some real-life, but apparently fantastic, facts about snakes
    (C) to show how dangerous and without purpose snakes are
    (D) to explain why authors like J. K. Rowling and Rudyard Kipling use snakes in their writing

16. *The author states that which of the following statements is true?*
    This question is a/an _____ question.

    (A) Rarely, snakes, like mammals, are born live from the body without passing through egg sacs.
    (B) Some snakes have jaws that can accommodate eating food larger than their heads.
    (C) No snakes can really paralyze their victims, like Nag in Kipling's "Rikki Tikki Tavi."
    (D) Some snakes are born through the skin of their living mother.

Over time, science and magic have frequently been confused one for the other. One can certainly understand why people might, superficially, be confused. The moon's gravity, for example, exerts a pull on the water along
Line the shorelines, creating something we now call tides—but we cannot see the
(5) pull of gravity; we only see the effect of that pull (e.g., tides). Without the benefit of scientific instruments to tell the difference, how wrong is it to attribute the waxing and waning of tides to a moon goddess (like the Roman deity Diana) or to the movements of a giant sea turtle (according to Rudyard Kipling's *Just So Stories*)?

(10) This idea that truth is often stranger than fiction becomes the basis of Mary Stewart's series retelling the Camelot cycle. Stewart creates a captivating series of four books that tell of the rise and ultimate fall of King Arthur and his Knights of the Round Table. Only, Stewart removes or otherwise explains away the magic associated with the tale. Stewart's Merlin is no magician—
(15) only a very perceptive, very gifted scientist, able to make accurate predictions regarding human behavior and to engineer large projects like Stonehenge.

Take, as one example, the first real test Merlin undertakes in the story. King Uther Pendragon wishes to erect a mighty castle. But the walls and foundation fall time and again. His wise men say that Merlin's blood,
(20) rubbed on the walls, will strengthen them. He confronts Merlin who, after

analyzing the situation, realizes that the royal architects and engineers are building on an unstable land fault. He saves his own life by <u>glibly</u> turning the tables on the so-called "wise men" and suggesting a new location.

(25) Stewart's series is an admirable work, balancing the difficult tasks of telling a good story and telling a realistic one. Only in the course of the final book, *The Wicked Day*, does her storytelling fall short.

17. *Based on the author's use of the word* <u>**glibly**</u> *in this passage, which of the following definitions is most appropriate?*
    This question is a/an _____ question.

    (A) clumsily
    (B) jokingly
    (C) skillfully
    (D) angrily

18. *According to the passage, to what force does Rudyard Kipling give credit for creating tides?*
    This question is a/an _____ question.

    (A) a giant turtle
    (B) Diana, goddess of the moon
    (C) the earth's gravity
    (D) Uther Pendragon

19. *The speaker's main purpose in writing this passage is most likely _____.*
    This question is a/an _____ question.

    (A) to warn people away from reading Mary Stewart's novels
    (B) to encourage people to read better fantasy books, like those by Rudyard Kipling
    (C) to argue that fiction is more fun and fulfilling to read than fact
    (D) to get people interested in reading Mary Stewart's King Arthur novels

20. *This piece would most likely get published in what type of publication?*
    This question is a/an _____ question.

    (A) an almanac
    (B) a social sciences magazine like *National Geographic*
    (C) the arts and leisure section of the local newspaper
    (D) a science fiction magazine like *Omni*

21. *How does the author feel about this book s/he is discussing?*
    This question is a/an _____ question.

    (A) generally pleased
    (B) disgusted
    (C) disappointed
    (D) exuberant

Perhaps one of the most captivating true stories of heroism, daring, and determination comes to us in the form of *Running a Thousand Miles for Freedom: The Story of William and Ellen Craft*. This story, lived and retold
Line by ex-slave William Craft, dates back to 1848, when William and his wife
(5) Ellen risked everything to gain their freedom. Almost any slave narrative has the ability to capture the attention; the story of the Crafts' escape offers even more drama and sensationalism than most. William and Ellen escaped using trickery: by having Ellen dress as an invalid white slave master, traveling to Philadelphia from Georgia for medical reasons, accompanied by her slave,
(10) William.

Why was this story so popular? One reason is because the tale fit so well with the values of its audience. The story pleased Abolitionists and European critics of the American slavery system. Such members of the audience thrilled to hear how two slaves escaped the chains of slavery: outsmarting
(15) their masters, finding appropriate and useful loopholes in the South's slavery system, and often traveling disguised in broad daylight under the watchful eyes of their would-be captors. On the other hand, slave owners could not hear the tale often enough, if only because of obsessive <u>self-denigration</u> for having allowed themselves to be tricked.

22. *The story of William and Ellen Craft took place before which of the following?*
This question is a/an _____ question.

(A) The Revolutionary War
(B) The Civil War
(C) World War I
(D) World War II

23. *The word **<u>self-denigration</u>** as used by the author most closely means _____.*
This question is a/an _____ question.

(A) sadness
(B) happiness
(C) anger
(D) self-hatred

24. *This passage most closely resembles which genre of literature?*
This question is a/an _____ question.

(A) critical review
(B) book report
(C) statistical analysis
(D) philosophical treatise

25. *The passage deals mainly with _____.*
    This question is a/an _____ question.

    (A) explaining why slave narratives in general are interesting
    (B) explaining why the story of William and Ellen Craft in particular is interesting
    (C) explaining why the South opted for a slave system in the first place
    (D) explaining why the North hated the Crafts' story so much

26. *Which of the following best summarizes the purpose of paragraph two?*
    This question is a/an _____ question.

    (A) an attempt to retell the major plot points of the book mentioned in paragraph one
    (B) an attempt to discourage future readers from reading this book by telling only boring details
    (C) an attempt to conclude an already overly long argument about the book
    (D) an attempt to explain a curiosity described in the preceding paragraph

    Authors have frequently shown themselves fascinated with the flaws found in human nature. In particular, they find human hypocrisy fascinating. Early medieval writers, who discuss the sins of the clergy and the wickedness of
Line kings and governmental rulers, have handed down the idea that people are
(5) <u>innately</u> evil and selfish; today, this message constantly appears in literature and media.

    Literary interest in hypocrisy reached a peak in the 1940s and 1950s, as World War II shook the world and all its beliefs. People suddenly found themselves faced with the uncertainty of the future. They grew fearful of
(10) wide-scale destruction of the war that loomed before them. Suddenly they failed to find fulfillment in the cookie-cutter life expectations represented by the nuclear family.

    It comes as no surprise, therefore, that J. D. Salinger's *The Catcher in the Rye* should have gotten so much attention—positive or negative. The main
(15) character shows complete scorn and irreverence for his cookie-cutter world, his preprogrammed life expectations, and the apparently artificial life goals toward which he seems headed. And he simply drops out of society, stops making "forward progress," and starts regressing toward childhood—the only truly happy time in his life.

(20)   What started with Salinger continues today. *Catcher* was followed soon after by Charles Webb's *The Graduate*, and more recently, we are offered *Igby Goes Down*. These "coming of age" novels show a consistent pattern: an enduring concern with morality combined with an inability to chart a satisfying path through the phony seas that surround us.

27. *Because of the author's discussion of J. D. Salinger's* <u>The Catcher in the Rye</u>, *and the overall topic of the passage, we can infer that _____.*
This question is a/an _____ question.

(A) Salinger is uninterested in studying human hypocrisy
(B) Charles Webb's *The Graduate* fails as a successful literary comment on human nature
(C) *The Catcher in the Rye* uses hypocrisy as a major theme
(D) people really loved *The Catcher in the Rye*

28. *The author's purpose in writing this passage is best described as _____.*
This question is a/an _____ question.

(A) drawing a correlation between the interests of society and the literature it produces
(B) reviewing several texts, identifying their themes and their literary merit
(C) bashing various so-called "popular" but ultimately bad texts
(D) discussing the hypocrisy of priests, politicians, and other prominent social figures

29. *The author uses the word **innately** in this passage to mean _____.*
This question is a/an _____ question.

(A) universally
(B) basically
(C) eagerly
(D) unavoidably

30. *When did literature show evidence that people were intensely interested in human hypocrisy?*
This question is a/an _____ question.

(A) 1940s
(B) 1840s
(C) 1740s
(D) 1640s

31. *Which of the following best describes the relationship of the second paragraph to the passage as a whole?*
This question is a/an _____ question.

(A) a way of introducing the message of the piece
(B) a way of communicating an interesting social event
(C) a way of showing how one author responded to current events
(D) a way of connecting the past with the present

   If you were looking for a way to study humanity, how would you go about doing it? Would you look at our literature? Our music? Would you search through decaying cities? What would be the best source of information about our ever-changing, ever-contradictory species?

(5) If you were Robert Hertz, a sociologist whose work dates back to 1907, you would study human funerary practices. He considered our death rituals to be our <u>most common denominator</u>. According to Hertz, our death rituals unite us, remaining relatively unchanged for far longer than other rituals or practices that unite us.

(10) Unfortunately, I do not think that Hertz was expecting the surprises that the 20th century would throw at him. Most of us follow the natural, pre-scribed funerary practices. Most of us will opt for burial or, for those of us who are a bit more daring, cremation. But increasingly, people are getting creative with their final moments.

(15) Take, for example, the last rites administered to Tony Mullan. Mullan died recently, at the relatively ripe age of 63. He was a shooting enthusiast, and, according to friends, wanted "to go out with a bang." Mullan left instructions to have himself cremated, packed into shotgun cartridges, and distributed to friends. Now, every time Mullan's friends go shooting, they
(20) ritually fire off a special "Mullan" cartridge, spreading his last remains over the grounds he revered most.

32. *What is the best concluding sentence for this passage?*
    This question is a/an _____ question.

    (A) "Tony would have done the same for us," says Mullan's friends.
    (B) Mullan's remaining ashes have been baked into clay pigeons and otherwise buried near his parent's gravestones in Dundalk, Ireland.
    (C) Groundskeepers are, needless to say, not happy with Mullan and his friends.
    (D) People interested in following in Mullan's footprints should contact . . .

33. *Which of the following options are listed in the passage as a source of data one could use to study human life?*
    This question is a/an _____ question.

    (A) art
    (B) music
    (C) cemeteries
    (D) spending habits

34. *Which of the following definitions most closely fits the words **most common denominator**?*
    This question is a/an _____ question.

    (A) two or more numbers into which a common number can be evenly divided
    (B) something that links two or more apparently different elements
    (C) several ethnic groups that are linked somehow
    (D) something that separates two or more apparently similar elements

35. *The passage mainly discusses* _____.
    This question is a/an _____ **question.**

    (A) how times are changing
    (B) the detailed and painstaking work of Hertz
    (C) the difficulty of substituting lead for ash in shotgun shells
    (D) a call for a return to common human decency in the form of traditional funeral rites

36. *The author speaks of people "getting creative with their final moments" with what kind of emotion?*
    This question is a/an _____ **question.**

    (A) hatred
    (B) enthusiasm
    (C) amusement
    (D) despair

    Audiences have loved L. Frank Baum's *The Wizard of Oz* for its captivating story, funny characters, and exciting adventures. Who can forget the sweet, Kansas-bred Dorothy, the clumsy but gallant Scarecrow, the warm-
Line hearted, empty-chested Tin Man, and the cowardly but determined Lion?
(5) The deadly field of poppies, the wicked but ultimately powerless Wicked Witch of the West, or the mercenary Winged Monkeys?

    Unfortunately many people have only enjoyed a third of the story's potential. Most readers (or watchers of the film) have missed out on the story's underlying symbolism. On the one hand, the story represents social
(10) criticism. Baum writes a story about a group of young people beset on all sides by wicked temptations and dangers in the outside world. Seen in this context, the references to poppy fields and "jitterbugs" take on new significance—the lures of drugs and mindless popular culture fads (like dancing or music) that lure us away from appropriate goals.

(15)   And, on the other hand, the story harbors political meaning. Historian Henry M. Littlefield interprets the wicked Witch of the East as Eastern industrialists and bankers who enslaved the good-hearted "little people" (the Munchkins). For Littlefield, the Scarecrow is a wise but naive Western farmer and the Tin Woodsman is a <u>dehumanized</u> industrial worker. He even
(20) sees significance in the colors used in the novel: The yellow of the Yellow Brick Road allegedly represents gold (the standard by which we controlled inflation back then), while Dorothy's silver shoes represent silver (an opposing solution to inflation—the coinage of silver money).

    Perhaps most vicious is the interpretation Littlefield finds lurking behind
(25) the gates of the Emerald City. He sees Emerald City as Washington, D.C., and its Wizard, "a little bumbling old man, hiding behind a facade of paper mache and noise, . . . able to be everything to everybody," a reference to many American presidents.

37. *What, according to the passage, does the Scarecrow represent?*
    This question is a/an _____ question.

    (A) a dehumanized industrial worker
    (B) a wise but naïve Western farmer
    (C) the gold standard
    (D) the American president

38. *What would be the best of the following title suggestions?*
    This question is a/an _____ question.

    (A) Lost in the Poppy Field
    (B) Lions! And Tigers! And Bears! Oh, My!
    (C) A Political Interpretation of L. Frank Baum's *The Wizard of Oz*
    (D) More than a Child's Bedtime Story: Deeper Meanings Within *The Wizard of Oz*

39. *Which of the following best defines the word **dehumanized***
    This question is a/an _____ question.

    (A) inhuman
    (B) automatic
    (C) bizarre
    (D) hardened

40. *What would be the best thing for the author to discuss next?*
    This question is a/an _____ question.

    (A) a continuation of the proof that the text is full of social criticism—it seems short-change compared to the political discussion
    (B) a continuation of the proof that the text is full of political meaning—it seems to need more proof
    (C) a conclusion of some sort—the author seems to have made his/her point
    (D) an introduction of a new level at which the story can be read—it's time for the fourth interpretation.

ANSWERS

MAIN IDEA ANSWERS

1. **(B)** The author does not list reasons why you should like pretzels—only interesting facts about their creation—so rule out option A. The author does not seem to be addressing marketers in general; the author seems to be talking to anyone who will listen. Rule out option C. Nor does the author list reasons why you shouldn't give little kids pretzels (although you shouldn't until kids are at least three years old because of choking risks); rule out option D. The final answer of the paragraph—which states "bakers made pretzels as a way of . . ." reveals

the answer. The main point of this passage is to tell the reader why pretzels were invented and why they have the shape they have. The answer is B.

2. **(B)** The author indeed discusses a little bit about odd things that happen during full moons, but this is not the focus of his/her passage, so rule out option A. Much as you would like to believe that odd behavior surrounding the coming of the full moon is bogus, scientists have actually documented proof that it is not; rule out option C. Nor does the author talk about misspellings, so rule out option D. Your only logical answer is B—the author wants to tell you about how the word *lunatic* came into being.

3. **(D)** Rule out any options that don't fit the situation. Does the author discuss all of Ayn Rand's dozens of written texts? No (see the first sentence). So you can't choose option A. Does the article define capitalism and tell about the pros and cons associated with it? No. Rule out option B. Does the article mention Rand's early life? Other than to mention that she was raised in communist Russia, no. Rule out option C. Your only reasonable answer is D—the article states that Rand was influenced by communism, an event that led to her later political stances.

WORD-IN-CONTEXT

4. **(B)** The word *substantiate* is a synonym for defend. Which of the options you are given means almost the same as defend? To undermine means to cut the legs out from under or refute. Clearly, these words do not share the same meaning; so rule out option A. Does defend mean refuse? No. Rule out option C. What about calculate? No. Back up. If you back up someone in a fight, are you defending them? Yes. So, B is your best choice. If you get stuck, try substituting your options for the word in the context of the sentence—nine times out of ten you can figure the word out this way.

5. **(D)** As we all know, the word plug usually refers to electricity—we plug in hair dryers and stereos all the time. But simple references to electricity don't work in the context of this paragraph. So, you can rule out A. Of course you've heard of—even possibly experienced—a clogged drain, the sort of plug discussed in option B. Does that fit in the context of the sentence? Shameless clogs for telephone payment plans? No! Now, you may have heard of people getting hair plugs to stimulate hair regrowth, but in context, having hair plugs doesn't make sense either. Rule out C. Surely you've heard of making a plug for someone (like a politician) or something (like a particular movie). Does that use of the word plug make sense here? Yes. Your best answer is option D; an advertisement for cheap telephone plans is just the definition for which we're searching.

6. **(B)** We've saved the trickiest word-in-context until last. Many times it's easy to figure out which definition of a word to use, but what about in a fantasy or science fiction book, when common words are, without

warning, given new definitions? Such is the case here. You really need to read between the lines on this one. Now, remember what you've been told. Ender comes from a war-torn world in which his people are being attacked by something called "Buggers." A person who turns traitor might conceivably be called "ender." Does that make sense given the rest of the passage? The rest of the text discusses how people hope Ender will save his planet—is he likely to become a traitor? Probably not. So rule out option A. What about option C? Is Ender the only person allowed to go to military school? No. You are specifically told that others like him are also attending military school. Does that necessarily help you define an Ender? No. Rule out option C. Choice D is really compelling, but—if the name Ender specifically refers to a messiah—when he hasn't had a chance to prove his worth as a messiah yet, why call Ender by that name now? That doesn't sound logical. Now consider option B. Ender is a boy who you have been told is the last child in his family—a family who has gotten official permission to expand beyond the typical two-kid limit. Consequently, the name Ender takes on extra meaningful significance—he is the end of his family. So option B is your best choice.

SUPPORTING IDEA/FACT

7. **(C)** Reread if you have to; the only way to answer fact-finding questions is to remember (or search out) facts. Remember also to relate facts only as they appear in the text—not as they might appear in your brain! The only fact you can find in both text and question here is C, severe burns.

8. **(B)** The same advice pertains here—the only answer is B, 1997.

9. **(C)** The only correct answer is C, Nancy Cunard.

INFERENCE

10. **(D)** Although sometimes inference questions seem like opinion, they're really not. The author leaves clues to help you figure out what you're supposed to realize; it's up to your logical processors to do the rest. Would it make sense for the text to discuss a whole history of women's activities since World War II? Not really. Such a discussion would have made far more sense placed *before* the text as you have read it begins. Rule out option B. What about C? A discussion of randomly selected niches in which women have proven successful could range from a discussion of culinary skills to a discussion of underwater scuba diving to educational prowess to, well, anything. You need to locate a topic that follows closely on the discussion that just ended. Option A is tempting—in some ways the article seems like it could stop here—but read on. Option D makes the best sense. The final sentence tantalizes you, suggesting that yet another woman needs honoring for her distinguishing work.

11. **(B)** Some of the options presented to you simply don't make logical sense. For example, based on the paragraph, you're likely to infer that because she loved primates she read *Tarzan* as a young girl; this is totally the opposite of option A. When in doubt, stick with the text: Rule out option A. Does it stand to logical reason that just because Jane loves primates she has a pet chimp? No. She could have many chimps—or a single gorilla—or a mixture of all sorts of primates. Nothing in the text should lead you to infer that she's got pets of any kind—much less of the primate variety. Rule out option C. Choice D also is not viable. You know nothing about Jane's mother other than that she accompanied Jane to the jungles to do research; therefore, you cannot make any kind of inference as to why she gave Jane her name. It may be an old family name—it may be a nickname. We simply do not know and cannot infer. You can, however, make an inference that leads to option B. We know that women could not, based on the information in the passage, go into the jungle alone; we are then told that Jane's mother went with her. We can infer, therefore, that Jane's mother went with her to allow her to conform to British rules regarding women in jungles.

TIP

Knowing your grammar really helps you identify structure in writing. Check out the Essay Writing chapter for more tips.

12. **(A)** The article spends a great deal of time telling you about one man's experiment with fast food, an experiment that ended with a great deal of health risk. Which of the titles make sense? Option B doesn't really make sense—does anyone, including the man who suffered the health risks, try to place blame on anyone? No. Rule out option B. How about option C? Well, unless you're a, pardon the pun, glutton for punishment (or being ironic), this title doesn't make sense. How about option D? This might work, but it's a little boring. Stick with option A. It's clever, it refers to fast food jargon currently in vogue, and it has great irony: supersizing the food servings led to a supersized human body.

ORGANIZATIONAL

13. **(B)** You can clearly see that the paragraph begins with a question. Therefore, you can rule out options A and D. Consider choices B and C. Both are correct, but you should select the answer that is most correct, which would be B. After all, an interrogative sentence expects an answer, whereas a rhetorical question does not. This question, as used in this paragraph, is asked of the audience and is not followed by an answer, nor does it expect one.

14. **(C)** You can see at a glance that options B and D are wrong; they refer to questions, and the passage has no questions. Consider choices A and C; quickly you can see that only option C is correct. The passage gives a clear set of directions on how to prepare the tasty, but tricky, chestnut.

15. **(D)** This question is testing your knowledge of grammar, specifically the relationship between nouns and pronouns. The *them* in line seven refers to the noun immediately preceding it; the answer is D.

TONE

16. **(C)** The author tells you about a governmental action that went into effect in 2009 that impacted every citizen's life. You can tell from references the author makes (the comment about having to choose between paying bills and buying a TV, the phrase "clunky converter box") that the author was not pleased with this event. Scan the list and check for words that mirror the tone of the author's attitude; of the choices listed, only option C, "disapproving," comes close.

17. **(D)** The author talks about how budget cuts and lack of staff support is damaging his/her department. His/her statement ends with a warning about what will happen if his/her department isn't given money or freedom to continue their good work. Clearly, then, the author does not think budget cuts are necessary; rule out options A and B. Nor does the author think the budget cuts being made are too small; rule out choice C. The correct answer is choice D because the author is against budget cuts of any sort.

18. **(A)** This question is the trickiest of the three presented; we saved the hardest for last. The author clearly states that Swift heavily identified with the plight of the Irish; therefore, he cannot seriously be asking the Irish to sell their children as food. Indeed, the author calls Swift's writing a satire. Therefore, three of the emotions listed don't make sense. Rule out joy (Swift is not happy with the way the English are treating the Irish) and greed (Swift does not advocate the sale of children as food, and he does not desire to profit from such trade). Swift does not use words that connote fear nor does he advise the Irish to run away; therefore, rule out fear, choice C. The best answer is choice A, anger.

MIXED BAG ANSWER KEY

1. **Main Idea**   D
2. **Word-in-Context**   C
3. **Fact**   C
4. **Inference**   B
5. **Fact**   D
6. **Inference**   A
7. **Word-in-Context**   D
8. **Main Idea**   B
9. **Word-in-Context**   C
10. **Main Idea**   A
11. **Fact**   D
12. **Inference**   D
13. **Inference**   C
14. **Word-in-Context**   D
15. **Main Idea**   B
16. **Fact**   D
17. **Word-in-Context**   C

18.	Fact	A
19.	**Main Idea**	D
20.	**Inference**	C
21.	**Tone**	A
22.	**Fact**	B
23.	**Word-in-Context**	D
24.	**Inference**	B
25.	**Main Idea**	B
26.	**Organizational**	D
27.	**Inference**	C
28.	**Main Idea**	A
29.	**Word-in-Context**	B
30.	**Fact**	A
31.	**Organizational**	B
32.	**Inference**	A
33.	**Fact**	B
34.	**Word-in-Context**	B
35.	**Main Idea**	A
36.	**Tone**	C
37.	**Fact**	B
38.	**Main Idea**	D
39.	**Word-in-Context**	D
40.	**Inference**	C

EXPLANATION OF ANSWERS TO MIXED BAG QUESTIONS

Note: We at Barron's want to help you feel confident that you can identify the type of reading comprehension question that will be asked of you; yet we hesitate to waste valuable book space explaining topics you can probably check for yourself by using the chart printed at the beginning of this chapter. We, therefore, strongly recommend that you verify which type of question is being asked with a quick reference to the chart at the beginning of this practice chapter. (We have used exactly the phrasing in our questioning here as we used to create the chart, to make your learning process easier.) Then check out our lengthy explanations of why certain answers are wrong and others are right. Good luck!

1. **(D)** You can rule out option A—it may be cute, but it does not bring any substantial meaning to the title; a title should be clever, but it should also convey meaningful information. You can also rule out C because the author does not mention Faberge eggs anywhere in the article. B is a more tempting solution, but the article goes beyond the question of what nests have to do with Easter. Your best answer is D, since the title mentions two major facts: the change in spelling from Ostara to Easter and the summation that the article will provide an overview of the Easter tradition.

2. **(C)** Choices A and B are designed to try and trick you into thinking that the word *allot* describes an amount. It does not—as your extensive vocabulary tells you. The word *allot* means to divide, to sort, to pass out so that all participating get an equal share. Choice D does not fit

this definition; rule it out. Your only answer is C. You can devote a share of jelly beans to each person, a way of restating the action of allotting a share of jelly beans to each person.

3. **(C)** You are reading for facts, and the only fact listed here and in the article is C, the statement that Americans spent $1.9 billion on Easter junk last year!

4. **(B)** Although it is true that it is unwise to spend money (and time, for that matter) on activities you don't fully understand, (A), this is not the main point of the article. Choices C and D are totally unsubstantiated; the article does not speculate as to what will happen in the future, nor is the subject of the previous year's spending even addressed by the article. Your only answer is B.

5. **(D)** Rereading the passage for factual detail reminds you that the only correct answer is D.

6. **(A)** You can rule out choice D because the passage clearly makes reference to several of Monet's works. You can also rule out choice C because Japanese art was *one* influence but by no means *the only* influence on Impressionist art. The passage discusses how Impressionism changed the type of art being produced typically. Previously the kind of art being created was highly realistic. Therefore, you can infer that the Impressionist art became increasingly fantastic as time went on. Your correct choice is A. Using this logic, therefore, you can see that choice B, which states just the opposite, is incorrect.

7. **(D)** The word *encapsulates* means to contract into one, precise explanation. That definition rules out options A, B, or C. The only answer that is remotely synonymous with *encapsulates* is D.

8. **(B)** You can rule out several choices right off the bat. First, why would an author spend so much time and energy discussing something that he or she considers to have little value? Rule out choice A. Nowhere in the article do you find evidence that the author thinks Impressionism is *the best* type of art around, nor do you get any direct order to go find out what Japanese art is like. Rule out choices C and D. Your only correct answer is B; the article sets out to define and give a few examples of Impressionist art, a goal at which it succeeds.

9. **(C)** You can rule out option D right off the bat; it doesn't make sense in context of the sentence if you substitute one word for another. The other three options are far more reasonable. They have the same general meaning—an assessment of a situation. How will you choose? If you look more closely, you will notice that diagnosis and evaluation (choices A and B) are awfully similar. It would be difficult, even impossible, to decide which of these choices to select. Now refer back to the sentence. Is the use of the word referring to an assessment of a situation? Or is it trying to focus on a future result of a current assessment? Using context clues like "long-term," you can see that you are looking for a word that discusses a situation that is yet to come. Refer back to your choices. Choices A and B are usually used in context of the present, but a prediction is usually used in context of the future. Choice C is the correct choice.

10. **(A)** Choices B and D are oversimplifications of points made in the article, but the fact that they are oversimplified rules them out. Choice C is just plain silly; a breathalyzer cannot evaluate fatigue—only alcohol consumption. The only real answer—and one that is rather clearly stated in the text—is choice A.

11. **(D)** Rereading the text—and doing a little addition—reveals to you that the only correct answer is D.

12. **(D)** Read these choices carefully. Some are worded so as to be self-contradictory. Check out, for example, Choice A. The article states that if you are sleeping too little you will be unproductive, the very opposite statement being expressed by option A. Choices B and C are equally ridiculous; they discuss situations that are not addressed by the article and for which you have no evidence, either factual or logical. Perhaps you are a person who needs eight hours of sleep a day; if you sleep nine hours, you may find yourself unproductive because you get too much sleep. In any case, the only statement that is consistent with the information *presented in the article* is D.

13. **(C)** This is a tricky question. Three of the four answers are logically flawed. Choices A and D confuse separately given facts—the story of the snake stealing the flower with the legend of a snake's paralyzing abilities and the snake stealing the flower with the story of the Garden of Eden. Choice B tries to make a false statement; paragraph one clearly sets out to discuss legendary information, while paragraph two sets out to discuss factual information. Note the author's intentional juxtaposition of fact *and* fiction, not merely a discussion of only fictional accounts regarding snakes. The only answer left is C, and the link makes sense—how would a snake use a flower of clothing regeneration? To ensure that when he grows out of his old skin, he's got a new skin waiting for him.

14. **(D)** If one is dubious, one has doubts. But even if you don't remember this definition, try plugging in the various words to see which ones make sense. Only choice D makes sense.

15. **(B)** The author by no means touches upon all of the millions of stories that use snakes. For example, you don't get any information about all the Native American lore that uses snakes as symbolic representation. Rule out choice A. The article does not discuss the dangerous abilities of snakes, like their venom sacs or quick striking ability. Rule out choice C. Even though the article mentions Kipling, it does not mention Rowling, so rule out choice D. Only choice B makes sense and is substantiated by the reading of the text.

16. **(D)** You are reading for facts; reread if you must. You will find that only D is accurately repeated.

17. **(C)** You may have heard of people being glib talkers—people who can easily talk their way out of tense situations. If you are good at talking, you are not clumsy (choice A). If you are glib, you *can* be either joking (B) or angry (D), but you are not necessarily so. The only thing you are consistently when you are glib is skillful. So the correct answer is C.

18. (A) Rereading for facts, you discover that Kipling's story tells of a giant turtle who moves the tides.

19. (D) This reading passage tells you various interesting things about the Mary Stewart books. Why would the author do this if s/he intended to get you *not* to read them? Rule out choices A and B, which state that the author is trying to get you to read something other than Mary Stewart books. The author simply does not get into a debate—or otherwise make a statement—regarding whether fiction is more fun than nonfiction. In fact, the article states that at times truth (nonfiction) is stranger than fiction; this is hardly support for choice C. Your only answer is D; the writer writes to get you to try out the Mary Stewart books.

20. (C) Because the article is trying to evaluate a text for you, with the intent of getting you to read it in your leisure time, you can rule out any choice that does not routinely address literary criticism or evaluation. Almanacs tell you about the weather; *National Geographic* tells you about other cultures; and *Omni* magazine specializes in science fiction—not fantasy. So, rule out choices A, B, and D, and select C as your choice.

21. (A) This question asks you to assess the author's emotional attachment to what s/he is writing. The words come across as professional and businesslike, and it neglects to include words with really dramatic connotations that convey disgust, disappointment, or exuberance. We can tell the author generally likes the book series, but we should not go so far as to say s/he is really excited by it. The best answer, therefore, is A.

22. (B) This question asks you to locate the reference to the setting of the book—a time when we still had slaves—and remember where that setting fits in chronologically with the periods listed here. America heavily relied on slavery near the Civil War period but not at any of the other periods. Choose answer B.

23. (D) The term *self-denigration* means hatred of the self, as the context of the reading passage will attest. So, choose the word listed that most closely resembles self-loathing; you will select choice D.

24. (B) The passage tells you about an interesting book that documents the real-life story of two slaves. The passage also tells you that people liked reading this book for long after it was published. Therefore, you are reading a text that deals with reporting on details important to a book and the public reaction to that book. Rule out any choices of texts that do not match with this data. Clearly, you can rule out choices C and D. Nowhere in the reading passage do you get figures or statistical analysis (choice C), nor do you get discussions of philosophical issues of morality or ethics (choice D). Choices A and B are more tricky. But you do not get an evaluation of things like the writing style. You are only given facts from the text and a bit of factual research on how people liked it. Therefore, choice B is more correct than choice A.

25. **(B)**   You have to decide why the author chose to write this piece. If you cannot immediately tell, try the process of elimination. Does the passage talk about why people liked reading slave narratives generally? No. Does the passage explain why the South relied on slavery so heavily? No. Is there any mention of the difficulty of managing large land tracts with little paid labor? No. Does the piece talk about why Northerners hated the Crafts' story? No. Does the text explain why the story of William and Ellen Craft is interesting? Yes, more than it explains why people hated it. So, rule out options A, C, and D. Your best answer is B.

26. **(D)**   The best way to figure out this question is to summarize quickly what each paragraph is doing. Choice B depends too much on what the reader considers exciting or boring, but most people, we think, would consider a daring escape somewhat exciting; omit B. You have no indication that either paragraph is a concluding one; omit choice C. Paragraph one indeed retells some major plot points of the book, but that doesn't matter because you have been questioned about paragraph two; rule out choice A. The best answer is D. The author has told you about a popular book and now attempts to convey *why* people found it interesting.

27. **(C)**   You don't get any information regarding the success or failure of *The Graduate*; you are only told that it existed and that it dealt with the theme of hypocrisy. Rule out option B. You are told that people loved *Catcher*, but you are also told that they hated it. Because you can only infer that you were given incomplete information, rule out option D. Option A goes against the message of the text; why mention Salinger in a discussion of people who like hypocrisy unless you mean for your reader to infer that he, too, waded into the discussion? Rule out option A. Your only real answer is C.

28. **(A)**   You can omit option B because even though the author discusses several texts, s/he does not thoroughly review them for content, literary merit, or any other significant data point. You can also omit option C because the author also does not put down the text s/he discusses. Indeed, other than mentioning a few key facts, the author does not evaluate the texts at all. You can also rule out option D because, aside from an opening hook designed to get your attention, the author does not spend much time discussing priests or politicians specifically. Your only real option is A. The author clearly states that society got interested in hypocrisy in the 1940s, and literary works catering to that taste soon appeared.

29. **(B)**   The word *innate* means instinctively or fundamentally—something that is extremely basic to human nature. However, the word *innate* does not necessarily refer to all people. Here is an illustration. He is rotten to the core; he is innately rotten. We are not saying that all people are rotten, merely that this one particular person is thoroughly rotten.

   Using the same logic, you can omit several choices. The word *innately* really has nothing to do with eagerness; rule out option C.

We use the word *universally* to refer to all people—if people are universally rotten, then they are all, without exception, rotten. This is not the appropriate context for the word *innate* as used in the passage. Rule it out. The word *innately* can be mistaken at times for unavoidably, (D), but because we generally believe (or like to believe) in free will, using the word *unavoidably* in the context of this passage is deeply unsatisfying and contrary to the speaker's intent. You should opt for choice B—basically means fundamentally, which in turn means innately.

30. **(A)** Rereading for fact tells you that the only correct answer is A.

31. **(B)** Again, this question is asking you to think about the organization of this passage. Each option describes the function of a specific paragraph in this reading selection; you just have to figure out which one describes paragraph two. Breaking down each paragraph and its function, you notice that option A describes paragraph one, option B describes paragraph two, and so on. Therefore the correct answer is B.

32. **(A)** Read the final paragraph, adding in the optional final statements to see which one sounds best. Choices C and D prove problematic; each one seems to begin a new portion of the story previously undiscussed. Because you are trying to find the best *ending* point—not the best *continuing* point—rule these out. A and B prove more tempting. But choice B seems relatively unnecessary, whereas choice A at least follows up on the story's mention of Mullan's friends, who were fundamental to his last wishes being carried out. It makes better sense to give them a voice than it does to tell you what happened to the rest of Mullan's ashes; go with choice A.

33. **(B)** Rereading for fact tells you that the only detail mentioned both in the article and in the question is B.

34. **(B)** The author is borrowing a phrase from mathematics to make a point. However, you do not want to select a mathematical definition to account for its use in this passage, for doing so simply makes no sense. We are not talking about numbers. So, rule out option A. Choice C simply doesn't make sense—denominators, even by extension, have nothing to do with ethnicity. You are left with choices B and D. Because you are looking for something that *links* two or more apparently different elements, rather than something that *separates* two or more elements, your choice is rather easy. Pick B.

35. **(A)** You can rule out some choices almost immediately. For example, while the author mentions Hertz, the author does not go into much detail regarding Hertz' work or his writing; rule out B. The author mentions that Mullan's friends packed his ashes into shotgun shells, but no one interviewed them about how difficult that task proved to be (or, if they did, no one included that information in this article). Rule out choice C. The author seems to find the piece amusing—if not revealing about human nature. Because s/he is not offended by the material discussed within, you can rule out option D. The piece does try to address the way that even our funeral practices are changing. Choose option A.

36. **(C)** This is another question that asks you to assess the tone of the writing. Again, the author is playing his/her feelings close to the vest; no words give such clearcut connotations that describe hatred or despair. Rule out options A and D. We also don't see anything that really connotes excitement or enthusiasm; rule out option B. Choice C is the best answer because the writer seems to be amused at how stupid we humans can be.

37. **(B)** Rereading for fact tells you that, while all of these definitions appear in the piece, they are usually applied to other characters. Only choice B, the Western farmer, refers to the Scarecrow, which makes sense from a simple process-of-elimination point of view, because a scarecrow is the only option listed that is usually found on a farm.

38. **(D)** Option B is simply a bad choice—it's cute, but remember a title should be cute *and* meaningful, and this title is not. Choice A is okay, but simply mentioning one minor point discussed in the text does not make a meaningful enough title. Choice C is even better, but it remains insufficient because it mentions only one portion of the interpretations discussed. It leaves out the whole discussion of the story as a vehicle for social criticism. D is your best option; it tells you that there is more than meets the eye in *The Wizard of Oz* and that this article intends to tell you about several of the story's interpretations.

39. **(D)** To become dehumanized is not necessarily to become inhuman, automatic, or bizarre, but only possibly so. By definition, to become dehumanized means to become accustomed to injustice, innured to pain, in short, to become hardened to adversity. Therefore, you should pick option D.

40. **(C)** If you had to pick what discussion should come next, certain of your choices simply don't make sense. To use option A would mean to return to a discussion of social criticism, but a good writer finishes one topic completely then moves on to another. There is no *good* reason to return to the topic of social criticism. If the author wants to include more discussion of social criticism, s/he should go back and edit that section, not add on a random discussion at the end of this particular discussion of the political meaning of the novel. The author could conceivably continue a discussion of the political meaning of the novel, but s/he has already spent a good deal of time discussing it. Why overbalance the piece by continuing what seems to be well established? Rule out choices A and B. The author, furthermore, could introduce a new level of interpretation—except for the fact that the author makes reference to readers who only get the surface plot of the tale, understanding *one-third* of the story. This implies three levels of meaning—the superficial meaning, the social criticism meaning, and the political interpretation meaning. The use of the phrase "a third" implies that there are no more interpretations to relate. Rule out option D. Option C seems best.

Essay Writing— SSAT and ISEE

CHAPTER 5

INTRODUCTION

The writing section of the SSAT and ISEE will appear as either the first or last section of the test you take. This portion will not be scored, but it may be sent to your high school so that they can evaluate your timed-writing ability.

ADVICE

Before we discuss the differences between the two tests, let's go over some common advice for both exams.

First of all, remember to write **legibly** and to use a pen with blue or black ink. This may not sound important, but keep in mind how many essays the examiners have to read! If your essay proves difficult to read, it will frustrate the reader. You want your reader to be in a good mood!

Grammar

Second, be aware of your grammar. No, it doesn't have to be perfect in timed writings, but it should make sense to the reader. Please don't underestimate the value of good grammar skills. You make your first impression on the reader by the look and legibility of your paper. However, this legibility must reveal that you can skillfully compose a sentence. Use complete sentences—not fragments. Your sentences should have subjects and verbs, **and** they should make sense standing alone.

Practice

Mark each of the following as a **complete sentence** or a **fragment**.

1. This is a complete sentence.
2. Is this a complete sentence?
3. Because I wonder sometimes.

ANSWERS

1. Yes, this is a complete sentence.
2. Yes, this question is a complete sentence.
3. No, this is not a complete sentence. It does have a subject and a verb ("**I wonder**"), but it can't stand alone.

> **TIP**
>
> Remember: sentence fragments are just that: parts of a sentence. A sentence must have a subject and a verb, **and** it must make sense standing alone.

If you have trouble identifying fragments, you might try this trick: add the words "*I heard that—*" or "*Is it true that—?*" at the beginning of a questionable phrase.

Because I wonder sometimes.

I heard that because I wonder sometimes.	No, it doesn't sound correct.
Is it true that because I wonder sometimes?	No, it doesn't sound correct.

Another common writing error is the use of comma splices and run-ons. In other words, be careful not to run more than one sentence together without the proper punctuation.

This is an example of a comma splice, it's really two sentences.
A run-on sentence doesn't even bother with any punctuation it just runs on.

You can correct these two examples by using either a period or a semicolon between the sentences. (A semicolon works just like a period. You can use it between two sentences that are closely related.)

This is a correction of the comma splice. It's really two sentences.
A run-on sentence doesn't even bother with any punctuation;
it just runs on.

You can also add words such as conjunctions to combine the sentences.

This is a correction of the comma splice, for now it's a compound
sentence.

Practice

Can you identify which of the following are comma splices? Correct the ones that need it.

1. This confuses some students, you know better.
2. Semicolons are not often used, most people don't understand how they work.
3. If you can do this, you will succeed.

POSSIBLE ANSWERS

1. Comma splice: This confuses some students, but you know better.
2. Comma splice: Semicolons are not often used; most people don't understand how they work.
3. This sentence is correct! You can't divide it into two sentences, or you'll create a fragment. *Is it true that if you can do this . . . ?*

Usage

Review the following words. Do you misuse them?

to/two/too

> Why are there three of these? **To** me, **two** is **too** many.

lose/loose

Why is this so difficult? *Lose* is a verb meaning "to be without something." *Loose* is an adjective meaning "not tight or not bound."

> I **lose** pages when writing on **loose**-leaf paper.

accept/except

> Don't **accept** credit cards **except** from people you know.

course/coarse

> The sand on the golf **course** felt **coarse**, of **course**.

lay/lie, set/sit, raise/rise

We **lay** or **set** something down. These require a direct object. (Test: You can replace these words with the word *put*.) We also **raise** something: a thing, a direct object. We *ourselves* **lie** or **sit** or **rise**.

> I am so tired that I have to **set** down my backpack and **sit**.
> Then I **lay** my head on my pillow and **lie** down.
> I **raise** my arms in a stretch before I **rise** in the morning.

This is simple. The problems occur when we get into tenses.

	Lay	**Lie**	**Raise**	**Rise**
Present Tense	I **lay** <u>it</u> down.	I **lie** down.	I **raise** <u>it</u> up.	I **rise**.
Past	I **laid** it down.	I **lay** down.	I **raised** it up.	I **rose**.
Past Participle	I had **laid** it down.	I had **lain** down.	I had **raised** it up.	I had **risen**.

Look at the past tense of *lie*, which causes all our troubles. Chances are, no one will mind if you mix these up in conversation; try to be more careful in your writing, however.

advise/advice

Advice is a noun; *advise* is a verb.

> I'd **advise** you never to give **advice**.

already/all ready
Already refers to time. I'm **already** prepared. (I was prepared beforehand.)
All ready means "completely prepared." I've been **all ready**. (I'm already all ready.)

> That's enough, already. If you're all ready, we'll continue.

affect/effect
This one causes a lot of trouble. *Affect* is usually a verb.

> Using this correctly can **affect** your writing positively.

Effect is usually a noun.

> It will cause a positive **effect**.

The problem occurs because *effect* is sometimes used as a verb, meaning "to cause." However, we already have a perfectly fine verb meaning "cause." It's called *cause*. Use it and forget about the other one for now. You can use *effect* as a verb after you're 18.

stationary/stationery
StationAry with an A means to stAy in one place. *StationEry* with an E is used to write lEtters.

> You should rem**a**in **stationary** when writing on **stationery**.

capital/capitol
Capital has many meanings, including a capital city, capital in the bank, and a capital letter. *CapitOl* with an O has Only One meaning: the actual *building* where governmental bodies meet. Picture the dome that sits on many capitol buildings. It's shaped like the top of the letter O.

desert/dessert

> After a week **desert**ed in the **desert**, you'd want some **dessert**.

Practice

Choose the correct word.

1. Michael is such a sore (looser/loser) in football.
2. After some thought, she (excepted/accepted) his apology.
3. Just (sit/set) your head on the pillow and (lay/lie) down.
4. Sometimes I feel stressed, but I try not to let it (affect/effect) me adversely.
5. The campers (rose/raised) at the crack of dawn.
6. Last night, I (lay/laid) awake.
7. This exercise has gone on (to/two/too) long.

ANSWERS/ANALYSIS

1. A *loser* doesn't win.
2. She *accepted* the apology.
3. Just *set* your head on the pillow and *lie* down.
    (Remember, your head is an object.)
4. *Affect* is the verb.
5. The campers *rose*.
6. In the past, I *lay* awake.
7. Yes, it has gone on a bit *too* long.

there/their/they're

They're (They are) so unsure of **their** destination that they don't go **there** without a map.

its/it's

Here it is: the pet peeve of English teachers. *It's* (with the apostrophe) is <u>always</u> a contraction. It's the way we say "it is." *Its* (without the apostrophe) is possessive. It is a possessive pronoun: his, its, hers, yours, theirs, ours, whose.

> **The wombat likes eating its meals at *his* house, not *hers*.**

whose/who's

See the above explanation for its/it's. *Who's* is the contraction for "who is"; *whose* is possessive.

> **Whose wombat won't eat at its own home? Who's keeping track of wombat dining habits, anyway?**

your/you're

You're is the contraction for "you are." *Your* is the possessive pronoun.

> **If you're tired of feeding your wombat, then send it to their house. They're always accepting marsupials there.**

principle/principal

The word *principle* is a noun; it has only one meaning: a rule.

> **We live by certain principles. (This means we live by certain rules. We do not live by certain chief school administrators.)**

The word *principal* can be an adjective, meaning "the most important."
    The **principal** rule is the most important rule, or the principal principle.
To demonstrate noun usage, people like to say, "Your **princi*pal*** is your *pal*." This serves as a useful mnemonic, but you cannot always rely on its truth. Try calling your principal late at night with a math problem. You'll find that he or she has limits on friendliness. Let's move on.

quite/quiet

You can remember this **quite** easily if you pronounce them correctly. If you can't pronounce them, then be **quiet**.

forth/fourth

Forth involves forward movement; *fourth* refers to the number four.

I am not the bravest member of the team. I was the fourth to go forth.

unique

This word is often misused. The prefix *uni-* means "one," so unique means "one of a kind." One of a kind can only be one of a kind, so you **cannot** say something is *very unique* or *more unique* or *most unique*. It can *only* be **unique**.

of/have

These sometimes sound alike when we use the word *have* as a helping verb. (If I had known that you were coming, I would **have** baked a cake.) The word *of* is never a verb.

I could have been a contender. Instead of a sentence fragment, which is what I am.

Finally, remember the following, and you will make great friends with your readers: the phrase *A LOT* is two words! *ALL RIGHT* is two words!

Practice writing them here—far apart.

a　　　　　lot　｜　　all　　　　　right

All right! I know a lot!

Practice

1. She said, "Thank you." I replied, "(Your/You're) welcome."
2. The pungent odor didn't (effect/affect) him at all.
3. The sharp aroma didn't have any (effect, affect) on him at all.
4. My grandparents allotted (alot/a lot) for that lot.
5. Victor Frankenstein (should of/should have) known better.
6. The creature never knew the truth about (it's/its) origins.
7. (All right! Alright!) We're done!

ANALYSIS

1. *You're* (You are) welcome.
2. *Affect* is still a verb!
3. *Effect* is a noun.

4. *A lot* is two words (unlike *allot*, which means "to distribute").
5. *Have* is a verb. He *should have known* better.
6. It's a shame it never discovered *its* origins.
7. *All right* is two words!

Combined Practice

Identify errors in usage and punctuation in the following sentences. Some sentences will contain more than one error.

1. I should of studied comma splices, then I couldn't loose.
2. We haven't gone over this problem word yet, but your smarter then you think.
3. In fact, you're very unique.
4. Your principle concern is the affect of concentrated study.
5. Of coarse, knowledge is it's own reward.
6. I've learned quiet alot, alright.

ANALYSIS

1. (This includes a comma splice, of course, but it contains two more errors.) I should **have** studied comma splices. Then I couldn't **lose**.
2. We haven't gone over this problem word, but **you're** (you are) smarter **than** you think. (The word *than* is used in comparisons. The word *then* refers to time. You know this; just be careful.)
3. You're one of a kind. You're **unique**.
4. Your **principal** concern is the **effect** of concentrated study. (Effect is a noun.)
5. Of **course**, knowledge is **its** own reward.
6. I've learned **quite a lot**, **all right**.

Tricks of the Trade

You can empower your writing with a simple technique: use exciting verbs. You probably learned the following list of verbs in elementary school.

is am are was were be being been have has had

They prove very useful as helping verbs, telling us **when** something happens.

I sing.	She sings.	They sing.
I am singing.	He is singing.	They are singing.
I was singing.	She was singing.	They were singing.
I have been singing.	He has been singing.	They have been singing.
I had been singing.	She had been singing.	They had been singing.

and so forth (I will sing, I would sing, I should sing, I might have sung, etc.).

However, when these verbs are used **alone**, they're not that exciting.

I **am** interesting.   They **are** not interesting.   We **are** different.

All the verbs are doing in this case is connecting the subject to an adjective. Look at how much more excitement you can generate by replacing this construction with some active verbs!

I **interest** people.   They **bore** me.   We **differ**.

This **is** a simple trick, but if you know it, your writing **will be** more exciting than all the rest!

OR

By mastering this simple trick, your writing will leap from the page!

Practice

Rewrite the following sentences, using more active verbs.

1. Sam is supportive of his sister.
2. She was appreciative of her teachers.
3. An error was committed by me.

POSSIBLE ANSWERS

1. Sam supports his sister.
2. She appreciated her teachers.
3. This sentence does contain an interesting verb (*was committed*), so what's the problem? This sentence illustrates **passive voice**. This simply means that the subject is not *performing* an action; it is *receiving* an action. You use this construction when you're trying to hide who is doing something. In this case, the most direct and active way of stating this sentence is "I committed an error" or, even more clearly, "I made a mistake." Remember: direct writing delivers a strong impact. A reader of many essays will especially appreciate clarity.

Bonus

When we write, we commonly begin many sentences with the words *There was*, *There were*, and *There are* (We call these <u>expletives</u>, by the way.) There is nothing really wrong with this practice, but it slows our writing down and makes it wordy. Be aware of this tendency, and avoid it when you can.

Practice ·

<u>Cross out</u> the first two words of the following sentences. Then rewrite them.

1. There is another trick you should know.
2. There is a common way of writing sentences that delays the subject.
3. There are a couple of empty words at the beginning of each of these sentences.
4. It is boring for readers to read these sentences.
5. Is there a way you can get rid of these dull expressions?

ANSWERS

1. You should know another trick.
2. A common way of writing sentences delays the subject.
3. Empty words just stand at the beginning of the sentences.
4. When the word *it* is not used as a pronoun, it also serves as an expletive. So you can rewrite the sentences as follows: *Readers are bored by these sentences.* However, if you want it to be an active sentence, write it this way: *These sentences bore readers.*
5. Can you get rid of these dull expressions?

Sentence Variation

Finally, try to be aware of this. Be aware of the rhythm of your writing. Don't use only short sentences. Don't use only long sentences. Vary the length. Give your reader some variety. Break up the monotony.

Practice

Please rewrite the previous paragraph!

THE ESSAY—SSAT and ISEE

On the SSAT, you will have 25 minutes to complete the writing section; on the ISEE, you will have 30 minutes. Both tests provide you with two lined pages on which to write the essay. You must use blue or black ink. Remember, you want the reader to have an easy time reading your essay, so follow the directions and write legibly.

The ISEE will ask you a question concerning yourself or society in general. The new SSAT will give you this same type of question as one of the writing options. (The other option is described on page 227.) In this section, we'll go over some writing strategies that will work for both tests.

The writing prompt may look like this:

What is your favorite subject in school? Why?

TIP

Good writing requires an opinion, but great writing requires knowing *why* as well as *what*.

The hardest part of developing your response will be answering the question; but since it concerns you and your experiences and opinions, that won't be too difficult! You cannot answer this incorrectly!

However, you must stick to the topic in the prompt, and you should remain *positive*. This is not the time to list why you *hate* certain classes, certain teachers, certain classmates, or (ahem!) certain standardized tests that include essays. Remember your audience: you want the reader to enjoy your essay in good spirits.

So, first of all, take a stand, and decide on an answer. You have an answer to any question the test asks; you've just got to put it into writing.

Practice

Read the following questions. Write a short answer next to each of them.

1. What people have inspired you in your life? How?

2. Where are your favorite places?

3. Do people change over time, or do our personalities remain the same?

4. What would be your ideal job? Why?

5. An old curse says, "May you live in interesting times." Do you live in interesting times?

6. Can science go too far in its advancements?

7. What are your favorite activities outside of school?

8. What books have influenced you the most? How?

9. How would you define success in life? What makes a person successful?

10. What community service would you recommend for yourself and your classmates? Why?

Prewriting

Now, ask yourself **why** you feel this way. Choose **one** of the practice topics and ask yourself what has happened to **you** personally that may have formed your opinion. Think. You've led an interesting life. Relax and let your memories enter your mind. (You might imagine yourself looking through a photo album of your life. What do you see?) Has anyone **else** had an experience that you know? Jot down a few key words to remind you of this story.

Personal Notes

Even though the question asks for your opinion, you can also bring in information from current events, books, and history. In fact, evidence from these sources can strongly support your opinion. For instance, if the question asks for your definition of a hero, you must give your choice and explain why, but, in doing so, you can also bring in similar examples from history and literature to further illustrate your point.

So, if it's appropriate to your question, try to think of a book, story, or poem that you've read that deals with or applies to this subject. Think of the works you've read for school. Do any of them stick out in your mind? Can you make a connection with the topic statement? Again, jot down a few key words to remind yourself.

Literature Notes

Think of history class. What stories or events interested you? Do they connect with the statement? What was on the news last night? What was in the newspaper?

History/Current Events Notes

If you still don't feel confident, you can try this: just start writing **something** on your note paper. Write **anything you feel about the topic**. Write single words with circles around them, or write phrases with arrows connecting them with other words and phrases; just brainstorm. Try it here and see if you discover some ideas.

Brainstorming Notes

Planning

By now, you should have plenty of material for an essay. Decide roughly in what order you'd like to place your stories. Should you build from your personal experience, to literature to current events? From history to literature to your experience? From literature to your experience?

Pick out your strongest stories. Don't worry if you don't write about all three; you're looking for the most interesting stories and the best quality writing you can produce in the time remaining. If it helps you, number your examples on your worksheet.

Writing

INTRODUCTION

Now it's time for your introduction. All this is going to do is **clearly** announce what your paper is about. You've got some choices here, too.

Some people **immediately** answer the prompt. The first sentence announces your opinion on the topic stated:

> *Two people have inspired me in my life.*

> **TIP**
>
> The Introduction clearly announces what your paper is about. The Thesis states the Topic and your Opinion on it.

Of course, your introduction should consist of more than one (or even two) sentences. After your opening, briefly expand and elaborate on what you've said. You might list the stories you know and the experiences you've had.

Another way to start a paper is open with a "hook." This just means you're going to hook the reader's interest, making him or her want to read more. You can start with a question:

> *What inspires a person in life? Who inspires a person?*

You can start with a colorful detail from one of the stories you're going to tell.

> *My grandmother looked at the smoldering wreckage where her home had once stood. With her nine children huddled around her, she made a decision that would change her family forever: "We will sell everything we have left," she told them, "and we will walk to the pier, where we will board a ship headed for the United States of America."*

You can also begin with a new anecdote (a short, amusing story):

When the famous hunter and explorer Daniel Boone was asked whether he had ever been lost, he replied, "No, I can't say I was ever lost, but I was bewildered once for three days." This confident attitude inspires me daily, and I have known a few people in my life who exemplify this state of mind.

Whatever way you choose to open, make sure you give your reader a clear idea of what your plan is. You might keep the acronym TOP in mind.

Topic
Opinion
Preview

You definitely need to state the topic, and you should clearly state your opinion on it. Together, this makes up your thesis statement. This is usually the last sentence or the first sentence of the paragraph. **Never lose sight** of your thesis statement. **Everything** you write must be about this statement. Do **not** stray off topic.

Furthermore, you **may** preview what you're going to cover in your paper. Give your readers any information they need to know in order to understand your paper (names of people involved, books, historical events). You can even preview your upcoming paragraphs in the thesis statement.

The people who inspire me keep trying their best at all times and endure no matter what the odds. I draw inspiration from the stories of King Arthur, the words of Martin Luther King, Jr., and the life of my grandmother.

Practice

On a piece of paper, write the introduction of your essay. If you like, you can try writing it a couple of different ways to see which method works best for you.

BODY PARAGRAPHS

Now comes the easy part. Look at the notes you wrote. Choose your first story and write a **topic sentence** for your first body paragraph. Simply state what you're going to write about:

I used to spend my summers at my grandmother's house, but I didn't realize until later what experiences had brought her to that home.

Then **tell your story**. This is your **specific example** that will support your thesis statement. This is your **evidence** showing why your opinion is what it is. This should be fun.

However, you're not done yet. The reader reads papers, not minds. Imagine that the readers are clueless drones whose minds have been melted away by reading stacks and stacks of student prose. You've got to **explain how** your example connects to your thesis/opinion. Don't leave the reader hanging at the end of the paragraph, saying, "Okay, why did this student tell me this story?" The third major component of a body paragraph is the **Analysis and Interpretation**. It can be simple:

Through her courageous example, I learned the importance of confidence and faith.

> **TIP**
>
> Each body paragraph should contain a topic sentence, a specific example, and an analysis of that example.

It can be more complex:

After hearing the story of her war experiences, I saw her in a different light: She was still the grandmother who baked me cookies, but she was also the most courageous and confident woman I'd ever known.

Body paragraphs, then, must contain three elements: a topic sentence, specific evidence to support it, and analysis and interpretation to explain how the evidence proves the topic and thesis. How can we remember these elements? How about another acronym? The cowboy will remind us: T-Ex-An (or TEA, if you prefer fewer letters).

Topic
Example
Analysis

Practice

Choose your first story and write a body paragraph. Make sure you include a topic sentence to tell us your first point. Illustrate this with your specific example. Then analyze and explain how that example proves your point.

If you need a reminder, try this formula:

Topic sentence:

For example, —

This means —

MORE WRITING (KEEP GOING!)

For your next body paragraph or paragraphs, work the same as you did for the first body paragraph. You might want to open with a transition word or phrase:

In addition,	Next,	However,	Therefore,
Furthermore,	Similarly,	Nevertheless,	Consequently,
Moreover,			Finally,

Furthermore, [topic sentence]

For example, —

This means —

CONCLUSION

Finally, your conclusion should restate what you've said in your essay and sum it all up. You definitely do want to restate your thesis. Just say it again using slightly different wording. You can even expand it a bit, showing its relevance to the world at large, to all of us, or to you personally.

You do not want to introduce new material here. You do not want to contradict what you've said earlier in any way. You do not want to apologize or use wishy-washy language ("I'm probably wrong about this." "It might be that this is true."). **Be bold.** Finish on a strong note.

If you're pressed for time and you start to panic about the conclusion, just relax. You've already written one. That's right—your introduction can serve as an excellent model for your conclusion. You can give your readers a sense of closure by echoing something from the beginning of your paper. Look at your introduction **in reverse** and find your ideas there. Remember, this is only a guide for your concluding ideas—and not one to take literally.

For instance, the introduction and conclusion do not even have to contain the same number of sentences. However, looking at the first and last sentences can give you an idea of what direction to move.

> **TIP**
>
> The Conclusion is like your Introduction in reverse. It restates and sums up your essay.

Example

INTRODUCTION

1. Writing an essay is a difficult and painstaking task.
2. You have to compose a strong thesis that previews your paper.
3. You have to organize your ideas and present them clearly, providing examples, interpretations, and transitions.
4. Finally, you've got to sum all of this up in a satisfying conclusion.
5. A good essay will contain all of these elements, plus a certain unclassifiable component—the writer's own voice.

[BODY PARAGRAPHS ILLUSTRATE AND EXPLAIN THESE IDEAS]

Topic   Example   Analysis

CONCLUSION

1. Obviously, the writer's voice is unique.
2. Therefore, a good essay contains more than just an introduction, thesis, examples, analysis, and conclusion.
3. It holds and reveals some of the author's own life and personality, flowing naturally and unhindered throughout the writing.
4. This freedom to express yourself makes writing one of the easiest and most enjoyable tasks of all.

Practice

After you've written another body paragraph (or two), conclude your essay. To check yourself, underline the thesis in your introduction and the topic sentences in each body paragraph. Then underline your thesis as it appears again in the conclusion. Read these underlined sentences. Do they focus on one topic? Do they fit together? If not, then you've gotten off track. Remember, everything you write must relate to the thesis statement.

Next, go through and find places where you used expletive expressions such as "*There is,*" "*There are,*" and "*It is. . . .*" Cross these out! With just a word or two of adjustment, you will vastly improve your writing and the reader's experience. [Review the exercises on pages 218–219.]

Furthermore, if you have included some of the problem usage words—and used them correctly—you will impress the reader with your writing skills. (Perhaps you'd like to purposely include one or two of these problem words, just to show the reader that they are NOT problems for YOU!)

Finally, take a deep breath to clear your head. Go back and proofread your essay, making sure that everything is clearly written. You can't catch every error, but you should recognize the most obvious ones and make corrections.

More Practice

Try writing on the other topics listed on page 220. Use the following outlines and notebook paper for practice. Time yourself. It's important to get a sense of how long you have and how much time you need. Give yourself 25 or 30 minutes to complete the prewriting, writing, and proofreading. Not only will practice improve your writing skills, but it will also relieve the anxiety over time. Remember, you don't have to use everything you noted during your brainstorming/prewriting. Pick out your best material and pace yourself. Above all, relax. All you're doing is talking on paper, and you've been telling stories all of your life.

Topic

Agree or Disagree

Personal Experience

Literature

History/News

Topic

Agree or Disagree

Personal Experience

Literature

History/News

The Essay—SSAT Option

The SSAT essay gives you two options: you can write about an issue or a personal opinion, as you've just practiced, or you can write an original story. This relatively new creative writing option can't adhere to clear-cut rules, making this easier in some ways and riskier in others.

You will be given an opening line or "story starter," like these:

1. When I entered the school, everything seemed to be as it always was: lockers stood in rows, classroom doors opened into the halls, the fluorescent lights hummed. It took me a minute to realize that I was the only person in the building.
2. I couldn't believe she was asking for my help!
3. Suddenly, its eyes opened:
4. The silence in the room was unbearable.
5. I don't want to get ahead of myself. Literally. I mean, I can travel through time.
6. My friend gave me that grin I had seen so many times before, and I knew we were going to get in trouble.
7. As far as superpowers go, mine might seem kind of lame.
8. We had no idea; my uncle's job had been kept secret by the government.
9. He looked at the key in his hand.
10. Well, THAT should confuse anyone looking for me!

Okay, at this point, you feel either panic or elation. If you're feeling anxious, remember you can write a straightforward essay. You've got the formulas, and you've got the skills. If you think this sounds like fun, then let's give this a try. However, you've got to realize that this writing exercise still must show the reader that you have mastered the basic skills of grammar and usage, organization, and clarity.

To that end, remember to write legibly in blue or black ink. And remain positive! This is not the time to write your gory zombie apocalypse extravaganza. Your bleak existential tragedy should probably wait for another opportunity. Put away your ideas for the vengeful thriller in which thinly disguised versions of your friends are given satisfying comeuppance. You want your reader to feel happy, pleasantly inclined, and impressed with your possibilities. The theme of your story should be a positive, hopeful one.

After reading the writing prompt, take a couple of minutes to map out your story. You'll want to have a beginning (an exposition introducing your characters and situation), a middle (the complications and problems that reach a climax), and an end (a resolution in which the outcome is revealed). Decide what characters to include (not many, given your time constraint) and give them some distinguishing traits.

Practice

Choose one of the prompts above and write some notes. Characters (and traits):

Opening situation and setting:

Conflict, problem, complications:

Climax:

Resolution:

Keep all of this fairly simple; you'll only have 15–20 minutes to write the story. Your opening sentence may thrust you right into the action. Keep that action going as you explain any necessary background information. Who is telling the story? Are you telling the story in the first person, or is a third-person narrator relating the tale? Whatever you choose, keep it consistent throughout. Let the reader meet the characters as this opening situation plays out.

Successful writers SHOW a story rather than tell a story. Use concrete details to describe the people and setting. Be direct rather than vague. You should create a vivid picture in the reader's mind; you're being evaluated on how strongly your writing affects him or her.

How can you do this? Well, you use the same techniques you learned in the previous section. Active verbs and specific nouns will help you achieve your goal.

TIP

Whenever you start to "tell" part of your story, try to find a way to SHOW that information through specific action.

Instead of this: *He was excited.*
                        She is happy.

Try this: *He quivered with excitement.*
                She radiates happiness.

Or this: *The little boy felt like jumping and catching a star.*
             My aunt's smile inspires everyone around her.

Practice

Replace the general noun with something more specific.

Ex. bird

sparrow, jay, vulture

1. horse
2. fruit
3. insect

Rewrite the following sentences with more active verbs.

Ex. He was angry.

His rage cleared the room.

1. The young woman was nervous.
2. The boy was very active.
3. My father is stern.
4. The teacher was stressed.
5. The cat was aloof.

Replace the expletive construction.

Ex. It was thundering.

Thunder split the sky.

1. There were three goals scored in last night's game.
2. It was a long wait in the lunch line.
3. It is a delicious lunch.

Once you start your story, introduce the problem quickly, and make everything specific: specific characters doing specific things in specific ways. A story requires conflict, and you must deal with it directly. Does the conflict rage within the character, or does the problem attack from the outside?

When a character speaks, not only must the paragraph change, but the character should do something, as well. Avoid overusing the expressions "she said" or "he said."

Use less of this: "Are you all right?" he asked.
"You're a little late in asking," she replied.

Use more of this: "Are you all right?" He looked back, still panting
in his fear, trying to find her on the dark path.
She picked herself off the ground. "You're a little late
in asking."

When your story reaches the high point or biggest conflict, the events should start winding down. This can (and should) happen much more quickly than the buildup to the climax. Has everything returned to normal? What has changed? Your story should have something to say about life (the THEME), and you can make that point more clearly here.

Practice

Time yourself and try writing stories about some of the prompts listed above. Allow for enough time to plan and proofread.

Practice Tests

CHAPTER 6

SSAT Practice Test 1
ANSWER SHEET

Section 2 Quantitative Skills

1 Ⓐ Ⓑ Ⓒ Ⓓ Ⓔ   6 Ⓐ Ⓑ Ⓒ Ⓓ Ⓔ   11 Ⓐ Ⓑ Ⓒ Ⓓ Ⓔ   16 Ⓐ Ⓑ Ⓒ Ⓓ Ⓔ   21 Ⓐ Ⓑ Ⓒ Ⓓ Ⓔ
2 Ⓐ Ⓑ Ⓒ Ⓓ Ⓔ   7 Ⓐ Ⓑ Ⓒ Ⓓ Ⓔ   12 Ⓐ Ⓑ Ⓒ Ⓓ Ⓔ   17 Ⓐ Ⓑ Ⓒ Ⓓ Ⓔ   22 Ⓐ Ⓑ Ⓒ Ⓓ Ⓔ
3 Ⓐ Ⓑ Ⓒ Ⓓ Ⓔ   8 Ⓐ Ⓑ Ⓒ Ⓓ Ⓔ   13 Ⓐ Ⓑ Ⓒ Ⓓ Ⓔ   18 Ⓐ Ⓑ Ⓒ Ⓓ Ⓔ   23 Ⓐ Ⓑ Ⓒ Ⓓ Ⓔ
4 Ⓐ Ⓑ Ⓒ Ⓓ Ⓔ   9 Ⓐ Ⓑ Ⓒ Ⓓ Ⓔ   14 Ⓐ Ⓑ Ⓒ Ⓓ Ⓔ   19 Ⓐ Ⓑ Ⓒ Ⓓ Ⓔ   24 Ⓐ Ⓑ Ⓒ Ⓓ Ⓔ
5 Ⓐ Ⓑ Ⓒ Ⓓ Ⓔ   10 Ⓐ Ⓑ Ⓒ Ⓓ Ⓔ   15 Ⓐ Ⓑ Ⓒ Ⓓ Ⓔ   20 Ⓐ Ⓑ Ⓒ Ⓓ Ⓔ   25 Ⓐ Ⓑ Ⓒ Ⓓ Ⓔ

Section 3 Reading Comprehension Skills

1 Ⓐ Ⓑ Ⓒ Ⓓ Ⓔ   9 Ⓐ Ⓑ Ⓒ Ⓓ Ⓔ   17 Ⓐ Ⓑ Ⓒ Ⓓ Ⓔ   25 Ⓐ Ⓑ Ⓒ Ⓓ Ⓔ   33 Ⓐ Ⓑ Ⓒ Ⓓ Ⓔ
2 Ⓐ Ⓑ Ⓒ Ⓓ Ⓔ   10 Ⓐ Ⓑ Ⓒ Ⓓ Ⓔ   18 Ⓐ Ⓑ Ⓒ Ⓓ Ⓔ   26 Ⓐ Ⓑ Ⓒ Ⓓ Ⓔ   34 Ⓐ Ⓑ Ⓒ Ⓓ Ⓔ
3 Ⓐ Ⓑ Ⓒ Ⓓ Ⓔ   11 Ⓐ Ⓑ Ⓒ Ⓓ Ⓔ   19 Ⓐ Ⓑ Ⓒ Ⓓ Ⓔ   27 Ⓐ Ⓑ Ⓒ Ⓓ Ⓔ   35 Ⓐ Ⓑ Ⓒ Ⓓ Ⓔ
4 Ⓐ Ⓑ Ⓒ Ⓓ Ⓔ   12 Ⓐ Ⓑ Ⓒ Ⓓ Ⓔ   20 Ⓐ Ⓑ Ⓒ Ⓓ Ⓔ   28 Ⓐ Ⓑ Ⓒ Ⓓ Ⓔ   36 Ⓐ Ⓑ Ⓒ Ⓓ Ⓔ
5 Ⓐ Ⓑ Ⓒ Ⓓ Ⓔ   13 Ⓐ Ⓑ Ⓒ Ⓓ Ⓔ   21 Ⓐ Ⓑ Ⓒ Ⓓ Ⓔ   29 Ⓐ Ⓑ Ⓒ Ⓓ Ⓔ   37 Ⓐ Ⓑ Ⓒ Ⓓ Ⓔ
6 Ⓐ Ⓑ Ⓒ Ⓓ Ⓔ   14 Ⓐ Ⓑ Ⓒ Ⓓ Ⓔ   22 Ⓐ Ⓑ Ⓒ Ⓓ Ⓔ   30 Ⓐ Ⓑ Ⓒ Ⓓ Ⓔ   38 Ⓐ Ⓑ Ⓒ Ⓓ Ⓔ
7 Ⓐ Ⓑ Ⓒ Ⓓ Ⓔ   15 Ⓐ Ⓑ Ⓒ Ⓓ Ⓔ   23 Ⓐ Ⓑ Ⓒ Ⓓ Ⓔ   31 Ⓐ Ⓑ Ⓒ Ⓓ Ⓔ   39 Ⓐ Ⓑ Ⓒ Ⓓ Ⓔ
8 Ⓐ Ⓑ Ⓒ Ⓓ Ⓔ   16 Ⓐ Ⓑ Ⓒ Ⓓ Ⓔ   24 Ⓐ Ⓑ Ⓒ Ⓓ Ⓔ   32 Ⓐ Ⓑ Ⓒ Ⓓ Ⓔ   40 Ⓐ Ⓑ Ⓒ Ⓓ Ⓔ

Section 4 Verbal Skills

1 Ⓐ Ⓑ Ⓒ Ⓓ Ⓔ   13 Ⓐ Ⓑ Ⓒ Ⓓ Ⓔ   25 Ⓐ Ⓑ Ⓒ Ⓓ Ⓔ   37 Ⓐ Ⓑ Ⓒ Ⓓ Ⓔ   49 Ⓐ Ⓑ Ⓒ Ⓓ Ⓔ
2 Ⓐ Ⓑ Ⓒ Ⓓ Ⓔ   14 Ⓐ Ⓑ Ⓒ Ⓓ Ⓔ   26 Ⓐ Ⓑ Ⓒ Ⓓ Ⓔ   38 Ⓐ Ⓑ Ⓒ Ⓓ Ⓔ   50 Ⓐ Ⓑ Ⓒ Ⓓ Ⓔ
3 Ⓐ Ⓑ Ⓒ Ⓓ Ⓔ   15 Ⓐ Ⓑ Ⓒ Ⓓ Ⓔ   27 Ⓐ Ⓑ Ⓒ Ⓓ Ⓔ   39 Ⓐ Ⓑ Ⓒ Ⓓ Ⓔ   51 Ⓐ Ⓑ Ⓒ Ⓓ Ⓔ
4 Ⓐ Ⓑ Ⓒ Ⓓ Ⓔ   16 Ⓐ Ⓑ Ⓒ Ⓓ Ⓔ   28 Ⓐ Ⓑ Ⓒ Ⓓ Ⓔ   40 Ⓐ Ⓑ Ⓒ Ⓓ Ⓔ   52 Ⓐ Ⓑ Ⓒ Ⓓ Ⓔ
5 Ⓐ Ⓑ Ⓒ Ⓓ Ⓔ   17 Ⓐ Ⓑ Ⓒ Ⓓ Ⓔ   29 Ⓐ Ⓑ Ⓒ Ⓓ Ⓔ   41 Ⓐ Ⓑ Ⓒ Ⓓ Ⓔ   53 Ⓐ Ⓑ Ⓒ Ⓓ Ⓔ
6 Ⓐ Ⓑ Ⓒ Ⓓ Ⓔ   18 Ⓐ Ⓑ Ⓒ Ⓓ Ⓔ   30 Ⓐ Ⓑ Ⓒ Ⓓ Ⓔ   42 Ⓐ Ⓑ Ⓒ Ⓓ Ⓔ   54 Ⓐ Ⓑ Ⓒ Ⓓ Ⓔ
7 Ⓐ Ⓑ Ⓒ Ⓓ Ⓔ   19 Ⓐ Ⓑ Ⓒ Ⓓ Ⓔ   31 Ⓐ Ⓑ Ⓒ Ⓓ Ⓔ   43 Ⓐ Ⓑ Ⓒ Ⓓ Ⓔ   55 Ⓐ Ⓑ Ⓒ Ⓓ Ⓔ
8 Ⓐ Ⓑ Ⓒ Ⓓ Ⓔ   20 Ⓐ Ⓑ Ⓒ Ⓓ Ⓔ   32 Ⓐ Ⓑ Ⓒ Ⓓ Ⓔ   44 Ⓐ Ⓑ Ⓒ Ⓓ Ⓔ   56 Ⓐ Ⓑ Ⓒ Ⓓ Ⓔ
9 Ⓐ Ⓑ Ⓒ Ⓓ Ⓔ   21 Ⓐ Ⓑ Ⓒ Ⓓ Ⓔ   33 Ⓐ Ⓑ Ⓒ Ⓓ Ⓔ   45 Ⓐ Ⓑ Ⓒ Ⓓ Ⓔ   57 Ⓐ Ⓑ Ⓒ Ⓓ Ⓔ
10 Ⓐ Ⓑ Ⓒ Ⓓ Ⓔ   22 Ⓐ Ⓑ Ⓒ Ⓓ Ⓔ   34 Ⓐ Ⓑ Ⓒ Ⓓ Ⓔ   46 Ⓐ Ⓑ Ⓒ Ⓓ Ⓔ   58 Ⓐ Ⓑ Ⓒ Ⓓ Ⓔ
11 Ⓐ Ⓑ Ⓒ Ⓓ Ⓔ   23 Ⓐ Ⓑ Ⓒ Ⓓ Ⓔ   35 Ⓐ Ⓑ Ⓒ Ⓓ Ⓔ   47 Ⓐ Ⓑ Ⓒ Ⓓ Ⓔ   59 Ⓐ Ⓑ Ⓒ Ⓓ Ⓔ
12 Ⓐ Ⓑ Ⓒ Ⓓ Ⓔ   24 Ⓐ Ⓑ Ⓒ Ⓓ Ⓔ   36 Ⓐ Ⓑ Ⓒ Ⓓ Ⓔ   48 Ⓐ Ⓑ Ⓒ Ⓓ Ⓔ   60 Ⓐ Ⓑ Ⓒ Ⓓ Ⓔ

SSAT Practice Test 1
ANSWER SHEET

Section 5 Quantitative Skills

1 Ⓐ Ⓑ Ⓒ Ⓓ Ⓔ   6 Ⓐ Ⓑ Ⓒ Ⓓ Ⓔ   11 Ⓐ Ⓑ Ⓒ Ⓓ Ⓔ   16 Ⓐ Ⓑ Ⓒ Ⓓ Ⓔ   21 Ⓐ Ⓑ Ⓒ Ⓓ Ⓔ
2 Ⓐ Ⓑ Ⓒ Ⓓ Ⓔ   7 Ⓐ Ⓑ Ⓒ Ⓓ Ⓔ   12 Ⓐ Ⓑ Ⓒ Ⓓ Ⓔ   17 Ⓐ Ⓑ Ⓒ Ⓓ Ⓔ   22 Ⓐ Ⓑ Ⓒ Ⓓ Ⓔ
3 Ⓐ Ⓑ Ⓒ Ⓓ Ⓔ   8 Ⓐ Ⓑ Ⓒ Ⓓ Ⓔ   13 Ⓐ Ⓑ Ⓒ Ⓓ Ⓔ   18 Ⓐ Ⓑ Ⓒ Ⓓ Ⓔ   23 Ⓐ Ⓑ Ⓒ Ⓓ Ⓔ
4 Ⓐ Ⓑ Ⓒ Ⓓ Ⓔ   9 Ⓐ Ⓑ Ⓒ Ⓓ Ⓔ   14 Ⓐ Ⓑ Ⓒ Ⓓ Ⓔ   19 Ⓐ Ⓑ Ⓒ Ⓓ Ⓔ   24 Ⓐ Ⓑ Ⓒ Ⓓ Ⓔ
5 Ⓐ Ⓑ Ⓒ Ⓓ Ⓔ   10 Ⓐ Ⓑ Ⓒ Ⓓ Ⓔ   15 Ⓐ Ⓑ Ⓒ Ⓓ Ⓔ   20 Ⓐ Ⓑ Ⓒ Ⓓ Ⓔ   25 Ⓐ Ⓑ Ⓒ Ⓓ Ⓔ

SECTION 1 WRITING SAMPLE

1 question   *25 minutes*

Directions: Read the two prompts below and choose the one that interests you more. Circle it.

A If you could live in any other country, which one would you choose? Why?

B What in the world was I doing onstage? I don't play the piano.

Use the space provided to complete your writing sample.

(Continue on the following page.)

STOP

SECTION 2 QUANTITATIVE SKILLS

25 questions   *30 minutes*

Directions: This section is a multiple-choice test. Work out the problems and, from the five choices given, select the best answer.

Sample Question:
What is the difference between the sum of the prime factors of 18 and the sum of the prime factors of 25?
(A) 6
(B) 5
(C) 3
(D) 4
(E) 2

Ⓐ Ⓑ Ⓒ Ⓓ ●

USE THIS SPACE FOR FIGURING

1. On the map, the symbol ⊢⊣ represents 12 miles. If Hailey drives at a speed of 60 miles per hour, how long will it take her to drive from city A to city B?

(A) 48 minutes
(B) 36 minutes
(C) 1 hour, 36 minutes
(D) 1 hour, 12 minutes
(E) 1 hour, 48 minutes

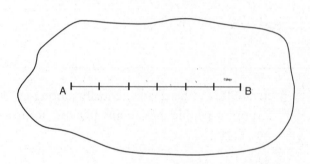

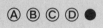

2. The car dealership sold 1,800 cars last year. According to the chart, how many Mazdas did the dealership sell?

(A) 648
(B) 306
(C) 324
(D) 522
(E) 486

Cars Sold by Car Dealership

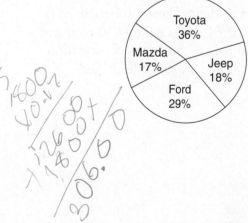

USE THIS SPACE FOR FIGURING

3. Henry wants to paint a wall 10 feet high by 24 feet long. If 1 quart of paint covers 40 square feet of wall space, how many quarts of paint does Henry need to paint the entire wall?

(A) 3 quarts
(B) 4 quarts
(C) 5 quarts
(D) 6 quarts
(E) 7 quarts

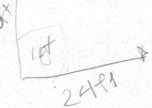

4. Describe the measure of side *AC*.

(A) *x*
(B) >*x*
(C) <*x*
(D) *y*
(E) >*y*

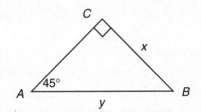

5. If $900 is to be divided equally among a group of people, how many persons are in the group?

(A) 17
(B) 19
(C) 21
(D) 15
(E) 27

6. The Crown Movie Theater collected $705 yesterday. If 54 adults paid $9.50 each and each child paid $3.50 less than each adult, how many children paid admissions?

(A) 32
(B) 38
(C) 29
(D) 25
(E) 42

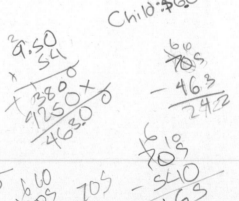

USE THIS SPACE FOR FIGURING

7. Simplify $6|-3|-4|5|$.

(A) 3
(B) 2
(C) −3
(D) −2
(E) 4

8. Hector Villanueva has a 0.300 batting average (hits/times at bat). If he gets a total of 10 more hits the next 10 times at bat, his batting average will jump to 0.400. Determine how many hits he had originally.

(A) 24
(B) 16
(C) 22
(D) 34
(E) 18

9. Given $5 > 3x \geq -2$, find a possible value for x.

(A) 2
(B) 1
(C) −2
(D) −1
(E) 3

10. Find the ratio of the number of residents of Middletown to the number of residents of Henderson in the year 2005.

(A) 1/5
(B) 2/5
(C) 3/8
(D) 5/8
(E) 4/9

 = 4,000 people

Residents in 2005	
Carson City	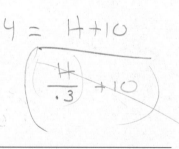
Middletown	
Newcastle	
Jamestown	
Henderson	

USE THIS SPACE FOR FIGURING

11. Find the value of y in the equation $y = 4x^3$ when $x = \dfrac{2}{3}$.

(A) $9\dfrac{1}{3}$

(B) $1\dfrac{5}{27}$

(C) $9\dfrac{4}{11}$

(D) $8\dfrac{12}{25}$

(E) $12\dfrac{2}{3}$

12. Review the following five algebraic expressions and then select the correct answer below.

(a) $4(r + s) + t$
(b) $4r + 4s$
(c) $4rst$
(d) $4r(s + t)$
(e) $4rt + 4rs$

(A) $a = b$
(B) $c > d$
(C) $e < a$
(D) $b > d$
(E) $d = e$

13. The table represents the frequency distribution of students' weights. Find the mean weight and round to the nearest tenth.

(A) 120.3
(B) 118.2
(C) 122.1
(D) 116.9
(E) 119.2

Pounds, p_i	Frequency, f_i	$p_i f_i$
98	2	
105	1	
109	1	
120	3	
126	2	
132	4	

USE THIS SPACE FOR FIGURING

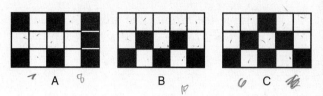

14. If the areas of all the inner squares are equal, select the correct answer among the following descriptions.

(A) The white area in B is less than the white area in A.
(B) The dark area in A is greater than the dark area in C.
(C) The white areas in A and B are equal.
(D) The dark area in C is greater than the white area in B.
(E) The white area in C is less than the dark area in B.

15. Represent the area of a triangle with a base of $2x + y$ and a height of $4z$.

(A) $2z(2x + y)$
(B) $2x(z + y)$
(C) $2xyz$
(D) $z(2x + y)$
(E) $2z + 4xy$

16. A container holds 3 yellow, 4 blue, and 2 white marbles. If 1 marble is drawn at random from the container, what is the possibility that it is either yellow or blue?

(A) 1/3
(B) 3/8
(C) 6/9
(D) 7/9
(E) 2/3

17. Determine the ratio of the area of a circle with radius 2 to the area of a circle with radius 4.

(A) $\frac{1}{4}$

(B) $\frac{1}{2}$

(C) $\frac{2}{3}$

(D) $\frac{3}{4}$

(E) $\frac{2}{5}$

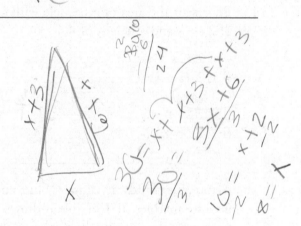

18. Each of the equal legs of an isosceles triangle is 3 more than the base, and the perimeter is 30. Find the measure of one of the equal legs.

(A) 12
(B) 10
(C) 7
(D) 11
(E) 15

19. If the area of a square is $4a^2$, find its perimeter.

(A) $6a$
(B) $8a^2$
(C) $12a$
(D) $6a^2$
(E) $8a$

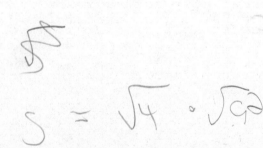

USE THIS SPACE FOR FIGURING

20. Hal spends $t + 4$ hours per day watching television. José spends t hours and Tony watches television $t - 2$ hours per day. Find the average number of hours of watching television for the three students.

   (A) $\dfrac{4t + 2}{3}$

   (B) $\dfrac{3t + 2}{3}$

   (C) $\dfrac{5t - 1}{3}$

   (D) $t + 12$

   (E) $\dfrac{3t - 2}{3}$

21–22.

Major Network Television Shows					
	2002	**2003**	**2004**	**2005**	**Summary**
Reality	2	3	12	14	31
Comedy	7	9	8	7	31
Law	3	6	7	5	21
Detective	8	9	6	12	35
Cartoons	10	12	14	16	52
News	20	24	21	15	80
Summary	50	63	68	69	250

21. In 2002, what percent of all television shows were detective stories?

   (A) 20%

   (B) 18%

   (C) 16%

   (D) 23%

   (E) 24%

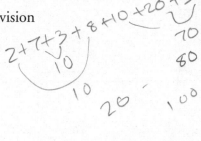

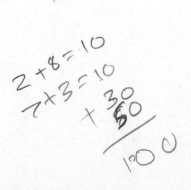

USE THIS SPACE FOR FIGURING

22. The total number of cartoons in the year 2004 and 2005 represent what percent of all shows in the years 2002 through and including 2005?

(A) 18%
(B) 24%
(C) 22%
(D) 12%
(E) 16%

23. If a is a negative integer and b is a positive one, which of the following statements is true?

(A) $ab < ba$
(B) $a + b > b - a$
(C) $a^2 < 0$
(D) $b^2 < 0$
(E) $ba \geq ab$

24. Express the linear relationship indicated in the table.

(A) $y = x + 1$
(B) $y = 2x + 1$
(C) $y = 3x - 1$
(D) $y = 2x - 1$
(E) $y = x + 4$

x	1	2	3	4	5
y	1	3	5	7	9

USE THIS SPACE FOR FIGURING

25. *ABCD* and *HIJK* are squares. *E*, *F*, and *G* are the midpoints of *AB*, *BC*, and *CD*, respectively. *EB* is the same length as *HI*. Which of the following statements is true?

(A) *AE* is equal to *BC*.

(B) Area *ABCD* is equal to area *EBCG* + area *HIJK*.

(C) Area *ABCD* is equal to area *AEGD* + twice area *HIJK*.

(D) *EG* is greater than twice the length of *HI*.

(E) Area *AEGD* + area *HIJK* is equal to area *ABCD*.

STOP

IF YOU FINISH BEFORE TIME IS UP, YOU MAY CHECK YOUR WORK ON THIS SECTION ONLY. DO NOT TURN TO ANY OTHER SECTION IN THE TEST.

SECTION 3 READING COMPREHENSION SKILLS

40 questions   *40 minutes*

Directions: Read each passage carefully and then answer the questions about it. For each question, decide on the basis of the passage which one of the choices best answers the question.

Ever wonder why we have wisdom teeth? If you're like most people, you'll have your wisdom teeth removed before they even start to surface. How can we just throw away teeth without their absence having some
Line impact on the state of our mouths? The science of dentistry studies
(5)   questions like this.

Although it dates back to 3700 B.C. in Egypt, dentistry as we know it did not emerge until the 19th century, when people began to study systematically the mouth, gums, jaw, and teeth. Modern dentistry is an intrinsic part of our lives. Nowadays, we cannot go a day without
(10)   hearing something about teeth care, if only through our television sets. If we have gingivitis, we can use mouthwash. If we have cavities, we can get fillings in a variety of colors and material types. If we have yellow teeth, we can make them white again in seven short days.

And, if we have crooked teeth, we can get braces. In fact, people
(15)   routinely get braces, so much so that we consider it an oddity if someone goes through their entire childhood without the experience of going to the orthodontist every month. Chances are that if someone does not get braces, they lack money or time, not interest in having work done.

The evolution of dentistry shows how medical science is changing the
(20)   human being. Because of increasingly good dental care, we don't lose our teeth and rely on our wisdom teeth coming in to give us a new set. To answer the question with which we began: We simply don't need those teeth anymore. Indeed, nowadays we have to pay to get our redundant teeth taken out.

1. The article says that we pull our wisdom teeth because _____.

   (A) we have gingivitis
   (B) they cause crooked teeth
   (C) we don't need them anymore
   (D) we listen to information about teeth care daily on the TV
   (E) they make our teeth yellow

2. Which of the following statements is true based on the reading?

   (A) Braces are a common solution to yellowing teeth.
   (B) Egyptian dentists conducted dentistry much as we do today.
   (C) If we have gingivitis, we can treat it with fillings.
   (D) We don't expect to lose our teeth because we have been taught how to care for them.
   (E) Braces are a rare experience while growing up.

3. When did dentists pull the first tooth?

   (A) 3700 B.C.
   (B) 17th century
   (C) 18th century
   (D) 19th century
   (E) The article does not say.

4. The writer's main purpose is apparently _____.

   (A) to answer frequently asked questions about teeth
   (B) to talk a little about the history of dentistry
   (C) to explain dreams about teeth
   (D) to write the section on dentistry for a medical school text
   (E) to encourage people to cut down on sweets

5. All but which of the following problems, according to the article, can dentists fix?

   (A) bad breath
   (B) yellowing teeth
   (C) crooked teeth
   (D) root canals
   (E) cavities

It's easy, nowadays, to blame others for bad things that happen to us. We complain that we don't have enough money because the government takes our taxes. We blame carbohydrates for our fat count. We blame society for our embarrassingly low educational scores.

Line
(5)   Well, I disagree. I say we could save money by skipping McDonald's and buying the non-name-brand food items at the grocery. I say we're fat because we don't exercise. I say we're stupid because we watch too much TV and never read anything more difficult than sixth grade reading material.

(10)   I say that it's in our own hands if we are operating at less than our potential.

So, sometime, when you're at a loss for something to do, change your life for the better. Crack open the dictionary at a random page and see what's inside.

(15)   <u>Seriously</u>.

Chances are you'll find something interesting you didn't know before. Reading the dictionary is like reading a thousand mininovels, for each word has a story.

For example, we often hear someone referred to as a "spinster." Most
(20)   of us know that we use this term to describe an old, unmarried woman, but few of us know that the name originally had more meaning. The reason that "spinster" came to refer to all old, unmarried women is because in earlier times old, unmarried women had to spin to earn their livings; old, unmarried women who could not spin nevertheless got
(25)   <u>lumped in</u> with the rest. Consider, also, the word "whirling dervish." We know that this word is used to refer to dancers or tornadoes. Originally, however, the word referred to Muslim priests who wandered the land as beggars; in addition to whirling dervishes, there existed also howling and dancing dervishes, too.

(30)   So, take five minutes and read the dictionary next time you're bored.

Seriously.

6. What is the best title for this passage?

   (A) Unexpected Discoveries
   (B) Through the Eye of a Needle
   (C) A Thousand and One Words
   (D) Boring Facts and Trivia
   (E) On the Origin of the Word "Dervish"

7. How would you describe the author's tone in this piece?

   (A) humorous and trivial
   (B) adamant and angry
   (C) friendly yet tired
   (D) amusing yet serious
   (E) sulky and sullen

8. Who does the author say is responsible for the state of our lives?

   (A) the government
   (B) McDonald's
   (C) television
   (D) educators
   (E) We, ourselves

9. Why does the author give the word *seriously* in line 12 its own paragraph?

   (A) The author thinks the reader will take his/her advice seriously; therefore s/he uses *seriously* to indicate s/he has made a joke.
   (B) The author must include nine paragraphs in the article and is cheating.
   (C) The author wishes the reader to look up the word *seriously* in a dictionary.
   (D) The author anticipates that the reader will scoff at the author's advice; the author wishes to convey serious intent of his/her advice.
   (E) The author desires to confuse the reader at all costs.

10. Which of the following words best defines the phrase *lumped in*?

   (A) left out
   (B) copied
   (C) combined with
   (D) evolved
   (E) destroyed

Pieter Brueghel, 16th century Flemish painter, has left for us a series of great paintings. One of his best works depicts the Greek myth of Icarus.

Line   To understand Brueghel's treatment of the piece, you must first recall
(5)   the facts of the Icarus story. Icarus was the son of Deadalus, the most brilliant thinker of his time. Deadalus had aided Ariadne in saving Theseus from the Minotaur. The king, angered by Deadalus' action, swiftly imprisoned Deadalus and his son in a lonely tower on a deserted shore, visited only by birds. Eager to escape, however, Deadalus used the
(10)   feathers and wax to create two sets of wings, and he and his son made plans to fly to freedom. Unfortunately, Icarus, <u>exhilarated</u> by the freedom he felt while flying, flew too close to the sun, despite his father's warnings. The sun's heat melted the wax on his wings, and he <u>plummeted</u> into the ocean and drowned. Deadalus, heartbroken,
(15)   nevertheless, made it to safety.

Brueghel's work depicts a huge, glorious scene of people working the land along a beautiful shoreline. Animals frolic; men work. Ships laden with goods plow through the waves. Amidst all the action captured in the scene, one is hard pressed to locate Icarus. Finally, after some
(20)   searching, we see him. He is located in the lower, right-hand side of the painting. Even so, his depiction is small. Indeed, all we see are two pale legs, kicking <u>frantically</u> in the surf.

Brueghel's work sends a clear message, one that underscores the largeness of the world and the relative insignificance of the individual
(25)   therein.

11. What will the author most likely discuss next?

    (A) artist Vincent van Gogh and how he cut off his ear
    (B) another artwork by Brueghel
    (C) an explanation of Brueghel's message regarding the insignificance in the world
    (D) an expanded discussion of the crime that landed Dedalus in jail
    (E) nothing, the article is complete

12. The author's purpose can best be described by which of the following statements?

    (A) to avoid discussing anything important
    (B) to advocate the talents of Brueghel
    (C) to relate the tale of Dedalus and Icarus
    (D) to argue that Brueghel is an untalented artist
    (E) to show how art can convey social comment

13. Which of the following words can be substituted for the word *exhilarated* in line 11 without changing the meaning of the sentence.

    (A) saddened
    (B) angered
    (C) joyous
    (D) frightened
    (E) advised

14. What is the tone of this piece?

    (A) solemn
    (B) understanding
    (C) sarcastic
    (D) joyous
    (E) unintelligent

15. All but which of the following words have the same meaning as *plummeted* in line 14?

    (A) fell
    (B) hung
    (C) dropped
    (D) sank
    (E) plunged

16. Which of the following words has a meaning most nearly opposite to the word *frantically* in line 22?

    (A) feebly
    (B) wildly
    (C) enthusiastically
    (D) vigorously
    (E) angrily

17. What caused Icarus' wings to melt?

    (A) the cold ocean spray
    (B) the swooping, swirling seagulls
    (C) the dampness of the water
    (D) the heat of Dedalus' wrath
    (E) the warmth of the sun

History documents the bloody habits of Vlad <u>Tepes</u> (or Vlad the Impaler), an infamous general who lived in Transylvania from 1431 to 1476. Stories about Vlad Tepes seem gruesome even by today's

Line standards. Consider this story about a group of generals whom Vlad
(5) Tepes was entertaining. Prior to their arrival, Vlad had punished several people by impaling them on long spikes surrounding the banquet area. One of the visiting generals complained of the smell; after all, he had been invited to a dinner. Vlad apologized and then had the general impaled on an even longer spike. His reason? So that the general, being
(10) suspended above the other rotting bodies, would not have to smell what offended him.

Other vampire tales come to us from this period, but they are clinical, historical accounts. The vampire legend grew popular only after the publication of Bram Stoker's *Dracula* in 1897. In his novel, Stoker
(15) creates a frightening combination of man and monster. His Dracula is striking in appearance, ruthless, calculating, and quite intelligent. Since then, vampire stories have grown in popularity over the years, inspiring both serious and tongue-in-cheek treatments.

The serious vampire offerings have grown increasingly enraptured by
(20) the idea of being undead. Take for example, the work of Anne Rice. Rice's books modernize the old vampire story. While Stoker's novel tells about the exploits of a single vampire, Rice's novels explore an entire vampiric underworld that coexists with—and preys upon—the human world. Rice's stories allow the old vampire lore to evolve into an entire
(25) world view; they work out in great detail the logistical and philosophical problems that come into play, if vampires really exist en masse. More importantly, however, Rice's stories humanize the vampire. Many of her characters are guilt-stricken to the point of madness because they must drink human blood to survive; some rail against their undead state, for
(30) they are frozen in time, unable to transition from one stage of human maturity to the next.

18. What does the word *Tepes* mean?

    (A) innocent
    (B) Dracula
    (C) impaler
    (D) bloody
    (E) ruler

19. Which statement gives an accurate description of Vlad Tepes' character?

    (A) He is a wise and caring ruler
    (B) He is a brilliant military strategist.
    (C) He was poor, despite his great power.
    (D) He was popular with women.
    (E) His sense of justice is very unconventional.

20. Which is the best title for this passage?

    (A) An American Werewolf in London
    (B) Witches, Warlocks, and Other Halloween Nasties
    (C) The Vlad Dynasty: A Family Tree
    (D) The Enduring Zombie
    (E) Still Hungry After All These Years

21. Which date approximates the time period when Anne Rice wrote?

    (A) 1431
    (B) 1476
    (C) 1789
    (D) 1897
    (E) 1990

22. The statement "Other vampire tales come to us from this period, but they are clinical, historical accounts" implies that _____.

    (A) vampire tales that come from this period are even more exciting than the Tepes story
    (B) interest in vampire lore died out altogether during this period
    (C) vampire stories that were written from this period were boring
    (D) stories about female vampires were especially popular during this period
    (E) Anne Rice was popular even during this period

Existentialism is a philosophy that focuses only on the actions that we humans make in the physical world that surrounds us. Because it admits no afterlife of any sort, Existentialism takes the world very
Line seriously; every decision forces the Existentialist to ponder deeply the
(5) consequences. She only gets one shot at life, so everything depends on her getting it right the first time. According to its <u>tenets</u>, life is absurd and filled with actions that seem pointless, futile, and ceaselessly endless.

Camus illustrates Existentialism using the example of Sisyphus from Greek mythology. Sisyphus vastly enjoyed life but held little respect for
(10) the gods. Upon his deathbed, Sisyphus instructed his wife to leave his body unburied as a gesture of anger and resentment at dying. She agreed to do as he said, but when he died, she reneged on her word. Upon waking in Hades, Sisyphus knew immediately that his wife had betrayed him, and he asked permission from King Hades to go revenge
(15) himself upon her. Hades agreed on condition that Sisyphus return to the underworld immediately after getting his revenge. However, as soon as Sisyphus reached the earth's surface, he chose to give up his revenge and refused to return to the underworld. Only after great efforts did King Hades recapture his prisoner.

(20) As punishment for his <u>hubris</u> or conceitedness, King Hades created a special task for Sisyphus. He now spends eternity rolling an enormous rock up a great hill, only to have it come crashing down immediately upon reaching the hill's summit. Sisyphus' task illustrates clearly the tenets of Existentialism outlined here. Let's see how.

23. According to the article, the story of Sisyphus comes from _____.

    (A) old wives' tales
    (B) Japanese tradition
    (C) Indian lore
    (D) Roman history
    (E) Greek myth

24. What does Sisyphus initially want to do when he returns to earth?

    (A) Stay alive.
    (B) Get revenge on his brother.
    (C) Punish his wife.
    (D) See his family.
    (E) Negotiate a treaty.

25. Which of the following most nearly means *tenets* as used in line 6?

    (A) beliefs
    (B) rules
    (C) portable buildings
    (D) woven strands of rope to catch fish
    (E) numbers

26. What will probably come after paragraph three?

    (A) background information about Camus
    (B) more information about Sisyphus' escapades
    (C) nothing; the author has made his/her point
    (D) a discussion of how Sisyphus' story illustrates the tenets of Existentialism
    (E) an opinion from a philosophy professor at the University of Kentucky

27. Which of the following words best represents an antonym for *hubris?*

    (A) daring
    (B) fearful
    (C) piety
    (D) miserable
    (E) perturbed

Have you ever wondered why you aren't supposed to wear white after Labor Day? It is a long-standing tradition, one that those of us from the South have had beaten into our heads from our very earliest memories. But from where does this rule come?

Line
(5)   People dispute the origin of this custom. Some say that the rule developed from practicality. After all, everyone knows that wearing white in the summer is wise because the white reflects heat and helps the wearer keep cool; wearing dark colors is wise in the winter because the dark material absorbs heat and keeps the wearer warm. The rule of
(10) thumb, they say, merely <u>solidifies</u> what was already well known, widely accepted common knowledge.

        Others say that the custom developed out of practical concerns, but for cleanliness reasons not for warmth purposes. They argue that the rule of white applies only to shoes, and that out of attempts to keep
(15) them clean grew the rule of wearing white only in the warm months.

        Still others say that the rule grew out of a class struggle that took place in the late 1800s. With the rise of manufacturing in America, a new class of wealthy people grew up, one that conflicted with the old money class that had existed since the founding of the colonies in the
(20) 18th century. The *nouveau riche* class wanted desperately to be accepted by the old money folk, but the old money people did not want to accept them. Therefore, the old money folk used knowledge that they had created for use among themselves, unwritten customs and accepted ways of doing things unknown to the *nouveau riche*, to keep the new
(25) money folk away.

        Whatever the reason, however, the rule remains in use today.

28. Which of the following words can be substituted for the word *solidifies* without changing the meaning of the sentence?

    (A) confirms
    (B) thickens
    (C) rebuilds
    (D) reconstitutes
    (E) goes against

29. This passage deals with all but which of the following topics?

    (A) social customs
    (B) historical data
    (C) human behavior
    (D) psychology
    (E) data analysis

30. Which of the following statements is supported by the information in the passage?

    (A) Customs became a weapon used by those with new money to force those with old money to let them become part of society.
    (B) Customs became a weapon used by those with old money to snub those with new money.
    (C) Customs regarding fashion quickly became out of date.
    (D) Customs regarding when to wear white changed to allow people to wear white year-round.
    (E) Customs always grow out of practical responses to issues of daily life.

31. Which of the following statements is not true according to the article?

    (A) The issue over when to wear white may have originated in the 1800s.
    (B) The *nouveau riche* had a hard time getting respect.
    (C) People should wear dark clothes in the winter.
    (D) Wearing white originally applied to shoes rather than clothes.
    (E) Concerns over keeping clean were never a concern when the rules for wearing white were developed.

32. All but which of the following inferences may be made about the author?

    (A) The author is willing to do research to find answers to interesting questions.
    (B) The author has studied some hisory.
    (C) The author is knowledgeable about fashion.
    (D) The author is female.
    (E) The author is from the South.

33. What will come next in this discussion?

    (A) nothing; the author has finished the article
    (B) a discussion of other instances in which the new money and old money clashed
    (C) an account of some famous Southern women who defied the "no-white-after-Labor-Day" rule
    (D) a complete list of instances in which one can break the "no-white-after-Labor-Day" rule
    (E) a handy mnemonic device to help us remember when to wear black

34. Based on your reading of the article, what does *nouveau riche* mean?

    (A) newly married
    (B) newly wealthy
    (C) newly graduated
    (D) newly born
    (E) newly bankrupted

35. This article sets out to _____.

    (A) set the record straight on old money in the South
    (B) supply interesting, but trivial, information
    (C) support new money people in the North
    (D) explain the cause of the Civil War
    (E) convince people to wear white after Labor Day

36. In which of the following publications would you most likely find this information?

    (A) the sports section of your local newspaper
    (B) the world news section of a weekly newsmagazine
    (C) the arts and leisure section of the Sunday paper
    (D) the science news section of a television news program
    (E) the comics page online

Most, if not all, Americans are familiar with the concept of *kamikaze*, special Japanese pilots who fought in World War II. These men were unique because they enlisted in the war effort knowing that they would
Line be fighting to the death. They trained to be suicide pilots, who
(5)   purposely drove their planes headlong into their targets, exploding themselves along with their planes and their targets.

Few of us, however, have heard of the *kaiten*. The *kaiten* were small vessels, carried on submarines; they weighed eight tons and were loaded with explosive warheads. They had limited range (traveling a distance
(10) ranging from 12 miles at top speed and 30 miles at low speed) and silent movement. But like the *kamikaze* planes, these *kaiten* were unrecoverable; if they reached their target, they exploded, captain and all, and if they didn't, they sank, carrying their captains with them.

Both of these military strategies depended heavily on the concept of
(15) honor. Honorable death, especially by suicide for the sake of the Emperor during battle, brought nobility to the soldier and his family. These fighters were idolized by their countrymen; they represented the highest ideals of the nation—that of total sacrifice on behalf of their ruler.

37. Based on the article, which of the following actions would be seen as honorable by Japanese warriors in World War II?

   (A) becoming a *kamikaze* pilot but pulling out of the final dive at the last minute
   (B) refusing to man the *kaiten* on which he had trained
   (C) defending Hiroshima as the atom bomb dropped
   (E) emigrating to Canada just after the war started
   (D) spying for the Americans

38. Which of the following words best describes the *kaiten?*

   (A) luxury liners
   (B) floating coffins
   (C) bamboo tubes
   (D) warrior flutes
   (E) underwater kayaks

39. What kind of ruler did Japan have during World War II, according to this article?

   (A) emperor
   (B) king
   (C) prince
   (D) president
   (E) chancellor

40. Which of the following gives an example of something that is *unrecoverable?*

   (A) a penny at the bottom of a wading pool
   (B) the moon when it is full
   (C) your shoe when it falls over a cliff
   (D) your book you left at your grandmother's house
   (E) a sand dune at high tide

STOP

IF YOU FINISH BEFORE TIME IS UP, YOU MAY CHECK YOUR WORK ON THIS SECTION ONLY. DO NOT TURN TO ANY OTHER SECTION IN THE TEST.

SECTION 4 VERBAL SKILLS

60 questions   *30 minutes*

Directions: The following 30 questions consist of one capitalized word followed by five choices. Select the choice that is closest in meaning to the word in capital letters.

Sample:
IRATE

(A) angry
(B) loyal
(C) calculating
(D) pleasant
(E) efficient

● Ⓑ Ⓒ Ⓓ Ⓔ

1. MALICE

(A) cunning
(B) forethought
(C) spite
(D) benevolence
(E) premeditation

2. WAN

(A) single
(B) lonely
(C) sanguine
(D) pale
(E) individual

3. BLATANT

(A) obvious
(B) fragrant
(C) odious
(D) airy
(E) subtle

4. DETER

(A) alternate
(B) beget
(C) curve
(D) discourage
(E) encourage

5. CONCUR

(A) agree
(B) refer
(C) breed
(D) race
(E) study

6. OATH

(A) vow
(B) fool
(C) grain
(D) vessel
(E) disagreement

7. CONTEMPORARY

(A) tardy
(B) rapid
(C) lengthy
(D) angry
(E) modern

8. CREDULOUS

(A) gullible
(B) nervous
(C) skittish
(D) outraged
(E) impossible

9. ARDOR

(A) passion
(B) disinterest
(C) closet
(D) difficulty
(E) list

10. APPARATUS

(A) magic
(B) alert
(C) awake
(D) device
(E) mistake

11. HOAX

(A) conflagration
(B) falsification
(C) imagination
(D) peregrination
(E) elation

12. OSTRACIZE

(A) blend
(B) fold
(C) exhaust
(D) enlarge
(E) exclude

13. PERUSE

(A) drive
(B) utilize
(C) know
(D) read
(E) understand

14. ELUCIDATE

(A) confuse
(B) speak
(C) escape
(D) make clear
(E) take care

15. MENDICANT

(A) pharmacist
(B) beggar
(C) epoxy
(D) bandage
(E) soporific

16. HAUGHTY

(A) arrogant
(B) uninterested
(C) humble
(D) attractive
(E) bored

17. SMITE

(A) strike
(B) defend
(C) burn
(D) sneer
(E) grin

18. DORMANT

(A) inactive
(B) exuberant
(C) collegial
(D) clean
(E) friendly

19. INCITE

(A) rouse
(B) cut
(C) bite
(D) burn
(E) illustrate

20. ZENITH

(A) appliance
(B) constellation
(C) negative
(D) summit
(E) nadir

SSAT Practice Test 1

21. JOVIAL

(A) happy
(B) plump
(C) lugubrious
(D) slow
(E) large

22. LEXICON

(A) route
(B) waterway
(C) river
(D) dictionary
(E) enclosure

23. CHAFF

(A) beverage
(B) companion
(C) irritation
(D) waste
(E) annoyance

24. RAZE

(A) fortify
(B) build
(C) elevate
(D) shave
(E) tear down

25. PERNICIOUS

(A) intelligent
(B) harmless
(C) false
(D) harmful
(E) entertaining

26. MINUTIAE

(A) trivia
(B) speed
(C) notes
(D) weaponry
(E) ammunition

27. PREHENSILE

(A) understanding
(B) grasping
(C) primitive
(D) antediluvian
(E) condescending

28. REPUGNANT

(A) offensive
(B) small
(C) hardy
(D) copied
(E) compact

29. TACITURN

(A) alien
(B) ubiquitous
(C) avian
(D) melodious
(E) silent

30. ABJURE

(A) announce
(B) rule
(C) judge
(D) renounce
(E) balance

Directions: The next 30 questions require you to find relationships between words. Select the answer choice that best completes the meaning of the sentence.

31. Nose is to face as finger is to _____.

(A) foot
(B) hand
(C) ear
(D) head
(E) ring

32. Bark is to tree as _____.

(A) grass is to seed
(B) peel is to banana
(C) body is to skin
(D) core is to apple
(E) coat is to pants

33. Flag is to country as _____.

(A) document is to nation
(B) cloth is to uniform
(C) comma is to pause
(D) state is to union
(E) president is to coin

34. Fork is to eat as _____.

(A) pencil is to paper
(B) pen is to write
(C) ink is to fill
(D) teacher is to instruct
(E) spoon is to soup

35. Epic is to haiku as _____.

(A) mural is to painting
(B) symphony is to song
(C) sketch is to still life
(D) novel is to book
(E) drop is to pond

36. Cap is to baseball as helmet is to _____.

(A) soccer
(B) tennis
(C) cycling
(D) golf
(E) head

37. Butterfly is to insect as _____.

(A) grasshopper is to cricket
(B) cardinal is to bird
(C) ant is to sparrow
(D) worm is to robin
(E) bee is to hummingbird

38. Idle is to employed as _____.

(A) graceful is to clumsy
(B) petite is to small
(C) elegant is to formal
(D) engine is to truck
(E) worker is to job

39. Noise is to irritate as _____.

(A) music is to calm
(B) cacophony is to appease
(C) singing is to singer
(D) speech is to text
(E) sound is to wave

40. Picture is to representation as _____.

(A) goat is to sheep
(B) mineral is to water
(C) painting is to sculpture
(D) apple is to orange
(E) perfume is to fragrance

41. Surgery is to hospital as _____.

    (A) illness is to infection
    (B) slippers is to ballet
    (C) lessons is to school
    (D) dormitory is to students
    (E) doctor is to office

42. Bush is to shrub as _____.

    (A) car is to automobile
    (B) tree is to flower
    (C) bud is to vase
    (D) fruit is to vegetable
    (E) stalk is to corn

43. Greet is to salute as _____.

    (A) hello is to goodbye
    (B) army is to navy
    (C) wag is to tail
    (D) suit is to tie
    (E) dress is to evening gown

44. Escape is to confinement as _____.

    (A) pursue is to safety
    (B) sing is to choir
    (C) eat is to buffet
    (D) educate is to school
    (E) run is to danger

45. Perspiration is to nervousness as _____.

    (A) heat is to weather
    (B) stress is to articulation
    (C) caffeine is to coffee
    (D) shivering is to cold
    (E) sweat is to water

46. Corporal is to sergeant as joey is to _____.

    (A) gosling
    (B) penguin
    (C) Josephine
    (D) emu
    (E) kangaroo

47. Funny is to hilarious as _____.

    (A) amusing is to joke
    (B) safe is to dangerous
    (C) hot is to sweltering
    (D) helpful is to courteous
    (E) terrifying is to scary

48. Library is to books as _____.

    (A) CD is to cassettes
    (B) ice is to freezer
    (C) computer is to circuits
    (D) can is to carton
    (E) tiger is to forest

49. Car is to key as television is to _____.

    (A) outlet
    (B) sound
    (C) remote control
    (D) cabinet
    (E) sound

50. Rain is to umbrella as draft is to _____.

    (A) wind
    (B) cold
    (C) thirst
    (D) door
    (E) military

51. Impressive is to inspiring as derogatory is to _____.

    (A) critical
    (B) praiseworthy
    (C) positive
    (D) elevating
    (E) dismal

52. Roof is to house as head is to _____.

    (A) thought
    (B) body
    (C) brain
    (D) foot
    (E) attic

53. Glorious is to exalted as _____.

    (A) esteemed is to serious
    (B) trivial is to unimportant
    (C) fatal is to mortal
    (D) insufferable is to kindly
    (E) tired is to vigilant

54. Meager is to abundant as _____.

    (A) slender is to skinny
    (B) rare is to medium
    (C) feeble is to rich
    (D) decrepit is to robust
    (E) weak is to slow

55. Period is to exclamation point as _____.

    (A) whale is to fish
    (B) turtle is to tortoise
    (C) elephant is to pachyderm
    (D) glance is to stare
    (E) comma is to quotation marks

56. Gem is to stone as _____.

    (A) opal is to jade
    (B) granite is to shale
    (C) pearl is to price
    (D) diamond is to mine
    (E) jewel is to rock

57. Destitute is to money as _____.

    (A) change is to coins
    (B) poor is to housing
    (C) confident is to doubt
    (D) nonplussed is to extravagance
    (E) putrid is to rot

58. Sign is to sing as _____.

    (A) hand is to heart
    (B) song is to mouth
    (C) applause is to shout
    (D) stop is to pots
    (E) rasp is to raps

59. Morose is to cheerful as _____.

    (A) clean is to hyperactive
    (B) happy is to ecstatic
    (C) hygienic is to contaminated
    (D) mud is to dirt
    (E) subtle is to torpid

60. Clue is to solution as _____.

    (A) period is to sentence
    (B) question is to resume
    (C) map is to vacation
    (D) signpost is to destination
    (E) obesity is to eating

STOP

IF YOU FINISH BEFORE TIME IS UP, YOU MAY CHECK YOUR WORK ON THIS SECTION ONLY. DO NOT TURN TO ANY OTHER SECTION IN THE TEST.

SECTION 5 QUANTITATIVE SKILLS

25 questions   *30 minutes*

Directions: At the end of each problem, you have a choice of five possible answers. Work out each problem and then choose the best possible answer.

Sample Question:
Simplify $-4(-2)^3$.

(A) -32
(B) 32
(C) 16
(D) -16
(E) -8

(A) ● (C) (D) (E)

USE THIS SPACE FOR FIGURING

1. In an auto manufacturing plant, the ratio of executives to assembly line workers is $1:15$. If there are 480 employees altogether, how many assembly line workers are there?

(A) 350
(B) 450
(C) 400
(D) 300
(E) 410

2. O and O' are the centers of their respective circles, with radii x and $2x$ respectively.

Choose the best answer.
(A) area $c >$ area a
(B) area $b >$ area d
(C) area $d >$ area c
(D) area $a +$ area $b =$ area d
(E) area $d = 2 \times$ area b

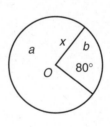

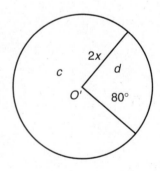

USE THIS SPACE FOR FIGURING

3. The quotient of 16 and *a* is greater than 4. What is a possible value of *a*?

(A) 2
(B) 4
(C) −2
(D) 8
(E) 5

---

4. Four cab drivers drive an average of 432 miles per day. Six other cab drivers drive an average of 486 miles per day. How many miles do all ten cabbies drive per day?

(A) 5,832
(B) 2,916
(C) 6,376
(D) 4,866
(E) 4,644

---

5. For all integers r and s, $r * s = r/s + s^2$. Find the value of $9 * 3$.

(A) 11
(B) 9
(C) 12
(D) 7
(E) 10

---

6. If the following sets of numbers represent three sides of a triangle, select the scalene triangle.

(A) 4, 4, 4
(B) 6, 7, 7
(C) 8, 11, 8
(D) 5, 6, 7
(E) 9, 9, 9

SSAT Practice Test 1

7. *ABCD* is a rectangle with length 12 and width 4. *RSTU* is a square, with *V* and *W* the midpoints of *RS* and *TU*, respectively. *RU* = 8.

Select the correct statement.

(A) The perimeter of *ABCD* is greater than the perimeter of *RSTU*.

(B) The perimeter of *RVWU* is greater than the perimeter of *ABCD*.

(C) One-half of the perimeter of *ABCD* is equal to the perimeter of *RVWU*.

(D) The perimeter of *RVWU* plus the perimeter of *VSTW* is greater than the perimeter of *ABCD*.

(E) The perimeter of *VSTW* is less than one-half the perimeter of *ABCD*.

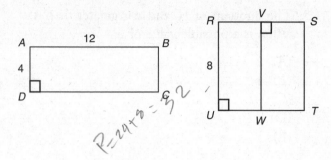

8. If $\dfrac{x}{5} = y + 2$, find the value of x when $y = 7$.

(A) 15
(B) 20
(C) 30
(D) 25
(E) 45

9. If *a* and *b* are integers and $a > 0$ and $b < 0$, select the statement that is true for all cases of *a* and *b*.

(A) $ab > 0$
(B) $ab \leq 0$
(C) $a^2 > b^2$
(D) $a^3 < b^3$
(E) $2a \leq b$

USE THIS SPACE FOR FIGURING

10. If the hypotenuse of a right triangle is 13 and one of its legs is 5, find the area of the triangle.

(A) 20
(B) 40
(C) 45
(D) 30
(E) 25

11. If the circumference of a circle is 31.4, find its radius. Use the formula $C = 2\pi r$ and let $\pi = 3.14$.

(A) 6
(B) 5
(C) 7
(D) 4
(E) 8

12. Malcolm and Dwayne start off running around the track at the same time. If Malcolm can run around the track in 5 minutes and Dwayne can cover the same distance in 3 minutes, when will they again meet at the start of the track?

(A) 12 minutes
(B) 16 minutes
(C) 15 minutes
(D) 18 minutes
(E) 13 minutes

13. Find the value of the expression $4xy + 5z^2$ when $x = 4$, $y = -3$, and $z = -2$.

(A) −28
(B) 32
(C) −16
(D) 22
(E) 30

USE THIS SPACE FOR FIGURING

14. The sum of the square of a number and 3 is equal to the product of 4 and 7. What is the number.

    (A) 3
    (B) 6
    (C) 5
    (D) 4
    (E) 7

15. If r, s, and t are positive consecutive odd integers, which of the following statements is true?

    (A) $r + t < 2s$
    (B) $r^2 > st$
    (C) $r + t > 2s$
    (D) $r^2 > 2s$
    (E) $rs > t^2$

16. If $x = 4/5$, $y = 2/3$, and $z = \sqrt{3}$, find the value of $10x - 9y - 4z^2$.

    (A) −6
    (B) −10
    (C) −8
    (D) 4
    (E) 2

17. Metal screws weigh 3 kilograms per cubic meter. The screws are packaged in a cube whose edge is 1.5 meter. Find the weight of the cube. Round the answer to the nearest tenth of a kilogram.

    (A) 9.6 kilograms
    (B) 10.125 kilograms
    (C) 10.1 kilograms
    (D) 9.65 kilograms
    (E) 12.5 kilograms

USE THIS SPACE FOR FIGURING

18. Examine the graph and then select the best answer.

    (A) $d > a + b + c$
    (B) $d = a + b + c$
    (C) $d = a + b$
    (D) $c - a < b + c$
    (E) $a + c < b + d$

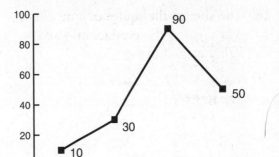

19. The areas of a rectangle and a square are equal. If one side of the square is twice the width of the rectangle and the length of the rectangle is 16, find the width of the rectangle.

    (A) 4
    (B) 10
    (C) 6
    (D) 8
    (E) 9

20. If a is a negative integer and b is a positive integer, which of the following statements is true?

    (A) $a^2 < 0$
    (B) $b^2 < 0$
    (C) $a^2 + b^2 > 0$
    (D) $ab^2 > 0$
    (E) $ab > b^2$

21. If $2^6 = 4^x$, find x.

    (A) 6
    (B) 5
    (C) 2
    (D) 4
    (E) 3

$64 = 4^x$

$2^6 = 4^x$
$2^6 = 2^{2(x)}$
$2^6 = 2^{2x}$

$2x = 6$

$x = \dfrac{6}{2} = 3$

USE THIS SPACE FOR FIGURING

22. Find the total area of the figure.

    (A) $4\sqrt{6}+4$

    (B) $3\sqrt{2}+4$

    (C) $5\sqrt{3}+12$

→ (D) $16+6\sqrt{2}$

    (E) $4\sqrt{3}+2\sqrt{2}$

$h=3\sqrt{2}$

4

4

23. Find the value of $\dfrac{3^9}{4\times3^7}$.

    (A) 3

    (B) $3\dfrac{1}{2}$

    (C) $2\dfrac{1}{4}$

    (D) $2\dfrac{3}{4}$

    (E) $3\dfrac{3}{4}$

24. Of the following expressions, which is the smallest?

    (A) $5 \times 3 - (2 + 7)$

    (B) $5(3) - 48/6$

    (C) $14 - 5 + 30/6$

    (D) $18/2 - 3(4 - 6) + 54/9$

    (E) $5(6 + 3) - 3^2$

USE THIS SPACE FOR FIGURING

25. Dwayne was on a diet. When he weighed himself at the start of his diet, Dwayne weighed 215 pounds. At the end of three months, Dwayne weighed 175 pounds. What fraction of his original weight did he lose? Reduce to lowest terms.

(A) 8/43
(B) 9/36
(C) 7/29
(D) 9/35
(E) 4/11

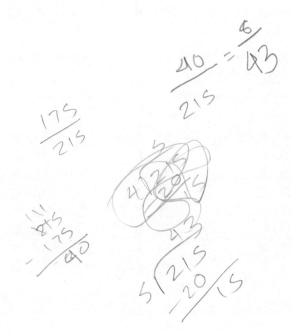

IF YOU FINISH BEFORE TIME IS UP, YOU MAY CHECK YOUR WORK ON THIS SECTION ONLY. DO NOT TURN TO ANY OTHER SECTION IN THE TEST.

SSAT Practice Test 1
ANSWER KEY

Section 2 Quantitative Skills

1. D	6. A	11. B	16. D	21. C
2. B	7. D	12. E	17. A	22. D
3. D	8. E	13. E	18. D	23. E
4. A	9. B	14. B	19. E	24. D
5. D	10. C	15. A	20. B	25. C

Section 3 Reading Comprehension Skills

1. C	9. D	17. E	25. A	33. A
2. D	10. C	18. C	26. D	34. B
3. E	11. C	19. E	27. C	35. B
4. B	12. E	20. E	28. A	36. C
5. D	13. C	21. E	29. E	37. C
6. A	14. A	22. C	30. B	38. B
7. D	15. B	23. E	31. E	39. A
8. E	16. A	24. C	32. D	40. C

Section 4 Verbal Skills

1. C	13. D	25. D	37. B	49. C
2. D	14. D	26. A	38. A	50. D
3. A	15. B	27. B	39. A	51. A
4. D	16. A	28. A	40. E	52. B
5. A	17. A	29. E	41. C	53. B
6. A	18. A	30. D	42. A	54. D
7. E	19. A	31. B	43. E	55. D
8. A	20. D	32. B	44. E	56. E
9. A	21. A	33. C	45. D	57. C
10. D	22. D	34. B	46. E	58. E
11. B	23. D	35. B	47. C	59. C
12. E	24. E	36. C	48. C	60. D

SSAT Practice Test 1
ANSWER KEY

Section 5 Quantitative Skills

1. **B**	6. **D**	11. **B**	16. **B**	21. **E**
2. **A**	7. **D**	12. **C**	17. **C**	22. **D**
3. **A**	8. **E**	13. **A**	18. **D**	23. **C**
4. **E**	9. **B**	14. **C**	19. **A**	24. **A**
5. **C**	10. **D**	15. **D**	20. **C**	25. **A**

ANSWER EXPLANATIONS

Section 1 Writing Sample Checklist

PROMPT A

☐ **Check your handwriting.** Is your text legible? Get used to forming your words clearly. Frustrated readers cannot score you highly if they cannot read your essay.

☐ **Proofread.** Correct the most glaring errors, especially run-ons, comma splices, and fragments. Make sure you capitalize when necessary and punctuate logically. Check your spelling, especially of easily confused words (to/too, their/there, your/you're, etc.). Notice how you use transition words.

☐ **Have someone else read this essay.** Choose a good writer and reader to comment on your work.

☐ **Read the question and writing prompt again.** Did you answer the question? You won't have time to rewrite the essay during the actual exam, so read the question carefully the first time and keep it in mind. Underline keywords in the questions to help you remember.

☐ **Read your introduction.** Did you include all of the information necessary for a reader to understand your essay? Does it include a thesis statement?

☐ **Underline your thesis statement in the introduction.** Does it address the question and give your opinion on it?

☐ **Underline the thesis statement in the conclusion.** Does it agree with your original thesis?

☐ **Underline the topic sentences of your body paragraphs.** Now read all of the underlined sentences in your practice essay. Do these sentences focus on the same topic? Do they fit together? Do they flow?

☐ **TExAn.** For each body paragraph, check to make sure you have a <u>*specific*</u> <u>Ex</u>ample to illustrate your <u>Topic sentence</u>. Again, make sure it is specific, rather than another general statement. Then make sure you <u>An</u>alyze or explain *how* this example proves your point.

    This is an important step, so get used to including this information **as you write** your paragraphs.

Practice writing more essays, and you will improve each time. During the actual exam, you will only have time to proofread and check your examples, so most items on this list will have to become second nature to you.

PROMPT B

☐ **Check your handwriting.** Is your text legible? Get used to forming your words clearly. Frustrated readers cannot score you highly if they cannot read your essay.

☐ **Proofread.** Correct the most glaring errors, especially run-ons, comma splices, and fragments. Make sure you capitalize when necessary and punctuate logically. Check your spelling, especially of easily confused words (to/too, their/there, your/you're, etc.). Notice how you use transition words.

☐ **Have someone else read this essay.** Choose a good writer and reader to comment on your work.

☐ **Did you give the reader enough exposition?** It's fine to jump right into the story (in fact, it's often a good idea), but in a story of such a short length, you need to establish the characters, setting, and situation quickly. **Show** the reader instead of **telling** the reader.

   – Setting
   – Character
   – Situation

☐ **What does the protagonist [main character] want or need to do?**

☐ **What obstacles are in his or her way?**

☐ **Did you start a new paragraph when a new speaker has dialogue?**

This helps the reader identify who is speaking. Remember, instead of writing she said each time, try substituting an action. *She shrugged.*

☐ **Does your story reach a high point in the conflict?**

This is called the climax. Everything should lead us here.

☐ **Does your resolution go on too long? Too short?**

The resolution should end the story quickly (especially in a story this short). However, make sure you allow enough time for your reader to feel satisfied. You can have a twist ending, of course, but that should come *after* the feeling of closure.

Practice writing more essays, and you will improve each time. During the actual exam, you will only have time to proofread and check your examples, so most items on this list will have to become second nature to you.

Section 2 Quantitative Skills

1.

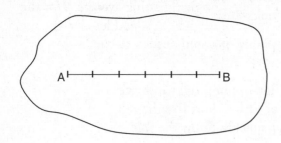

ANALYSIS

To determine the number of miles between cities A and B, count the number of symbols and multiply by 12. Then divide the number of miles by 60 miles per hour, the speed of the car.

WORK

$$6 \times 12 = 72 \text{ miles}$$

$$\frac{72 \text{ miles}}{60 \text{ miles per hour}} = 1\frac{12}{60} = 1 \text{ hour, 12 minutes}$$

ANSWER: (D)

2.

Cars Sold by Car Dealership

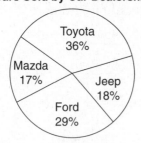

ANALYSIS

Since 17% of all cars were Mazdas, multiply 17% (.17) by 1,800.

WORK

$$0.17 \times 1,800 = 306$$

ANSWER: (B)

3.

ANALYSIS

First find the area of the wall by multiplying length by height. Then, in order to find the number of quarts required, divide the area (the number of square feet) by 40.

WORK

$$\text{area} = \text{length} \times \text{height} =$$
$$24 \times 10 = 240 \text{ square feet}$$
Number of quarts required =
$$\frac{\text{area}}{40 \text{ sq ft per quart}} = \frac{240}{40} = 6 \text{ quarts}$$

ANSWER: (D)

4.

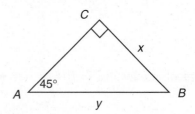

ANALYSIS

The measure of angle C is 90° and the measure of angle A is 45°. The angles of a triangle add up to 180°.

WORK

$$m\angle A + m\angle B + m\angle C = 180°$$
$$45° + m\angle B + 90° = 180°$$
$$135° + m\angle B = 180°$$
Subtract 135°: $\quad m\angle B = 45°$

If $m\angle A = m\angle B = 45°$, the triangle is isosceles and the measures of sides AC and BC are equal, so $AC = BC = x$.

ANSWER: (A)

5.

ANALYSIS

Divide 900 by each of the choices and see which answer results in an answer without a remainder.

WORK

$$15\overline{)900} \quad \begin{array}{r} 60 \\ \underline{900} \end{array}$$

ANSWER: (D)

6.

ANALYSIS

Add up the total paid by adults and children and set that amount equal to $705.

WORK

Each child paid $2.50 less than an adult admission: $9.50 − $3.50 = $6.00. Let x = the number of children.

$$54 \cdot \$9.50 + x \cdot \$6.00 = \$705$$
$$\$513 + 6x = \$705$$

Subtract $459: \qquad\qquad $6x = \$192$

Divide by 6: \qquad\qquad\qquad $x = 32$

ANSWER: (A)

7.

ANALYSIS

$$|-3| = 3$$

WORK

$$6|-3|-4|5|$$
$$6(3) - 4(5)$$
$$18 - 20$$
$$-2$$

ANSWER: (D)

8.

ANALYSIS

Let BA_O = original batting average, H = the number of original hits, and let G = the total number of original times at bat.

$$BA_O = \frac{H}{G}$$

WORK

Original batting average

$$BA_O = 0.300: \qquad\qquad 0.300 = \frac{H}{G}$$
$$H = 0.3G$$

New batting average

$$BA_N = 0.400: \qquad 0.400 = \frac{H+10}{G+10}$$
$$0.4(G + 10) = H + 10$$
$$H = 0.3G: \qquad 0.4G + 4 = 0.3G + 10$$
$$0.1G = 6$$
$$G = 60$$
$$H = 0.3G = 0.3(60) = 18$$

ANSWER: (E)

9.

ANALYSIS

Split the inequality into two parts.

WORK

$$5 > 3x \qquad\qquad 3x \geq -2$$
$$\frac{5}{3} > x \qquad\qquad x \geq \frac{-2}{3}$$
$$1\frac{2}{3} > x$$

x is located in between $1\frac{2}{3}$ and $-\frac{2}{3}$.

One is the only number satisfying these conditions.

ANSWER: (B)

10.

Residents in 2005	
Carson City	👥 👥
Middletown	👥 👤
Newcastle	👥 👥 👤
Jamestown	👥 👥 👥 👥 👥
Henderson	👥 👥 👥 👥

👥 = 4,000 people

ANALYSIS

Each symbol represents 4,000 people.

WORK

$$\frac{\text{Middletown residents in 2005}}{\text{Henderson residents in 2005}} =$$
$$\frac{1.5 \times 4{,}000 = 6{,}000}{4 \times 4{,}000 = 16{,}000} = \frac{6{,}000}{16{,}000} = \frac{3}{8}$$

ANSWER: (C)

11.
ANALYSIS

Substitute 2/3 into the equation.

WORK

$$x = 2/3: \quad \begin{aligned} y &= 4x^3 \\ &= 4(2/3)^3 \\ &= 4(2/3)(2/3)(2/3) \\ &= 4(8/27) \\ &= (32)/27 \\ &= 1\ 5/27 \end{aligned}$$

ANSWER: (B)

12.
ANALYSIS

Simplify (a), (b), (c), (d), and (e) and then substitute the results into (A), (B), (C), (D), and (E) in order to see which statement is true.

WORK

$$(d) = (e)$$
$$4r(s + t) = 4rt + 4rs$$
$$4rs + 4rt = 4rs + 4rt \checkmark$$

ANSWER: (E)

13.

Pounds, p_i	Frequency, f_i	$p_i f_i$
98	2	
105	1	
109	1	
120	3	
126	2	
132	4	

ANALYSIS

Multiply the pounds, p_i, by the frequencies, f_i, total all the $p_i f_i$s and then divide by the total frequencies.

WORK

pounds, p_i	Frequency, f_i	$p_i f_i$
98	2	$2 \times 98 = 196$
105	1	$1 \times 105 = 105$
109	1	$1 \times 109 = 109$
120	3	$3 \times 120 = 360$
126	2	$2 \times 126 = 252$
132	4	$4 \times 132 = 528$
Totals	13	1,550

$$\frac{p_i f_i}{f_i} = \frac{1{,}550}{13} = 119.23 \approx 119.2$$

ANSWER: (E)

14.

A   B   C

ANALYSIS

Count the number of white and dark boxes in each figure and then substitute into each of the given statements.

WORK

The dark area in A is greater than the dark area in C.

$$7 > 6 \checkmark$$

ANSWER: (B)

15.
ANALYSIS

Use the formula $A = \left(\dfrac{1}{2}\right)bh$, where A = the area, b = the base, and h = the height of the triangle.

WORK

$$A = \left(\dfrac{1}{2}\right)bh$$

$b = 2x + y,$

$h = 4z$ $\qquad = \dfrac{1}{\cancel{2}}(2x + y)(\cancel{4}^{2}z) = 2z(2x + y)$

ANSWER: (A)

16.
ANALYSIS

Out of nine marbles, find the possibility of drawing a yellow or a blue marble and then add the two numbers.

WORK

$$
\begin{aligned}
&\text{possibility of a yellow marble} = 3/9 \\
+\ &\underline{\text{possibility of a blue marble} = 4/9} \\
&\hphantom{\text{possibility of a blue marble} = }7/9
\end{aligned}
$$

ANSWER: (D)

17.
ANALYSIS

The formula for the area of a circle is $A = \pi r^2$, where A = area and r = radius. Because we don't need an exact answer and we're just comparing areas, let's just use π in the problems.

WORK

Area of circle with radius 2

$A = \pi r^2$
$\quad = \pi(2)^2$
$\quad = 4\pi$

Area of circle with radius 4

$A = \pi r^2$
$\quad = \pi(4)^2$
$\quad = 16\pi$

$$\frac{\text{area of circle with radius 2}}{\text{area of circle with radius 4}} = \frac{4\pi}{16\pi} = \frac{1}{4}$$

ANSWER: (A)

18.
ANALYSIS

Let the base = x and let each of the equal legs = $x + 3$. Add up all the sides and set the sum equal to the perimeter, 30. Then find each of the legs.

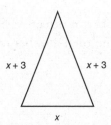

$$
\begin{aligned}
x + (x + 3) + (x + 3) &= 30 \\
3x + 6 &= 30
\end{aligned}
$$

Subtract 6: $\qquad\qquad 3x = 24$
Divide by 3: $\qquad\qquad\quad x = 8 \text{ (the base)}$
$\qquad\qquad\qquad\qquad x + 3 = 11 \text{ (each leg)}$

ANSWER: (D)

19.

ANALYSIS

Using the given information, draw a diagram of a square and label it. Then add up all the sides.

WORK

$A = s^2$, where A = area, s = side

$A = 4a^2$: $\quad 4a^2 = s^2$

Take the
square root: $\quad 2a = s$

$s = 2a$

Perimeter $= 4(2a) = 8a$

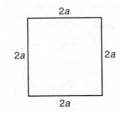

ANSWER: (E)

20.

ANALYSIS

Add up all the hours and divide by 3, the number of students.

WORK

$$\overline{x} = \frac{(t+4)+(t)+(t-2)}{3} = \frac{3t+2}{3}$$

ANSWER: (B)

21–22.

Major Network Television Shows					
	2002	2003	2004	2005	Summary
Reality	2	3	12	14	31
Comedy	7	9	8	7	31
Law	3	6	7	5	21
Detective	8	9	6	12	35
Cartoons	10	12	14	16	52
News	20	24	21	15	80
Summary	50	63	68	69	250

21.

ANALYSIS

Locate the number of detective stories in 2002 and divide by the total number of shows in 2002, 50.

WORK

$$\frac{\text{number of detective shows in 2002}}{\text{total number of television shows in 2002}} =$$

$$\frac{8}{50} = 16\%$$

ANSWER: (C)

22.

ANALYSIS

Determine the total number of cartoons in 2004 and 2005 and then divide by the total number of shows in the years 2002 through and including 2005.

WORK

	Cartoons
2004	14
2005	16
Total:	30

Total number of television shows in the years 2002 through and including 2005: 250

$$\frac{30}{250} = 0.12 = 12\%$$

ANSWER: (D)

23.

ANALYSIS

The best way to solve this problem is to substitute integers for *a* and *b* into the inequalities. Since *a* is negative, let *a* = −2, and since *b* is positive, let *b* = 5.

WORK

$$(E)\ ba \geq ab$$
$$5(-2) \geq (-2)(5)$$
$$-10 \geq -10$$

ANSWER: (E)

24.

x	1	2	3	4	5
y	1	3	5	7	9

ANALYSIS

A linear equation is represented by the general formula $y = mx + b$. Let's arbitrarily select several values for *x* and *y* and plug them into the general formula.

WORK

$$y = mx + b$$

$x = 1, y = 1$: (equation i) $1 = m(1) + b$

$x = 2, y = 3$: (equation ii) $3 = m(2) + b$

Subtract equation ii from equation i:

(equation i)	$1 = m + b$
(equation ii)	$-(3 = 2m + b)$
	$-2 = -1m$
	$2 = m$
	$m = 2$

Substitute 2 for *m* in equation i:

(equation i)	$1 = m + b$
$m = 2$:	$1 = 2 + b$
	$-1 = b$
	$b = -1$

Substitute 2 for *m* and −1 for *b* in the general equation.

$$y = mx + b$$
$$y = 2x - 1$$

ANSWER: (D)

25.

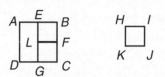

ANALYSIS

Since *E*, *F*, *G*, and *L* are midpoints of sides *AB*, *BC*, *CD*, and *EG* respectively, and *ABCD* is a square, *EBFL* and *LFCG* are also squares. If *EB* is the same length as *HI*, *EBLF*, *LFCG*, and *HIJK* are squares with equal areas.

WORK

area *ABCD* = area *AEGD* + 2 × area *HIJK*

ANSWER: (C)

Section 3 Reading Comprehension Skills

1. **(C)** The last paragraph says that we don't need our wisdom teeth anymore. The article also says that for gingivitis we use mouthwash (A); for crooked teeth we use braces (B); for yellow teeth we use teeth whiteners (E). How we get our information about dental care doesn't matter.

2. **(D)** The article states that braces fix crooked, not yellow, teeth (A) and that mouthwashes fix bad breath, not cavity fillings (C). Therefore, choices A and C are wrong. The article states,

too, that braces are an increasingly common part of growing up; choice D is, therefore, wrong. Given what we know about Egyptian dental care, we can infer that we know more than, not the same as, they did; rule out choice B. The only correct inference we can make is that we don't expect to lose our teeth because modern dental care keeps them working well for our entire lifespans.

3. **(E)** We might assume that the first dentists probably first pulled teeth, but the article does not make this clear.

4. **(B)** The author does not set out to answer questions about teeth, although s/he might cover information about which the reader might have wondered; rule out A. Talking about tooth-related dreams might have been a good idea because they do frequently occur, but this author does not do so. Rule out C. The article is not factual or thorough enough to be part of a medical text. Rule out D. Nor does the author go to great lengths trying to convince the reader to cut down on sweets (choice E). The article does tell a bit about the history of dentistry; choose B.

5. **(D)** Dentists can indeed perform root canals, but the article does not discuss this fact.

6. **(A)** Choice B does not make sense; neither does choice D, since the author is trying to make the argument that reading a dictionary can be fun (not boring) as well as useful (not trivial). Choices C and E are too limited; dictionaries contain well more than a thousand words, and the text discusses more than just the meaning of the word "dervish." The best answer is A because reading the dictionary, according to this author, can result in many "unexpected" but pleasant "discoveries."

7. **(D)** The passage is not angry or sullen; therefore, omit choices B and E. The

passage is, hopefully, a little bit amusing, so you might be tempted by A, C, or D. However, two of these choices just don't fit. How might you convey a "tired" feeling? Not using any of the words in this article; in fact, the author seems to be trying to be lighthearted and energetic to get your attention. So rule out C. Is the author seriously trying to get you to read a dictionary? Yes (see paragraphs five and nine), so you can omit choice A; the author is not trying to be trivial. The best answer, therefore, is D; the author is trying to be amusing (to get your attention) but serious (to get you to better yourself).

8. **(E)** Paragraph two states that the author thinks we have personal responsibility for our situation.

9. **(D)** Choices B and E don't make sense; usually when a person takes the time to write, s/he tries to be clear and succinct, and these choices would simply waste the reader's time. Choice C also doesn't work; the author might want the reader to look up the word, but there's no reason why s/he should want that when s/he is trying to make a more important point. Choices A and D are opposites. Because the author wants the reader to take the message seriously, choice D makes more sense. Fearing that the reader might think the author is joking, the author reinforces his/her serious intent.

10. **(C)** Substitute the various options for the phrase *lumped in*; you'll find that only choice C makes sense.

11. **(C)** The author makes a claim, in the last section of the piece, that s/he does not explain fully; therefore, the author should take the time to explain that claim. Because *something* should come next in the piece, choice E is wrong. Discussions of Van Gogh (A), other art by Brueghel (B), or Dedalus' crime (C) should only come into the

discussion if doing so is helpful to making the author's claim clear.

12. **(E)** The author clearly sets out to discuss something important to him/her; choice A is incorrect. Talking about Brueghel's talents (B and D) and the tale of Dedalus and Icarus (C) are secondary to the author's purpose. This author intends to make a comment about the way the world works through his/her discussion of "the largeness of the world and the relative insignificance of the individual therein," a message that comes to the public, not through writing or speech, but through art.

13. **(C)** Substitute the various vocabulary options for "exhilarated," and you will see that only "joyous" makes a good match.

14. **(A)** The author wants the reader to pay attention, so s/he strives for a neutral, educated tone. The lack of words that connote understanding (B), sarcasm (C), joy (D), or stupidity (E) supports this claim.

15. **(B)** Fell (A), dropped (C), sank (D), and plunged (E) all mean plummet. Hung (B) means to be suspended in air; therefore, it is the odd man out.

16. **(A)** Wildly (B), enthusiastically (C), vigorously (D), and angrily (E) all connote some form of frantic action. The only option that does not do so is "feebly" (A). Feebly means to move without energy or vigor.

17. **(E)** According to paragraph two, Icarus' wings melted because he flew too close to the sun, and the sun's heat melted the wax that held them together.

18. **(C)** The author refers to Vlad Tepes in paragraph one as if using a first and last name—"Vlad <u>Tepes</u> (or Vlad the Impaler)"—therefore, the reader can infer that *Tepes* means impaler.

19. **(E)** The anecdote about Vlad Tepes impaling a guest on a long post implies that choice A cannot be correct. The

other descriptors—his military ability (B), his wealth (C), his popularity with women (D)—may be true, but they are not addressed in the passage. However, because Vlad Tepes metes out punishment to the guest for something Vlad Tepes considers offensive, we can conclude that his sense of justice is very unconventional (E).

20. **(E)** The article does not discuss werewolves (A), witches (B), or zombies (D). The article does mention Vlad Tepes, but it does not dwell on his entire family (C). Indeed, the article goes on to discuss vampires and vampire stories across the years; therefore, E is the best answer.

21. **(E)** The passage does not say exactly what dates Rice writes, but it does say that she is a modern writer. Of the dates listed here, 1990 is the most modern of the bunch.

22. **(C)** The key word in this sentence is "clinical," a term which means technical or without passion. Therefore, we may infer that something clinical is not very exciting. Options A, D, and E all refer to vampire stories as being "popular"— not a good match with "clinical"; besides, the time period in option E is all wrong. Option B goes too far; if vampire lore died out, we would not be enjoying it today. Option C says vampire stories from this period were boring; this is the best answer.

23. **(E)** Paragraph two states that the myth of Sisyphus comes from Greek mythology.

24. **(C)** See paragraph two for details.

25. **(A)** Choice C wants to trick you into thinking *tenets* has something to do with tents; choice D wants to make you think of nets. Both are incorrect. Substituting "numbers" for "tenets" also makes no sense; rule out option E. Rule (B) is a close competitor, but tenets has more to do with beliefs, not rules.

26. **(D)** The third paragraph tells us that the myth of Sisyphus illustrates the beliefs of Existentialism, but it does not give us any details. We need to know more about the author's theory, or we cannot judge the correctness of the argument. (Rule out option C.) The author seems to be saving this part of the discussion for paragraph four. We don't need any more information about Camus at this point; skip choice A. We already know enough about Sisyphus, so omit option B. And, unless the author happens to be from the University of Kentucky, we don't need option E either.

27. **(C)** Paragraph three tells you that *hubris* means conceited, so find the word in this list that is an antonym for conceited. The answer is C; if one is pious, one does not have hubris.

28. **(A)** Substituting the words for *solidifies* in the passage, you find that "confirms" (A) is the best answer.

29. **(E)** The article mentions social rules of fashion (A) and in doing so mentions historical fact (B). It discusses human behavior—especially in being catty with each other (C) and reveals much about human psychology, even if it makes no direct reference to it (D). But at no point does the author discuss numbers or data crunching.

30. **(B)** The article claims that old money and new money clashed over having to hang out together. Old money began using unwritten rules (like those having to do with fashion) to ensure that they didn't have to deal with new money. The other statements just don't agree with the information contained in the essay.

31. **(E)** All of the statements, except that contained in option E, appear in the essay.

32. **(D)** The author has clearly done research for this article by finding the answer to a popular question (A), and in doing that history s/he has had to bone up on history (B). The author is knowledgeable about fashion (C), and s/he says early on that s/he is from the South (E). But at no point do we get a clear read on whether the author is male or female; after all, males and females care equally for fashion—either they like it, are neutral toward it, or don't care. Nothing about an interest in fashion demands that you be female.

33. **(A)** The article has covered what it set out to cover, and it has come to an end. The clash of new and old money is not the main topic of this article, and we don't need more information about it (B). It might be interesting to hear about Southern women who wore white after Labor Day, but we don't need it (C). And the article is not set up to give specific fashion advice; therefore, omit D and E.

34. **(B)** The phrase comes in opposition to the phrase "old money." We can infer, therefore, that *nouveau riche* has an opposing meaning.

35. **(B)** The article sets out to discuss a fashion rule, something by definition frivolous. It does not take sides on old money (A) or new money (C), nor does it discuss the Civil War (D). And it does more to reinforce the rule rather than try to get people to break it (E).

36. **(C)** As we said in question 35, this is a trivial issue about fashion. We do not discuss fashion in the sports section (A) or in the world news section (B). The discussion does not address science in any way (D) or intentionally try to be humorous (E). However, fashion is frequently discussed in a newspaper's leisure section.

37. **(C)** To be considered honorable by WWII Japanese society, a soldier had to do something noble, chivalrous, and self-sacrificing. Avoiding one's duty, as is

described in choices A, B, D, and E does not constitute honorable action. But fighting in Hiroshima despite certain death does constitute honorable action by World War II Japanese standards.

38. **(B)** The *kaiten* were watercraft and held no escape route; therefore, the best correlation would be floating coffins.

39. **(A)** Paragraph three states that Japan during World War II was ruled by an emperor.

40. **(C)** For something to be unrecoverable, it must have been possessed at one time and then permanently lost. Examples A, B, and E involve items that do not belong to anyone and therefore cannot be owned then lost. Example D involves something owned but easily recovered. The only example that involves something owned then permanently lost is example C.

Section 4 Verbal Skills

1. **(C)** Something done with malice is done with ill-will. It may be done with intent (B and E), but those choices do not mention *harmful* intent.

2. **(D)** A very famous poem begins, "Why so pale and wan, fond lover?"

3. **(A)** Something blatant is conspicuous. *Obvious* is the best choice.

4. **(D)** *Deter* means to discourage in order to keep something from happening.

5. **(A)** To **concur** means to act together, or more precisely, to agree.

6. **(A)** An oath is a declaration of truth or a promise.

7. **(E)** Contemporary has a couple of meanings, but it literally breaks down to "with the time." However, it does not mean tardy, rapid, or lengthy. Something modern is up to date.

8. **(A)** The root *cred* means believe, and one who is credulous believes something too easily. This is also the meaning of

gullible, someone who is easily gulled, or fooled.

9. **(A)** Ardor means heat—in this case, emotional heat or passion.

10. **(D)** An apparatus is a device, an appliance, a tool, or an implement to do a particular job.

11. **(B)** A hoax is a deception. Think of the magician's term *hocus-pocus.*

12. **(E)** Ostracize means to exclude from a group. The ostrich was ostracized because of its size.

13. **(D)** Peruse means to read closely. Choices C and E (know and understand) are so close in meaning that you can eliminate them. They can't both be correct.

14. **(D)** The root *luc* means light, so to elucidate is to make something clear.

15. **(B)** This is a word you see on several tests, so you might as well make a note card if you don't know it. A mendicant is a beggar. The other choices are tricks.

16. **(A)** *Haughty* shares a root with *high*, so if you feel higher than everyone else, you are arrogant.

17. **(A)** To smite is to strike something. Past tenses are *smote* and *smitten.*

18. **(A)** The root of dormant is *dormire*, to sleep. (People sleep in a dormitory.) Something dormant is inactive.

19. **(A)** To incite is to stir up or move someone to action. *Rouse* (to awaken) is the only synonym listed.

20. **(D)** A zenith is a high point, as is a summit. (A nadir, by the way, is the lowest point.)

21. **(A)** The Roman god Jove (or Jupiter) was said to be the source of joy. A jovial person is jolly.

22. **(D)** The root *lexis* means word, so a lexicon is a dictionary. Because graph means to write or draw, what do you suppose a lexicographer does?

23. **(D)** When you separate the wheat from the chaff, you winnow away the husks from the edible part of the grain. These inedible husks are called chaff.

By extension, anything worthless is called chaff.

24. **(E)** Raze means to tear down completely, as in "The old building was razed." It shares the same root (*radere*, to scrape) as the word *razor*. Think of a bulldozer scraping the debris of an old house off the ground like a shaver. (That's a lot of shaving cream.)

25. **(D)** Pernicious means extremely harmful or destructive. Hence, we get the following sports cheer: "Pernicious, pernicious, stop being malicious; but if you persist, we will also get vicious. We'll get all seditious—revenge is delicious." (Okay, we were never cheerleaders. Now you know why.)

26. **(A)** This contains the word *minute*, or small. Minutiae are small, unimportant details. *Trivia* is the best match.

27. **(B)** If you remember that the roots of the word *comprehend* mean to grasp together, you know that **prehen**sile means able to grasp.

28. **(A)** Something repugnant is distasteful or offensive to you.

29. **(E)** The word *tacit* means silent. Sometimes in a piece of music you'll see the direction "tacit," which means to stop playing. A taciturn person does not like to talk. (If you are given tacit approval to do something, that means no one told you **not** to do it!)

30. **(D)** This one is difficult, as the choices all *sound* reasonable. You'll just have to learn the word. To abjure something means to give it up, or renounce it.

31. **(B)** Your nose is part of your face; your finger is part of your hand.

32. **(B)** Bark covers a tree. A peel covers a banana.

33. **(C)** A flag represents or stands for a country. A comma represents a pause.

34. **(B)** A fork is used to eat; a pen is used to write. You could argue that a teacher is used to instruct or ink is used to fill. Making the sentence more specific can

clear this up: A fork is a **utensil** used to eat; a pen is a **utensil** used to write.

35. **(B)** An epic is a **large**-scale work (of poetry), whereas a haiku is a **small** work (of poetry). A symphony is a large-scale work (of music), whereas a song is a small work (of music).

36. **(C)** You wear a cap when playing baseball. The only sport listed where you wear a helmet is cycling.

37. **(B)** A butterfly is a specific kind of insect. A cardinal is a specific kind of bird.

38. **(A)** If you are idle, you are **not** employed. If you are graceful, you are **not** clumsy.

39. **(A)** A noise irritates. The only other pair that fits this relationship is *Music can calm.*

40. **(E)** A picture is a representation; a perfume is a fragrance.

41. **(C)** Surgery **takes place** in a hospital. Yes, slippers are in a ballet, doctors are in an office, and a dorm contains students. These do not represent the same relationship as Lessons **take place** in a school.

42. **(A)** Bush and shrub are synonyms, as are car and automobile.

43. **(E)** A more formal greeting is a salute. A more formal dress is an evening gown.

44. **(E)** You escape from confinement; you run from danger.

45. **(D)** Nervousness can cause perspiration. Cold can cause shivering.

46. **(E)** A corporal becomes or progresses to a sergeant. A joey becomes a kangaroo.

47. **(C)** Something extremely funny is hilarious. Choice A makes sense (Something really amusing is a joke), but it's not the same relationship of degree. E is a tempting choice, but the order is backward. (It should read: Something extremely scary is terrifying.) Something extremely hot is sweltering.

48. **(C)** A library contains books; a computer contains circuits.

49. **(C)** A car is started by a key. A television is started by a remote control. Outlet

is not quite right, as you are not looking for the power source, but to the instrument that turns it on.

50. **(D)** An umbrella keeps out rain. A door keeps out a draft.

51. **(A)** Something impressive is inspiring, while something derogatory is critical.

52. **(B)** A roof is the top of a house. A head is the top of the body. You wouldn't choose brain (top of the attic) or foot (top of the foundation).

53. **(B)** Something glorious is exalted; something trivial is unimportant.

54. **(D)** Meager is the opposite of abundant. Decrepit is the opposite of robust. Look these words up if you don't know them. Write them down and make cards if you need to do so.

55. **(D)** An exclamation point is more intense than a period. A stare is more intense than a glance.

56. **(E)** A gem is a jewel; a stone is a rock.

57. **(C)** Someone who is destitute is without money. Someone who is confident is without doubt. (Someone who is poor is not necessarily without housing.)

58. **(E)** This is one of those odd analogies that has nothing to do with the meanings of the words. In each pair, the last two letters are transposed: sign/sing, rasp/raps.

59. **(C)** Morose is the opposite of cheerful. Hygienic is the opposite of contaminated. Look up the words in this question if you don't know them.

60. **(D)** A clue leads to a solution, as a signpost leads to destination. (Choice E is backwards: obesity does not lead to eating.)

Section 5 Quantitative Skills

1.

ANALYSIS

Let x = the number of executives and $15x$ = the number of assembly line workers. The total number of employees is 480, so let $15x + x =$ 480.

WORK

$$15x + x = 480$$
$$16x = 480$$
$$x = 30$$
$$15x = 15(30) = 450$$

ANSWER: (B)

2.

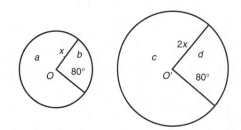

ANALYSIS

First determine the areas of O and O'. Then find the areas of sectors a, b, c, and d and substitute into the given equalities or into the inequalities.

WORK

Area Circle $O = \pi r^2 = \pi x^2$

Area sector $a = \dfrac{280°}{360°} \cdot \pi x^2 = \dfrac{7}{9}\pi x^2$

Area sector $b = \dfrac{80°}{360°} \cdot \pi x^2 = \dfrac{2}{9}\pi x^2$

Area Circle $O' = \pi r^2 = \pi(2x)^2 = \pi 4x^2$

Area sector $c = \dfrac{280°}{360°} \cdot \pi 4x^2 = \dfrac{7}{9}\pi 4x^2 = 3\dfrac{1}{9}\pi x^2$

Area sector $d = \dfrac{80°}{360°} \cdot \pi 4x^2 = \dfrac{2}{9} \cdot \pi 4x^2 = \dfrac{8}{9}\pi x^2$

(A) Area c > Area a

$3\dfrac{1}{9}\pi x^2 > \dfrac{7}{9}\pi x^2$ ✔

ANSWER: (A)

3.

ANALYSIS

Substitute the possible values into the given inequality.

WORK

$$\frac{16}{a} > 4$$

$a = 2:$ $\frac{16}{2} > 4$

$$8 > 4 \checkmark$$

ANSWER: (A)

4.

ANALYSIS

Multiply 432 by 4 and 486 by 6 and add the results.

WORK

$$4 \times 432 = 1,728$$
$$+6 \times 486 = 2,916$$
$$\overline{\hspace{2em}4,644}$$

ANSWER: (E)

5.

ANALYSIS

Substitute 8 and 3 for r and s.

WORK

$$r * s = r/s + s^2$$
$r = 9, s = 3:$ $9 * 3 = 9/3 + 3^2$
$$= 3 + 9$$
$$= 12$$

ANSWER: (C)

6.

ANALYSIS

In a scalene triangle, all the sides are of different lengths.

WORK

5, 6, 7

ANSWER: (D)

7.

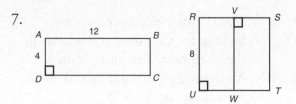

ANALYSIS

Find the perimeters of *ABCD*, *RSTU*, *RVWU*, and *VSTW*. Since *RSTU* is a square and *RU* = 8, all the sides are equal to 8. The midpoints, *V* and *W*, divide *RS* and *TU* in half, respectively.

WORK

Perimeter of $ABCD = 2 \times 4 + 2 \times 12$
$$P(ABCD) = 8 + 24$$
$$P(ABCD) = 32$$
$$P(RSTU) = 32$$
$$P(RVWU) = 24$$
$$P(VSTW) = 24$$

The perimeter of *RVWU* plus the perimeter of *VSTW* is greater than the perimeter of *ABCD*.

$$P(RVWU) + P(VSTW) > P(ABCD)$$
$$24 + 24 > 32$$
$$48 > 32 \checkmark$$

ANSWER: (D)

8.

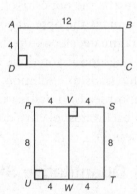

ANALYSIS

Substitute 7 for *y* in the given equation.

WORK

$$\frac{x}{5} = y + 2$$

$y = 7$:
$$\frac{x}{5} = 7 + 2$$

$$\frac{x}{5} = 9$$

Multiply by 5: $x = 45$

ANSWER: (E)

9.
ANALYSIS

Since it is given that $a > 0$ and $b < 0$, let's substitute some specific numbers for a and b. For example, let $a = 2$, $b = -3$.

WORK

$$ab \le 0$$
$$(2)(-3) \le 0$$
$$-6 \le 0 \checkmark$$

ANSWER: (B)

10.
ANALYSIS

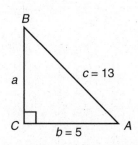

WORK

$b = 5$:
$$a^2 + b^2 = c^2$$
$$a^2 + 5^2 = 13^2$$
$$a^2 + 25 = 169$$

Subtract 25: $a^2 = 144$
Take the square root: $a = 12$

Now use the area formula.

$b = 5$, $h = 12$:
$$A = (1/2)b \cdot h$$
$$A = (1/2)(5)(12)$$
$$A = 30$$

ANSWER: (D)

11.
ANALYSIS

Use the formula $C = 2\pi r$ and substitute 31.4 for C and 3.14 for π.

WORK

$$C = 2\pi r$$
$$31.4 = 2(3.14)r$$
$$31.4 = 6.28r$$
Divide by 6.28: $5 = r$

ANSWER: (B)

12.
ANALYSIS

They'll meet again at the start of the track whenever 3 and 5 share a common multiple.

WORK

$3 \times 1 = 3$	$5 \times 1 = 5$
$3 \times 2 = 6$	$5 \times 2 = 10$
$3 \times 3 = 9$	$5 \times 3 = \underline{15}$
$3 \times 4 = 12$	$5 \times 4 = 20$
$3 \times 5 = \underline{15}$	$5 \times 5 = 25$

ANSWER: (C)

13.
ANALYSIS

Substitute the values for x, y, and z into the given expression.

WORK

$x = 4$, $y = -3$, $z = -2$:
$$4xy + 5z^2$$
$$4(4)(-3) + 5(-2)^2$$
$$16(-3) + 5(-2)(-2)$$
$$-48 + 5(4)$$
$$-48 + 20$$
$$-28$$

ANSWER: (A)

14.
ANALYSIS

Let x = the number.

WORK

$$x^2 + 3 = 4 \times 7$$
$$x^2 + 3 = 28$$

Subtract 3: $\qquad\qquad x^2 = 25$

Take the square root: $\qquad x = \pm\, 5$

ANSWER: (C)

15.

ANALYSIS

Assign r, s, and t values as consecutive odd integers. For example, let $r = 5$, $s = 7$, and $t = 9$.

WORK

$$r^2 > 2s$$
$$(5)^2 > 2(7)$$
$$25 > 14 \; \checkmark$$

ANSWER: (D)

16.

ANALYSIS

Substitute the values for the variables into the given expression.

WORK

$$10x - 9y - 4z^2$$

$x = 4/5$, $y = 2/3$,
$z = \sqrt{3}$

$$10(4/5) - 9(2/3) - 4\left(\sqrt{3}\right)^2$$
$$\quad 8 \;\; - \;\; 6 \;\; -4(3)$$
$$\qquad 2 \qquad -12$$
$$\qquad\quad -10$$

ANSWER: (B)

17.

ANALYSIS

First determine the volume of the cube. Then multiply 3 kilograms per cubic meter by the number of cubic meters.

WORK

$$V = e^3$$

$e = 1.5$: $\qquad V = (1.5)^3 = 3.375$ cubic meters

Weight $= 3.375 \times 3 = 10.125 \approx 10.1$

ANSWER: (C)

18.

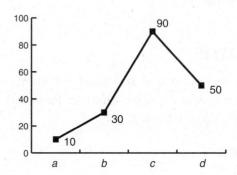

ANALYSIS

Determine the values of a, b, c, and d and then substitute into (A), (B), (C), and (D).

WORK

$$a = 10$$
$$b = 30$$
$$c = 90$$
$$d = 50$$
$$c - a < b + c$$
$$90 - 10 < 30 + 90 \; \checkmark$$
$$80 < 120$$

ANSWER: (D)

19.

ANALYSIS

Let A_S = area of the square and let A_R = area of the rectangle. Let x = the width of the rectangle and $2x$ = one side of the square. Since all sides of a square are equal, all of the sides are equal to $2x$.

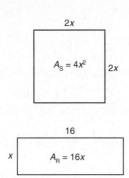

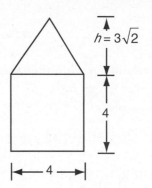

WORK

$$A_S = A_R$$

The areas are equal: $4x^2 = 16x$

Divide by 4: $x^2 = 4x$

Divide by x: $x = 4$ (width of the rectangle)

ANSWER: (A)

20.
ANALYSIS

Let's substitute -2 for a and 3 for b.

WORK

$$a^2 + b^2 > 0$$
$$(-2)^2 + (3)^2 > 0$$
$$4 + 9 > 0 \checkmark$$

ANSWER: (C)

21.
ANALYSIS

Change 4 to a power of 2. Then set the exponents equal.

WORK

$4 = 2^2$:
$$2^6 = 4^x$$
$$2^6 = (2^2)^x$$
$$2^6 = 2^{2x}$$
$$6 = 2x$$

Divide by 2: $x = 3$

ANSWER: (E)

ANALYSIS

Separately, find the areas of the two figures and add them.

WORK

Area of the square: $A = s^2$, where $A = $ area and $s = $ side.

$14s = 4$:
$$A = 4^2$$
$$A = 16$$

Area of triangle: $A = \dfrac{1}{2}bh$, where $A = $ area, $b = $ base, and $h = $ height.

$b = 4$, $h = 3\sqrt{2}$:
$$A = \dfrac{1}{2}(\overset{2}{\cancel{4}})(3\sqrt{2})$$
$$A = 6\sqrt{2}$$
Total area $= 16 + 6\sqrt{2}$

ANSWER: (D)

23.
ANALYSIS

Divide 3^9 by 3^7 and then simplify.

WORK

$$\frac{\overset{3^2}{\cancel{3^9}}}{4 \times \underset{1}{\cancel{3^7}}} = \frac{9}{4} = 2\frac{1}{4}$$

ANSWER: (C)

24.

ANALYSIS

Simplify expressions within the parentheses and then work from left to right.

WORK

(A) $5 \times 3 - (2 + 7) = 15 - (9) = 6$
(B) $5(3) - 48/6 = 15 - 8 = 7$
(C) $14 - 5 + 30/6 = 9 + 5 = 14$
(D) $18/2 - 3(4 - 6) + 54/9 = 9 - 3(-2) + 6 = 9 + 6 + 6 = 21$
(E) $5(6 + 3) - 3^2 = 5(9) - 9 = 45 - 9 = 36$

ANSWER: (A)

25.

ANALYSIS

Determine how much weight Dwayne lost and then let the result be the numerator of a fraction with the original weight the denominator.

WORK

Weight Lost: 215 pounds − 175 pounds = 40 pounds

Weight Lost: $\dfrac{40}{215} = \dfrac{\cancel{5} \times 8}{\cancel{5} \times 43} = \dfrac{8}{43}$
Original Weight:

ANSWER: (A)

SSAT Practice Test 2
ANSWER SHEET

Section 2 Quantitative Skills

1 ⒶⒷⒸⒹⒺ	6 ⒶⒷⒸⒹⒺ	11 ⒶⒷⒸⒹⒺ	16 ⒶⒷⒸⒹⒺ	21 ⒶⒷⒸⒹⒺ
2 ⒶⒷⒸⒹⒺ	7 ⒶⒷⒸⒹⒺ	12 ⒶⒷⒸⒹⒺ	17 ⒶⒷⒸⒹⒺ	22 ⒶⒷⒸⒹⒺ
3 ⒶⒷⒸⒹⒺ	8 ⒶⒷⒸⒹⒺ	13 ⒶⒷⒸⒹⒺ	18 ⒶⒷⒸⒹⒺ	23 ⒶⒷⒸⒹⒺ
4 ⒶⒷⒸⒹⒺ	9 ⒶⒷⒸⒹⒺ	14 ⒶⒷⒸⒹⒺ	19 ⒶⒷⒸⒹⒺ	24 ⒶⒷⒸⒹⒺ
5 ⒶⒷⒸⒹⒺ	10 ⒶⒷⒸⒹⒺ	15 ⒶⒷⒸⒹⒺ	20 ⒶⒷⒸⒹⒺ	25 ⒶⒷⒸⒹⒺ

Section 3 Reading Comprehension Skills

1 ⒶⒷⒸⒹⒺ	9 ⒶⒷⒸⒹⒺ	17 ⒶⒷⒸⒹⒺ	25 ⒶⒷⒸⒹⒺ	33 ⒶⒷⒸⒹⒺ
2 ⒶⒷⒸⒹⒺ	10 ⒶⒷⒸⒹⒺ	18 ⒶⒷⒸⒹⒺ	26 ⒶⒷⒸⒹⒺ	34 ⒶⒷⒸⒹⒺ
3 ⒶⒷⒸⒹⒺ	11 ⒶⒷⒸⒹⒺ	19 ⒶⒷⒸⒹⒺ	27 ⒶⒷⒸⒹⒺ	35 ⒶⒷⒸⒹⒺ
4 ⒶⒷⒸⒹⒺ	12 ⒶⒷⒸⒹⒺ	20 ⒶⒷⒸⒹⒺ	28 ⒶⒷⒸⒹⒺ	36 ⒶⒷⒸⒹⒺ
5 ⒶⒷⒸⒹⒺ	13 ⒶⒷⒸⒹⒺ	21 ⒶⒷⒸⒹⒺ	29 ⒶⒷⒸⒹⒺ	37 ⒶⒷⒸⒹⒺ
6 ⒶⒷⒸⒹⒺ	14 ⒶⒷⒸⒹⒺ	22 ⒶⒷⒸⒹⒺ	30 ⒶⒷⒸⒹⒺ	38 ⒶⒷⒸⒹⒺ
7 ⒶⒷⒸⒹⒺ	15 ⒶⒷⒸⒹⒺ	23 ⒶⒷⒸⒹⒺ	31 ⒶⒷⒸⒹⒺ	39 ⒶⒷⒸⒹⒺ
8 ⒶⒷⒸⒹⒺ	16 ⒶⒷⒸⒹⒺ	24 ⒶⒷⒸⒹⒺ	32 ⒶⒷⒸⒹⒺ	40 ⒶⒷⒸⒹⒺ

Section 4 Verbal Skills

1 ⒶⒷⒸⒹⒺ	13 ⒶⒷⒸⒹⒺ	25 ⒶⒷⒸⒹⒺ	37 ⒶⒷⒸⒹⒺ	49 ⒶⒷⒸⒹⒺ
2 ⒶⒷⒸⒹⒺ	14 ⒶⒷⒸⒹⒺ	26 ⒶⒷⒸⒹⒺ	38 ⒶⒷⒸⒹⒺ	50 ⒶⒷⒸⒹⒺ
3 ⒶⒷⒸⒹⒺ	15 ⒶⒷⒸⒹⒺ	27 ⒶⒷⒸⒹⒺ	39 ⒶⒷⒸⒹⒺ	51 ⒶⒷⒸⒹⒺ
4 ⒶⒷⒸⒹⒺ	16 ⒶⒷⒸⒹⒺ	28 ⒶⒷⒸⒹⒺ	40 ⒶⒷⒸⒹⒺ	52 ⒶⒷⒸⒹⒺ
5 ⒶⒷⒸⒹⒺ	17 ⒶⒷⒸⒹⒺ	29 ⒶⒷⒸⒹⒺ	41 ⒶⒷⒸⒹⒺ	53 ⒶⒷⒸⒹⒺ
6 ⒶⒷⒸⒹⒺ	18 ⒶⒷⒸⒹⒺ	30 ⒶⒷⒸⒹⒺ	42 ⒶⒷⒸⒹⒺ	54 ⒶⒷⒸⒹⒺ
7 ⒶⒷⒸⒹⒺ	19 ⒶⒷⒸⒹⒺ	31 ⒶⒷⒸⒹⒺ	43 ⒶⒷⒸⒹⒺ	55 ⒶⒷⒸⒹⒺ
8 ⒶⒷⒸⒹⒺ	20 ⒶⒷⒸⒹⒺ	32 ⒶⒷⒸⒹⒺ	44 ⒶⒷⒸⒹⒺ	56 ⒶⒷⒸⒹⒺ
9 ⒶⒷⒸⒹⒺ	21 ⒶⒷⒸⒹⒺ	33 ⒶⒷⒸⒹⒺ	45 ⒶⒷⒸⒹⒺ	57 ⒶⒷⒸⒹⒺ
10 ⒶⒷⒸⒹⒺ	22 ⒶⒷⒸⒹⒺ	34 ⒶⒷⒸⒹⒺ	46 ⒶⒷⒸⒹⒺ	58 ⒶⒷⒸⒹⒺ
11 ⒶⒷⒸⒹⒺ	23 ⒶⒷⒸⒹⒺ	35 ⒶⒷⒸⒹⒺ	47 ⒶⒷⒸⒹⒺ	59 ⒶⒷⒸⒹⒺ
12 ⒶⒷⒸⒹⒺ	24 ⒶⒷⒸⒹⒺ	36 ⒶⒷⒸⒹⒺ	48 ⒶⒷⒸⒹⒺ	60 ⒶⒷⒸⒹⒺ

SSAT Practice Test 2
ANSWER SHEET

Section 5 Quantitative Skills

1 Ⓐ Ⓑ Ⓒ Ⓓ Ⓔ	6 Ⓐ Ⓑ Ⓒ Ⓓ Ⓔ	11 Ⓐ Ⓑ Ⓒ Ⓓ Ⓔ	16 Ⓐ Ⓑ Ⓒ Ⓓ Ⓔ	21 Ⓐ Ⓑ Ⓒ Ⓓ Ⓔ
2 Ⓐ Ⓑ Ⓒ Ⓓ Ⓔ	7 Ⓐ Ⓑ Ⓒ Ⓓ Ⓔ	12 Ⓐ Ⓑ Ⓒ Ⓓ Ⓔ	17 Ⓐ Ⓑ Ⓒ Ⓓ Ⓔ	22 Ⓐ Ⓑ Ⓒ Ⓓ Ⓔ
3 Ⓐ Ⓑ Ⓒ Ⓓ Ⓔ	8 Ⓐ Ⓑ Ⓒ Ⓓ Ⓔ	13 Ⓐ Ⓑ Ⓒ Ⓓ Ⓔ	18 Ⓐ Ⓑ Ⓒ Ⓓ Ⓔ	23 Ⓐ Ⓑ Ⓒ Ⓓ Ⓔ
4 Ⓐ Ⓑ Ⓒ Ⓓ Ⓔ	9 Ⓐ Ⓑ Ⓒ Ⓓ Ⓔ	14 Ⓐ Ⓑ Ⓒ Ⓓ Ⓔ	19 Ⓐ Ⓑ Ⓒ Ⓓ Ⓔ	24 Ⓐ Ⓑ Ⓒ Ⓓ Ⓔ
5 Ⓐ Ⓑ Ⓒ Ⓓ Ⓔ	10 Ⓐ Ⓑ Ⓒ Ⓓ Ⓔ	15 Ⓐ Ⓑ Ⓒ Ⓓ Ⓔ	20 Ⓐ Ⓑ Ⓒ Ⓓ Ⓔ	25 Ⓐ Ⓑ Ⓒ Ⓓ Ⓔ

SECTION 1 WRITING SAMPLE

1 question   *25 minutes*

Directions: Read the two prompts below and choose the one that interests you more. Circle it.

A What career interests you most? Why?

B "Ten - Nine - Eight . . ." Nothing could stop this now. "Seven - Six - Five . . ."

Use the space provided to complete your writing sample.

STOP

IF YOU FINISH BEFORE TIME IS UP, YOU MAY CHECK YOUR WORK ON THIS SECTION ONLY. DO NOT TURN TO ANY OTHER SECTION IN THE TEST.

SECTION 2 QUANTITATIVE SKILLS

25 questions *30 minutes*

Directions: This section is a multiple-choice test. Work out the problems and, from the five choices given, select the best answer.

Sample Question:
Of the following expressions, which is the largest?

(A) $4 \times 3 - (5 + 3)$
(B) $27/3 + 2(9 - 4)$
(C) $29 - 4 + 64/8$
(D) $8(7) - 54/3$
(E) $54/9 + 3(8 - 4)$

Ⓐ Ⓑ Ⓒ ● Ⓔ

USE THIS SPACE FOR FIGURING

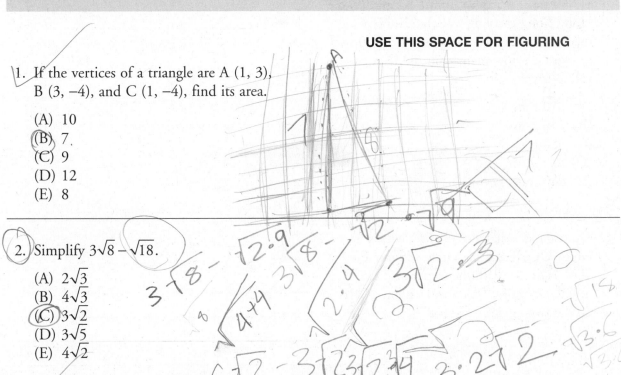

1. If the vertices of a triangle are A (1, 3), B (3, −4), and C (1, −4), find its area.

   (A) 10
   (B) 7
   (C) 9
   (D) 12
   (E) 8

2. Simplify $3\sqrt{8} - \sqrt{18}$.

   (A) $2\sqrt{3}$
   (B) $4\sqrt{3}$
   (C) $3\sqrt{2}$
   (D) $3\sqrt{5}$
   (E) $4\sqrt{2}$

3. Describe the following line graph.

   (A) $-4 > x > 1$
   (B) $-4 < x < 1$
   (C) $-4 \leq x \leq 1$
   (D) $-4 < x \leq 1$
   (E) $1 < x \leq -4$

SSAT Practice Test 2

USE THIS SPACE FOR FIGURING

4. Mitch drives for 30 minutes at 50 miles per hour. He then drives for an additional 45 minutes at 60 miles per hour. How many miles did he drive altogether?

(A) 60 miles
(B) 80 miles
(C) 50 miles
(D) 65 miles
(E) 70 miles

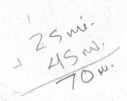

5. An ocean-going cargo ship has a capacity of 800 tons. If it sails from Los Angeles to Hong Kong carrying five-eighths of its capacity and returns carrying three-fifths of its capacity, how many tons did it carry round-trip?

(A) 650 tons
(B) 760 tons
(C) 980 tons
(D) 870 tons
(E) 840 tons

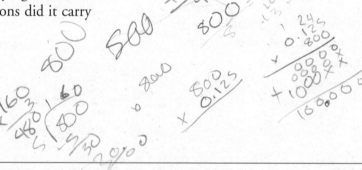

6. A circle has a diameter of 10″, with a radius OC. If another circle with a radius of 6″ is drawn with the center at the middle of radius OC, at how many points do the two circles intersect?

(A) 3
(B) 4
(C) 2
(D) 0
(E) 1

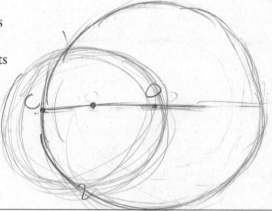

7. Excluding 1, what is the difference between the sum of the prime factors of 35 and 30?

(A) 5
(B) 4
(C) 2
(D) 3
(E) 5

USE THIS SPACE FOR FIGURING

8. If *a*, *b*, and *c* are consecutive odd integers in the given order and *c* = 11, what is the product of *a* and *b*?

(A) 55
(B) 45
(C) 72
(D) 87
(E) 63

9. Simplify $\dfrac{a\sqrt{42}}{b\sqrt{7}}$.

(A) $\dfrac{a}{b}\sqrt{6}$

(B) $a\sqrt{6}$

(C) $ab\sqrt{7}$

(D) $\dfrac{b}{a}\sqrt{7}$

(E) $ab\sqrt{6}$

10. Julissa drives from Central City to Marbury, a distance of 154 miles. If she leaves Central City at 8 A.M. and arrives in Marbury at 10:45 A.M., what is her average rate of speed?

(A) 58 mph
(B) 62 mph
(C) 54 mph
(D) 56 mph
(E) 59 mph

11. If *x* and *y* are negative integers and *y* > *x*, which of the following statements is true?

(A) $xy < 0$
(B) $x + y > 0$
(C) $xy > 0$
(D) $y - x < 0$
(E) $\dfrac{y}{x} < 0$

12. Find the value of the expression $3rs - 2t$ when $r = 2$, $s = 3$, and $t = 4$.

   (A) 12
   (B) 10
   (C) 14
   (D) 8
   (E) 18

13. O is the center of the circle. Which of the following statements is true?

   (A) $AB > CD$
   (B) $CO < OB$
   (C) $AB - OB = DO$
   (D) $CD - OB < OD$
   (E) $CD > OA + OC$

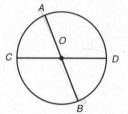

14. $\overrightarrow{SR}$ is perpendicular to $\overrightarrow{ST}$. $m\angle TSU = 22°$. Find x.

   (A) 54°
   (B) 66°
   (C) 22°
   (D) 68°
   (E) 48°

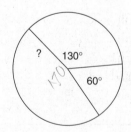

15. If two central angles of a triangle are 60° and 130°, find the average of all three central angles.

   (A) 60°
   (B) 120°
   (C) 65°
   (D) 95°
   (E) 85°

16. Mary Lou is pumping oxygen into an emergency room at the rate of 3 cubic meters per minute. If the room is 9 meters long by 6 meters wide by 4 meters high, how long will it take for the room to be filled with oxygen?

(A) 64 minutes
(B) 72 minutes
(C) 86 minutes
(D) 44 minutes
(E) 58 minutes

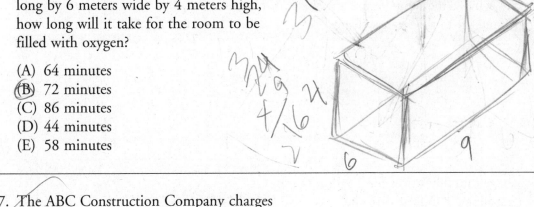

17. The ABC Construction Company charges $2.58 a square foot to cement a driveway. At this rate, what is the cost of cementing a driveway 11 feet by 34 feet? Round off your answer to the nearest dollar.

(A) $965
(B) $966
(C) $961
(D) $964
(E) $963

18. What happens to the area of a triangle when its base is doubled and its height is tripled?

(A) it is doubled
(B) it is tripled
(C) it is quadrupled
(D) it is increased fivefold
(E) it is increased sixfold

19. If the following sets of numbers represent the three sides of various triangles, select the scalene triangle.

(A) 4, 4, 4
(B) 6, 7, 7
(C) 8, 11, 8
(D) 5, 6, 7
(E) 6, 9, 6

USE THIS SPACE FOR FIGURING

20. The temperature is 90°F at 3 P.M. If it decreases by 40 percent by midnight and then increases by 26 percent by 10 A.M. the next day, what is the temperature at 10 A.M.? Round off to the nearest degree.

(A) 68°F
(B) 54°F
(C) 66°F
(D) 42°F
(E) 58°F

21–22. The average monthly prices for a gallon of regular gasoline are indicated in the chart.

21. Find the average price of a gallon of gasoline for the months of April and August.

(A) $3.10
(B) $3.40
(C) $3.70
(D) $4.10
(E) $3.50

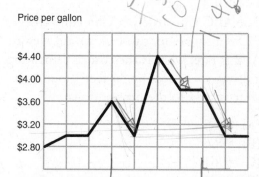

Price per gallon

22. How much was the steepest drop in the average price per gallon of gasoline between two consecutive months?

(A) $.40
(B) $.60
(C) $.30
(D) $.80
(E) $.50

23. The measure of the vertex angle of an isosceles triangle is 50°. Find the measure of an exterior angle to one of the base angles of the triangle.

(A) 65°
(B) 125°
(C) 115°
(D) 80°
(E) 75°

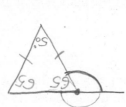
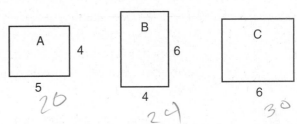

24. Examine the figures and choose the best answer.

(A) Area A is greater than area C.
(B) Area A is greater than area B.
(C) Area B is greater than area C.
(D) Area C is less than area A.
(E) Area B is less than area C.

25. The Missoula Manatees scored 12, 7, 10, 6, and 9 runs in their last five games. If they want to maintain an average of 9 runs per game for six games, how much do they have to score on their next game?

(A) 6
(B) 8
(C) 10
(D) 4
(E) 12

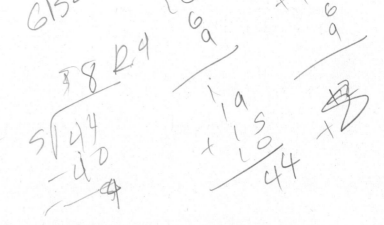

STOP

IF YOU FINISH BEFORE TIME IS UP, YOU MAY CHECK YOUR WORK ON THIS SECTION ONLY. DO NOT TURN TO ANY OTHER SECTION IN THE TEST.

SSAT Practice Test 2

SECTION 3 READING COMPREHENSION SKILLS

40 questions   *40 minutes*

> **Directions:** Read each passage carefully and then answer the questions about it. For each question, decide on the basis of the passage which one of the choices best answers the question.

UFO enthusiasts often attempt to prove the existence of aliens. They show fuzzy photos of floating white cigars and point to oddities in the way the world works as proof that "we are not alone." They also point
Line to the mysterious Anasazi culture. The Anasazi, historians say, were an
(5) ancient Native American tribe located near the desert area we now call Area 51 that suddenly began experiencing a huge cultural revolution. Some people attribute such miraculous cultural growth to a decision to farm beans, but others prefer to give credit to assistance to friendly aliens.

(10)   Now, alien fans can add some weight to their argument that aliens exist—from the writings of Washington Irving. Irving (1783–1859) wrote the first fiction works in the colonial America. Among other things, Irving wrote about the history of New York and mythological stories; he also wrote satires, a powerful tool given the fledgling nation's
(15) political turmoil. However, he is best known for his stories, like "The Legend of Sleepy Hollow" and "Tales of a Traveler."

Of Irving's *ouvre*, it is Irving's "Rip Van Winkle" to which UFO fans should direct their attention, for the argument has been made that Van Winkle's twenty-year sleep is actually a case of alien abduction. As odd
(20) as this sounds, the case deserves some investigation.

1. What is the function of paragraph two?

   (A) to hook the reader's attention so that s/he will continue reading
   (B) to move the discussion from the introduction to the highlight of the article
   (C) to give a detailed argument that "Rip Van Winkle" describes a UFO abduction
   (D) to tell biographical information about Washington Irving
   (E) to tell the story of "The Legend of Sleepy Hollow"

2. Which of the following events happened around the time of Irving's lifetime?

   (A) the Civil War
   (B) the Vietnam War
   (C) World War I
   (D) the American Revolution
   (E) World War II

3. Which of the following inferences can be made about the Anasazi?

   (A) The beans probably gave them additional energy and cultural stability.
   (B) They lived near New England.
   (C) They all disappeared mysteriously.
   (D) They sacrificed children to the aliens.
   (E) They migrated freely until the 1980s.

4. According to the article, for which of his writings was Irving famous?

   (A) "Tale of a Tub"
   (B) "Old Mother Hubbard"
   (C) "The Headless Horseman"
   (D) "Rip Van Winkle"
   (E) "The Life of Washington"

5. Which of the following best describes the author's tone?

   (A) rude but informative
   (B) knowledgeable but playful
   (C) Conceited but angry
   (D) Skeptical but pious
   (E) Sarcastic but rigorous

6. The author's main purpose in writing this piece is _____.

   (A) to embarrass Washington Irving's successors
   (B) to get the reader interested in reading mythology
   (C) to bring to light a little-known theory about Irving's work
   (D) to argue that aliens do not exist
   (E) to refute the argument that George Washington believed in alien life.

In the 1980s, theaters presented a new animated film called *Anastasia*. It told the story of a young, poverty-stricken Russian girl who comes to find out that she is the long-lost Princess Anastasia, daughter of Czar
Line Nicholas II. By the end of the movie, she ascends her throne as a
(5) benevolent ruler. But fans of that movie must face an unpleasant truth: Either the writers got it all wrong, or they intentionally ignored history. On July 17, 1918, Anastasia, along with the rest of her family, was murdered before she reached the age of 18; there were no survivors. And although the film correctly targets Rasputin as a disreputable
(10) villain, it nevertheless caricatures his character and his ambitions.

It's time to set the record straight.

Rasputin, born Grigory Yefimovisc Novykh, was born in Siberia in 1872. He came from poverty-stricken, illiterate people, and he soon earned for himself a bad reputation for his wild lifestyle; indeed, his
(15) nickname "Rasputin" means debauched. For a time, Rasputin studied at a monastery, but he came to believe that the only means of salvation came through indulging one's appetites. He then became a wandering, self-proclaimed holy man, and he traveled extensively, even into Greece and Jerusalem. Upon his return to Russia, Rasputin traveled to St.
(20) Petersburg. There he met Czar Nicholas II and his family. Unbelievably, despite his salacious lifestyle and his distaste for bathing, Rasputin ingratiated himself with the Czarina. For whatever reason, Rasputin proved repeatedly that he could comfort the crown prince Alexis, who was afflicted with hemophilia.

(25) Naturally, his close relationship with the ruling family threw a sour taste into the mouths of the Russian nobility. They eventually plotted against Rasputin with the goal of engineering his death. On December 29, 1916, a nobleman invited Rasputin to his home for drinks and conversation. There, he poisoned Rasputin's drink and waited for him
(30) to die. Rasputin proved stronger than anticipated, and so the noble and his friends tried to shoot him instead. Again, Rasputin clung to life. Finally, the nobles had to drag him down to the river and drown him.

Rasputin had his drawbacks. He was selfish. He was corrupt. He was politically ambitious. However, he does not deserve to be represented as
(35) he is in *Anastasia*.

7. The author's intent in writing this passage is _____.

    (A) to further confound the information people have about Anastasia and her family
    (B) to desecrate Rasputin's reputation
    (C) to praise the film *Anastasia* for its historical accuracy
    (D) to restore a little dignity to a powerful historical figure
    (E) to talk about Czar Nicholas II and his family

8. When were Anastasia and her family murdered?

    (A) 1872
    (B) 1890
    (C) 1916
    (D) 1918
    (E) 1929

9. What did Rasputin consider himself?

    (A) a politician
    (B) a holy man
    (C) a czar
    (D) a noble
    (E) a spy

10. Who, according to the article, had hemophilia?

    (A) Anastasia
    (B) the czar
    (C) the czarina
    (D) The crown prince
    (E) Rasputin

11. The author writes this passage with _____.

    (A) humility
    (B) fear
    (C) anxiety
    (D) serenity
    (E) outrage

Turning and turning in the widening gyre
The falcon cannot hear the falconer;
Things fall apart; the center cannot hold;
Line Mere anarchy is loosed upon the world,
(5) The blood-dimmed tide is loosed, and everywhere
The ceremony of innocence is drowned;
The best lack all conviction, while the worst
Are full of passionate intensity . . .

—William Butler Yeats (1920)

12. Which of the following events take place in this poem?

    (A) The volcanoes are beginning to explode.
    (B) The falcon cannot hear the falconer.
    (C) The animals cannot find their way home.
    (D) The people cannot see the sun.
    (E) The tidal wave dashes the shore to pieces.

13. What is let loose upon the world?

    (A) the blood-dimmed tide
    (B) the widening gyre
    (C) the falconer
    (D) the ceremony of innocence
    (E) mere anarchy

14. What cannot hold?

    (A) the moon
    (B) the tide
    (C) the center
    (D) the world
    (E) the worst

15. This poem tries to express the _____.

    (A) fine skill of falconry
    (B) understandable injustice of death
    (C) great joy about life
    (D) deep pessimism about the world
    (E) appreciation for anarchy as a political system

16. Why do you think that the author uses words like "blood-dimmed," "anarchy," and "drowned innocence"?

    (A) to give a happy tone to the poem
    (B) to give a sad tone to the poem
    (C) to give a menacing tone to the poem
    (D) to give a light-hearted tone to the poem
    (E) to give a proud tone to the poem

Scattered across the United States are countless statues of men on horseback. You can find them in cemeteries, in parks, and outside public service buildings. Normally, these statues depict men in uniform
Line sitting astride horses. The main difference among these statues are the
(5) position the horses hold; they rear back on their hind legs with both hooves in the air, or hold one hoof aloft, or plant all four hooves firmly on the ground.

Legend has it that you can look at statues of men on horseback, anywhere in the United States, and know how they died. If the rider sits
(10) atop a horse with one hoof held up, then that person was wounded in battle and later died of his wounds. If the horse rears back on both hind legs, then that person died in battle. And if the horse stands on all four hooves, the rider died of natural causes.

Unfortunately, this story is a load of horse manure. It's pretty to
(15) think that all sculptors adhered to this rule, but they did not. A simple scan across the horse-and-rider statues will prove this point. In fact, the lore generally is true only for Civil War battlefields.

17. You are in a graveyard located in Los Alamos, New Mexico. You see many statues of men on horseback. One in particular catches your attention; it is made of bronze, and the man sits astride a horse reared back on both hind legs. You infer that _____.

(A) this man died in battle
(B) this man was wounded in battle and later died
(C) this man died of natural causes
(D) this man was a public servant
(E) this man liked horses

18. In what sort of publication would you likely find this article?

(A) a science text
(B) an almanac
(C) a book of trivia
(D) a history book
(E) a comic book

19. The best title for this passage would be _____.

(A) Urban Legends Explained
(B) Ripley's Believe It or Not
(C) Secrets of Civil War Battlegrounds
(D) The Story of the Civil War
(E) The Art of Making Statues

20. The author's tone can be described as _____.

(A) heavyhanded
(B) mathematical
(C) dour
(D) lighthearted
(E) loquacious

Line
(5)
It has been said that "History is written by the winners," and to a certain extent this statement is true. If nothing else, history has a very selective memory. As we study the events of World War II, stories continue to surface. Some of these are happy; others are sad. Still others are merely intriguing.

(10)
One such story is that of Vasili Zeitsev, who fought for the Russian army against the invading Germans. Zeitsev, a deer hunter from the Urals, became a hero for his marksmanship; in one ten-day period, he shot 40 Germans. He was so good a shot, and so demoralizing for German soldiers, that the Germans shipped in their own sharpshooter, Colonel Heinz Thornwald, for the express purpose of killing Zeitsev. Unfortunately for Thornwald, Zeitsev proved the better soldier. Thornwald, after attempting a shot, stuck up his head for a quick look around; Zeitsev took the advantage and eliminated Thornwald. By the

(15)
end of the war, Zeitsev alone defeated 242 Germans before he was blinded by a land mine.

(20)
Anyone interested in Zeitsev's story can watch the recent film *Enemy at the Gates*, starring Joseph Fiennes, Jude Law, and Ed Harris. Even though some details have been changed, for example the inclusion of a love triangle, the movie is quite exciting and informative.

21. How many Germans did Zeitsev kill?

    (A) 142
    (B) 242
    (C) 342
    (D) 442
    (E) 542

22. What does the phrase "History is written by the winners" mean?

    (A) The losers, because of their suffering, are more interesting to listen to.
    (B) The soldiers, because of their sacrifice, are ignored.
    (C) The winners, because they are now more powerful, can control information flow.
    (D) The generals, because of their military skill, can remain silent.
    (E) The artists, because of their skill, will listen to the soldiers.

23. What ended Zeitsev's career?

    (A) He stepped on a land mine and blew himself up.
    (B) He went deaf after standing too near a tank when it fired its shot.
    (C) He drowned in the attack on Normandy.
    (D) He was blinded by a land mine.
    (E) He was paralyzed when the cavalry stampeded his tent.

24. Zeitsev was _____.

    (A) American
    (B) French
    (C) German
    (D) neutral
    (E) Russian

25. The author intended _____.

    (A) to anger the reader
    (B) to relate an interesting historical tidbit
    (C) to plug the movie *Enemy at the Gates*
    (D) to praise the Germans
    (E) to document the story of Heinz Thornwald

26. What can we infer from Thornwald's defeat?

    (A) If Thornwald had aimed to the left, Zeitsev would be dead.
    (B) If Zeitsev had been more careful about checking his shot, Thornwald would be alive.
    (C) If Thornwald had not eaten 15 minutes before making his shot, Zeitsev would be alive.
    (D) If Thornwald had not joined the German army, Zeitsev would not have joined the Russian army.
    (E) If Thornwald had been more careful about checking to see whether he hit, Zeitsev might not have gotten a shot.

27. Because of his great aim, which of the following jobs was Zeitsev assigned?

    (A) sniper
    (B) radio man
    (C) gunner
    (D) pilot
    (E) cook

Anyone who has lived in the United States for any length of time has seen, or heard of, graffiti. Graffiti is the scrawled artwork that defaces public buildings, street signs, and roadways. The subjects depicted by graffiti artists range widely; sometimes the graffiti is just gang names *Line* and logos, other times it is the artist's name. Sometimes the graffiti is *(5)* vaguely attractive, but more often than not, it is just a mass of obscene words.

Linguists will tell you that the term *graffiti* comes from the Italian word *graffito*, which means to scratch. Artists will tell you that the art *(10)* form (They call it an art form!) dates back to the dawn of humanity; even the cave men used graffiti on their cave walls, and don't forget the caricature of Jesus on the *Domus Gelotiana* in Rome, now on display in a museum.

These modern, politically correct yahoos would have you believe the *(15)* garbage we see scrawled on sidewalks and mailboxes every day is somehow contributing to our quality of life. By ridding ourselves of these "urban artworks," they say, we are discriminating against those whose artistic ideals are different from ours.

Well, I say, our ideals are different—and theirs are wrong. Art does *(20)* not deface property. Art is not vulgar. Art is not commercialism for gangland activities. And I urge you to join my opinion.

28. From what language does the word *graffiti* come?

    (A) English
    (B) Russian
    (C) Italian
    (D) Latin
    (E) Hebrew

29. In what context are you likely to find this kind of writing?

    (A) the headlines
    (B) the opinions/editorial page
    (C) the gossip columns
    (D) the sports page
    (E) the real estate section

30. Which position does the author likely endorse?

    (A) The city should set aside funding for grants to graffiti artists so they can continue their work.
    (B) The Museum of Modern Art should consider having a showcase for graffiti art.
    (C) Young children should be allowed to express their artistic impulses on sidewalks and school buildings.
    (D) Urban artists should create their own wrapping paper design.
    (E) Graffiti artists should receive jail sentences.

31. In what place does this author likely live?

    (A) a rural town in Mississippi
    (B) a village in eastern Kentucky
    (C) New York City
    (D) the seaside in Florida
    (E) a resort in Alaska

32. With what emotion does the author write?

    (A) satisfaction
    (B) joy
    (C) fear
    (D) exasperation
    (E) sorrow

Students study the theory of communism in school. They know that it was created and popularized by Marx and Engels. They know that it advocates putting the state's needs above the individual's needs. They *Line* know many of the Russian leaders—like Stalin, Khrushchev, and (5) Gorbachev. They also know that, to many people's way of thinking, communism is a failed philosophy; if nothing else, it has proven that people are too selfish to conform to a system based on altruism.

What they may not realize is that, in the late 1890s, many great European and American thinkers adamantly advocated communism. (10) This was a time during which one could see class division taking place. At that time, people generally fit into one of two categories; either they were rich, or striving to be rich, or they were dirt poor. The poor desired to be rich, and the rich had no desire to come into any contact with the poor. Communism offered a way out for the poor at the (15) expense of the wealthy; classlessness offered a hopeful future for many.

Take, for example, British author H. G. Wells. Wells, one of the first science fiction writers, wrote *The Time Machine* with the tenets of communism firmly in mind. *The Time Machine* warns about what will (20) happen if society continues to split into two factions—the rich and the poverty-stricken. The book shows the poverty-stricken class finally rising up and taking revenge upon the rich. By contrast, Wells argues, communism, with its classless society, offers a much more hopeful future.

(25) Another writer who favored communism was American author John Steinbeck. In his *The Grapes of Wrath*, for example, he sets up a story in which poverty-stricken folk are offered a dream—the American Dream—that will never come true for them. Steinbeck holds capitalism accountable for the poverty and despair that exists in the world. He (30) does this by depicting the horrible events that befall the Joad family on their way to find work in California. Bankers take over their farm. Their car breaks down, and salesmen try to gyp them out of their cash. The Joads can't find work in California because there is always someone willing to work at a lower wage. All of these traumas, Steinbeck (35) insinuates, will come true under capitalism. Steinbeck offers only one harmonious event for the Joads; a camp that runs on the principles of communism.

33. According to the passage, what text did John Steinbeck write?

    (A) *Marx and Engels*
    (B) *The Adventures of Huckleberry Finn*
    (C) *The Time Machine*
    (D) *Communism: The Way to Go*
    (E) *The Grapes of Wrath*

34. Which statement outlines the organization of these four paragraphs?

    (A) An introduction and an example with two opposite claims.
    (B) A conclusion, two supporting paragraphs, and an introduction.
    (C) An introduction, a claim, and two supporting paragraph-long examples.
    (D) Two claims with a supporting example.
    (E) An introduction, two supporting paragraphs, and a conclusion.

35. We can infer from the passage that the author _____.

    (A) is neutral
    (B) is a communist
    (C) is a capitalist
    (D) is a novelist
    (E) is poor

36. The author sets out to _____.

    (A) argue that communism is an evil theory
    (B) give an explanation as to why people once took a great interest in communism
    (C) advocate a return to communism
    (D) recommend some good books to read
    (E) eradicate capitalism from the world

Line
(5)

(10)

(15)

(20)

(25)

(30)

If you are a fan of such shows as *Days of Our Lives* or *Passions*, you are enjoying a dramatic tradition over a thousand years old. Any fan of a soap opera knows that certain trademark characters will be a part of the show, whether or not you want them to be. Every soap opera has a naïve, innocent character (usually female) who runs into trouble with an evil, conniving, manipulative character (also usually female) who has set her sights on the innocent character's boyfriend. Every soap opera, additionally, has an earnest young man who, because he is in love with the naïve, innocent character, finds himself in conflict with a calculating, boastful man. These recurring character types are modern versions of archetypes created by *commedia dell'arte.*

Commedia dell'arte evolved from the standards set by Roman comedies that became particularly popular during the Renaissance. Roman comedy had become highly formalized, and it used six main types of characters around whom the story unfolded. These characters included the Sweet Young Thing (a naïve, innocent, young female character), the *Miles Gloriosus* (the superficially bold but secretly cowardly soldier), the Old Man (who takes a highly inappropriate interest in the Sweet Young Thing), the Old Woman (usually a nurse or chaperone of the Sweet Young Thing), the Brave Young Man (who eventually weds the Sweet Young Thing), and the Clever Slave (who comically but cleverly aids the Brave Young Man and the Sweet Young Thing in their attempts to escape the evil clutches of the Old Man).

Commedia dell'arte adopted these main characters, in particular the Clever Slave (often called the *zanni*) and the Brave Young Man and the Sweet Young Thing (also called The Lovers or Harlequin and Columbine) and expanded their number. Eventually, a typical *commedia dell'arte* company consisted of 10 or 12 actors, each specializing in one or two character types, who ad-libbed performances. Over time, people grew tired of these stereotypical characters, and drama turned to more realistic depictions of human traumas. Nevertheless, remnants of *commedia dell'arte* exist—such as those in modern soap operas, as we shall see as we analyze some modern day examples.

37. The author wants to make the point that
_____.

    (A) soap operas are a complete waste of
    time
    (B) *commedia dell'arte* is a modern art
    form
    (C) *Days of our Lives* is the best soap opera
    on TV
    (D) old things can sometimes be recreated
    in new ways
    (E) *commedia dell'arte* was a highly
    scripted art form

38. The character in *commedia dell'arte* who is
a secret coward is the _____.

    (A) Sweet Young Thing
    (B) *Miles Gloriosus*
    (C) Clever Slave
    (D) Old Man
    (E) Brave Young Man

39. What is the purpose of paragraph one?

    (A) to tell about the *commedia dell'arte*
    (B) to discuss the latest plot developments
    of *Days of Our Lives*
    (C) to talk about specific *commedia
    dell'arte* characters
    (D) to engage the reader's attention
    (E) to waste the reader's time

40. What is the name of the pair of lovers in
commedia dell'arte?

    (A) Romeo and Juliet
    (B) Abbot and Costello
    (C) Punch and Judy
    (D) Betty and Veronica
    (E) Harlequin and Columbine

STOP

IF YOU FINISH BEFORE TIME IS UP, YOU MAY CHECK YOUR WORK ON THIS
SECTION ONLY. DO NOT TURN TO ANY OTHER SECTION IN THE TEST.

SSAT Practice Test 2

SECTION 4 VERBAL SKILLS

60 questions   *30 minutes*

Directions: The following 30 questions consist of one capitalized word followed by five choices. Select the choice that is closest in meaning to the word in capital letters.

Sample:
MANNERLY

(A) insolent
(B) polite
(C) pompous
(D) sly
(E) aloof

1. FOE

   (A) author
   (B) warrior
   (C) poet
   (D) spy
   (E) enemy

2. FRACTION

   (A) piece
   (B) break
   (C) breach
   (D) disagreement
   (E) opposing side

3. DISCARD

   (A) reject
   (B) acquire
   (C) offend
   (D) play
   (E) amass

4. EMPLOY

   (A) deceive
   (B) use
   (C) trick
   (D) pay
   (E) fall

5. CONTORT

   (A) twist
   (B) accompany
   (C) legislate
   (D) dine
   (E) diet

6. EXALT

   (A) elevate
   (B) breathe
   (C) insult
   (D) denigrate
   (E) fatigue

7. SOMNOLENT

   (A) liquid
   (B) flexible
   (C) spartan
   (D) fluid
   (E) sleepy

8. TERRAIN

   (A) land
   (B) water
   (C) justice
   (D) storm
   (E) atmosphere

9. MEDDLESOME

   (A) nosy
   (B) noisome
   (C) confusing
   (D) addled
   (E) unbalanced

10. BOON

   (A) interruption
   (B) explosion
   (C) gift
   (D) deviation
   (E) fool

11. STERN

   (A) stem
   (B) sterile
   (C) stout
   (D) strict
   (E) stressed

12. DUBIOUS

   (A) welcome
   (B) slow
   (C) random
   (D) doubtful
   (E) hearty

13. FALLACY

   (A) plunge
   (B) credit
   (C) fancy
   (D) style
   (E) error

14. ABODE

   (A) home
   (B) augury
   (C) container
   (D) design
   (E) prediction

15. INDEFATIGABLE

   (A) unknown
   (B) friendless
   (C) inflated
   (D) undefinable
   (E) tireless

16. TOXIC

   (A) void
   (B) free
   (C) poisonous
   (D) concealing
   (E) hidden

17. MALICIOUS

   (A) odorous
   (B) spiteful
   (C) inedible
   (D) atypical
   (E) hungry

18. CONTOUR

   (A) expedition
   (B) incarceration
   (C) texture
   (D) duty
   (E) outline

19. HERALD

   (A) announcer
   (B) paper
   (C) tribute
   (D) monarch
   (E) jester

20. AVARICE

   (A) snow
   (B) beauty
   (C) envy
   (D) serenity
   (E) greed

SSAT Practice Test 2

21. COLOSSAL

    (A) misplaced
    (B) sloppy
    (C) grieving
    (D) gigantic
    (E) clumsy

22. AFFABLE

    (A) friendly
    (B) fiery
    (C) unintelligent
    (D) casual
    (E) truculent

 23. AMBULATORY

    (A) injured
    (B) walking
    (C) conservative
    (D) scientific
    (E) medical

 24. ANTITHESIS

    (A) control
    (B) formula
    (C) statement
    (D) similarity
    (E) opposite

25. CRUDE

    (A) physical
    (B) refined
    (C) crass
    (D) mental
    (E) weak

26. CHIDE

    (A) scold
    (B) wager
    (C) nick
    (D) chip
    (E) bet

 27. FOIBLE

    (A) bone
    (B) feeling
    (C) being
    (D) sport
    (E) weakness

28. ALOOF

    (A) reserved
    (B) intelligent
    (C) diligent
    (D) dogged
    (E) alien

 29. INNOCUOUS

    (A) repugnant
    (B) immune
    (C) medical
    (D) harmless
    (E) sharp

 30. VERACIOUS

    (A) lawful
    (B) legal
    (C) true
    (D) mature
    (E) angry

Directions: The next 30 questions require you to find relationships between words. Select the answer choice that best completes the meaning of the sentence.

31. Dark is to light as _____.

    (A) big is to heavy
    (B) clean is to dirty
    (C) bar is to soap
    (D) pure is to immaculate
    (E) simple is to easy

32. Negative is to positive as _____.

    (A) valley is to mountain
    (B) dominant is to overbearing
    (C) height is to weight
    (D) neutral is to flat
    (E) ocean is to sea

33. Pack is to suitcase as _____.

    (A) jump is to plane
    (B) fuel is to car
    (C) read is to magazine
    (D) eat is to restaurant
    (E) buy is to groceries

34. Bus is to car as whale is to _____.

    (A) fish
    (B) plankton
    (C) dolphin
    (D) ocean
    (E) ship

35. Tile is to mosaic as _____.

    (A) tire is to car
    (B) sand is to box
    (C) musician is to orchestra
    (D) flower is to plant
    (E) colony is to ant

36. Golf is to course as _____.

    (A) hockey is to net
    (B) football is to goal
    (C) course is to basketball
    (D) baseball is to diamond
    (E) volleyball is to spike

37. Coat is to jacket as chair is to _____.

    (A) stool
    (B) table
    (C) couch
    (D) counter
    (E) sofa

38. Modest is to vanity as innocent is to _____.

    (A) happiness
    (B) reason
    (C) fear
    (D) guilt
    (E) purity

39. Recluse is to publicity as _____.

    (A) pragmatist is to practicality
    (B) politician is to votes
    (C) anarchist is to order
    (D) spider is to web
    (E) equivocator is to hunger

40. Zoo is to animals as _____.

    (A) school is to education
    (B) prison is to policemen
    (C) circus is to tightrope
    (D) letter is to mailbox
    (E) factory is to workers

41. Blossom is to bloom as _____.

    (A) fruit is to tree
    (B) quiver is to vibrate
    (C) run is to hide
    (D) fast is to slow
    (E) wax is to wane

42. Desert is to arid as _____.

    (A) sand is to beach
    (B) saturated is to desiccated
    (C) wet is to dry
    (D) continent is to unexplored
    (E) rain forest is to humid

43. Hero is to villain as antagonist is to
_____.

   (A) character
   (B) protagonist
   (C) mentor
   (D) companion
   (E) sidekick

44. Zebra is to skunk as _____.

   (A) rhinoceros is to hippopotamus
   (B) horse is to cow
   (C) leopard is to Dalmatian
   (D) mammoth is to wool
   (E) dinosaur is to bird

45. Grizzly is to bear as _____.

   (A) butter is to bur
   (B) night is to mare
   (C) mint is to herb
   (D) spear is to pepper
   (E) puppy is to dog

46. Square is to pentagon as _____.

   (A) triad is to chord
   (B) quartet is to quintet
   (C) circle is to sphere
   (D) multiply is to divide
   (E) cube is to root

47. Recess is to play as breakfast is to _____.

   (A) dress
   (B) pancakes
   (C) juice
   (D) eat
   (E) lunch

48. Walk is to stroll as _____.

   (A) run is to race
   (B) sing is to orate
   (C) converse is to chat
   (D) dance is to twirl
   (E) rattle is to roll

49. Helter is to skelter as _____.

   (A) wishy is to washy
   (B) in is to out
   (C) back is to forth
   (D) mish is to mash
   (E) harem is to scarem

50. Odd is to agenda as _____.

   (A) strange is to tent
   (B) plan is to point
   (C) weird is to wired
   (D) quirky is to schedule
   (E) list is to nomination

51. Drill is to hole as blender is to _____.

   (A) flour
   (B) batter
   (C) eggs
   (D) milk
   (E) blades

52. Sanitary is to clean as _____.

   (A) empathy is to ethereal
   (B) heinous is to inane
   (C) elegy is to copious
   (D) cogent is to haphazard
   (E) earnest is to serious

53. Imagination is to thought as _____.

   (A) song is to bird
   (B) music is to sound
   (C) art is to painting
   (D) theatre is to auditorium
   (E) engineering is to train

54. Parade is to march as _____.

   (A) circus is to walk
   (B) swim is to meet
   (C) meet is to eat
   (D) race is to run
   (E) sweat is to sweet

55. Record is to document as _____.

  (A) excel is to feign
  (B) excuse is to pardon
  (C) conceal is to exempt
  (D) inundate is to wilt
  (E) challenge is to venture

56. Financial is to money as psychological is to _____.

  (A) mind
  (B) spirit
  (C) body
  (D) academics
  (E) psychiatric

57. Pencil is to lead as _____.

  (A) pen is to paper
  (B) tube is to straw
  (C) stem is to pith
  (D) graphite is to mineral
  (E) wood is to mill

58. Monday is to Thursday as _____.

  (A) February is to May
  (B) eight is to six
  (C) March is to May
  (D) 12:00 is to 1:00
  (E) first is to third

59. Bath is to water as _____.

  (A) soap is to tub
  (B) tub is to popcorn
  (C) popcorn is to movie
  (D) movie is to picture
  (E) picture is to frame

60. Fiend is to friend as _____.

  (A) enemy is to foe
  (B) hart is to wart
  (C) tuck is to truck
  (D) height is to weight
  (E) monster is to critic

STOP

IF YOU FINISH BEFORE TIME IS UP, YOU MAY CHECK YOUR WORK ON THIS SECTION ONLY. DO NOT TURN TO ANY OTHER SECTION IN THE TEST.

SSAT Practice Test 2

SECTION 5 QUANTITATIVE SKILLS

25 questions *30 minutes*

Directions: At the end of each problem, you have a choice of five possible answers. Work out each problem and then choose the best possible answer.

Sample Question:
If the circumference of a circle is 37.68, find its radius. Use the formula C = 2πr and let π = 3.14.

(A) 6
(B) 5
(C) 7
(D) 4
(E) 8

SSAT Practice Test 2

USE THIS SPACE FOR FIGURING

1. Find the quotient of 2.112 and .6.

   (A) 2.54
   (B) .349
   (C) 3.52
   (D) 4.118
   (E) 2.47

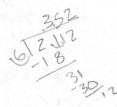

2. Sides *AB* and *BC* in Δ*ABC* are equal in measure. If the exterior angle at *C* measures 96°, find the measure of angle *B*.

   (A) 18°
   (B) 24°
   (C) 12°
   (D) 16°
   (E) 19°

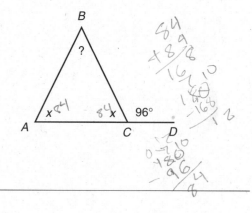

3. The price of a computer dropped 10% and then dropped another 20% of the reduced price. What percent of the original price was the computer selling for after the second drop?

   (A) 72%
   (B) 87%
   (C) 56%
   (D) 67%
   (E) 48%

USE THIS SPACE FOR FIGURING

4. Determine the value of x in the equation
   $62 + 2(8 - x) = 72$.

   (A) 2
   (B) 6
   (C) 4
   (D) 5
   (E) 3

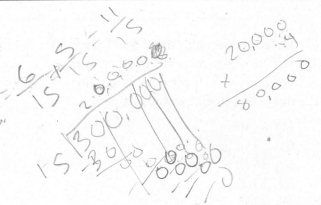

5. What is the greatest common factor of 70
   and 14?

   (A) 10
   (B) 7
   (C) 15
   (D) 14
   (E) 28

6. Ruben, Shelly, and Malcolm have recorded
   a hit song. If Ruben gets 2/5 of the income
   and Shelly gets 1/3 and they earn
   $300,000, how much does Malcolm get?

   (A) $90,000
   (B) $250,000
   (C) $210,000
   (D) $80,000
   (E) $110,000

7. On the real number line, if the distance
   between two numbers is 5.6, which of the
   following sets correctly represents the two
   numbers?

   (A) 4.7 and 11.3
   (B) 9.5 and 1.8
   (C) 12.4 and 6.5
   (D) 9.3 and 3.7
   (E) 2.4 and 5.9

USE THIS SPACE FOR FIGURING

8. Find the value of $5.3 \times 10^3 - 1.3 \times 10^2$.

   (A) 3,450
   (B) 5,170
   (C) 1,300
   (D) 5,400
   (E) 4,260

9. Twenty-four students in a class are right-handed and six are left-handed. If these figures represent the entire class, what percent is left-handed?

   (A) 15%
   (B) 25%
   (C) 20%
   (D) 30%
   (E) 35%

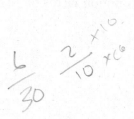

10. Henry receives a salary of $530 per week. José gets 30% more than Henry. If they both receive $70 per week raises, how much will José be earning?

    (A) $650
    (B) $458
    (C) $548
    (D) $568
    (E) $759

11. A ticket to the movies is $8.00. If the price increases 10% this year and 20% the following year, how much will a movie ticket be at the end of two years?

    (A) $9.48
    (B) $10.12
    (C) $9.76
    (D) $10.56
    (E) $12.43

USE THIS SPACE FOR FIGURING

12. The three-digit number $49x$ is divisible by
    4 with no remainders. If the sum of the
    digits is divisible by 5 with no remainders,
    what is the number?

    (A) 492
    (B) 497
    (C) 493
    (D) 498
    (E) 491

13. Two-thirds of what number is equal to 7
    less than 5 squared?

    (A) 12
    (B) 18
    (C) 27
    (D) 24
    (E) 20

14. Simplify $\sqrt[3]{64a^3b^9}$.

    (A) $4ab^3$
    (B) $4a^3b$
    (C) $16a^3b$
    (D) $16ab^3$
    (E) $4a^2b^2$

15. If $x = \dfrac{4}{5}$, $y = \dfrac{2}{3}$, and $z = \sqrt{3}$, find the value

    of $10x - 9y - 4z^2$.

    (A) 4
    (B) −8
    (C) −10
    (D) 6
    (E) 7

USE THIS SPACE FOR FIGURING

16. Which of the following statements is false?

    (A) $3^2 + 6 \leq 3(5 + 2)$
    (B) $4 \cdot 5 - 2 > 3^3$
    (C) $2(8 + 3) < (3 + 4)^2$
    (D) $5(8 - 5) \geq (5 \times 3)$
    (E) $4^3 - 3^2 < 5(6 + 2) + 3^3$

17. Simplify $4|-3|-2|-5|$.

    (A) 3
    (B) −2
    (C) 2
    (D) −3
    (E) 1

18. Select the set of values for x and y that will make the statement $3x + 5 < y$ true.

    (A) (2, 6)
    (B) (4, 8)
    (C) (3, 10)
    (D) (2, 5)
    (E) (1, 9)

19. Add: $(4c - 6b + 7a) + (5c - 3a - 8b)$

    (A) $1a + 11b - 11c$
    (B) $4a - 14b + 9c$
    (C) $1a - 11b + 11c$
    (D) $-1a - 11b + 11c$
    (E) $4a - 2b + 9c$

20. Mildred weighs $x - 3$ pounds. Her brother, Hector, weighs 8 pounds more than Mildred while her sister, Stacey, weighs 12 pounds less than Hector. Find their total weight.

    (A) $4x - 5$
    (B) $5x + 3$
    (C) $x + 12$
    (D) $3x - 5$
    (E) $2x + 5$

USE THIS SPACE FOR FIGURING

21. Simplify $-2|5|\cdot3|-4|$.

    (A) 100
    (B) 120
    (C) −120
    (D) −80
    (E) 70

22. The height of the front door on a blueprint of a one-family house measures $\frac{3}{4}''$. If the actual door is 8 feet tall, what is the ratio of the blueprint diagram to the actual dimensions of the house?

    (A) 2/65
    (B) 1/96
    (C) 2/55
    (D) 1/128
    (E) 3/13

23. If a is a positive even integer and b and c are the following consecutive integers, which of the following statements is false?

    (A) ab is even
    (B) $a + b$ is odd
    (C) ac is odd
    (D) $b + c$ is odd
    (E) $c - a$ is even

24. Find the measure of the angle between the hour hand and the minute hand when a clock reads 9:05. Select the closest answer.

    (A) 120°
    (B) 150°
    (C) 90°
    (D) 110°
    (E) 130°

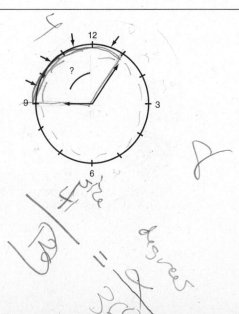

25. In the diagram, $\overrightarrow{MN}$ is perpendicular to $\overrightarrow{ML}$, $\angle NMO$ measures 71°, and $\angle LMO$ is represented by $2x - 5$. Determine the value of x.

   (A) 16°
   (B) 18°
   (C) 24°
   (D) 32°
   (E) 12°

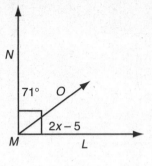

$$
\begin{array}{r}
\overset{8}{9}\overset{10}{0} \\
-71 \\
\hline
19
\end{array}
$$

$$19 = 2x - 5$$
$$+5 \qquad +5$$

$$\frac{24}{2} = \frac{2x}{2}$$

$$12 = x$$

STOP

SSAT Practice Test 2

ANSWER EXPLANATIONS

Section 1 Writing Sample Checklist

PROMPT A

☐ **Check your handwriting.** Is your text legible? Get used to forming your words clearly. Frustrated readers cannot score you highly if they cannot read your essay.

☐ **Proofread.** Correct the most glaring errors, especially run-ons, comma splices, and fragments. Make sure you capitalize when necessary and punctuate logically. Check your spelling, especially of easily confused words (to/too, their/there, your/you're, etc.). Notice how you use transition words.

☐ **Have someone else read this essay.** Choose a good writer and reader to comment on your work.

☐ **Read the question and writing prompt again.** Did you answer the question? You won't have time to rewrite the essay during the actual exam, so read the question carefully the first time and keep it in mind. Underline keywords in the questions to help you remember.

☐ **Read your introduction.** Did you include all of the information necessary for a reader to understand your essay? Does it include a thesis statement?

☐ **Underline your thesis statement in the introduc.** Does it address the question and give your opinion on it?

☐ **Underline the thesis statement in the conclusion.** Does it agree with your original thesis?

☐ **Underline the topic sentences of your body paragraphs.** Now read all of the underlined sentences in your practice essay. Do these sentences focus on the same topic? Do they fit together? Do they flow?

☐ **TExAn.** For each body paragraph, check to make sure you have a *specific* <u>Ex</u>ample to illustrate your <u>Topic</u> sentence. Again, make sure it is specific, rather than another general statement. Then make sure you <u>An</u>alyze or explain *how* this example proves your point.

   This is an important step, so get used to including this information **as you write** your paragraphs.

Practice writing more essays, and you will improve each time. During the actual exam, you will only have time to proofread and check your examples, so most items on this list will have to become second nature to you.

PROMPT B

☐ **Check your handwriting.** Is your text legible? Get used to forming your words clearly. Frustrated readers cannot score you highly if they cannot read your essay.

☐ **Proofread.** Correct the most glaring errors, especially run-ons, comma splices, and fragments. Make sure you capitalize when necessary and punctuate logically. Check your spelling, especially of easily confused words (to/too, their/there, your/you're, etc.). Notice how you use transition words.

☐ **Have someone else read this essay.** Choose a good writer and reader to comment on your work.

☐ **Did you give the reader enough exposition?** It's fine to jump right into the story (in fact, it's often a good idea), but in a story of such a short length, you need to establish the characters, setting, and situation quickly. **Show** the reader instead of **telling** the reader.

– Setting
– Character
– Situation

☐ **What does the protagonist [main character] want or need to do?**

☐ **What obstacles are in his or her way?**

☐ **Did you start a new paragraph when a new speaker has dialogue?**

This helps the reader identify who is speaking. Remember, instead of writing she said each time, try substituting an action. *She shrugged.*

☐ **Does your story reach a high point in the conflict?**

This is called the climax. Everything should lead us here.

☐ **Do**ˌ ~~~~ ˌˌˌ **too long? Too short?**

The resolution should end the sto**ˌ**y quickly (especially in a story this short). However, make sure you allow enough time for your reader to feel satisfied. You can have a twist ending, of course, but that should come *after* the feeling of closure.

Practice writing more essays, and you will improve each time. During the actual exam, you will only have time to proofread and check your examples, so most items on this list will have to become second nature to you.

Section 2 Quantitative Skills

1.

ANALYSIS

Draw the diagram on a graph and find the base and height of the triangle.

WORK

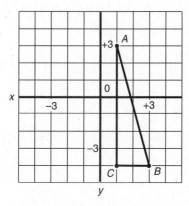

$$\text{base} = 2, \text{ height} = 7$$

$$A = \frac{1}{2}bh, \text{ where } A = \text{area},$$

$$b = \text{base, and } h = \text{height}$$

$$b = 2, h = 7: \qquad = \frac{1}{2}(2)(7) = 7$$

ANSWER: (B)

2.

ANALYSIS

Simplify both radicals and subtract.

WORK

$$3\sqrt{8} - \sqrt{18}$$
$$= 3\sqrt{2 \cdot 4} - \sqrt{2 \cdot 9}$$
$$= 3\sqrt{2} \cdot \sqrt{4} - \sqrt{2} \cdot \sqrt{9}$$
$$= 3 \cdot 2\sqrt{2} - 3\sqrt{2}$$
$$= 6\sqrt{2} - 3\sqrt{2}$$
$$= 3\sqrt{2}$$

ANSWER: (C)

3.

ANALYSIS

We want to include all numbers greater than −4 and less than or equal to 1.

WORK

$$-4 < x \le 1$$

ANSWER: (D)

4.

ANALYSIS

Use the formula $d = rt$, where $d =$ distance, $r =$ rate, and $t =$ time. Find the two distances and then add them.

WORK

$$\text{First time } (t) = 30 \text{ minutes} = \frac{1}{2} \text{ hr}$$

$$\text{First rate } (r) = 50 \text{ mph}$$
$$d = rt$$
$$= 50\left(\frac{1}{2}\right)$$
$$= 25 \text{ miles}$$

$$\text{Second time} = 45 \text{ minutes} = \frac{3}{4} \text{ hr}$$

$$\text{Second rate} = 60 \text{ mph}$$
$$d = rt$$
$$= 60\left(\frac{3}{4}\right)$$
$$= 45 \text{ miles}$$
$$\text{Total distance} = 25 \text{ miles} + 45 \text{ miles}$$
$$= 70 \text{ miles}$$

ANSWER: (E)

5.

ANALYSIS

First multiply 800 tons by $\frac{5}{8}$. Then multiply 800 tons by $\frac{3}{5}$ and add the two answers.

WORK

$$\frac{5}{8} \times 800 \text{ tons} = 500 \text{ tons}$$

$$+\frac{3}{5} \times 800 \text{ tons} = 480 \text{ tons}$$

$$\overline{\hspace{2cm} 980 \text{ tons}}$$

ANSWER: (C)

6.
ANALYSIS

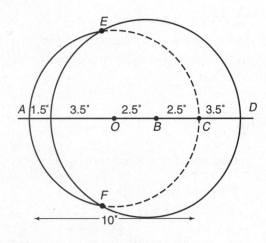

Radius $OC = 5''$ and $BC = 2.5''$.

WORK

Extend BC to D so that $CD = 3.5''$ and $BD = 6''$. A circle with radius $BD = 6$ will intersect the original circle, O, at two points, E and F.

ANSWER: (C)
7.

ANALYSIS

Determine the prime factors of 35 and 30. Then find the difference of their sums.

WORK

$$35 = 7 \cdot 5 \qquad 30 = 2 \cdot 5 \cdot 3$$

$$7 + 5 = 12 \qquad 2 + 5 + 3 = 10$$

$$12 - 10 = 2$$

ANSWER: (C)

8.
ANALYSIS

c is the last odd integer in the series. Find the two preceding odd integers and multiply.

WORK

$$c = 11, \ b = 9, \ a = 7$$
$$a \cdot b = (7)(9) = 63$$

ANSWER: (E)

9.
ANALYSIS

Divide the whole numbers and the radicals separately.

WORK

$$\frac{a\sqrt{42}}{b\sqrt{7}} = \frac{a}{b}\sqrt{\frac{42}{7}} = \frac{a}{b}\sqrt{6}$$

ANSWER: (A)

10.
ANALYSIS

There are 2 hours and 45 minutes (2 45/60) or $2\frac{3}{4}$ hours of time between 8 A.M. and 10:45 A.M.

Divide 154 miles by $2\frac{3}{4}$ in order to obtain the average speed.

WORK

$$154 \div 2\frac{3}{4} = 154 \div \frac{11}{4} = 154 \times \frac{4}{11} = \frac{616}{11} = 56$$

ANSWER: (D)

11.
ANALYSIS

In cases when we are given a generalized statement, make the problem concrete by using actual numbers fitting the description. The two unknowns, x and y, are negative and $y > x$, so let's try using $x = -2$ and $y = -1$.

WORK

Let $x = -2$, $y = -1$:
$$xy > 0$$
$$(-2)(-1) = +2$$
$$+2 > 0$$

ANSWER: (C)

12.
ANALYSIS

Substitute the values for r, s, and t in the given expression.

WORK

$$3rs - 2t$$
$r = 2$, $s = 3$, $t = 4$:
$$= 3(2)(3) - 2(4)$$
$$= 18 - 8$$
$$= 10$$

ANSWER: (B)

13.

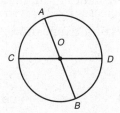

ANALYSIS

CO, OD, AO, and OB are radii and are therefore equal in length. AB and CD are diameters and are also equal in length.

WORK

$$AB - OB = DO$$
$$\text{diameter } AB - \text{radius } OB = \text{radius } DO$$

DO is a radius, and all radii in the same circle are equal in length.

ANSWER: (C)

14.

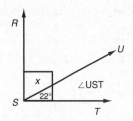

ANALYSIS

$\angle TSU$ and $\angle RSU$ are complementary.

WORK

$$m\angle TSU + m\angle RSU = 90°$$
$m\angle TSU = 22°$:
$$22° + m\angle RSU = 90°$$
$$m\angle RSU = 68°$$

ANSWER: (D)

15.

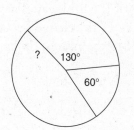

ANALYSIS

All of the central angles add up to 360°, so find the missing third angle (call it x) and then find the average of all three angles.

WORK

$$x + 60 + 130 = 360$$
$$x + 190 = 360$$
Subtract 190:
$$x = 170$$

Find the average of the three central angles:

$$(60 + 130 + 170)/3 = 360/3 = 120$$

ANSWER: (B)

16.
ANALYSIS

Find the volume of the room and then divide by the rate the oxygen fills the room, 3 cubic meters per minute.

WORK

$$V = l \cdot w \cdot h$$

$l = 9$, $w = 6$, $h = 4$: $= (9)(6)(4)$
$= 216$ cubic meters

Divide by 3
cubic meters: $216/3 = 72$

ANSWER: (B)

17.
ANALYSIS

Find the area of the driveway. Then multiply the area by \$2.58, the charge per square foot, and round off to the nearest dollar.

WORK

$$A = bh$$
$$A = 11 \times 34 = 374 \text{ square feet}$$

$$\$2.58 \times 374 = \$964.92 \approx \$965$$

ANSWER: (A)

18.
ANALYSIS

Assign the base and height arbitrary numbers and then see what happens to the area when the base and height are increased. To begin, let $b_1 = 2$ and $h_1 = 3$. Then double the base so that $b_2 = 4$ and triple the height so that $h_2 = 9$.

WORK

$A = \dfrac{1}{2}bh$, where A = area, b = base, and h = height

$$b_1 = 2,\ h_1 = 3: \quad A_1 = \frac{1}{2}(2)(3) = 3$$

$$b_2 = 4,\ h_2 = 9: \quad A_2 = \frac{1}{2}(4)(9) = 18$$

The area is increased sixfold.

ANSWER: (E)

19.
ANALYSIS

In a scalene triangle, all the sides are different.

WORK

5, 6, 7 ✔

ANSWER: (D)

20.
ANALYSIS

On the first day, if the temperature decreases by 40%, it is 60% of the original temperature (100% − 40% = 60%). The next day, the temperature increases by 26%, so it is now 126% of the second temperature.

WORK

$$0.60 \times 1.26 \times 90° = 68.04°$$

ANSWER: (A)

21–22.

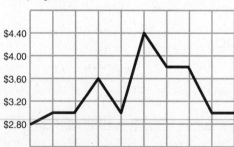

Price per gallon

Jan. Feb. Mar. Apr. May Jun. Jul. Aug. Sep. Oct.

21.

ANALYSIS

Add the April and August prices and divide by 2.

WORK

$$\frac{\$3.60 + \$3.80}{2} = \frac{\$7.40}{2} = \$3.70$$

ANSWER: (C)

22.

ANALYSIS

Determine the two consecutive months with the greatest drop in average price per gallon of gasoline.

WORK

August price − September price
= \$3.80 − \$3.00 = \$.80

ANSWER: (D)

23.

ANALYSIS

Draw a diagram of an isosceles triangle. Let each of the base angles = x. Then set the sum of the measures of all three angles equal to 180°.

WORK

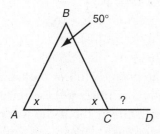

$$x + x + 50° = 180°$$
$$2x + 50° = 180°$$

Subtract 50°: $\qquad\qquad 2x = 130°$
Divide by 2: $\qquad\qquad\quad x = 65°$

$\angle BCD$ and $\angle BCA$ are supplementary:

$$m\angle BCA + m\angle BCD = 180°$$

m$\angle BCA = 65°$: $\qquad 65° + m\angle BCD = 180°$
Subtract 65°: $\qquad\qquad\quad m\angle BCD = 115°$

ANSWER: (C)

24.

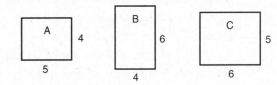

ANALYSIS

Find all the areas and then substitute the results into the four inequalities.

WORK

area A = $bh = 5 \cdot 4 = 20$
area B = $bh = 4 \cdot 6 = 24$
area C = $bh = 6 \cdot 5 = 30$

Area B is less than area C.
$$24 < 30 \checkmark$$

ANSWER: (E)

25.

ANALYSIS

Let y = the number of runs the team has to score on the last game, and set up an equation to solve for the mean, $\bar{x}$.

WORK

$$\bar{x} = \frac{12 + 7 + 10 + 6 + 9 + y}{6}$$

$\bar{x} = 9$: $\qquad\qquad 9 = \dfrac{44 + y}{6}$

Multiply
by 6: $\qquad\qquad 54 = 44 + y$
Subtract 44: $\quad 10 = y$

ANSWER: (C)

Section 3 Reading Comprehension Skills

1. **(B)** The article tries to engage the reader's attention (A), but it does so in paragraph one. The article might go on to discuss in detail ways in which "Rip Van Winkle" describes an alien abduction (C), but if it will, it will do so in paragraphs not included in this selection. The article does not discuss biographical information about Irving (D) or the entire plot of one of his short stories (E), and it should not do so unless this information is pertinent to the discussion.

2. **(D)** Irving, according to the article, lived from 1783–1859. Compare these dates to the events listed as options: the Civil War (1861–1865), the Vietnam War (1955–1975), World War I (1914–1918), the American Revolution (1775–1783), and World War II (1941–1945). You will see that Irving lived more closely to the American Revolution than to any of the other events.

3. **(A)** The Anasazi lived in the desert, nowhere near New England; rule out B. The Anasazi experienced exponential growth, not sudden disappearance; omit C. The remaining claims are not supported by the article; rule out D and E. The only logical claim is A. Most likely the beans they farmed gave them better nutrition, which led to more cultural development.

4. **(D)** "Tale of a Tub" was written by Jonathan Swift, so rule out option A. "Old Mother Hubbard" comes from an anonymous source; skip B. The Headless Horseman is a character in Irving's "The Legend of Sleepy Hollow"; rule out C. Irving did write "The Life of Washington," but it is not well known. The best answer is D.

5. **(B)** Only someone with a sense of humor, despite their great education, would write about alien abduction with any seriousness. Besides, the author's tone is not rude (A), conceited or angry (C), pious (D), or sarcastic (E).

6. **(C)** The author does not, according to what s/he has written, intend to embarrass anyone (A), get people to read mythology (B), give a position on alien existence (D), or make any claim about George Washington (E). Instead, the author intends to tell people about a theory that is interesting but little known.

7. **(D)** The author tells you that s/he is disappointed that a film intended for children would present false information; therefore, option A and C cannot be true for this author. Nor does the author set out to discuss Czar Nicholas II; s/he seems much more interested in discussing Rasputin. The author tries to restore Rasputin's character rather than make it worse (B).

8. **(D)** Paragraph one states that Anastasia was murdered on July 17, 1918.

9. **(B)** Paragraph two states that Rasputin considered himself a holy man.

10. **(D)** Paragraph two states that Alexis, the crown prince, suffered from hemophilia.

11. **(E)** The author seems very upset that a film for children would intentionally give out false information. The best answer is E.

12. **(B)** Check out line two.

13. **(A)** Check out line five.

14. **(C)** Check out line three.

15. **(D)** The poem is full of dark, stress-inducing images; these images convey a pessimism about the world.

16. **(C)** Using such dark images instills a menacing tone to the poem; the poem is definitely not happy (A), sad (B), light-hearted (D), or proud (E).

17. **(E)** Watch yourself on this one. The final paragraph tells you that this legend about horse statues only pertains in Civil War battlefields. You are not in a Civil War battlefield; therefore, all you can really tell is that the person buried may have liked horses.

18. **(C)** Science texts don't discuss statuary; skip A. Almanacs discuss the weather; skip B. Looking at statues is not part of a history text or a comic book; skip D and E.

19. **(A)** Answering this question demands that you have some knowledge of the world around you. Choice B deals with truths that are stranger than fiction; it tends to publish stories about the Elephant Man or the man with the longest fingernails in the world. An interesting story about the secret code of statues probably won't make the cut. Choices C and D are tempting because they mention the Civil War, but neither necessarily deals with statues. Choice E might also tempt you, but because it talks about statue construction in general, you have no reason to think that it might discuss codes. The best title is A. After all, an urban legend is a story that seems true but really isn't; the passage clearly states that the idea of a secret code of statue making isn't true—so, essentially this passage debunks a popular urban legend.

20. **(D)** You have to know the definitions of these words to choose the correct answer. Heavyhanded (A) means language that is difficult to read; this article is not heavyhanded. Neither is the passage dour or grumpy; rule out choice C. The article mentions no numbers; rule out choice B. The passage does not ramble on for pages and pages; therefore, we can assume that it is not loquacious (or talkative). The best answer is D. (Get real: how many articles have you read in which the author calls something a load of horse manure?)

21. **(B)** Paragraph two states that Zeitsev killed 242 Germans before ending his sniping career.

22. **(C)** The phrase implies that the winners, having killed off (or beaten into submission) the enemy, can say anything they want about what happened during the conflict because the enemy will not be powerful enough to stop them. Therefore, choice C is the best answer.

23. **(D)** Paragraph two states that Zeitsev was blinded by a land mine; this does not necessarily mean that Zeitsev stepped on the land mine, and, moreover, we know he survived. Rule out choices A and C. Option B, deafness, although inconvenient, would not necessarily have stopped Zeitsev from sniping; omit it. And choice E is simply wrong.

24. **(E)** Paragraph two states that Zeitsev was part of the Russian army; you can infer that he was Russian.

25. **(B)** The author does not want to anger the reader; most writers don't. Skip option A. Nor does the author particularly want to advertise *Enemy at the Gates* (C) or document Thornwald's life (E); however, s/he does mention these topics during the course of telling about Zeitsev's history. And, the author does not try to praise the Germans; the piece is mostly praise for Zeitsev.

26. **(E)** Be careful when reading these options; make sure you keep straight who was shooting whom and when. The main inference we can make is this: Thornwald got shot while checking to see if he had hit Zeitsev; therefore, if Thornwald had been more careful, he would not have exposed his position, and Zeitsev might not have seen him and gotten such good aim.

27. **(A)** This question demands that you know what skills people who perform this list of jobs must have. A radio man (B) must know how to work a radio.

A gunner (C) must know how to work guns on aircraft. A pilot (D) must know how to fly, and a cook (E) must know how to cook. A sniper (A) must know how to shoot well, as Zeitsev did.

28. **(C)** Paragraph two tells you that *graffiti* is an Italian word.

29. **(B)** The article is very opinionated, and it attempts to get the reader to agree with the author that graffiti is bad. The two answers most tempting are B and E. One might realistically expect an article on graffiti to appear in the real estate section because the presence of graffiti might bring property values down—a real concern for current or future property owners. But, such an article would probably not be so emotional or opinionated. Such writing as that usually appears in editorials—so the best answer is B, the op ed page.

30. **(E)** We know that the author hates graffiti; choices A through D all deal with pleasant things happening to graffiti artists; indeed, they all deal with encouraging graffiti artists to ply their trade. E is the only sentence that asks for something bad to happen to graffiti artists. Clearly, the author agrees with this position.

31. **(C)** The author sees graffiti on a daily basis; most graffiti takes place in urban areas. Choices A, B, D, and E all mention places that are rural; therefore, pick the place that is urban—C, New York City.

32. **(D)** The author clearly hates graffiti and is impatient with those who like it and those who create it. D is the best descriptor for the author's emotions.

33. **(E)** Paragraph four states that Steinbeck wrote *The Grapes of Wrath.* (It's a good book; give it a try sometime.)

34. **(C)** Break down the passage into a sentence outline, and you will see that C is the correct answer. Your outline should look something like this:

a. Students study communism.
b. Students don't realize that communism was a tempting plan in the late 1890s.
c. H. G. Wells, for example, supported communism.
d. John Steinbeck, as well, supported communism.

35. **(A)** The author strives not to take a position on the topic of whether communism is viable; s/he strives for neutrality.

36. **(B)** The author neither argues against communism (A) or for it (C), nor does s/he give an opinion on capitalism (E). The author does mention some books worth reading, but this is not his/her main goal. The author does, however, attempt to explain why people took communism seriously at the turn of the century (i.e., "What they may not realize . . .").

37. **(D)** The author does not advocate soap operas (C) or deride them (A). However, s/he does mention them to make a larger point—that parts of modern day life find their roots in ages past (D). The author, by the way, in giving an overview of *commedia dell'arte*, says that it was a spontaneous art form (so skip E) from the Renaissance (skip B).

38. **(B)** Paragraph two states that the *Miles Gloriosus*, the "brave soldier," was secretly a coward.

39. **(D)** You'll see this time and time again— an author mentions a modern topic or broaches a topic from a weird angle— to grab the reader's attention. Did you have any idea, when the author started talking about soap operas, that s/he would tie that subject in to an ancient dramatic form? We thought not!

40. **(E)** Paragraph three states that the lovers were sometimes called "Harlequin and Columbine."

Section 4 Verbal Skills

1. **(E)** A foe is an enemy. It doesn't necessarily have to be a warrior or a spy.

2. **(A)** A fraction is a piece of something. A **fract**ure is a break or a breach. They both come from a root that means break; the fraction is the broken piece.

3. **(A)** In a card game, you discard when you throw out a card you don't need.

4. **(B)** To employ is to use or utilize.

5. **(A)** To contort is to twist. The word *distort* is related.

6. **(A)** The root *alt* means high, so to exalt is to elevate or raise. C (insult) and D (denigrate) are synonyms for each other.

7. **(E)** Somnolent means sleepy. If you have in**somnia**, you have trouble sleeping.

8. **(A)** The root *terra* means land.

9. **(A)** People who are meddlesome don't mind their own business. The best choice is nosy.

10. **(C)** A boon is an older word for a gift, reward, or blessing. Think of the French word *bon* (good) or the word *bonus.*

11. **(D)** Someone who is stern is strict.

12. **(D)** Dubious and doubt share the same root.

13. **(E)** A fallacy is an error. Someone who is fallible is capable of making mistakes.

14. **(A)** The word *bide* means to stay or dwell. You dwell in your home or abode.

15. **(E)** Something indefatigable is not fatigue-able, or tireless.

16. **(C)** Toxic means poisonous. Those labels that say *nontoxic* are safe.

17. **(B)** The "bad" prefix *mal* should tell us that this is a negative word.

18. **(E)** Contour literally means "with the turns," so it is the outline of something.

19. **(A)** A herald is an announcer and messenger. That's why some newspapers use this word in their titles.

20. **(E)** Specifically, avarice is greed for money or wealth.

21. **(D)** Huge Roman and Greek statues were called colossi, so anything of great size is called colossal.

22. **(A)** Affable means friendly and pleasant.

23. **(B)** Ambulatory means able to walk. Think of the word *amble*, which means to walk leisurely. Choices A and E are tricks to make you think of the word *ambulance.*

24. **(E)** The antithesis is the direct opposite of something. Remember that *anti* means against; E is the only negative choice.

25. **(C)** One of the meanings of *crude* is tasteless, which is also the meaning of *crass*. (Crude can also mean in a natural state or roughly made.)

26. **(A)** To chide is to scold.

27. **(E)** *Foible* and *feeble* share the same root. It's a small defect or weakness.

28. **(A)** Aloof means cool and reserved, or distant.

29. **(D)** Something innocuous is harmless. It is not noxious (hazardous to health). The word is related to innocent.

30. **(C)** Veracity is truth or honesty, so veracious means true. (Voracious means hungry!)

31. **(B)** Dark is the opposite of light; clean is the opposite of dirty.

32. **(A)** Negative is the opposite of positive. (Negative is low; positive is high.) A valley is low, while a mountain is high.

33. **(B)** This one is kind of tricky. You pack a suitcase, you fuel a car, you read a magazine, and you buy groceries. Make the sentence more specific: When you pack a suitcase, you fill it. When you fuel a car, you fill it. (Fuel is a verb here.)

34. **(C)** A bus is a larger vehicle than a car. A whale is a larger aquatic mammal than a dolphin.

35. **(C)** Tiles make up a mosaic. Musicians make up an orchestra.

36. **(D)** You play golf on a course, while you play baseball on a diamond.

37. **(A)** A jacket is a small type of coat. A stool is a small type of chair.

38. **(D)** Someone modest is without vanity. Someone innocent is without guilt.

39. **(C)** A recluse shuns publicity. An anarchist rejects order.

40. **(E)** Animals make up a zoo. Workers make up a factory.

41. **(B)** To blossom means to bloom, and to quiver means to vibrate.

42. **(E)** The desert is arid, while the rainforest is humid.

43. **(B)** A hero is the opposite of a villain; an antagonist is the opposite of a protagonist.

44. **(C)** Zebras and skunks share a physical characteristic: They are both striped. Leopards and Dalmatians are both spotted.

45. **(C)** A grizzly is a type of bear. Mint is a type of herb.

46. **(B)** A square has four sides, while a pentagon has five. A quartet contains four members, while a quintet contains five.

47. **(D)** You play at recess. You eat at breakfast.

48. **(C)** A casual walk is a stroll; a casual conversation is a chat.

49. **(E)** Helter and skelter rhyme. So do harem and scarem.

50. **(D)** This is an odd pair that do not relate, so you'll have to look at the answer choices. *Odd* means *quirky* and *agenda* means *schedule*.

51. **(B)** A drill makes a hole. A blender makes batter. (It does not **make** flour, eggs, milk, or blades.)

52. **(E)** Something sanitary is clean; something earnest is serious.

53. **(B)** Imagination requires thought; music requires sound.

54. **(D)** You march in a parade, and you run in a race.

55. **(B)** This is difficult if you don't look at the words as **verbs**. To *record* is to *document*. To *excuse* is to *pardon*.

56. **(A)** Financial matters deal with your money. Psychological matters deal with your mind.

57. **(C)** The core of a pencil is the lead. The center of a stem is the pith.

58. **(A)** Monday and Thursday are **three** days apart. February and May are **three** months apart.

59. **(D)** If you said, "A bath contains water," then you have two answers that fit: "A tub contains popcorn" and "A movie contains a picture." Make the sentence more specific. "A bath **must** contain water" (or "Water is a **necessary part** of a bath") is more like "A movie **must** contain a picture."

60. **(C)** Here's one of those odd analogies that has more to do with spelling than the meanings of the words. Add the letter *r* after the *f* in *fiend* to spell *friend*. Add an *r* after the *t* in *tuck* to spell *truck*.

Section 5 Quantitative Skills

1.

ANALYSIS

Move the decimal places one place to the right and divide.

WORK

$$
\begin{array}{r}
3.52 \\
\wedge 6.\overline{)2 \wedge 1.12} \\
1\ 8\ \text{xx} \\
3\ 1 \\
3\ 0 \\
\hline
1\ 2 \\
1\ 2 \\
\end{array}
$$

ANSWER: (C)

2.

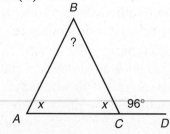

ANALYSIS

Step 1: The measure of ∠*BCA* + the measure of ∠*BCD* = 180° because the angles lie on a straight line and, together, add up to a straight angle. Then find m∠*BCA*.

Step 2: Interior angles *A* and *BCA* are the same measure, so let m∠*A* = *x* and let m∠*BCA* = *x*. Then add up all three interior angles of Δ*ABC* and set the sum equal to 180°.

Step 3: Now find the measure of ∠*B*.

WORK

Step 1:	m∠*BCA* + m∠*BCD* = 180
	x + 96 = 180
Subtract 96:	*x* = 84

| *Step 2:* | m∠*A* + m∠*B* + m∠*BCA* = 180 |
| m∠*A* = m∠*BCA* = *x*: | *x* + m∠*B* + *x* = 180 |

Step 3:	2*x* + m∠*B* = 180
x = 84:	2(84) + m∠*B* = 180
	168 + m∠*B* = 180
Subtract 168:	m∠*B* = 12

ANSWER: (C)

3.
ANALYSIS

If the price drops 10%, it is then selling at 90% (or .90) of the original price. If the price then drops another 20%, it is then selling at 80% (.80) of the reduced price or .80(.90).

WORK

0.80(0.90) = 0.72 = 72% of the original price

ANSWER: (A)

4.
ANALYSIS

First, multiply the expression inside the parentheses by 2 and combine similar terms. Then subtract 78 from both sides of the equation and, finally, divide by −2.

WORK

$$62 + 2(8 - x) = 72$$
$$62 + 16 - 2x = 72$$
$$78 - 2x = 72$$
$$\underline{-78 \qquad = -78}$$
$$-2x = -6$$
$$\frac{-2x}{-2} = \frac{-6}{-2}$$
$$x = 3$$

ANSWER: (E)

5.
ANALYSIS

Find the greatest common factor of 70 and 14.

WORK

70 = 14 × 5
14 = 14 × 1   greatest common factor = 14

ANSWER: (D)

6.
ANALYSIS

Add 2/5 and 1/3 and then subtract the result from 1 (the total amount). The answer is Malcolm's portion. After we determine Malcolm's portion, multiply that fraction by $300,000, the total income.

WORK

$$\frac{2}{5} = \frac{6}{15} \qquad 1 = \frac{15}{15}$$
$$+\frac{1}{3} = \frac{5}{15} \qquad -\frac{11}{15}$$
$$\frac{11}{15} \qquad \frac{4}{15}$$

$$\frac{4}{15} \cdot 300{,}000 = 80{,}000$$

ANSWER: (D)

7.

ANALYSIS

Subtract each set of numbers in order to find a difference of 5.6.

WORK

$$9.3 - 3.7 = 5.6 ✔$$

ANSWER: (D)

8.

ANALYSIS

Simplify each term and then subtract.

WORK

$$5.3 \times 10^3 = 5.3 \times 10 \times 10 \times 10$$
$$= 5.3 \times 1,000 \quad\quad = 5,300$$
$$-1.3 \times 10^2 = \quad\quad 1.3 \times 10 \times 10$$
$$= 1.3 \times \underline{\quad 100 \quad\quad = \quad 130}$$
$$ 5,170$$

ANSWER: (B)

9.

ANALYSIS

Add the right and left-handed numbers of students in order to obtain the total number. Then divide the total into the number of left-handed students.

WORK

Total number of students: $6 + 24 = 30$
Left-handed students/total: $6/30 = .20$
$ .20 = 20\%$

ANSWER: (C)

10.

ANALYSIS

José is earning 30% more than Henry, or 130% of Henry's wage. Once we determine José's current wage, add $70.

WORK

Henry's wage:

$$\$530$$

José's wage:

$$130\% \times \$530 \text{ or } 1.30 \times \$530 = \$689$$

Jose's wage after a $70 raise:

$$\$689 + \$70 = \$759$$

ANSWER: (E)

11.

ANALYSIS

If the price first increases by 10%, the new price is 110% or 1.10 of the original price. The price at the end of the second increase is 20% more than the price at the end of the first price increase, so multiply the previous year's price by 1.20.

WORK

$$1.10 \times 1.20 \times \$8.00 = \$10.56$$

ANSWER: (D)

12.

ANALYSIS

Substitute the possible answers into the given information.

WORK

The three-digit number 49x is divisible by 4:

$$\frac{492}{4} = 123$$

The sum of the digits is divisible by 5:

$$\frac{4+9+2}{5} = \frac{15}{5} = 3$$

ANSWER: (A)

13.

ANALYSIS

Let $x =$ the unknown number.

WORK

$$\frac{2}{3}x = 5^2 - 7$$

$$\frac{2}{3}x = 25 - 7$$

$$\frac{2}{3}x = 18$$

Multiply by $\frac{3}{2}$:

$$\frac{3}{2} \times \frac{3}{2}x = 18 \times \frac{3}{2}$$

$$x = 27$$

ANSWER: (C)

14.
ANALYSIS

We want to find a monomial that, when multiplied by itself three times, is equal to $64a^3b^9$.

WORK

$$\sqrt[3]{64a^3b^9} = 4ab^3$$
$$4ab^3 \cdot 4ab^3 \cdot 4ab^3 = 64a^3b^9 ✔$$

ANSWER: (A)

15.
ANALYSIS

Substitute the values for the variables into the given expression.

WORK

$$10x - 9y - 4z^2$$
$$x = \frac{4}{5}, \quad y = \frac{2}{3},$$
$$z = \sqrt{3}: \quad = 10\left(\frac{4}{5}\right) - 9\left(\frac{2}{3}\right) - 4\left(\sqrt{3}\right)^2$$
$$= 8 \quad -6 \quad -4(3)$$
$$= 2 \quad\quad -12$$
$$= -10$$

ANSWER: (C)

16.
ANALYSIS

Check each statement.

WORK

$$4 \cdot 5 - 2 > 3^3$$
$$20 - 2 > 3 \cdot 3 \cdot 3$$
$$18 > 27 ✗$$

ANSWER: (B)

17.
ANALYSIS

$$|-3| = 3$$
$$|-5| = 5$$

WORK

$$4|-3| - 2|-5|$$
$$4(3) - 2(5)$$
$$12 - 10 = 2$$

ANSWER: (C)

18.
ANALYSIS

Substitute the possible answers into the given inequality.

WORK

$x = 1, y = 9:$
$$3x + 5 < y$$
$$3(1) + 5 < 9$$
$$3 + 5 < 9$$
$$8 < 9 ✔$$

ANSWER: (E)

19.
ANALYSIS

Arrange both polynomials in the same alphabetical order and then use the rules of addition.

WORK

$$7a - 6b + 4c$$
$$+ \; -3a - 8b + 5c$$
$$\overline{4a - 14b + 9c}$$

ANSWER: (B)

20.

ANALYSIS

Develop a chart for all the given information and then add all their weights.

WORK

Mildred's weight: $\qquad x - 3$
Hector's weight: $(x-3) + 8 = x - 3 + 8 = x + 5$
Stacey's weight: $(x+5) - 12 = x + 5 - 12 = x - 7$
Total weights: $\qquad 3x - 5$

ANSWER: (D)

21.

ANALYSIS

Remove the absolute value signs and then multiply all the numbers.

WORK

$$-2|\,5| \cdot 3\,|-4| = (-2)(5)(3)(4) = -120$$

ANSWER: (C)

22.

ANALYSIS

$$\text{ratio} = \frac{\text{height of door in the blueprint}}{\text{height of actual door}}$$

WORK

$$\text{ratio} = \frac{\frac{3}{4} \text{ inch}}{8 \text{ ft}}$$

1 foot = 12 inches: $= \dfrac{\frac{3}{4} \text{ inch}}{8 \times 12} = \dfrac{\frac{3}{4} \text{ inch}}{96 \text{ inches}}$

$$= \left(\frac{3}{4}\right) \div (96)$$

$$= \frac{3}{4} \times \frac{1}{96} = \frac{1}{128}$$

ANSWER: (D)

23.

ANALYSIS

The best way to solve an abstract example like this is to substitute some numbers. We need a first positive consecutive even integer, so let's let $a = 4$. Then we need two following integers, so let $b = 5$ and $c = 6$. Now we can test all the statements and determine which one is false.

WORK

$$ac \text{ is odd}$$
$$4(6) \text{ is odd}$$
$$24 \text{ is odd; False}$$

ANSWER: (C)

24.

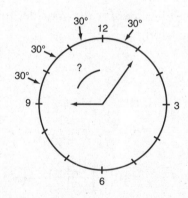

ANALYSIS

There are 360° in a circle and the hours 1–12 divide the circle into 12 sections. If we divide 360° by 12, we find that there are 30° in each section.

WORK

As the diagram clearly shows, there are four sections between the hands of the clock at 9:05, so 4 × 30° = 120°.

ANSWER: (A)

Note: This example is a simplification, for at 9:05, the hour hand is slightly higher than the 9 and the real answer is slightly smaller than 120°.

25.

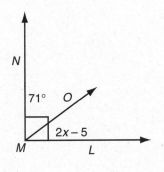

ANALYSIS

The two angles are complementary.

WORK

$$(2x - 5) + 71 = 90$$
$$2x + 66 = 90$$
$$2x = 24$$
$$x = 12$$

ANSWER: (E)

ISEE Practice Test 1
ANSWER SHEET

Section 1 Verbal Reasoning

1 Ⓐ Ⓑ Ⓒ Ⓓ	9 Ⓐ Ⓑ Ⓒ Ⓓ	17 Ⓐ Ⓑ Ⓒ Ⓓ	25 Ⓐ Ⓑ Ⓒ Ⓓ	33 Ⓐ Ⓑ Ⓒ Ⓓ
2 Ⓐ Ⓑ Ⓒ Ⓓ	10 Ⓐ Ⓑ Ⓒ Ⓓ	18 Ⓐ Ⓑ Ⓒ Ⓓ	26 Ⓐ Ⓑ Ⓒ Ⓓ	34 Ⓐ Ⓑ Ⓒ Ⓓ
3 Ⓐ Ⓑ Ⓒ Ⓓ	11 Ⓐ Ⓑ Ⓒ Ⓓ	19 Ⓐ Ⓑ Ⓒ Ⓓ	27 Ⓐ Ⓑ Ⓒ Ⓓ	35 Ⓐ Ⓑ Ⓒ Ⓓ
4 Ⓐ Ⓑ Ⓒ Ⓓ	12 Ⓐ Ⓑ Ⓒ Ⓓ	20 Ⓐ Ⓑ Ⓒ Ⓓ	28 Ⓐ Ⓑ Ⓒ Ⓓ	36 Ⓐ Ⓑ Ⓒ Ⓓ
5 Ⓐ Ⓑ Ⓒ Ⓓ	13 Ⓐ Ⓑ Ⓒ Ⓓ	21 Ⓐ Ⓑ Ⓒ Ⓓ	29 Ⓐ Ⓑ Ⓒ Ⓓ	37 Ⓐ Ⓑ Ⓒ Ⓓ
6 Ⓐ Ⓑ Ⓒ Ⓓ	14 Ⓐ Ⓑ Ⓒ Ⓓ	22 Ⓐ Ⓑ Ⓒ Ⓓ	30 Ⓐ Ⓑ Ⓒ Ⓓ	38 Ⓐ Ⓑ Ⓒ Ⓓ
7 Ⓐ Ⓑ Ⓒ Ⓓ	15 Ⓐ Ⓑ Ⓒ Ⓓ	23 Ⓐ Ⓑ Ⓒ Ⓓ	31 Ⓐ Ⓑ Ⓒ Ⓓ	39 Ⓐ Ⓑ Ⓒ Ⓓ
8 Ⓐ Ⓑ Ⓒ Ⓓ	16 Ⓐ Ⓑ Ⓒ Ⓓ	24 Ⓐ Ⓑ Ⓒ Ⓓ	32 Ⓐ Ⓑ Ⓒ Ⓓ	40 Ⓐ Ⓑ Ⓒ Ⓓ

Section 2 Quantitative Reasoning

1 Ⓐ Ⓑ Ⓒ Ⓓ	9 Ⓐ Ⓑ Ⓒ Ⓓ	17 Ⓐ Ⓑ Ⓒ Ⓓ	25 Ⓐ Ⓑ Ⓒ Ⓓ	33 Ⓐ Ⓑ Ⓒ Ⓓ
2 Ⓐ Ⓑ Ⓒ Ⓓ	10 Ⓐ Ⓑ Ⓒ Ⓓ	18 Ⓐ Ⓑ Ⓒ Ⓓ	26 Ⓐ Ⓑ Ⓒ Ⓓ	34 Ⓐ Ⓑ Ⓒ Ⓓ
3 Ⓐ Ⓑ Ⓒ Ⓓ	11 Ⓐ Ⓑ Ⓒ Ⓓ	19 Ⓐ Ⓑ Ⓒ Ⓓ	27 Ⓐ Ⓑ Ⓒ Ⓓ	35 Ⓐ Ⓑ Ⓒ Ⓓ
4 Ⓐ Ⓑ Ⓒ Ⓓ	12 Ⓐ Ⓑ Ⓒ Ⓓ	20 Ⓐ Ⓑ Ⓒ Ⓓ	28 Ⓐ Ⓑ Ⓒ Ⓓ	36 Ⓐ Ⓑ Ⓒ Ⓓ
5 Ⓐ Ⓑ Ⓒ Ⓓ	13 Ⓐ Ⓑ Ⓒ Ⓓ	21 Ⓐ Ⓑ Ⓒ Ⓓ	29 Ⓐ Ⓑ Ⓒ Ⓓ	37 Ⓐ Ⓑ Ⓒ Ⓓ
6 Ⓐ Ⓑ Ⓒ Ⓓ	14 Ⓐ Ⓑ Ⓒ Ⓓ	22 Ⓐ Ⓑ Ⓒ Ⓓ	30 Ⓐ Ⓑ Ⓒ Ⓓ	
7 Ⓐ Ⓑ Ⓒ Ⓓ	15 Ⓐ Ⓑ Ⓒ Ⓓ	23 Ⓐ Ⓑ Ⓒ Ⓓ	31 Ⓐ Ⓑ Ⓒ Ⓓ	
8 Ⓐ Ⓑ Ⓒ Ⓓ	16 Ⓐ Ⓑ Ⓒ Ⓓ	24 Ⓐ Ⓑ Ⓒ Ⓓ	32 Ⓐ Ⓑ Ⓒ Ⓓ	

Section 3 Reading Comprehension

1 Ⓐ Ⓑ Ⓒ Ⓓ	9 Ⓐ Ⓑ Ⓒ Ⓓ	17 Ⓐ Ⓑ Ⓒ Ⓓ	25 Ⓐ Ⓑ Ⓒ Ⓓ	33 Ⓐ Ⓑ Ⓒ Ⓓ
2 Ⓐ Ⓑ Ⓒ Ⓓ	10 Ⓐ Ⓑ Ⓒ Ⓓ	18 Ⓐ Ⓑ Ⓒ Ⓓ	26 Ⓐ Ⓑ Ⓒ Ⓓ	34 Ⓐ Ⓑ Ⓒ Ⓓ
3 Ⓐ Ⓑ Ⓒ Ⓓ	11 Ⓐ Ⓑ Ⓒ Ⓓ	19 Ⓐ Ⓑ Ⓒ Ⓓ	27 Ⓐ Ⓑ Ⓒ Ⓓ	35 Ⓐ Ⓑ Ⓒ Ⓓ
4 Ⓐ Ⓑ Ⓒ Ⓓ	12 Ⓐ Ⓑ Ⓒ Ⓓ	20 Ⓐ Ⓑ Ⓒ Ⓓ	28 Ⓐ Ⓑ Ⓒ Ⓓ	36 Ⓐ Ⓑ Ⓒ Ⓓ
5 Ⓐ Ⓑ Ⓒ Ⓓ	13 Ⓐ Ⓑ Ⓒ Ⓓ	21 Ⓐ Ⓑ Ⓒ Ⓓ	29 Ⓐ Ⓑ Ⓒ Ⓓ	
6 Ⓐ Ⓑ Ⓒ Ⓓ	14 Ⓐ Ⓑ Ⓒ Ⓓ	22 Ⓐ Ⓑ Ⓒ Ⓓ	30 Ⓐ Ⓑ Ⓒ Ⓓ	
7 Ⓐ Ⓑ Ⓒ Ⓓ	15 Ⓐ Ⓑ Ⓒ Ⓓ	23 Ⓐ Ⓑ Ⓒ Ⓓ	31 Ⓐ Ⓑ Ⓒ Ⓓ	
8 Ⓐ Ⓑ Ⓒ Ⓓ	16 Ⓐ Ⓑ Ⓒ Ⓓ	24 Ⓐ Ⓑ Ⓒ Ⓓ	32 Ⓐ Ⓑ Ⓒ Ⓓ	

ISEE Practice Test 1

ANSWER SHEET

Section 4 Mathematics Achievement

1 Ⓐ Ⓑ Ⓒ Ⓓ 11 Ⓐ Ⓑ Ⓒ Ⓓ 21 Ⓐ Ⓑ Ⓒ Ⓓ 31 Ⓐ Ⓑ Ⓒ Ⓓ 41 Ⓐ Ⓑ Ⓒ Ⓓ
2 Ⓐ Ⓑ Ⓒ Ⓓ 12 Ⓐ Ⓑ Ⓒ Ⓓ 22 Ⓐ Ⓑ Ⓒ Ⓓ 32 Ⓐ Ⓑ Ⓒ Ⓓ 42 Ⓐ Ⓑ Ⓒ Ⓓ
3 Ⓐ Ⓑ Ⓒ Ⓓ 13 Ⓐ Ⓑ Ⓒ Ⓓ 23 Ⓐ Ⓑ Ⓒ Ⓓ 33 Ⓐ Ⓑ Ⓒ Ⓓ 43 Ⓐ Ⓑ Ⓒ Ⓓ
4 Ⓐ Ⓑ Ⓒ Ⓓ 14 Ⓐ Ⓑ Ⓒ Ⓓ 24 Ⓐ Ⓑ Ⓒ Ⓓ 34 Ⓐ Ⓑ Ⓒ Ⓓ 44 Ⓐ Ⓑ Ⓒ Ⓓ
5 Ⓐ Ⓑ Ⓒ Ⓓ 15 Ⓐ Ⓑ Ⓒ Ⓓ 25 Ⓐ Ⓑ Ⓒ Ⓓ 35 Ⓐ Ⓑ Ⓒ Ⓓ 45 Ⓐ Ⓑ Ⓒ Ⓓ
6 Ⓐ Ⓑ Ⓒ Ⓓ 16 Ⓐ Ⓑ Ⓒ Ⓓ 26 Ⓐ Ⓑ Ⓒ Ⓓ 36 Ⓐ Ⓑ Ⓒ Ⓓ 46 Ⓐ Ⓑ Ⓒ Ⓓ
7 Ⓐ Ⓑ Ⓒ Ⓓ 17 Ⓐ Ⓑ Ⓒ Ⓓ 27 Ⓐ Ⓑ Ⓒ Ⓓ 37 Ⓐ Ⓑ Ⓒ Ⓓ 47 Ⓐ Ⓑ Ⓒ Ⓓ
8 Ⓐ Ⓑ Ⓒ Ⓓ 18 Ⓐ Ⓑ Ⓒ Ⓓ 28 Ⓐ Ⓑ Ⓒ Ⓓ 38 Ⓐ Ⓑ Ⓒ Ⓓ
9 Ⓐ Ⓑ Ⓒ Ⓓ 19 Ⓐ Ⓑ Ⓒ Ⓓ 29 Ⓐ Ⓑ Ⓒ Ⓓ 39 Ⓐ Ⓑ Ⓒ Ⓓ
10 Ⓐ Ⓑ Ⓒ Ⓓ 20 Ⓐ Ⓑ Ⓒ Ⓓ 30 Ⓐ Ⓑ Ⓒ Ⓓ 40 Ⓐ Ⓑ Ⓒ Ⓓ

SECTION 1 VERBAL REASONING

40 questions   *20 minutes*

Directions: Choose the word that means the same or most nearly the same as the capitalized word.

Sample:
IRATE

(A) angry
(B) loyal
(C) calculating
(D) pleasant

● Ⓑ Ⓒ Ⓓ

1. MALIGNANT

   (A) possessive
   (B) deadly
   (C) positive
   (D) parallel

2. LIBERATE

   (A) weigh
   (B) think
   (C) listen
   (D) free

3. SEVER

   (A) torment
   (B) divide
   (C) repair
   (D) agree

4. STATIONARY

   (A) unmoving
   (B) writing
   (C) guarding
   (D) driving

5. UNIFORMITY

   (A) sameness
   (B) stubbornness
   (C) diversity
   (D) wardrobe

6. OBSCURE

   (A) vague
   (B) transparent
   (C) clear
   (D) perfect

7. PREJUDICE

   (A) legality
   (B) bias
   (C) opinion
   (D) decision

8. CONGENIAL

   (A) suitable
   (B) intelligent
   (C) magical
   (D) supernatural

9. RESILIENT

   (A) flexible
   (B) rigid
   (C) unmoving
   (D) serene

10. LETHARGY

    (A) inactivity
    (B) speed
    (C) efficiency
    (D) poison

11. DONOR

    (A) hermit
    (B) doctor
    (C) contributor
    (D) misanthrope

12. SHRILL

    (A) piercing
    (B) melodious
    (C) low
    (D) rumbling

13. PUNCTUAL

    (A) prompt
    (B) late
    (C) rude
    (D) careless

14. DEVISE

    (A) startle
    (B) bluff
    (C) create
    (D) outwit

15. NOTORIOUS

    (A) infamous
    (B) honorable
    (C) hopeful
    (D) fast

16. JEOPARDY

    (A) game
    (B) peril
    (C) twice
    (D) knowledge

17. SCRUTINY

    (A) revision
    (B) ignorance
    (C) examination
    (D) liability

18. BIODEGRADE

    (A) reminisce
    (B) investigate
    (C) divulge
    (D) decay

19. VORACIOUS

    (A) hungry
    (B) loud
    (C) foolish
    (D) vast

20. REVERSAL

    (A) inversion
    (B) agreement
    (C) indecision
    (D) regret

Part Two Sentence Completion

Directions: Fill in the word or words that best complete the following sentences.

Sample:
Although Edwards was shown to be driven and unforgiving throughout the novel, he shows_____ in the closing moments.

(A) anger
(B) stubbornness
(C) fear
(D) mercy

Ⓐ Ⓑ Ⓒ ●

21. Because he was a dedicated_____, Darrell opposed using any military action in the troubled area.

    (A) soldier
    (B) industrialist
    (C) agitator
    (D) pacifist

22. The author did not live to see his work completed, but his children published the novel_____.

    (A) anonymously
    (B) posthumously
    (C) consecutively
    (D) carefully

23. Everyone seemed afraid to talk, so I finally_____the topic.

    (A) disproved
    (B) chose
    (C) broached
    (D) researched

24. Even though I am a patient reader, I couldn't follow the_____directions.

    (A) laconic
    (B) specific
    (C) incorrect
    (D) verbose

25. No one has discovered a practical use for the appendix in the human body, so it seems to be a_____organ.

    (A) superfluous
    (B) crucial
    (C) functioning
    (D) decaying

26. Greg always puts off mowing the lawn because it is such a/an_____task for him.

    (A) odious
    (B) attractive
    (C) meditative
    (D) exhilarating

27. Itoro and Daisy made up quickly; their argument was really a _____ disagreement.

    (A) serious
    (B) violent
    (C) stunning
    (D) petty

28. It was a perfect afternoon for a picnic: a warm sun, a clear sky, and a gentle _____.

    (A) zephyr
    (B) caress
    (C) whisper
    (D) animal

29. Many cartoon animals are _____, talking, wearing clothing, and walking on two legs.

    (A) anthropomorphic
    (B) intelligent
    (C) omnipotent
    (D) inanimate

30. We were all relieved when the doctor found her condition to be _____.

    (A) malingering
    (B) benign
    (C) munificent
    (D) choleric

31. Did you hear Ms. Lichtenfeld speak yesterday? It was an interesting _____.

    (A) book
    (B) rhetoric
    (C) melody
    (D) lecture

32. After a long, hard day at work, Serafina finds a hot bath to be a welcome _____.

    (A) aversion
    (B) solace
    (C) responsibility
    (D) reconciliation

33. I was so bored during the presentation that I found it difficult to _____ interest.

    (A) feign
    (B) reproduce
    (C) manipulate
    (D) inhibit

34. When I need advice, I go to my grandfather, who is known for his _____.

    (A) sagacity
    (B) health
    (C) frailty
    (D) age

35. After years of saving and investing, Barney managed to _____ a great deal of wealth.

    (A) amass
    (B) spread
    (C) distribute
    (D) detest

36. He never knew who paid for his scholarship, for Pip's education was supplied by an anonymous _____.

    (A) author
    (B) benefactor
    (C) request
    (D) antagonist

37. Paulina never_____, but pressed on_____.

    (A) faltered . . . resolutely
    (B) failed . . . uselessly
    (C) finished . . . until the end
    (D) spoke . . . garrulously

38. The discipline in her classroom was too_____, resulting in an atmosphere of total_____.

    (A) strict . . . lassitude
    (B) loose . . . restriction
    (C) ambiguous . . . clarity
    (D) lax . . . anarchy

39. Mrs. Duncan was a_____worker, known for her_____and eye for detail.

    (A) tireless . . . dreaming
    (B) careful . . . lethargy
    (C) meticulous . . . precision
    (D) sloppy . . . zeal

40. The senator refused to take a side, remaining_____as he tried to reach a_____.

    (A) belligerent . . . point
    (B) nonpartisan . . . compromise
    (C) calm . . . milestone
    (D) biased . . . decision

STOP

IF YOU FINISH BEFORE TIME IS UP, YOU MAY CHECK YOUR WORK ON THIS SECTION ONLY. DO NOT TURN TO ANY OTHER SECTION IN THE TEST.

ISEE Practice Test 1

SECTION 2 QUANTITATIVE REASONING

37 questions   *35 minutes*

Directions: This section is a multiple-choice test. Work out the problems and, from the four choices given, select the best answer.

Sample:
If the volume of a cube is 0.216, find one edge.

(A) 6
(B) 0.06
(C) 0.6
(D) 0.006

1. Let k represent the length of a rectangle. Represent the perimeter when the width is 8 less than the length.

   (A) $6k - 6$
   (B) $2k + 16$
   (C) $4k - 10$
   (D) $4k - 16$

2. In the three digit number $49x$, x represents units. The number is divisible by 4. If the sum of the digits is divisible by 5, what is the number?

   (A) 493
   (B) 498
   (C) 496
   (D) 492

3. Find the shaded area if the radius of the outer circle is 8 inches and the radius of the inner circle is 5 inches. Let $\pi = 3.14$.

   (A) 198.44
   (B) 234.82
   (C) 122.46
   (D) 202.56

4. $5\sqrt{2} \times 3\sqrt{8} =$

   (A) $10\sqrt{24}$
   (B) $\sqrt{10}\sqrt{16}$
   (C) 60
   (D) 40

5. Thirty math books were distributed to an algebra class at the beginning of the semester. Four books were lost, and the rest were returned. In simplest terms, what is the ratio of returned books to lost books?

   (A) 5/4
   (B) 17/9
   (C) 5/13
   (D) 13/2

6. If x is a positive number and y is a negative number, which of the following statements is true?

   (A) $\dfrac{x}{y} > 0$
   (B) $xy < 0$
   (C) $x^2 < 0$
   (D) $y^2 < 0$

7. The sum of 6 and the quotient of 60 and a number is equal to the product of two-thirds and 15. Find the number.

   (A) 10
   (B) 20
   (C) 6
   (D) 15

8. Henry receives a salary of $530 per week. José gets 30% more than Henry. If they both receive $70 per week raises, how much will José be earning?

   (A) $650 (B) $458 (C) $759 (D) $568

9. This circle graph indicates how the average high school student spends his/her 24-hour day.

   How many hours does the average student spend on personal items?

   (A) 4.2 hours
   (B) 2.7 hours
   (C) 1.9 hours
   (D) 3.6 hours

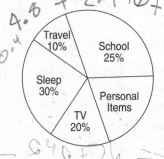

Travel 10%
School 25%
Sleep 30%
Personal Items
TV 20%

10. A 25-foot tree casts a shadow of 15 feet. How long is the shadow of a nearby 300-foot building if the tree and its shadow are in the same ratio as the building and its shadow?

    (A) 180 ft
    (B) 120 ft
    (C) 200 ft
    (D) 140 ft

11. Twenty-four students in a class are right-handed and 6 are left-handed. If these figures represent the entire class, what percent is left-handed?

    (A) 15%
    (B) 25%
    (C) 20%
    (D) 30%

12. Find side *BC* of the adjoining right angle.

    (A) 12
    (B) 18
    (C) 19
    (D) 15

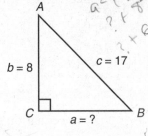

$b = 8$ $c = 17$ $a = ?$ A C B

13. Find the value of $5.3 \times 10^3 - 1.3 \times 10^2$.

    (A) 3,450
    (B) 5,170
    (C) 660
    (D) 5,480

14. Excluding the number 1, what is the sum of all the prime factors of 50?

    (A) 12
    (B) 9
    (C) 15
    (D) 10

15. Find the value of the expression $4xy + 5z^2$ when $x = 4$, $y = -3$, and $z = -2$.

    (A) −6
    (B) 18
    (C) −18
    (D) −28

16. Find 20% of 30% of 180.

    (A) 12.4
    (B) 6.6
    (C) 9.4
    (D) 10.8

17. Determine the answers to the following problems and then choose the correct statement.

    (a) 0.15/3
    (b) 15/0.3
    (c) 1.5/0.3

    (A) *a* is less than *b* and also greater than *c*.
    (B) *b* is greater than *c*, and *a* is less than *c*.
    (C) *c* is greater than *b* or less than *a*.
    (D) *a* is less than *c*, which is greater than *b*.

18. Which of the following numbers can satisfy the inequality $-2.4 < 3x \le 3.6$?

(A) 0

(B) -2.4

(C) -1.8

(D) 2

19. Write the equation of a line that has a slope of 3 and passes through the point (2, 5).

(A) $y = 4x + 1$

(B) $y = 2x + 3$

(C) $y = x + 4$

(D) $y = 3x - 1$

20. Change 5.003% to a decimal.

(A) 0.05003

(B) 5.003

(C) 0.5003

(D) 50.03

21. Which of the the following expressions is the **smallest**?

(A) $4^2 + 5(9 - 3)$

(B) $3 \cdot 17 - 4 \cdot 6$

(C) $7 + 9 \cdot 4 - 6(9 - 7)^3$

(D) $6 - 2 + 48/6$

22. Find the value of $5.3 \times 10^3 - 1.3 \times 10^2$.

(A) 345

(B) 5,310

(C) 5,170

(D) 540

Directions for Questions 23–37.

In each question, simplify both expressions and then compare them.

Select A if the expression in column A is the greater one.

Select B if the expression in column B is the greater one.

Select C if the two expressions are equal.

Select D if the relationship cannot be determined.

Column A	Column B
23. $3 \times (0.4)^2$	$4 \times (0.3)^2$
24. The area of a triangle whose base is 6 and whose height is 5.	The area of a rectangle with a base of 5 and a height of 4.

25.

Column A	Column B
The measure of $\angle A$.	The measure of $\angle B$.
26. $15\% \times 25\% \times \$56$	$\dfrac{7}{9} \times \$2.70$

<u>Column A</u>	<u>Column B</u>
27. $(0.8)^3$	$(0.5)^4$
28. Excluding the number 1, the sum of the prime factors of 20.	Excluding the number 1, the sum of the prime factors of 18.

29. Let $y = 4$.

$3y + 8$	$7y - 12$
30. x^3	x^2
31. The distance traveled at the rate of 56 mph from 9:30 A.M. to 1 P.M.	430 miles
32. $4\sqrt{8}$	$2\sqrt{32}$

33.

The absolute distance from 3 to −2.	The absolute distance from −1 to 4.
34. If two unbiased coins are tossed, the probability of obtaining two heads.	$\dfrac{1}{4}$
35. 2 kilograms	1,800 grams
36. Eight more than two-fifths of 35.	$\sqrt{625}$
37. The average of $\dfrac{1}{3}$ and $\dfrac{3}{8}$.	$\dfrac{1}{4}$

STOP

IF YOU FINISH BEFORE TIME IS UP, YOU MAY CHECK YOUR WORK ON THIS SECTION ONLY. DO NOT TURN TO ANY OTHER SECTION IN THE TEST.

ISEE Practice Test 1

SECTION 3 READING COMPREHENSION

36 questions   *35 minutes*

> **Directions:** Each passage is followed by questions based on its content. Answer the questions following the passage on the basis of what is **stated** or **implied** in that passage.

Passage for Questions 1–5

They're called typhoons in China and *baquios* in the Philippines. They're called willy-willies in Australia and cyclones in India. Whichever of these names you prefer, they all refer to the same phenomenon: hurricanes.
Line Meteorologists define hurricanes as windstorms in which the air currents
(5) blow more than 75 miles per hour. They come from deep within the West Indies, moving west with the trade winds. However, the Earth's rotation causes them to veer right, moving across the Caribbean into the Atlantic Ocean. Here they often increase in size and strength, nourished by the warm waters. They vary in intensity, containing winds that can blow up
(10) to 150 miles per hour.

Hurricanes, though slow moving, can be quite devastating. They bring with them enormous amounts of rainfall, usually resulting in widespread flooding. They also bring high winds, winds that can knock down buildings, throw planes off course, and send normally earth-bound objects into
(15) the topmost branches of trees. While they are not as capricious as their tornado counterparts, they can have a malicious nature, leaving some houses merely water damaged while completely destroying others.

Despite these dire facts, people, even those who must deal with hurricanes annually, often do not take hurricanes seriously enough; folks in
(20) Louisiana, for example, have been known to have "Hurricane Parties" upon hearing of an approaching storm. Rather than preparing for the onslaught by putting masking tape on windows, filling bathtubs with fresh water, and storing up extra batteries and flashlights, people spike tropical punch and foolishly sit out on their porches, watching for the eye of the
(25) storm.

1. The writer's main purpose is apparently_____.

   (A) to encourage people to take hurricane preparations lightly
   (B) to convince people that hurricanes are more deadly than tornados
   (C) to inform people about basic facts about hurricanes
   (D) to talk about 1968's Hurricane Camille's effects on Southern Louisiana

2. Why do you think that the author includes synonyms for the name "hurricane" in the opening statement?

   (A) to show how stupid some of the names sound
   (B) to grab the reader's attention
   (C) to increase his/her word count
   (D) to explain why hurricanes have such high winds

3. Which of the following best describes how the author feels about Hurricane Parties?

   (A) scornful
   (B) eager to join
   (C) jealous
   (D) excited

4. According to the article, where do hurricanes develop?

   (A) the West Indies
   (B) the Philippines
   (C) India
   (D) Australia

5. Based on the information in this passage, the reader can infer that_____.

   (A) the author is from Louisiana
   (B) the author is a meteorologist
   (C) the author has studied hurricanes quite a bit
   (D) the author always boards up his/her windows during a storm

Passage for Questions 6–10

Line
(5)

Setting tables with knife (edge in) and spoon on the right side of the plate and the fork on the left. Using salad forks *and* regular forks, teaspoons *and* tablespoons *and* dessert spoons. Drinking out of water *and* wine glasses. Rinsing our fingertips in perfumed fingerbowls. These are all examples of what Americans consider polite behavior at mealtime. They are customs that we follow—or of which we are aware, even if we do not follow them. But where did they come from?

(10)

These niceties are by-products of advanced cultures. When a population is breaking its back trying to establish a stable economy and decent housing, it doesn't have any time to spare making sure people aren't spitting on the carpet. Only after the majority of a culture's population reaches a stable, reasonably affluent level can members of that society think about luxuries like multiple clean outfits, nice possessions, and good manners.

(15)

(20)

But, how cultures choose the manners they choose remains a mystery. Why do we use the right hand when shaking hands rather than the left? Why is it not okay to wear white after Labor Day? Why do men remove their hats in the presence of ladies, but ladies wear theirs in all situations? Why is it not okay to point? Often what we consider polite conflicts with what other nations think is polite. We think it is rude to burp during a meal, but *not* burping after a meal in some cultures is a deep insult. We think it polite to maintain eye contact here in the states, whereas it is rude to do so in other parts of the world.

(25)

It would be convenient if we all used the same standards of polite behavior, but it would also be less interesting. Humanity has created a wide variety of amazing and wonderful permanent things. It has tamed wildernesses, constructed sprawling cities, and brought forth beautiful musical and artistic works. But in the process, it has also brought forth things that are confusing and inconsistent, like manners. And, really, we wouldn't want it any other way.

6. Which of the following is considered impolite in some countries?

   (A) not burping after a meal
   (B) making eye contact
   (C) women wearing hats
   (D) putting the knife (edge in) on the right side of the plate

7. Which of the following can we infer about the author?

   (A) S/he has traveled abroad.
   (B) S/he hates other cultures.
   (C) S/he is intrigued by human nature.
   (D) S/he is very unmannered much of the time.

8. The title that best expressed the ideas of this passage is?

   (A) To Spit or Not to Spit
   (B) The Ugly American
   (C) Anything Goes
   (D) Handsome Is as Handsome Does

9. Based on the information in the passage, which of the following is permissible in some parts of the world but not in America?

   (A) making eye contact
   (B) using water and wine glasses during a meal
   (C) chewing with the mouth open
   (D) burping

10. Which of the following is most likely to be true, based on the passage?

   (A) The standards of polite behavior in Australia are better than those in England.
   (B) We cannot keep track of all the various etiquette systems in the world.
   (C) Polite behavior in Africa will be the same as that in the United States.
   (D) Manners in Cuba will likely be different from those in the United States.

Passage for Questions 11–15

Line

(5)

(10)

(15)

(20)

Many people walk away from science and math classes wondering when they will ever need the skills they learn there. Although it's easy to see the practicality of English, keyboarding, and business marketing classes, it's difficult to see the value of learning that force equals mass multiplied by distance; it's hard to understand how we'll ever use differential calculus again. All most of us need is the ability to balance our checkbooks.

Science and math classes put into perspective millions of events that occur in our daily lives, events that we take for granted. The force of two cars colliding at high speeds, the calculations necessary for planes to take off, the chemical reactions that allow flour, yeast, egg, and water to become hot bread from the oven—all of these combine infinite amounts of scientific and mathematical data.

Take, for example, esters. Scientists define esters as compounds formed when an acid combines with a solid. Most oils, waxes, and plastics fall into this category. Now, this definition of esters is quite accurate; however, it is too clinical for most of us to wrap our heads around. What kind of acid? What kind of solid? What kind of reaction?

Yet, you run into esters in your daily life—more often than you might think. Every room deodorizer you plug in, every squirt of dish detergent you squeeze into the kitchen sink, every piece of gum you pop into your mouth—they all contain esters. Esters, in short, provide odors, especially the odors of bananas, oranges, and pineapples.

11. The passage mainly sets out to convince the reader that_____.

    (A) science and math classes are useless to everyone but science and math majors
    (B) science and math classes are useful, even to people who are not science and math majors
    (C) esters are harmful and should be eradicated
    (D) the calculations necessary for planes to take off are the result of magical incantations

12. What is an example of an ester?

    (A) the color of fruit-flavored gum
    (B) the texture of fruit-flavored gum
    (C) the taste of fruit-flavored gum
    (D) the smell of fruit-flavored gum

13. Which of the following definitions most closely fits the word *clinical* in line 16?

    (A) technical
    (B) medical
    (C) cold
    (D) operational

14. How does the author feel about science and math classes?

    (A) S/he finds them dull and useless.
    (B) S/he finds them difficult to understand.
    (C) S/he finds them easy to understand.
    (D) S/he finds them useful in most areas of life.

15. The author would most likely include _____ next in his/her discussion.

    (A) more information about esters
    (B) some information about flying planes
    (C) an example of something learned in math class that takes place routinely
    (D) a discussion of why most room deodorizers smell like citrus fruits

Passage for Questions 16–22

As the world grows more complex and more chaotic, we humans find events spinning increasingly beyond our control. Natural disasters, disease, and, more recently, terrorist attacks and abductions plague our daily inter-
Line actions. It becomes more and more difficult for us to treat activities like
(5) riding on an airplane or opening the mail like the simple tasks they once were.

Now more than ever, psychologists say, people desire control over their personal lives. Because they can't get control of the big things, people are increasingly settling for control over smaller things—like organizing the
(10) sock drawer and uncluttering the kitchen. In our small way, therefore, we're trying to make order out of chaos.

This need to create a haven from the outside world is starting to affect how we build our houses, in particular, our bathrooms. Increasingly, we find things in the bathrooms that we once associated with entertainment
(15) rooms. People now install wide screen television sets and surround sound stereo systems. They replace the old 5½ by 3 foot, white porcelain tub with Jacuzzis that can hold five people. Some people even shell out big bucks for showerheads that create colored light displays as the water falls; feeling excited about going out? Switch on the red light. Feeling stressed?
(20) Click on the blue light. Contractors even offer grandiose toilets that do all the work for you; you don't need toilet paper, and you don't have to flush.

Now, the idea of creating the perfect bathroom may strike you as strange. Yet, consider how much time we spend in the bathrooms. From
(25) getting clean to getting dressed to just relaxing in hot water, we spend huge amounts of time in the porcelain palace. Doesn't it make sense to indulge in <u>accoutrements</u> that enhance the places in which we spend time—and to cut back in places in which we don't?

16. What does the article say triggers such extravagant attention to the bathroom?

    (A) stress about the workplace
    (B) stress about world events
    (C) stress about gaining weight
    (D) stress about entertainment systems

17. The main idea of this selection may be expressed as_____.

    (A) when times get tough, the tough get going.
    (B) when the going gets tough, the tough take a bath.
    (C) when the road is weary, the traveler presses on.
    (D) when time runs out, the first one across the finish line is the winner.

18. Which of the following is not something that causes people stress, according to the article?

    (A) terrorist attacks
    (B) opening the mail
    (C) working late hours
    (D) riding in an airplane

19. Which of the following best describes the author of this passage?

    (A) an emotional hypochondriac who fears much about the world
    (B) an agile, tough-minded leader who trains people in stress-relief through yoga
    (C) an unbiased observer of human behavior
    (D) an outgoing, enthusiastic huntsman who believes in military readiness

20. The first paragraph primarily consists of a description of_____.

    (A) various stresses affecting people today
    (B) people's reaction to the stresses affecting them
    (C) a specific example that illustrates clearly people's reaction to stress
    (D) the author's justification of people's reaction to stress

21. Based on the information in this passage, the reader can infer that_____.

    (A) people probably eat out more than they once did.
    (B) people probably listen to music more than they once did.
    (C) people probably spend more money on bubble bath than they once did.
    (D) people probably spend more time watching TV than they once did.

22. The word *accoutrements*, as used in line 27, can best be described as_____.

    (A) furnishings.
    (B) admonishments.
    (C) compliments.
    (D) hair care items.

Passage for Questions 23–30

Line
(5)

(10)

(15)

(20)

It is the year 1994 in the city of Surat in the northwest region of India. You are the child of a poor family without any means of transportation; otherwise, you would have left the city weeks ago. Now, it's too late; you cannot leave, though you dearly wish you could. A police-enforced quarantine has the city locked down. Plague has struck the city.

You hear horror stories daily about how the victims die—burning to death with fever, breathless, with lymph nodes at the underarm and leg area sometimes swelling to the size of grapefruits. Doctors have been treating the disease with antibiotics, specifically tetracycline, but the success the drugs are having in 1994 is eclipsed by the dread that grips the remaining population. You seem to be one of the lucky ones who will live to tell this tale, for you seem to have escaped the clutches of the pneumonic plague.

You learn later that pneumonic plague, often called simply "plague" or "the black death," is caused by *Pasteurella pestis* or sometimes *Yersinia pestis*. It is a bacillus carried by the fleas that live on rats, squirrels, and other rodents. The bacillus is versatile and can take on three different forms. It can attack the lymph nodes (bubonic), the lungs (pneumonic), and the blood (septicemic). Although all three types of plague are deadly, the worst by far is the septicemic variety, which attacks the bloodstream so severely and so quickly that the victim dies before the bubonic or pneumonic varieties can develop. Even though plague has mostly been eradicated, it rears its ugly head in regions that lack good insect and rodent control and water purification.

23. Which of the following best summarizes the purpose of paragraph three?

    (A) It personalizes the discussion by using direct address.
    (B) It broadens the discussion by bringing in information about other diseases, like malaria.
    (C) It enhances the discussion by incorporating factual detail about plague.
    (D) It summarizes the discussion by bringing the debate to an end.

24. What is another name for plague?

    (A) *Erstina pestis*
    (B) *Pulcinella pestis*
    (C) *Jersine pestis*
    (D) *Yersinia pestis*

25. What form of plague is called septicemia?

    (A) Plague that strikes the lungs worst.
    (B) Plague that strikes the bloodstream worst.
    (C) Plague that strikes the heart worst.
    (D) Plague that strikes the lymph nodes worst.

26. What can be done by the city of Surat to ensure that plague doesn't strike as easily next time?

    (A) encourage the growth of the city's rat population
    (B) close down the ports
    (C) build more hospitals and train more doctors
    (D) fund more programs that eradicate rodents and insects

27. Why would quarantining the city of Surat help stop the transmission of plague?

    (A) Quarantining reduces the number of rats that enter the city.
    (B) Quarantining increases the number of insects that enter the city.
    (C) Quarantining reduces the number of human carriers that can leave the city.
    (D) Quarantining increases the amount of medicine that can enter the city.

28. In what year did the city of Surat suffer an outbreak of plague?

    (A) 2004
    (B) 1894
    (C) 1994
    (D) It has never experienced an outbreak of plague.

29. This selection sets out to inform people about_____.

    (A) an outbreak of plague
    (B) quarantine
    (C) the city of Surat
    (D) rats

30. The use of the word *eradicated* in line 23 can be best defined as_____.

    (A) exposed to radiation
    (B) caused to grow
    (C) engineered to multiply
    (D) wiped out completely.

Passage for Questions 31–36

Kentucky residents periodically go to the voting booth to decide upon the fate of alcohol sales there. Kentucky is one of many states that still have "dry" counties, or counties that forbid the sale of alcoholic beverages.
Line
(5) Like other "sinful" luxuries, the sale of alcohol is sure to bring controversy wherever it goes.

This statement has been true simply forever. The use of alcohol, since its discovery by the Egyptian dynasties, has been highly contested. By the 19th century, excessive drinking was common, to the point that it was considered a social problem. Its presence led to the creation of temperance
(10) societies in America and abroad. Populated primarily by women, temperance societies set out to stomp out the sale and use of alcohol.

Often these societies would publish stories meant to frighten people out of using drink. One popular, probably untrue, story told of a young boy of 14 who worked as a waiter for a New England bar, something that
(15) commonly happened at that time. This boy was in the habit of finishing patrons' unfinished drinks. The boy consumed so much during his shift one Friday evening that he eventually passed out in the cellar—only to be eaten alive by the rats. The bar owner didn't find his body until Monday.

(20) But temperance society members were not content merely to tell salacious stories. Women like Carry Nation would appear in person at saloons and give the customers a severe tongue-lashing. Then she would damage as much of the place as she could with her hatchet. At six feet tall, Nation, in particular, became <u>anathema</u> to tavern owners and drinkers across the
(25) United States.

31. Paragraph three makes the assumption that if one drinks, one will_____.

    (A) become rich
    (B) be imprisoned
    (C) lose all self-control
    (D) grow angry

32. The story about the boy eaten by rats allegedly took place in_____.

    (A) England
    (B) Egypt
    (C) Kentucky
    (D) New England

33. In what century did alcoholism become a social problem?

    (A) Egyptian dynasty period
    (B) 18th century
    (C) 19th century
    (D) 20th century

34. Based on its use in the selection, what is the best definition of *anathema*?

    (A) something to be watched
    (B) something to be dreaded
    (C) something to be welcomed
    (D) something to be repeated

35. Why did temperance societies tell stories like the one in the passage?

    (A) so people would drink more
    (B) so people would go to church
    (C) so people would fear drinking
    (D) so people would vote for "wet" counties

36. The best title for this reading selection would be_____.

    (A) Vote and Sin No More
    (B) One Man's Pleasure Is Another Man's Poison
    (C) Temperance Carries the Nation
    (D) The History of Drinking in America

STOP

IF YOU FINISH BEFORE TIME IS UP, YOU MAY CHECK YOUR WORK ON THIS SECTION ONLY. DO NOT TURN TO ANY OTHER SECTION IN THE TEST.

ISEE Practice Test 1

SECTION 4 MATHEMATICS ACHIEVEMENT

47 questions   *40 minutes*

Directions: At the end of each problem, you have a choice of four possible answers. Work out each problem and then choose the best possible answer.

Sample:
How many pints are there in 8 gallons?

(A) 32
(B) 16
(C) 24
(D) 64

Ⓐ Ⓑ Ⓒ ●

1. Given parallel lines *AB* and *CD*. If the measure of ∠1 is 49°, find the measure of ∠*x*.

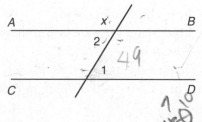

(A) 49°
(B) 118°
(C) 131°
(D) 98°

2. The Aztec Chemical Company wants to repackage 1,159 ounces of one of their chemicals into one-pound containers. How many ounces remain after all the chemicals are repackaged? (Sixteen ounces equal one pound.)

(A) 7 ounces
(B) 48 ounces
(C) 64 ounces
(D) 72 ounces

3. Determine the value of *x* in the equation 62 + 2(8 − *x*) = 72.

(A) 3
(B) 4
(C) 7
(D) 6

4. Simplify $(2a^2 + 5a - 3) - (4a - 7a^2 + 6)$.

(A) $4a^2 - 3a + 9$
(B) $9a^2 - 5a + 9$
(C) $7a^2 + 3a - 9$
(D) $9a^2 + 1a - 9$

5. Seven times a certain number is 64.4. What is the result if we divide the original number by 2?

(A) 3.4
(B) 5.6
(C) 2.7
(D) 4.6

6. The formula $d = 16t^2$ represents the distance in feet, *d*, an object falls in *t* seconds. Find the distance an object drops in 3 seconds.

(A) 144 ft
(B) 96 ft
(C) 166 ft
(D) 128 ft

7. Simplify $\dfrac{a\sqrt{42}}{b\sqrt{7}}$

(A) $\dfrac{b}{a}\sqrt{6}$

(B) $\dfrac{a}{b}\sqrt{6}$

(C) $ab\sqrt{6}$

(D) $6ab$

8. If the circumference of a circular amphitheater is 628 feet, find the distance across its center (the diameter). Use the formula $C = 2\pi r$ and let $\pi = 3.14$.

   (A) 60 feet
   (B) 100 feet
   (C) 200 feet
   (D) 400 feet

9. Jarmel is shipping some sports equipment in a box 15″ long × 8″ wide × 6″ high. He wants to ship some other equipment in another box that measures 12″ long × 8″ wide. How high should this second box be in order to contain the same volume as the first box?

   (A) 8.2″
   (B) 8.4″
   (C) 7.5″
   (D) 6.4″

10. The quotient of 36 and a number is equal to the product of five-eighths and 80 reduced by 41. Find the number.

    (A) 6
    (B) 4
    (C) 8
    (D) 12

11. In parallelogram $ABCD$, the height is 9″, and the base is 15″. Find the area.

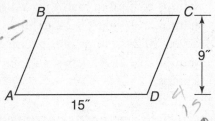

    (A) 135
    (B) 67.5
    (C) 270
    (D) 60

12. Determine the third root of $-27a^6$.

    (A) $3a^3$
    (B) $3a^2$
    (C) $-3a^3$
    (D) $-3a^2$

13. Find the value of the expression $3rs - 2t$ when $r = 2$, $s = -3$, and $t = 4$.

    (A) 14
    (B) -10
    (C) 19
    (D) -26

14. Jennifer receives a base salary of $500 per week plus an 8% commission on sales over $2,000 for the week. If she sold $3,500 for the week, what was her total salary?

    (A) $620
    (B) $710
    (C) $540
    (D) $460

15. A 15-foot tree casts a shadow of 20 feet. How long is the shadow of a nearby 450-foot building if the tree and its shadow are in the same ratio as the building and its shadow?

    (A) 180 ft
    (B) 120 ft
    (C) 200 ft
    (D) 600 ft

16. The perimeter of a ranch is 23,760 feet. If Lois walks at the rate of 3 miles per hour, how long will it take for her to walk around the ranch? (One mile = 5,280 feet.)

    (A) 2.3 hours
    (B) 1.8 hours
    (C) 2.4 hours
    (D) 1.5 hours

17. What number is 17 more than 5% of 420?

   (A) 26
   (B) 64
   (C) 44
   (D) 38

18. Which of the following numbers is 8 less than 2/3 of 27?

   (A) 10
   (B) 8
   (C) 6
   (D) 4

19. For all integers x and y, $x \# y = \dfrac{x+y}{2}$. If $5 \# y$ is an integer, what is a possible value for y?

   (A) 2
   (B) 6
   (C) 7
   (D) 4

20. The height of the front door in a blueprint of a one-family house measures $\dfrac{3}{4}$″. If the actual door is 8 feet tall, what is the ratio of the blueprint to the actual dimensions of the house?

   (A) 1/128
   (B) 2/5
   (C) 3/32
   (D) 1/64

21. Which of the following angles can represent the three angles of a triangle?

   (A) 43°, 56°, 47°
   (B) 58°, 29°, 68°
   (C) 56°, 72°, 38°
   (D) 59°, 53°, 68°

22. Larry places $2,400 in a bank account for a period of two years and six months at a simple annual interest rate of 4%. How much is in the account at the end of the time period?

   (A) $2,640
   (B) $2,510
   (C) $2,960
   (D) $2,750

23. Examine the diagram and then choose the best answer. *O* is the center of the circle.

   (A) *JL* > *MP*
   (B) *ON* < *OK*
   (C) *NQ* < *JL*
   (D) *OP* > *ON*

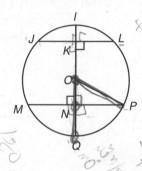

24. Which one of the following statements is true?

   (A) Nine $0.15 stamps plus six $0.37 stamps cost more than five $0.65 stamps.
   (B) Sixteen $0.15 stamps plus eight $0.37 stamps is less than seven $0.30 stamps plus nine $0.24 stamps.
   (C) Four $0.30 stamps plus five $0.37 stamps cost more than thirteen $0.15 stamps and eight $0.24 stamps.
   (D) Seven $0.24 stamps plus twelve $0.30 stamps cost $0.45 less than four $0.37 stamps.

25. Patricia, Holly, and Juwan are partners in a dress shop. If Patricia gets 1/4 of the income and Holly gets 1/3 and, altogether, they earn $480,000, how much does Juwan get?

   (A) $120,000
   (B) $180,000
   (C) $200,000
   (D) $220,000

26. Marcia leaves her home at 10 A.M. and drives to her sister's house. If she drives at an average speed of 53 mph and the distance between their homes is 238.5 miles, at what time will she arrive?

    (A) 1 P.M.
    (B) 1:30 P.M.
    (C) 2 P.M.
    (D) 2:30 P.M.

27. Review the diagram and then select the best answer. The squares indicate right angles.

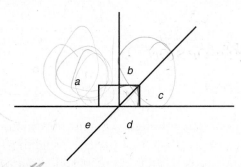

    (A) m∠c = m∠b
    (B) m∠a + m∠d < 90°
    (C) m∠c = m∠d
    (D) m∠b + m∠c = 90°

28. If ■ = 4, □ = 3, * = 2, · = multiplication, + = addition, and − = subtraction, find the value of 5 · ■ + 3 · □ − 4 · *.

    (A) 23
    (B) 34
    (C) 21
    (D) 18

29. Which of the following numbers cannot satisfy the inequality −2.4 < x ≤ 3.8?

    (A) 0
    (B) −2.4
    (C) −1.8
    (D) −2.39

30. If the measures of angles A and C are, respectively, 32° and 59°, find the measure of exterior angle *CBD*.

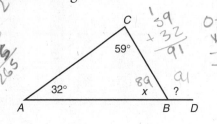

    (A) 59°
    (B) 91°
    (C) 89°
    (D) 98°

31. Simplify $3\sqrt{7} - 4\sqrt{3} + 11\sqrt{7} - 6\sqrt{3}$.

    (A) $9\sqrt{7} - 10\sqrt{3}$
    (B) $14\sqrt{7} + 7\sqrt{3}$
    (C) $14\sqrt{7} - 10\sqrt{3}$
    (D) $14\sqrt{21} - 10\sqrt{3}$

32. A plate of glass $4\frac{1}{2}$ inches long and 3 inches wide weighs 10.8 ounces. If the glass weighs 0.4 ounces per cubic inch, how thick is the glass?

    (A) 3 in.
    (B) 2.5 in.
    (C) 1 in.
    (D) 2 in.

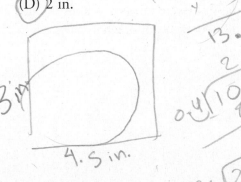

33. The bar graph summarizes the numbers of cartoons, dramas, and comedies produced in the United States in the years 2007–2009. Use the information provided in the bar graph to determine which of the following statements is false.

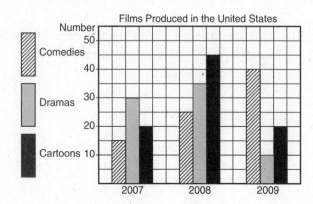

(A) The number of cartoons in 2009 is less than the number of dramas in 2007.

(B) The number of cartoons in 2007 is more than the number of dramas in 2008.

(C) The number of dramas in 2009 is less than the number of comedies in 2007.

(D) The number of comedies in 2008 is greater than the number of cartoons in 2009.

34. Simplify $\dfrac{7}{17\frac{1}{2}}$.

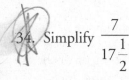

(A) 3/7
(B) 2/5
(C) 5/9
(D) 7/8

35. If the real estate taxes on a house valued at $108,000 are $4,320, what is the tax rate?

(A) 4%
(B) 3%
(C) 3.5%
(D) 5%

36. Which point lies 4 units above the *x*-axis and 2 units to the left of the *y*-axis?

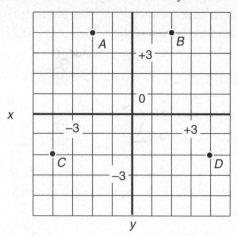

(A) *A*
(B) *B*
(C) *C*
(D) *D*

37. If one screw weighs 2 grams, how many screws are there in a package weighing 78 kilograms? (1,000 grams = 1 kilogram.)

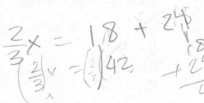

(A) 25,000
(B) 39,000
(C) 41,000
(D) 53,000

38. Two-thirds of what number is equal to 18 more than 60% of 40.

(A) 27
(B) 33
(C) 36
(D) 63

39. Given parallelogram, select the best answer.

(A) *a* = *b*
(B) *b* = *d*
(C) *a* > *c*
(D) *a* = *d*

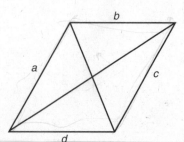

40. Find the dark area in the diagram. The area of a circle is equal to πr^2, where $\pi = 3.14$. Round off the answer to the nearest tenth.

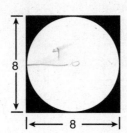

(A) 12.8
(B) 13.8
(C) 13.76
(D) 12.83

41. Forty-eight divided by what number equals $2/3 \times 9$?

(A) 6
(B) 12
(C) 4
(D) 8

42. Based on the information in the diagram, select the best answer.

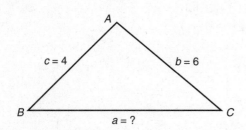

(A) $a = 10$
(B) $a < 10$
(C) $a = 11$
(D) $a > 10$

43. Find the value of x in the figure.

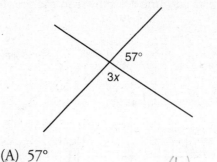

(A) 57°
(B) 41°
(C) 39°
(D) 3°

44. Simplify the following powers and then select the correct answer below.

(a) 5^2 (b) 2^5 (c) 2^3

(A) $a > b$ or $c > a$
(B) $c = a$ or $b < c$
(C) $c > b$ and $a = b$
(D) $b < a$ or $c < b$

45. Find side BC of the adjoining right angle.

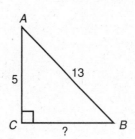

(A) 12
(B) 18
(C) 19
(D) 15

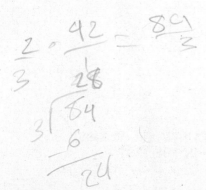

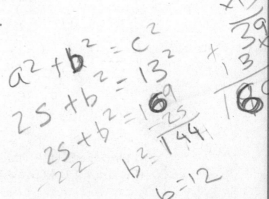

46. The average monthly prices for a gallon of regular gasoline are shown in the graph.

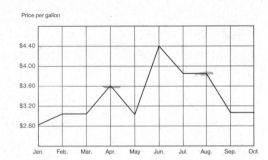

Price per gallon

Find the average price of a gallon of gasoline for the months of April and August.

(A) $3.90
(B) $3.70
(C) $4.10
(D) $3.60

47. The price of a computer dropped from $1,500 to $1,200. What was the percent drop?

(A) 30%
(B) 20%
(C) 38%
(D) 34%

STOP

IF YOU FINISH BEFORE TIME IS UP, YOU MAY CHECK YOUR WORK ON THIS SECTION ONLY. DO NOT TURN TO ANY OTHER SECTION IN THE TEST.

Section 5 Essay

1 question   *30 minutes*

Directions: Write an essay responding to the following topic. Please write legibly and use only blue or black ink.

TOPIC: Do we make history, or does it make us?

_____

_____

_____

_____

_____

_____

_____

_____

_____

_____

_____

_____

_____

_____

_____

_____

_____

_____

_____

_____

_____

_____

_____

_____

_____

_____

_____

_____

_____

_____

_____

_____

_____

_____

_____

STOP

IF YOU FINISH BEFORE TIME IS UP, YOU MAY CHECK YOUR WORK ON THIS SECTION ONLY. DO NOT TURN TO ANY OTHER SECTION IN THE TEST.

ANSWER EXPLANATIONS

Section 1 Verbal Reasoning

1. **(B)** Remember that "bad" prefix *mal*? It's deadly.

2. **(D)** To liberate something is to free it. Think of the Statue of Liberty, symbolizing freedom.

3. **(B)** To sever something is to cut it or separate it. *Divide* is the closest word to this meaning.

4. **(A)** This is one of those tricky words. Stationary (spelled with an *a*) means unmoving. Stationery (spelled with an *e*) is writing paper.

5. **(A)** You might be tricked into guessing (D) *wardrobe*, but remember that *uni* means one. One form means sameness. When you wear a uniform, you dress the same as many other people.

6. **(A)** Something obscure is vague. You can eliminate B (transparent) and C (clear) because they are synonyms.

7. **(B)** If you are prejudiced, you prejudge something. You are biased.

8. **(A)** Magic and supernatural are similar, so you can eliminate them; they can't both be the correct choice. The prefix *con* means with or together. Things that go together are suitable for one another.

9. **(A)** Something resilient springs back. The closest match to this is flexible. Choices B and C mean the opposite of this. Choice D means calm.

10. **(A)** Something lethargic is slow and drowsy. In Greek mythology, drinking from the river Lethe would cause forgetfulness. This might make you inactive.

11. **(C)** A donor donates or gives or contributes.

12. **(A)** A high, piercing sound is shrill.

13. **(A)** If you are punctual, you are prompt, or on time **to a point**. (Think of *puncture* or *punctuation*, which also involve points.)

14. **(C)** To devise something is to plan or invent it.

15. **(A)** Notorious and infamous both mean well-known for something bad.

16. **(B)** Jeopardy and peril mean danger.

17. **(C)** If you scrutinize something, you examine it closely.

18. **(D)** *Bio* means life, and the degradation of life would be decay.

19. **(A)** If you remember that the root *vor* has to do with eating, you'll know that voracious means ravenously hungry.

20. **(A)** Reversal and inversion both involve backward movement.

21. **(D)** If you tried to fill in the blank, you would have put in something like "peace-lover." That's what a pacifist is.

22. **(B)** In the first part of the sentence, we are told that the author is no longer living. Therefore, his children published the novel **after his death**. Posthumously (*post*, after + *humus*, earth or ground) means after death or burial.

23. **(C)** The first part of the sentence tells us that everyone was afraid to talk. To broach a topic is to bring it up for the first time. (A brooch is a decorative pin. *I was afraid to broach the subject of her brooch because it was so ugly.*)

24. **(D)** **Even though** I am a **patient reader**, I couldn't follow the **wordy** (verbose) directions.

25. **(A)** No one has discovered a practical use, so it's extra. Something superfluous is unnecessary—more than sufficient.

26. **(A)** Greg doesn't like to mow the lawn. A is the only choice that is not positive. Odious means hateful, repugnant, or detestable.

27. **(D)** Because the girls made up quickly, you probably said their disagreement

was small or unimportant. Petty means small; think of the word *petite*.

28. **(A)** The sentence lists descriptions of the weather. A zephyr is a breeze.

29. **(A)** If you remember your roots, *anthropomorphic* means man-shaped. That describes cartoon animals who walk on two legs, talk, and wear clothes. Choice B, intelligent, might work, but it doesn't take much intelligence to wear clothes. Omnipotent means all-powerful, and inanimate means not alive.

30. **(B)** We were all **relieved** because her condition was positive. Remember that the prefix *bene* means good.

31. **(D)** Lecture and rhetoric both concern speech, but lecture (D) fits better in context.

32. **(B)** Solace is a word worth knowing. It means relief, comfort, or consolation. After a hard day, Serafina wants relief.

33. **(A)** To feign means to pretend.

34. **(A)** If someone is sage, he or she is wise. You would go to a sage person for advice.

35. **(A)** Choices B and C are similar, so they cannot both be correct. To accumulate or amass is to collect something into a mass or pile.

36. **(B)** There's that good *bene* prefix again! What a kind prefix it is.

37. **(A)** Because Paulina pressed on, she never stopped. This leaves only choices A and B. However, the second word in choice B makes no sense in context. (She pressed on uselessly?), so the answer is A. (She pressed on resolutely.)

38. **(D)** The other choices all contradict themselves when put into the sentence.

39. **(C)** The clue phrase is that Mrs. Duncan has an "eye for detail." Meticulous and precision concern attention to detail.

40. **(B)** The senator refused to take a side, so he was **neutral**. A (belligerent) and D (biased) are obviously incorrect. B is the best choice. C makes little sense when both words are plugged in.

Section 2 Quantitative Reasoning

1.

ANALYSIS

Let P = the perimeter. Let k = the length of the rectangle, and let $k - 8$ = the width of the rectangle.

WORK

$$P = 2 \cdot \text{length} + 2 \cdot \text{width}$$

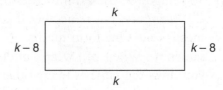

$$P = 2(k) + 2(k - 8) = 2k + 2k - 16$$
$$P = 4k - 16$$

ANSWER: (D)

2.

ANALYSIS

Set up two equations. Since the three-digit number and the sum of the digits are divisible by 4 and 5, respectively, we have no remainders.

WORK

The original number $\dfrac{\overset{12}{\cancel{4}\cancel{9}^1 x}}{4}$ is divisible by 4:

In order for $1x$ to be divisible by 4, x has to be either

$$2\frac{(12)}{4} \text{ or } 6\frac{(16)}{4}.$$

Because the last digit has to be either 2 or 6 and the sum of the digits is divisible by 5, let's try substitution.

$$\frac{4+9+2}{3}=\frac{15}{3}=3 \;\checkmark$$ (The sum of the digits is divisible by 5.)

$$\frac{4+9+6}{5}=\frac{19}{5}=3\frac{4}{5} \;\times$$ (The sum of the digits is not divisible by 5.)

The digit is 492.

ANSWER: (D)

3.

ANALYSIS

Subtract the area of the inner circle from the area of the outer circle.

WORK

$$A=\pi r^2$$

$A_{\text{Outer circle}}, \; r=8:$
$$A_O = 3.14 \cdot 8^2 = 3.14 \cdot 64 = 200.96$$

$A_{\text{Inner circle}}, \; r=5:$
$$-A_I = -3.14 \cdot 5^2 = -3.14 \cdot 25 = -78.50$$

Shaded area: 122.46

ANSWER: (C)

4.

ANALYSIS

Multiply the whole numbers and the radicals separately and then simplify.

WORK

$$5\sqrt{2} \times 3\sqrt{8}=15\sqrt{16}=15\times 4=60$$

ANSWER: (C)

5.

ANALYSIS

Find the number of returned books and compare that number to the number of lost books.

WORK

Original number of books:	30
−Number of books lost:	4
Number of books returned:	26

Ratio of returned books to lost books:

$$\frac{26}{4}=\frac{13}{2}$$

ANSWER: (D)

6.

ANALYSIS

Whenever we are given a general statement, make it concrete by using actual numbers. Because we are given that x is a positive number and y negative, let's arbitrarily set $x=2$ and $y=-3$.

WORK

Let $x=2$, $y=-3$:

$$xy<0$$
$$(2)(-3)=-6$$
$$-6<0 \;\checkmark$$

ANSWER: (B)

7.

ANALYSIS

Let y = the unknown number.

WORK

$$6+\frac{60}{y}=\frac{2}{3}\times 15$$

Multiply by y: $6+\dfrac{60}{y}=10$

Subtract $6y$: $6y+60=10y$

Divide by 4: $60=4y$

$$y=15$$

ANSWER: (D)

8.

ANALYSIS

José is earning 30% more than Henry, or 10% of Henry's wage. Once we determine José's current wage, add $70.

WORK

Henry's wage: $530

José's wage: $130\% \times \$530$ or $1.30 \times \$530 = \$689$

Jose's wage after a $70 raise: $\$689 + \$70 = \$759$

ANSWER: (C)

9.

ANALYSIS

Add up the different percentages and subtract from a total of 100%. Then multiply the answer by 24 hours.

WORK

$30\% + 10\% + 25\% + 20\% = 85\%$
$100\% - 85\% = 15\% = 0.15$

$0.15 \times 24 = 3.6$

ANSWER: (D)

10.
ANALYSIS

Since the sun casts its light on both structures, set up a proportion between the tree and its shadow and the building and its shadow, x.

WORK

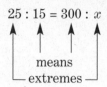

tree shadow = building : shadow

$$25 : 15 = 300 : x$$

means
extremes

The product of the means is equal to the product of the extremes:

$$25x = 15(300)$$
$$25x = 4500$$

Divide by 25: $\quad x = 180$

ANSWER: (A)

11.
ANALYSIS

Add the right- and left-handed numbers of students in order to obtain the total number. Then divide the total into the number of left-handed students.

WORK

Total number of students:	$6 + 24 = 30$
Left-handed students/total:	$6/30 = 0.20$
	$0.20 = 20\%$

ANSWER: (C)

12.

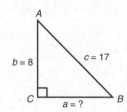

ANALYSIS

Use the Pythagorean Theorem.

WORK

	$a^2 + b^2 = c^2$
$b = 8$, $c = 17$:	$a^2 + 8^2 = 17^2$
	$a^2 + 64 = 289$
Subtract 64:	$a^2 = 225$
Take the square root of both sides:	$a = 15$

ANSWER: (D)

13.

ANALYSIS

Simplify each term and then subtract.

WORK

$$5.3 \times 10^3 = 5.3 \times 10 \times 10 \times 10 = 5.3 \times 1,000 = 5,300$$
$$-1.3 \times 10^2 = 1.3 \times 10 \times 10 \quad\quad = 1.3 \times 100 \quad = \quad 130$$
$$\overline{ 5,170}$$

ANSWER: (B)

14.

ANALYSIS

Excluding 1, $50 = 2 \times 5 \times 5$

WORK

The sum of the prime factors $= 5 + 2 + 5 = 12$

ANSWER: (A)

15.

ANALYSIS

Substitute the values for x, y, and z into the given expression.

WORK

$$4xy + 5z^2$$
$x = 4, y = -3, z = -2:$
$$= 4(4)(-3) + 5(-2)^2$$
$$= 16(-3) + 5(-2)(-2)$$
$$= -48 + 5(4)$$
$$= -48 + 20$$
$$= -28$$

ANSWER: (D)

16

ANALYSIS

Change percents to decimals and multiply.

WORK

$$20\% \times 30\% \times 180$$
$$0.20 \times 0.30 \times 180$$
$$10.8$$

ANSWER: (D)

17.

ANALYSIS

Find the value of each expression and then substitute into the inequalities.

WORK

(a) $0.15/3 = 0.05$
(b) $15/0.3 = 50$
(c) $1.5/0.3 = 5$

b is greater than c, and a is less than c.

$$50 > 5 \text{ and } 0.05 < 5 \checkmark$$

ANSWER: (B)

18.

ANALYSIS

Separate the inequality into two inequalities.

WORK

$$\quad\quad\quad -2.4 < 3x \quad\quad 3x \leq 3.6$$
Divide by 3: $\quad -0.8 < x \quad\quad\quad x \leq 0.9$

The number x is larger than -0.8 and less than or equal to 0.9.

$$-2.4 < 3x \leq 3.6$$
$$-2.4 < 3(0) \leq 3.6 \checkmark$$

ANSWER: (A)

19.

ANALYSIS

We can either use the equation $y = mx + b$ and find the slope and the y-intercept, b, or else we can substitute the point $(2, 5)$ into the given equations in order to find which one fits.

Method 1

The generic formula for a linear equation is $y = mx + b$, where m is the slope and b is the y-intercept. We know that the slope is 3, but we don't know the y-intercept. However, we can substitute 2 for x and 5 for y in the generic linear equation.

$$y = mx + b$$
$$m = 3, x = 2, y = 5: \quad 5 = 3(2) + b$$
$$5 = 6 + b$$
Subtract 5: $\quad -1 = b$
$y = mx + b$ $m = 3$, $b = -1$: $\quad y = 3x - 1$

Method 2

See whether the point $(2, 5)$ lies on each of the given lines.

WORK

$$y = mx + b$$
$$y = 3x - 1$$
$x = 2, y = 5: \quad 5 = 3(2) - 1$
$$5 = 6 - 1$$
$$5 = 5 \checkmark$$

ANSWER: (D)

20.

ANALYSIS

Move the decimal two places to the left.

WORK

$$5.003\% = 0.05003$$

ANSWER: (A)

21.

ANALYSIS

A. $4^2 + 5(9 - 3) = 16 + 5 \cdot 6 = 16 + 30 = 46$
B. $3 \cdot 17 - 4 \cdot 6 = 51 - 24 = 27$
C. $7 + 9 \cdot 4 - 6(9 - 7)^3 = 7 + 36 - 6(2)^3 =$
    $43 - 6(8) = 43 - 48 = -5$
D. $6 - 2 + 48/6 = 4 + 8 = 12$

ANSWER: (C)

22.

ANALYSIS

Simplify the expression and then subtract.

WORK

$$5.3 \times 10^3 = 5.3 \times 10 \times 10 \times 10$$
$$= 5.3 \times 1,000 \qquad = 5,300$$
$$-1.3 \times 10^2 = -1.3 \times 10 \times 10$$
$$= -1.3 \times 100 \qquad \underline{= -130}$$
$$= 5,170$$

ANSWER: (C)

23.

ANALYSIS

A. $3 \times (0.4)^2 = 3(0.16) = 0.48$
B. $4 \times (0.3)^2 = 4(0.09) = 0.36$

ANSWER: (A)

24.

ANALYSIS

area of a triangle $= \dfrac{1}{2}bh$, where $b = $ base and $h = $ height.

area of a rectangle $= bh$, where $b = $ base and $h = $ height.

WORK

A. Area of triangle

$$b = 6, h = 5: \qquad A = \frac{1}{2}(6)(5) = 3(5) = 15$$

B. Area of rectangle

$$b = 5, h = 4: \qquad A = (5)(4) = 20$$

ANSWER: (B)

25.

ANALYSIS

First, find the measure of interior angle ACB by subtracting $102°$ from $180°$. Then find the measure of $\angle B$ and compare the two angles.

WORK

A. $\qquad$ m$\angle ACB = 180° - 102° = 78°$
B. $\qquad$ m$\angle A$ + m$\angle B$ + m$\angle ACB = 180°$
m$\angle A = 35°$,
m$\angle ACB = 78°$: $\qquad$ $35°$ + m$\angle B$ + $78° = 180°$
$\qquad\qquad\qquad\qquad\qquad$ $113°$ + m$\angle B = 180°$
Subtract $113°$: $\qquad\qquad$ m$\angle B = 67°$

ANSWER: (B)

26.
ANALYSIS

A. $0.15 \times 0.25 \times \$56 = 0.0375 \times \$56 = \$2.10$
B. $\dfrac{7}{\cancel{9}} \times \$\cancel{2.70}\,^{0.30} = \$2.10$

ANSWER: (C)

27.
ANALYSIS

A. $(0.8)^3 = (0.8)(0.8)(0.8) = 0.512$
B. $(0.5)^4 = (0.5)(0.5)(0.5)(0.5) = 0.0625$

ANSWER: (A)

28.
ANALYSIS

A. Excluding 1, list the prime factors of 20 and then determine their sum.
B. Excluding 1, list the prime factors of 18 and then determine their sum.

WORK

A. $20 = 10 \times 2 = 5 \times 2 \times 2$
Sum of the prime factors $= 5 + 2 + 2 = 9$

B. $18 = 9 \times 2 = 3 \times 3 \times 2$
Sum of the prime factors $= 3 + 3 + 2 = 8$

ANSWER: (A)

29.
ANALYSIS

A. $3y + 8 = 3(4) + 8 = 12 + 8 = 20$
B. $7y - 12 = 7(4) - 12 = 28 - 12 = 16$

ANSWER: (A)

30.
ANALYSIS

We don't know what value x assumes, so we can't really determine the value of either expression.

ANSWER: (D)

31.
ANALYSIS

A. Determine the number of hours traveled and then multiply that time by 56 mph.

WORK

Time between 9:30 A.M. and 1 P.M. $= 3\dfrac{1}{2}$ hours

$$3\dfrac{1}{2} \times 56 = \dfrac{7}{\cancel{2}} \times \cancel{56}\,^{28} = 196 \text{ miles}$$

B. 430 miles

ANSWER: (B)

32.
ANALYSIS

A. $4\sqrt{8} = 4\sqrt{4 \cdot 2} = 4\sqrt{4}\sqrt{2} = 4 \cdot 2 \cdot \sqrt{2} = 8\sqrt{2}$
B. $2\sqrt{32} = 2\sqrt{16 \cdot 2} = 2\sqrt{16}\sqrt{2} = 2 \cdot 4 \cdot \sqrt{2} = 8\sqrt{2}$

ANSWER: (C)

33.
ANALYSIS

Just find the distance between the two points.

WORK

A.

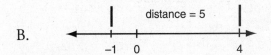

B.

ANSWER: (C)

34.

ANALYSIS

To obtain the probability of obtaining two heads is the product of the probability of obtaining one head and then another head.

WORK

A. Probability of one head: $\dfrac{1}{2}$

Probability of two heads: $\dfrac{1}{2} \times \dfrac{1}{2} = \dfrac{1}{4}$

B. $\dfrac{1}{4}$

ANSWER: (C)

35.

ANALYSIS

One kilogram equals 1,000 grams.

WORK

A. 2 kilograms = 2 × 1,000 = 2,000 grams
B. 1,800 grams

ANSWER: (A)

36.

WORK

A. $\dfrac{2}{\cancel{5}} \times \cancel{35}^{7} + 8 = 14 + 8 = 22$

B. $\sqrt{625} = 25$

ANSWER: (B)

37.

ANALYSIS

A. Add $\dfrac{1}{3}$ and $\dfrac{3}{8}$ and divide by 2.

WORK

A.
$$\begin{array}{r} \dfrac{1}{3} = \dfrac{8}{24} \\[2mm] +\dfrac{3}{8} = \dfrac{9}{24} \\ \hline \dfrac{17}{24} \end{array}$$

$$\dfrac{17}{24} \div \dfrac{2}{1} = \dfrac{17}{24} \times \dfrac{1}{2} = \dfrac{17}{48}$$

B. $\dfrac{1}{4} \times \dfrac{12}{12} = \dfrac{12}{48}$

ANSWER: (A)

Section 3 Reading Comprehension

1. **(C)** If the passage were intended only to give people advice on how to survive hurricanes, the piece would have a decidedly different tone—a much more businesslike way of speaking. This article is too chatty and full of trivia. Rule out choice A. If the article were intended to communicate how deadly hurricanes are, the piece would include many more gory and horrific details designed to scare the reader into being more careful; rule out choice B. The article does not even mention Hurricane Camille, so rule out choice D. The article does give an overview of basic hurricane facts; the correct answer is C.

2. **(B)** Choices A and C are ridiculous, so avoid them. The article does address how the hurricane develops such high winds, however not in paragraph one. B is the correct answer.

3. **(A)** The author makes it clear that s/he does not approve of Hurricane Parties because they involve people playing around when they should be finding shelter. So, the author is neither

excited by them, eager to join in, nor jealous of those who attend. In fact, you can rule out choices B, C, and D. The only answer is A.

4. **(A)** Checking the passage, you can see that hurricanes develop strength in the West Indies.

5. **(C)** The author may be from Louisiana, but knowing a lot about hurricanes does not mean you necessarily come from Louisiana. Rule out choice A. Lots of people can know about hurricanes; you don't have to be a meteorologist. You can rule out choice B. The author probably boards up his/her windows, but again, this is not necessarily true; the author may live in New York where hurricanes never come. Get rid of choice D. However, it is clear that the author does know quite a bit about hurricanes. Therefore, the correct answer is C.

6. **(B)** Reread the passage; you will notice that although all of these actions are mentioned, only making eye contact is listed as being *rude* in some countries.

7. **(C)** An author can know much about etiquette in various places yet never visit these areas; moreover, one can know much about something one hates. Neither choice A nor B are necessarily true. The manners of the writer don't matter when what you're trying to determine is how well the writer understands etiquette; so, forget choice D. The best answer is C.

8. **(A)** The phrase "Handsome Is as Handsome Does" and "The Ugly American" really don't have much to do with manners; omit them. The title "Anything Goes" implies that anything someone does is okay, yet the passage makes it clear that some actions are not okay. The only good choice is A; it may be that it is polite to spit in one country but not in another. Knowing whether to do so or not is a real concern.

9. **(D)** A quick scan of the passage reveals that burping after a meal is considered a compliment in some countries but offensive in America.

10. **(D)** Judging manners is a no-win situation. Because there exists no real logic behind their evolution, it's really impossible to decide which actions are "good" and which are "bad." So, rule out choice A. The idea of two countries sharing exactly the same rules of etiquette is nice to envision but difficult to find in reality. Omit choice C. And, the task of keeping track of all manners in the world might be difficult, but it can certainly be done. Omit choice B. The only thing that is fairly certain is that any two countries (unless one has come under the influence of another) are likely to have different systems of polite behavior. The correct answer is D.

11. **(B)** The author clearly has an opinion on the usefulness of math and science classes. Choices A and C indicate that the author's opinion is negative, but a quick read of the passage states that s/he feels that such classes are positive. Omit choices A and C. Choice D is not addressed by the passage; magic has no place in the study of mathematics and science. Skip choice D. The author clearly approves of math and science classes, so choice B is correct.

12. **(D)** The article clearly states that esters contribute smells; the correct answer is D.

13. **(A)** The word *clinical* can have all four connotations listed in this question. Substitute the different options for the word *clinical*, however, and only one option works well—technical.

14. **(D)** Question 13 already prepped you for this one; the author may find math and science classes difficult or easy— it doesn't matter. The main point is that the author thinks they are useful.

15. **(C)** Because the author sets out to prove that information learned in class has real-world effects, it makes sense that s/he should provide examples of this claim. S/he has already provided a science example; it makes sense that s/he would now provide a math example. We don't need more information about esters (A) or any data about planes (B), and a discussion of room deodorizers at this point would not be useful (D).

16. **(B)** According to the article, stress about world events causes people to consider renovating their bathrooms.

17. **(B)** Since the article discusses changes to the bathroom, it makes sense to mention that in selecting an answer.

18. **(C)** The article mentions various causes of stress, including terrorist attacks, mail delivery, and air travel. Even though working late hours also might contribute, the article does not mention the possibility. Remember, you are asked to report answers listed in the passage, not answers that you know from outside sources or things that seem like logical answers.

19. **(C)** If you are trying to identify the tone of the article, you will notice that it is generally unbiased. Therefore, it holds no words that connote fear (A), advocate a particular behavior (B), or encourage becoming a militant (D). The best answer is C.

20. **(A)** The article begins by discussing sources of stress; the rest of the passage touches upon the other three points listed here.

21. **(C)** Since the article spends a great deal of time discussing people's bathrooms, it makes sense that one would draw an inference that involves the bathroom. If people are trying to destress themselves, they are likely to indulge in showers or bathing. Naturally, then, one might be indulging in bath salts or bubble bath more frequently. The

other competitive options are options B and D; you might select one of these because they mention music and TV and the article talked about people installing entertainment equipment in their bathrooms. But the majority of people who increase their time in bathrooms probably did not also install TVs or stereos there. The best answer is still C.

22. **(A)** If you don't know the word *accoutrements*, plug in the various options and see which one makes the best sense. A does.

23. **(C)** The article uses all the tactics listed in this question; but in paragraph three is where we find factual detail about plague—its cause, its symptoms, its scientific name, and so on.

24. **(D)** Just reread the passage; you'll see that *Yersina pestis* is the scientific name for the plague.

25. **(B)** Paragraph three discusses septicemia, which attacks the bloodstream.

26. **(D)** Since pests introduce plague bacteria into the population, Surat would do well to work harder to get rid of their rodent and insect population. Closing down the ports (B) and building more hospitals (C) would be a good idea if the city was trying to keep the plague from spreading. And, certainly, Surat would not encourage a rat population (A) if they were trying to prevent plague.

27. **(C)** Pay attention to the verbs. Quarantining reduces the number of human carriers that can leave the city and possibly spread the disease to other populations; it doesn't help fight the influx of rats (A) or insects (B), and it has nothing to do with the transmission of medicine (D).

28. **(C)** The article states in paragraph one that Surat suffered a plague outbreak in 1994.

29. **(A)** While the article mentions all of these topics during its discussion, it sets out

to tell people about plague, so as to make people aware of its deadly existence.

30. **(D)** Three of these options are here to trick you into associating the word *eradicated* with other words. The correct definition is D.

31. **(C)** Temperance societies believed alcohol was evil and likely to possess the user. Even though one would be unlikely to get rich (A), they believed it quite likely that one would be imprisoned (B) or angered (D) while under the influence. The best answer is C, however, because losing self-control might cause one to get angry and do something for which one gets imprisoned.

32. **(D)** Paragraph three states that the boy worked in a New England bar.

33. **(C)** Paragraph two states that alcoholism was a problem by the 19th century.

34. **(B)** Substitute the various choices for *anathema*, and you will see that *dreaded* makes the most sense. Think about it: Imagine the giantess Carry Nation striding into your bar wielding an axe; you're still paying off the repairs that stemmed from her last visit. Wouldn't you be dreading her arrival? We thought so.

35. **(C)** People tell stories like this one to make people too scared to do "bad" things. People who hate alcohol will not do things to get people to drink more (A) or vote for counties that support drinking (D); indeed, such a result is counterproductive to members of temperance societies. Although members of temperance societies might advocate going to church (B), their primary goal is to scare people into going sober.

36. **(B)** You should not choose D because the article does not address all of the issues involving drinking all across America. Choice C is cute but does not address the entire article; indeed,

Carry Nation only appears late in the passage. Voting is mentioned in paragraph one, but the author does not sustain this topic throughout. Omit choice A. The best answer is B because the article discusses a conflict over how to treat drinking—it is both bane and boon.

Section 4 Mathematics Achievement

1.

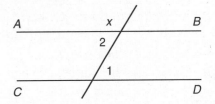

ANALYSIS

Since the two lines are parallel, angles 1 and 2 are alternate interior angles, and their measures are equal. Together, angles 2 and x form a straight angle and are therefore supplementary.

WORK

$$m\angle 1 = m\angle 2 = 49°$$

$\angle 2 = 49°$:
$$m\angle 2 + m\angle x = 180°$$
$$49° + m\angle x = 180°$$
$$m\angle x = 131°$$

ANSWER: (C)

2.

ANALYSIS

Since one pound equals 16 ounces, divide 1,159 by 16.

WORK

$$
\begin{array}{r}
72\text{R}7 \\
16\overline{)1,159} \\
\underline{112} \\
39 \\
\underline{32} \\
7
\end{array}
$$

ANSWER: (A)

3.

ANALYSIS

First, multiply the expression inside the parentheses by 2. Then subtract 78 from both sides of the equation and, finally divide by −2.

WORK

$$62 + 2(8 - x) = 72$$
$$62 + 16 - 2x = 72$$
$$78 - 2x = 72$$
$$\underline{-78 \qquad = -78}$$
$$-2x = -6$$
$$\frac{-2x}{-2} = \frac{-6}{-2}$$
$$x = 3$$

ANSWER: (A)

4.

ANALYSIS

Line up the terms in descending order of powers of *a*. Change the signs in front of the subtrahend and add.

WORK

$$2a^2 + 5a - 3$$
$$\underline{+ \quad - \quad -}$$
$$\underline{- \ \ominus 7a^2 \oplus 4a \oplus 6}$$
$$9a^2 + 1a - 9$$

ANSWER: (D)

5.

ANALYSIS

Let *x* = the unknown number. Find the original number and then divide by 2.

WORK

$$7x = 64.4$$

Divide by 7: $\qquad x = 9.2$

Divide 9.2 by 2: $\qquad \dfrac{9.2}{2} = 4.6$

ANSWER: (D)

6.

ANALYSIS

Substitute 3 for *t* in the given formula.

WORK

$t = 3$:
$$d = 16t^2$$
$$= 16(3)^2$$
$$= 16(9)$$
$$= 144$$

ANSWER: (A)

7.

ANALYSIS

Divide variables and radicals separately.

WORK

$$\frac{a\sqrt{42}}{b\sqrt{7}} = \frac{a}{b}\sqrt{\frac{42}{7}} = \frac{a}{b}\sqrt{6}$$

ANSWER: (B)

8.

ANALYSIS

Use the formula $C = 2\pi r$ and substitute 628 for *C* and 3.14 for π.

WORK

$$C = 2\pi r$$
$$628 = 2(3.14)r$$
$$628 = 6.28r$$

Divide by 6.28: $\qquad 100 = r$

Diameter = 2*r*: $\qquad 2(100) = D$
$$D = 200$$

ANSWER: (C)

9.

ANALYSIS

Find the volume of the first box and then use that volume to determine the height of the second box.

WORK

First box: $\qquad V = l \cdot w \cdot h$

where *V* = volume, *l* = length, *w* = width, and *h* = height.

$l = 15$, $w = 8$,
$h = 6$: $V = 15 \cdot 8 \cdot 6 = 720$

Second box: $V = l \cdot w \cdot h$
$V = 720$, $l = 12$,
$w = 8$: $720 = 12 \cdot 8 \cdot h$
                          $720 = 96h$
Divide by 96: $7.5 = h$

ANSWER: (C)

10.
ANALYSIS

Let x = the unknown number.

WORK

$$\frac{36}{x} = \frac{5}{8} \cdot 80 - 41$$

$$\frac{36}{x} = 50 - 41$$

$$\frac{36}{x} = 9$$

Multiply by x: $36 = 9x$

Divide by 9: $4 = x$

ANSWER: (B)

11.
ANALYSIS

Use the formula $A = b \cdot h$, where A = area, b = base, and h = height of the parallelogram.

WORK:

$$A = b \cdot h$$
$$A = 15 \cdot 9$$
$$A = 135$$

ANSWER: (A)

12.
ANALYSIS

Determine which number, when multiplied by itself three times, is equal to $-27d^6$.

WORK

$$\sqrt[3]{-27d^6} = -3d^2$$
$$(-3d^2)(-3d^2)(-3d^2) = -27d^6$$

ANSWER: (D)

13.
ANALYSIS

Substitute the values for r, s, and t in the given expression.

WORK

$r = 2$, $s = -3$, $t = 4$:
$$3rs - 2t$$
$$= 3(2)(-3) - 2(4)$$
$$= -18 - 8$$
$$= -26$$

ANSWER: (D)

14.
ANALYSIS

Find 8% of the excess money over $2,000, and add the result to the $500 base salary.

WORK

$$\$3,500 - \$2,000 = \$1,500$$
$$8\% = 0.08$$
$$0.08 \times \$1,500 = \$120$$
$$\$500 + \$120 = \$620$$

ANSWER: (A)

15.
ANALYSIS

If we set up two similar triangles, their corresponding sides are in proportion.

WORK

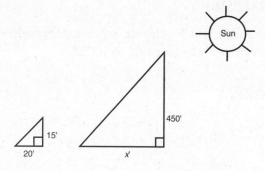

$$\frac{15}{20} = \frac{450}{x}$$

Multiply by 15x: $15x = 9,000$
Divide by 15: $x = 600$

ANSWER: (D)

16.
ANALYSIS

Change both units of distance to the same measure. In this case, let's just change 3 miles per hour to feet per hour and then divide.

WORK

3 miles per hour = 3 · 5,280 feet per hour = 15,840 feet per hour

$$\frac{23,760}{15,840} = 1.5$$

ANSWER: (D)

17.
ANALYSIS

Find 5% of 420 and add 17.

WORK

$$5\% = 0.05$$
$$0.05 \times 420 = 21$$
$$21 + 17 = 38$$

ANSWER: (D)

18.
ANALYSIS

Subtract 8 from the product of 2/3 and 27.

WORK

$$\frac{2}{3} \times 27 - 8 = 18 - 8 = 10$$

ANSWER: (A)

19.
ANALYSIS

Substitute the given values for y in order to determine when $5 \, \# \, y$ results in an integer.

WORK

(A) $5 \# 2 = \dfrac{5+2}{2} = \dfrac{7}{2} = 3\dfrac{1}{2}$ (not an integer)

(B) $5 \# 6 = \dfrac{5+6}{2} = \dfrac{11}{2} = 5\dfrac{1}{2}$ (not an integer)

(C) $5 \# 7 = \dfrac{5+7}{2} = \dfrac{12}{2} = 6$ (an integer)

(D) $5 \# 4 = \dfrac{5+4}{2} = \dfrac{9}{2} = 4\dfrac{1}{2}$ (not an integer)

ANSWER: (C)

20.
ANALYSIS

$$\text{ratio} = \frac{\text{height of the door in the blueprint}}{\text{height of actual door}}$$

Change 8 feet to inches and then simplify the ratio.

WORK

$$\text{ratio} = \frac{\dfrac{3}{4} \text{ inch}}{8 \, \text{ft}}$$

1 foot = 12 inches:
$$= \frac{\frac{3}{4} \text{ inch}}{8 \times 12} = \frac{\frac{3}{4} \text{ inch}}{96 \text{ inches}}$$
$$= \left(\frac{3}{4}\right) \div (96)$$
$$= \frac{3}{4} \times \frac{1}{96} = \frac{1}{128}$$

ANSWER: (A)

21.

ANALYSIS

The measures of the three angles of a triangle add up to 180°.

WORK

$$59 + 53 + 68 = 180$$

ANSWER: (D)

22.

ANALYSIS

Let A = amount of money in the account after two years and six months, P = the principal, R = the rate per year, and T = the number of years.

4% = 0.04; 2 years, 6 months = 2.5 years

We want to find the total amount in the bank account, A, so use the formula $A = P + PRT$.

WORK

$$A = P + PRT$$
$P = \$2{,}400,$
$R = 0.04,$
$T = 2.5:$
$$A = 2{,}400 + 2{,}400(0.04)(2.5)$$
$$A = 2{,}400 + 240$$
$$A = 2{,}640$$

ANSWER: (A)

23.

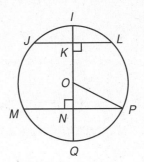

ANALYSIS

OQ, OP, and OI are all radii and are congruent.

WORK

$OP > ON$: OP is a radius, while ON is only a part of radius OQ. Therefore, the statement is true. ✓

ANSWER: (D)

24.

ANALYSIS

Set up inequalities to determine the true statement.

WORK

Nine $0.15 stamps plus six $0.37 stamps cost more than five $0.65 stamps.

$$9 \times \$0.15 + 6 \times \$0.37 > 5 \times \$0.65$$
$$\$1.35 + \$2.22 > \$3.25$$
$$3.57 > \$3.25 ✓$$

ANSWER: (A)

25.

ANALYSIS

Add $\frac{1}{4}$ and $\frac{1}{3}$ and then subtract the result from 1 (the total amount). The answer is Juwan's portion. Once we determine Juwan's portion, multiply that fraction by $480,000, the total income.

WORK

$$\begin{array}{rl} \frac{1}{4} &= \frac{3}{12} \\ +\frac{1}{3} &= \frac{4}{12} \\ \hline &\frac{7}{12} \end{array} \qquad \begin{array}{rl} 1 &= \frac{12}{12} \\ -&\frac{7}{12} \\ \hline &\frac{5}{12} \end{array}$$

$$\frac{5}{12} \times \$480{,}000 = \$200{,}000$$

ANSWER: (C)

26.

ANALYSIS

Let d = the distance driven, r = the rate of speed, t = the time for the trip. Find the number of hours it took Jacqueline to drive the distance and then add the answer to 10 A.M.

WORK

	$d = rt$
$d = 238.5$, $r = 53$:	$238.5 = 53t$
Divide by 53:	$4.5 = t$
Symmetric property:	$t = 4.5$

Add 4.5 hours to
10 A.M.:   10 A.M. + 4.5 hours
          = 2:30 P.M.

ANSWER: (D)

27.

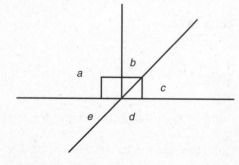

ANALYSIS

From the diagram, m∠$a°$ = 90° and m∠b + m∠c = 90°.

WORK

$$\text{m}\angle b + \text{m}\angle c = 90°$$

ANSWER: (D)

28.

ANALYSIS

Just substitute the given numbers for the symbols in the algebraic expression.

WORK

$$\begin{array}{l} 5 \cdot \blacksquare + 3 \cdot \square - 4 \cdot * \\ \blacksquare = 4, \square = 3 \text{ and } * = 2: \quad = 5 \cdot 4 + 3 \cdot 3 - 4 \cdot 2 \\ \qquad\qquad\qquad\qquad\qquad = 20 + 9 - 8 \\ \qquad\qquad\qquad\qquad\qquad = 21 \end{array}$$

ANSWER: (C)

29.

ANALYSIS

The number that does not satisfy the inequality cannot be greater than −2.4 and less than or equal to 3.8.

WORK

$$-2.4 < -2.4 \le 3.8 \ \text{✗}$$

ANSWER: (B)

30.

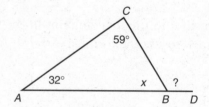

ANALYSIS

The sum of the angles of a triangle equals 180°, so, in order to determine the measure of angle *ABC*, add up the two given angles and subtract from 180°. Then, since the measure of straight angle *ABD* is 180°, subtract the answer from 180°.

WORK

Let $x = m\angle ABC$:
$$32° + 59° + x = 180°$$
$$91° + x = 180°$$
$$x = 89°$$
$$m\angle ABC = 89°$$

$$m\angle ABC + m\angle CBD = 180°$$
$m\angle ABC = 89°$: $\quad 89° + m\angle CBD = 180°$
Subtract 89°: $\quad m\angle CBD = 91°$

ANSWER: (B)

31.
ANALYSIS

Combine similar terms.

WORK

$$3\sqrt{7} + 11\sqrt{7} = 14\sqrt{7}$$
$$\underline{-4\sqrt{3} - 6\sqrt{3} = -10\sqrt{3}}$$
$$14\sqrt{7} - 10\sqrt{3}$$

ANSWER: (C)

32.
ANALYSIS

The total weight (TW) is equal to the product of the volume (V or $l \cdot w \cdot h$) and the weight per cubic inch (Wt/cu in.) of the glass.

WORK

$$TW = (l \cdot w \cdot h)(\text{Wt/cu in.})$$

TW = 10.8,
$l = 4.5$, $w = 3$,
Wt/cu in. = 0.4: $\quad 10.8 = (4.5)(3)(h)(0.4)$
$$10.8 = 5.4h$$
Divide by 5.4: $\quad 2 = h$

ANSWER: (D)

33.

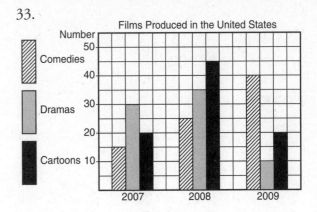

ANALYSIS

First, make a table indicating the numbers of cartoons, dramas, and comedies produced in each of the indicated years. Then you're in a position to check the given statements for their validity. Each horizontal line represents five films.

	2007	2008	2009
Comedies	15	25	40
Dramas	30	35	10
Cartoons	20	45	20

WORK

The number of cartoons in 2007 is more than the number of dramas in 2008.

$$20 > 35 \; ✗$$

ANSWER: (B)

34.
ANALYSIS

Divide 7 by $17\frac{1}{2}$.

WORK

$$7 \div 17\frac{1}{2}$$

$$\frac{7}{1} \div \frac{35}{2}$$

$$\frac{\overset{1}{7}}{1} \times \frac{2}{\underset{5}{35}} = \frac{2}{5}$$

ANSWER: (B)

35.

ANALYSIS

Divide $4,320 by $108,000.

WORK

$$\frac{4,320}{108,000}$$

$$108,000\overline{)4320.000} \quad 0.04 = 4\%$$
$$\underline{4320\ 00}$$

ANSWER: (A)

36.

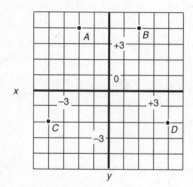

ANALYSIS

The points above the *x*-axis have positive *y*-values, whereas the points below the *x*-axis have negative *y*-values. The points to the left of the *y*-axis have negative *x*-values, whereas the points to the right of the *y*-axis have positive *x*-values.

WORK

Points *A* and *B* are both 4 units above the *y*-axis. Point *A* is also 2 units to the left of the *y*-axis.

ANSWER: (A)

37.

ANALYSIS

Change 78 kilograms to grams and then divide by 2 grams.

WORK

$$78 \text{ kilograms} = 78 \times 1,000 \text{ grams} = 78,000 \text{ grams}$$

$$\frac{78,000}{2} = 39,000$$

ANSWER: (B)

38.

ANALYSIS

Let *x* = the unknown number and change 60% to 0.60.

WORK

$$\frac{2}{3}x = 0.60 \cdot 40 + 18$$

$$\frac{2}{3}x = 24 + 18$$

Multiply by 3: $\frac{2}{3}x = 42$

Divide by 2: $2x = 126$
$$x = 63$$

ANSWER: (D)

39.

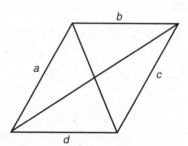

ANALYSIS

The opposite sides of parallelogram are equal.

WORK

$$b = d$$

ANSWER: (B)

40.

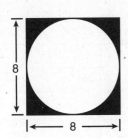

ANALYSIS

Find the areas of the square and the circle and subtract. The diameter of the circle is 8, so the radius is 4.

WORK

Area of square, A_S:
$s = 8$:

$$A_S = s^2$$
$$= 8^2 = 64$$

Area of circle, A_C:
$\pi = 3.14$, $r = 4$:

$$A_C = \pi r^2$$
$$= 3.14(4)^2$$
$$= 3.14(16)$$
$$= 50.24$$

$$A_S - A_C = 64 - 50.24$$
$$= 13.76$$
$$\approx 13.8$$

ANSWER: (B)

41.
ANALYSIS

Let y = the unknown number.

WORK

$$\frac{48}{y} = \frac{2}{3} \times 9$$

Multiply by y:

$$\frac{48}{y} = 6$$

Divide by 6:

$$6y = 48$$
$$y = 8$$

ANSWER: (D)

42.

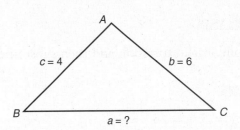

ANALYSIS

The sum of two sides of a triangle is always larger than the third side.

WORK

(A) $a = 10$: If $a = 10$, then $6 + 4$ will form a straight line and will coincide with side a. No triangle will be formed.
(B) $a < 10$: If $a < 10$, then sides 6 and 4 will form a triangle. ✔
(C) $a = 11$: If $a = 11$, then sides 4 and 6 will never meet, and no triangle will be formed.
(D) $a > 10$: If $a > 10$, then sides 4 and 6 will never meet, and no triangle will be formed.

ANSWER: (B)

43.

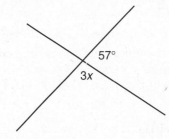

ANALYSIS

The two angles lie on a straight line, so they add up to 180°.

WORK

$$3x + 57 = 180$$
Subtract 57:
$$3x = 123$$
Divide by 3:
$$x = 41$$

ANSWER: (B)

44.

ANALYSIS

Simplify each expression and then substitute.

WORK

(a) $5^2 = 5 \cdot 5 = 25$
(b) $2^5 = 2 \cdot 2 \cdot 2 \cdot 2 \cdot 2 = 32$
(c) $2^3 = 2 \cdot 2 \cdot 2 = 8$

$$b < a \text{ or } c < b$$
$$32 < 25 \text{ or } 8 < 32 \checkmark$$

ANSWER: (D)

45.

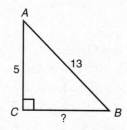

ANALYSIS

Use the Pythagorean Theorem.

WORK

$b = 5, c = 13$:

$$a^2 + b^2 = c^2$$
$$a^2 + 5^2 = 13^2$$
$$a^2 + 25 = 169$$
$$a^2 = 144$$

Take the square
root of both sides: $a = 12$

ANSWER: (A)

46.

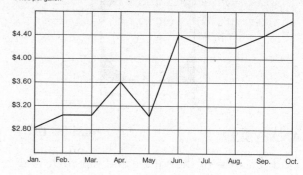

ANALYSIS

Add the April and August prices and divide by 2.

WORK

$$\frac{\$3.60 + \$4.20}{2} = \frac{\$7.80}{2} = \$3.90$$

ANSWER: (A)

47.

ANALYSIS

The price dropped $300.

WORK

$$\frac{300}{1500} = \frac{1}{5} = 0.20 = 20\%$$

ANSWER: (B)

Section 5 Writing Sample Checklist

☐ **Read the question and writing prompt again.** Did you answer the question? You won't have time to rewrite the essay during the actual exam, so read the question carefully the first time and keep it in mind. Underline keywords in the questions to help you remember.

☐ **Read your introduction.** Did you include all of the information necessary for a reader to understand your essay? Does it include a thesis statement?

☐ **Underline your thesis statement in the introduction.** Does it address the question and give your opinion on it?

☐ **Underline the thesis statement in the conclusion.** Does it agree with your original thesis?

☐ **Underline the topic sentences of your body paragraphs.** Now read all of the underlined sentences in your practice essay. Do these sentences focus on the same topic? Do they fit together? Do they flow?

☐ **TExAn.** To illustrate your <u>**T**opic sentence</u> in each body paragraph, check to make sure you have a <u>*specific* **Ex**ample</u>. Again, make sure it is specific, rather than another general statement. Then make sure you <u>**An**alyze or explain</u> *how* this example proves your point.

   This is an important step, so get used to including this information **as you write** your paragraphs.

☐ **Check your handwriting.** Is your text legible? Get used to forming your words clearly. Frustrated readers cannot score you highly if they cannot read your essay.

☐ **Proofread.** Correct the most glaring errors, especially run-ons, comma splices, and fragments. Make sure you capitalize when necessary and punctuate logically. Check your spelling, especially of easily confused words (to/too, their/there, etc.). Notice how you use transition words.

☐ **Have someone else read this essay.** Choose a good writer and reader to comment on your work.

Practice writing more essays, and you will improve each time. During the actual exam, you will only have time to proofread and check your examples, so most items on this list will have to become second nature to you.

ISEE Practice Test 2
ANSWER SHEET

Section 1 Verbal Reasoning

1 Ⓐ Ⓑ Ⓒ Ⓓ	9 Ⓐ Ⓑ Ⓒ Ⓓ	17 Ⓐ Ⓑ Ⓒ Ⓓ	25 Ⓐ Ⓑ Ⓒ Ⓓ	33 Ⓐ Ⓑ Ⓒ Ⓓ
2 Ⓐ Ⓑ Ⓒ Ⓓ	10 Ⓐ Ⓑ Ⓒ Ⓓ	18 Ⓐ Ⓑ Ⓒ Ⓓ	26 Ⓐ Ⓑ Ⓒ Ⓓ	34 Ⓐ Ⓑ Ⓒ Ⓓ
3 Ⓐ Ⓑ Ⓒ Ⓓ	11 Ⓐ Ⓑ Ⓒ Ⓓ	19 Ⓐ Ⓑ Ⓒ Ⓓ	27 Ⓐ Ⓑ Ⓒ Ⓓ	35 Ⓐ Ⓑ Ⓒ Ⓓ
4 Ⓐ Ⓑ Ⓒ Ⓓ	12 Ⓐ Ⓑ Ⓒ Ⓓ	20 Ⓐ Ⓑ Ⓒ Ⓓ	28 Ⓐ Ⓑ Ⓒ Ⓓ	36 Ⓐ Ⓑ Ⓒ Ⓓ
5 Ⓐ Ⓑ Ⓒ Ⓓ	13 Ⓐ Ⓑ Ⓒ Ⓓ	21 Ⓐ Ⓑ Ⓒ Ⓓ	29 Ⓐ Ⓑ Ⓒ Ⓓ	37 Ⓐ Ⓑ Ⓒ Ⓓ
6 Ⓐ Ⓑ Ⓒ Ⓓ	14 Ⓐ Ⓑ Ⓒ Ⓓ	22 Ⓐ Ⓑ Ⓒ Ⓓ	30 Ⓐ Ⓑ Ⓒ Ⓓ	38 Ⓐ Ⓑ Ⓒ Ⓓ
7 Ⓐ Ⓑ Ⓒ Ⓓ	15 Ⓐ Ⓑ Ⓒ Ⓓ	23 Ⓐ Ⓑ Ⓒ Ⓓ	31 Ⓐ Ⓑ Ⓒ Ⓓ	39 Ⓐ Ⓑ Ⓒ Ⓓ
8 Ⓐ Ⓑ Ⓒ Ⓓ	16 Ⓐ Ⓑ Ⓒ Ⓓ	24 Ⓐ Ⓑ Ⓒ Ⓓ	32 Ⓐ Ⓑ Ⓒ Ⓓ	40 Ⓐ Ⓑ Ⓒ Ⓓ

Section 2 Quantitative Reasoning

1 Ⓐ Ⓑ Ⓒ Ⓓ	9 Ⓐ Ⓑ Ⓒ Ⓓ	17 Ⓐ Ⓑ Ⓒ Ⓓ	25 Ⓐ Ⓑ Ⓒ Ⓓ	33 Ⓐ Ⓑ Ⓒ Ⓓ
2 Ⓐ Ⓑ Ⓒ Ⓓ	10 Ⓐ Ⓑ Ⓒ Ⓓ	18 Ⓐ Ⓑ Ⓒ Ⓓ	26 Ⓐ Ⓑ Ⓒ Ⓓ	34 Ⓐ Ⓑ Ⓒ Ⓓ
3 Ⓐ Ⓑ Ⓒ Ⓓ	11 Ⓐ Ⓑ Ⓒ Ⓓ	19 Ⓐ Ⓑ Ⓒ Ⓓ	27 Ⓐ Ⓑ Ⓒ Ⓓ	35 Ⓐ Ⓑ Ⓒ Ⓓ
4 Ⓐ Ⓑ Ⓒ Ⓓ	12 Ⓐ Ⓑ Ⓒ Ⓓ	20 Ⓐ Ⓑ Ⓒ Ⓓ	28 Ⓐ Ⓑ Ⓒ Ⓓ	36 Ⓐ Ⓑ Ⓒ Ⓓ
5 Ⓐ Ⓑ Ⓒ Ⓓ	13 Ⓐ Ⓑ Ⓒ Ⓓ	21 Ⓐ Ⓑ Ⓒ Ⓓ	29 Ⓐ Ⓑ Ⓒ Ⓓ	37 Ⓐ Ⓑ Ⓒ Ⓓ
6 Ⓐ Ⓑ Ⓒ Ⓓ	14 Ⓐ Ⓑ Ⓒ Ⓓ	22 Ⓐ Ⓑ Ⓒ Ⓓ	30 Ⓐ Ⓑ Ⓒ Ⓓ	
7 Ⓐ Ⓑ Ⓒ Ⓓ	15 Ⓐ Ⓑ Ⓒ Ⓓ	23 Ⓐ Ⓑ Ⓒ Ⓓ	31 Ⓐ Ⓑ Ⓒ Ⓓ	
8 Ⓐ Ⓑ Ⓒ Ⓓ	16 Ⓐ Ⓑ Ⓒ Ⓓ	24 Ⓐ Ⓑ Ⓒ Ⓓ	32 Ⓐ Ⓑ Ⓒ Ⓓ	

Section 3 Reading Comprehension

1 Ⓐ Ⓑ Ⓒ Ⓓ	9 Ⓐ Ⓑ Ⓒ Ⓓ	17 Ⓐ Ⓑ Ⓒ Ⓓ	25 Ⓐ Ⓑ Ⓒ Ⓓ	33 Ⓐ Ⓑ Ⓒ Ⓓ
2 Ⓐ Ⓑ Ⓒ Ⓓ	10 Ⓐ Ⓑ Ⓒ Ⓓ	18 Ⓐ Ⓑ Ⓒ Ⓓ	26 Ⓐ Ⓑ Ⓒ Ⓓ	34 Ⓐ Ⓑ Ⓒ Ⓓ
3 Ⓐ Ⓑ Ⓒ Ⓓ	11 Ⓐ Ⓑ Ⓒ Ⓓ	19 Ⓐ Ⓑ Ⓒ Ⓓ	27 Ⓐ Ⓑ Ⓒ Ⓓ	35 Ⓐ Ⓑ Ⓒ Ⓓ
4 Ⓐ Ⓑ Ⓒ Ⓓ	12 Ⓐ Ⓑ Ⓒ Ⓓ	20 Ⓐ Ⓑ Ⓒ Ⓓ	28 Ⓐ Ⓑ Ⓒ Ⓓ	36 Ⓐ Ⓑ Ⓒ Ⓓ
5 Ⓐ Ⓑ Ⓒ Ⓓ	13 Ⓐ Ⓑ Ⓒ Ⓓ	21 Ⓐ Ⓑ Ⓒ Ⓓ	29 Ⓐ Ⓑ Ⓒ Ⓓ	
6 Ⓐ Ⓑ Ⓒ Ⓓ	14 Ⓐ Ⓑ Ⓒ Ⓓ	22 Ⓐ Ⓑ Ⓒ Ⓓ	30 Ⓐ Ⓑ Ⓒ Ⓓ	
7 Ⓐ Ⓑ Ⓒ Ⓓ	15 Ⓐ Ⓑ Ⓒ Ⓓ	23 Ⓐ Ⓑ Ⓒ Ⓓ	31 Ⓐ Ⓑ Ⓒ Ⓓ	
8 Ⓐ Ⓑ Ⓒ Ⓓ	16 Ⓐ Ⓑ Ⓒ Ⓓ	24 Ⓐ Ⓑ Ⓒ Ⓓ	32 Ⓐ Ⓑ Ⓒ Ⓓ	

ISEE Practice Test 2
ANSWER SHEET

Section 4 Mathematics Achievement

1 Ⓐ Ⓑ Ⓒ Ⓓ   11 Ⓐ Ⓑ Ⓒ Ⓓ   21 Ⓐ Ⓑ Ⓒ Ⓓ   31 Ⓐ Ⓑ Ⓒ Ⓓ   41 Ⓐ Ⓑ Ⓒ Ⓓ
2 Ⓐ Ⓑ Ⓒ Ⓓ   12 Ⓐ Ⓑ Ⓒ Ⓓ   22 Ⓐ Ⓑ Ⓒ Ⓓ   32 Ⓐ Ⓑ Ⓒ Ⓓ   42 Ⓐ Ⓑ Ⓒ Ⓓ
3 Ⓐ Ⓑ Ⓒ Ⓓ   13 Ⓐ Ⓑ Ⓒ Ⓓ   23 Ⓐ Ⓑ Ⓒ Ⓓ   33 Ⓐ Ⓑ Ⓒ Ⓓ   43 Ⓐ Ⓑ Ⓒ Ⓓ
4 Ⓐ Ⓑ Ⓒ Ⓓ   14 Ⓐ Ⓑ Ⓒ Ⓓ   24 Ⓐ Ⓑ Ⓒ Ⓓ   34 Ⓐ Ⓑ Ⓒ Ⓓ   44 Ⓐ Ⓑ Ⓒ Ⓓ
5 Ⓐ Ⓑ Ⓒ Ⓓ   15 Ⓐ Ⓑ Ⓒ Ⓓ   25 Ⓐ Ⓑ Ⓒ Ⓓ   35 Ⓐ Ⓑ Ⓒ Ⓓ   45 Ⓐ Ⓑ Ⓒ Ⓓ
6 Ⓐ Ⓑ Ⓒ Ⓓ   16 Ⓐ Ⓑ Ⓒ Ⓓ   26 Ⓐ Ⓑ Ⓒ Ⓓ   36 Ⓐ Ⓑ Ⓒ Ⓓ   46 Ⓐ Ⓑ Ⓒ Ⓓ
7 Ⓐ Ⓑ Ⓒ Ⓓ   17 Ⓐ Ⓑ Ⓒ Ⓓ   27 Ⓐ Ⓑ Ⓒ Ⓓ   37 Ⓐ Ⓑ Ⓒ Ⓓ   47 Ⓐ Ⓑ Ⓒ Ⓓ
8 Ⓐ Ⓑ Ⓒ Ⓓ   18 Ⓐ Ⓑ Ⓒ Ⓓ   28 Ⓐ Ⓑ Ⓒ Ⓓ   38 Ⓐ Ⓑ Ⓒ Ⓓ
9 Ⓐ Ⓑ Ⓒ Ⓓ   19 Ⓐ Ⓑ Ⓒ Ⓓ   29 Ⓐ Ⓑ Ⓒ Ⓓ   39 Ⓐ Ⓑ Ⓒ Ⓓ
10 Ⓐ Ⓑ Ⓒ Ⓓ   20 Ⓐ Ⓑ Ⓒ Ⓓ   30 Ⓐ Ⓑ Ⓒ Ⓓ   40 Ⓐ Ⓑ Ⓒ Ⓓ

SECTION 1 VERBAL REASONING

40 questions   *20 minutes*

Directions: Choose the word that means the same or most nearly the same as the capitalized word.

Sample:
MANNERLY

(A) insolent
(B) polite
(C) pompous
(D) sly

1. LUCID

   (A) confusing
   (B) clear
   (C) weak
   (D) irrelevant

2. SUMPTUOUS

   (A) rich
   (B) paltry
   (C) vegetarian
   (D) hypothetical

3. COUNTERFEIT

   (A) imaginary
   (B) opposite
   (C) false
   (D) ambiguous

4. INOPPORTUNE

   (A) untimely
   (B) convenient
   (C) quick
   (D) inconclusive

5. MALADROIT

   (A) clumsy
   (B) cruel
   (C) adept
   (D) dexterous

6. PROCLAIM

   (A) support
   (B) hear
   (C) dismiss
   (D) declare

7. EQUITABLE

   (A) fair
   (B) biased
   (C) financial
   (D) worthy

8. CRUCIAL

   (A) necessary
   (B) extra
   (C) optional
   (D) rare

9. PERPETUITY

   (A) eternity
   (B) regularity
   (C) purity
   (D) vanity

10. IRE

   (A) confusion
   (B) anger
   (C) exhaustion
   (D) joy

11. DEPLETE

   (A) proclaim
   (B) finish
   (C) conclude
   (D) empty

12. BELLICOSE

   (A) warlike
   (B) happy
   (C) overweight
   (D) loud

13. VALOR

   (A) royalty
   (B) myth
   (C) fame
   (D) courage

14. PIED

   (A) knotted
   (B) baked
   (C) multicolored
   (D) keen

15. OBDURATE

   (A) unclear
   (B) stubborn
   (C) vague
   (D) rewarding

16. WHIMSICAL

   (A) adaptable
   (B) mechanical
   (C) playful
   (D) difficult

17. TRAVAIL

   (A) labor
   (B) travel
   (C) expedition
   (D) pride

18. BLITHE

   (A) happy
   (B) simple
   (C) slender
   (D) uncomplicated

19. PENULTIMATE

   (A) most difficult
   (B) final
   (C) second to last
   (D) first

20. UTILITY

   (A) usefulness
   (B) electricity
   (C) power
   (D) washer

Part Two Sentence Completion

Directions: Fill in the word or words that best complete the following sentences.

Sample:
Although Edwards was shown to be driven and unforgiving throughout the novel, he shows_____in the closing moments.

(A) anger
(B) stubbornness
(C) fear
(D) mercy

Ⓐ Ⓑ Ⓒ ●

21. Even though I hated to agree with the opposition, I had to _____with him.

   (A) digress
   (B) concur
   (C) clash
   (D) dispute

22. Kyoko knew exactly how many miles she had walked because she was wearing _____.

   (A) an abacus
   (B) a pedometer
   (C) a geographer
   (D) a hydrometer

23. The violence onscreen had me looking for the nearest _____.

   (A) egress
   (B) usher
   (C) cashier
   (D) receptacle

24. A _____bird, the owl hunts mostly at night.

   (A) sleepy
   (B) nocturnal
   (C) blind
   (D) wise

25. In order to complete the obstacle course successfully, the runner had to possess strong _____.

   (A) agility
   (B) magnanimity
   (C) variety
   (D) satiety

26. Readers comprehend more easily when what they read is divided into sections, so poets often divide their work into _____.

   (A) paragraphs
   (B) stanzas
   (C) caesuras
   (D) periods

27. A dedicated _____, Rachel grew parsley, sage, rosemary, and thyme.

   (A) carnivore
   (B) industrialist
   (C) balladeer
   (D) herbalist

28. The spokesperson delivered an _____: Take it or leave it.

   (A) answer
   (B) ordinance
   (C) explanation
   (D) ultimatum

29. Sophie is a fine watchdog: loyal, brave, and always _____.

    (A) loving
    (B) vigilant
    (C) somnolent
    (D) abstemious

30. Mrs. Grundy will not tolerate tardiness, so her students must be _____.

    (A) prompt
    (B) succinct
    (C) late
    (D) neat

31. The guide's directions seemed _____ to me; in fact, I ended up where I began.

    (A) misleading
    (B) inconsequential
    (C) circuitous
    (D) linear

32. Ben's frequent boasting is a good indication of his _____.

    (A) arrogance
    (B) humility
    (C) charity
    (D) eloquence

33. I was inspired by the _____ speaker.

    (A) peripatetic
    (B) corporeal
    (C) heinous
    (D) motivational

34. Dr. Moore is an excellent _____; my sore throat was indeed due to an infection, just as she predicted.

    (A) malpractitioner
    (B) empathizer
    (C) diagnostician
    (D) pediatrician

35. Mr. DiCastro's outburst was unexpected; his personality is usually _____.

    (A) placid
    (B) tumultuous
    (C) boisterous
    (D) ebullient

36. One would think that with all of his wealth, Mr. Blake would lead an opulent lifestyle; on the contrary, he lives very _____.

    (A) frugally
    (B) logically
    (C) wastefully
    (D) thoughtlessly

37. Because worms, like us, _____ oxygen to breath, they must come out when the ground is _____ with rain.

    (A) decline . . . devoid
    (B) separate . . . pulsating
    (C) require . . . saturated
    (D) enjoy . . . external

38. The _____ of the house was tastefully decorated, contrasting sharply with the _____ appearance of the outside.

    (A) impression . . . awkward
    (B) exterior . . . cheap
    (C) interior . . . tawdry
    (D) inside . . . lovely

39. The judge was forced to _____ the case because the prosecution could not produce a single _____ witness.

    (A) dismiss . . . credible
    (B) withdraw . . . unreliable
    (C) hear . . . believable
    (D) endure . . . expert

40. The wizard's _____ demeanor was initially off-putting, yet his underlying _____ soon became evident.

    (A) hideous . . . ugliness
    (B) sickly . . . malevolence
    (C) innocent . . . sincerity
    (D) gruff . . . tenderness

9:03 sec. left.

STOP

IF YOU FINISH BEFORE TIME IS UP, YOU MAY CHECK YOUR WORK ON THIS SECTION ONLY. DO NOT TURN TO ANY OTHER SECTION IN THE TEST.

SECTION 2 QUANTITATIVE REASONING

37 questions   *35 minutes*

Directions: This section is a multiple-choice test. Work out the problems and, from the four choices given, select the best answer.

Sample:
Four centimeters are what part of a meter?

(A) 3%
(B) 1/25
(C) 1/30
(D) 5%

Ⓐ ● Ⓒ Ⓓ

1. This graph represents the percentage of federal income tax based upon annual income.

   What is the best estimate of the income tax of someone earning $90,000 per year?

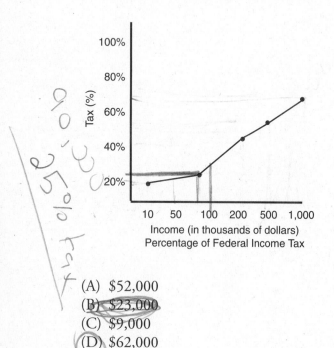

Income (in thousands of dollars)
Percentage of Federal Income Tax

   (A) $52,000
   (B) $23,000
   (C) $9,000
   (D) $62,000

2. The library has a policy of ordering 5 fiction, 2 historical, 3 biographical, and 3 science books in that order. If 124 books were ordered, what subject was the last book?

   (A) fiction
   (B) historical
   (C) biographical
   (D) science

3. Find side *BC* of this right triangle.

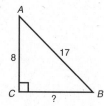

   (A) 12
   (B) 18
   (C) 19
   (D) 15

4. A square pool is 22 feet on each side. Fernando wants to place 6-inch square tiles around the pool. How many tiles does he need to complete the job?

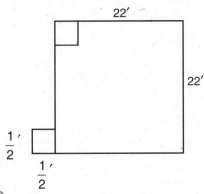

(A) 88
(B) 176
(C) 110
(D) 44

5. $\overrightarrow{BA}$ is perpendicular to $\overrightarrow{BD}$. Angle *ABE* measures 17°, and angle *DBC* measures 54°. Find the measure of angle *EBC*.

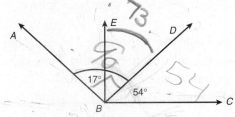

(A) 125°
(B) 71°
(C) 127°
(D) 144°

6. Find the shaded area.

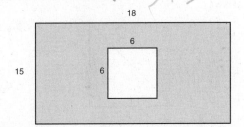

(A) 234
(B) 123
(C) 342
(D) 188

7. Simplify $\sqrt[3]{64a^3b^9}$.

(A) $8ab^3$
(B) $4a^3b^3$
(C) $4a^3b$
(D) $4ab^3$

8. If 16 people, with a total weight of 2,085 pounds, are standing on a floor measuring 20 feet by 32 feet, what is the average weight each square foot of the floor is supporting? Round your answer to the nearest hundredth of a pound.

(A) 4.28 lb
(B) 5.34 lb
(C) 6.03 lb
(D) 3.26 lb

9. Add: $(-4) + (+9) + (-6) + (+3)$

(A) −4
(B) +2
(C) −6
(D) +3

10. Find the value of $\dfrac{4 \times 5^8}{2 \times 5^6}$.

(A) 50
(B) 40
(C) 25
(D) 100

11. What are the coordinates of point *A*?

(A) (−2, 3)
(B) (4, −1)
(C) (−1, 4)
(D) (4, 1)

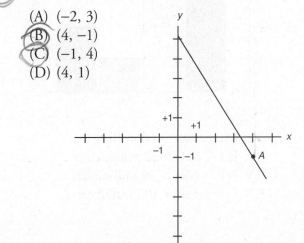

12. Determine the value of x in the equation
$4(x + 2) - 3(x + 1) = 12$.

    (A) 7
    (B) 3
    (C) 4
    (D) 8

13. The measure of the vertex angle of an isosceles triangle is 50°. Find the measure of an exterior angle at the base of the triangle.

    (A) 65°
    (B) 125°
    (C) 115°
    (D) 80°

14. The length of a rectangle is 4 more than twice its width. If the width is represented by w, find the perimeter of the rectangle in terms of w.

    (A) $6w + 12$
    (B) $6w + 8$
    (C) $6w - 6$
    (D) $4w + 8$

15. Examine the bar graph below and select the correct answer.

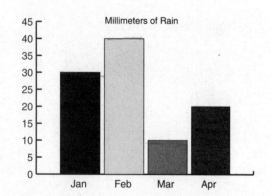

    (A) Mar + Apr = 60 millimeters
    (B) Jan − Mar = 20 millimeters
    (C) Feb − Mar > 40 millimeters
    (D) Apr + Feb > 100 millimeters

16. Change $5\frac{1}{4}\%$ to a fraction.

    (A) 21/400
    (B) 5/100
    (C) 21/100
    (D) 25/150

17. O and O' are the centers of their respective circles.

    Choose the best answer.

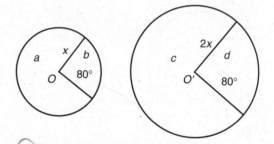

    (A) area c > area a
    (B) area a + area b > area c + area d
    (C) area c − area a > area a + area d
    (D) area c − area b = area d + area a

18. Pedro wants to repackage 212 quarts of cooking oil into liter bottles. How many liter bottles does Pedro need?
(1.06 liters = 1 quart)

    (A) 210
    (B) 180
    (C) 190
    (D) 200

19. Based on the diagram, select the best answer.

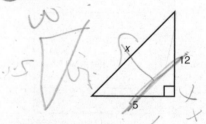

    (A) $5 + 12 < x$
    (B) $x + 5 < 12$
    (C) $x^2 > 5^2 + 12^2$
    (D) $5 + 12 > x$

20. Determine the perimeter of the right triangle.

(A) 5
(B) 24
(C) 9
(D) 17

$a = 8$ $c = ?$ $b = 6$

21. What number is equal to 15 more than two thirds of 30?

(A) 35
(B) 30
(C) 25
(D) 20

Directions: Use the graph below to answer the following question.

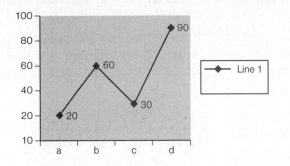

22. Which statement is true?

(A) a + b > d
(B) b + c < d
(C) b + c = d
(D) a + c = d

Directions for Questions 23–37.

In each question, simplify both expressions and then compare them.

Select A if the expression in column A is the greater one.
Select B if the expression in column B is the greater one.
Select C if the two expressions are equal.
Select D if the relationship cannot be determined.

Column A   Column B

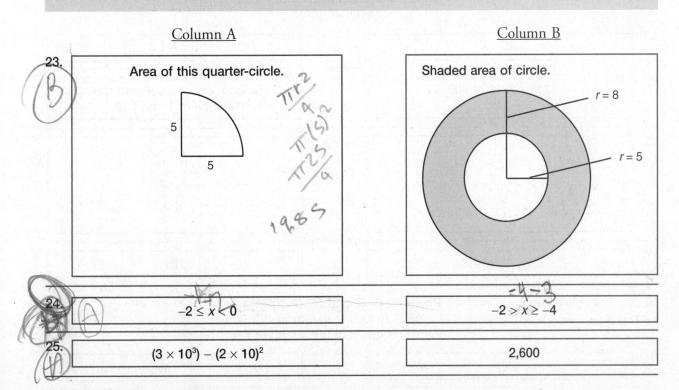

23. Area of this quarter-circle.   Shaded area of circle.

$\frac{\pi r^2}{4}$ $\frac{\pi (5)^2}{4}$ $\frac{\pi 25}{4}$ 1968

5   5 $r = 8$ $r = 5$

24. $-2 \le x < 0$ $-2 > x \ge -4$

25. $(3 \times 10^3) - (2 \times 10)^2$ 2,600

In each question, simplify both expressions and then compare them.

Select A if the expression in column A is the greater one.
Select B if the expression in column B is the greater one.
Select C if the two expressions are equal.
Select D if the relationship cannot be determined.

Column A   Column B

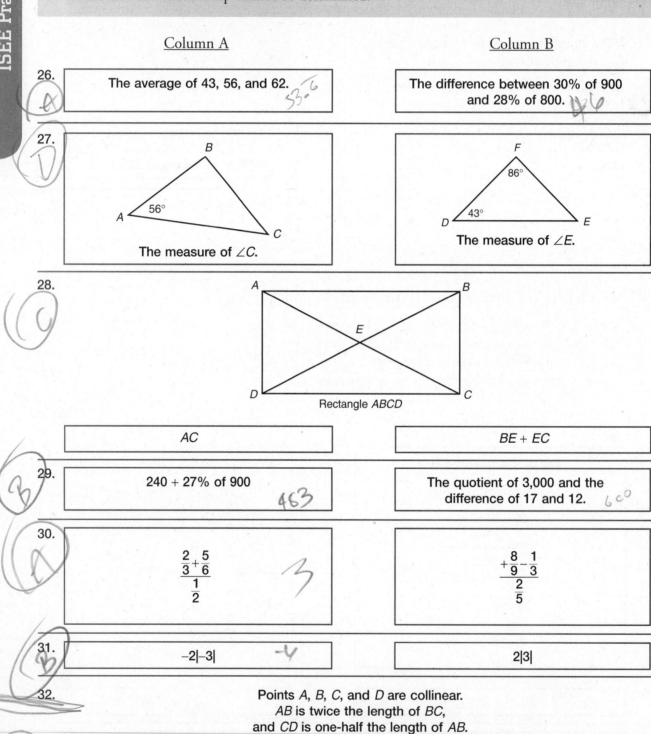

26.

| The average of 43, 56, and 62. | The difference between 30% of 900 and 28% of 800. |

27.

| The measure of ∠C. | The measure of ∠E. |

28.

Rectangle *ABCD*

| AC | BE + EC |

29.

| 240 + 27% of 900 | The quotient of 3,000 and the difference of 17 and 12. |

30.

| $\dfrac{\frac{2}{3}+\frac{5}{6}}{\frac{1}{2}}$ | $\dfrac{+\frac{8}{9}-\frac{1}{3}}{\frac{2}{5}}$ |

31.

| −2|−3| | 2|3| |

32.

Points *A*, *B*, *C*, and *D* are collinear.
AB is twice the length of *BC*,
and *CD* is one-half the length of *AB*.

| BC | CD |

	Column A	Column B
33.	$4x^2 + 3x - 8$	$9x^3$
34.	The greatest common prime factor of 30 and 20.	4
35.	Twenty-one and six-tenths divided by the product of 0.8 and 0.3.	120% of 75.
36.	Besides 1, the number of distinct prime factors of 168.	6
37.	The positive root of the equation $2x^2 = 242$	The root of the equation $5x + 2 = 62$

STOP

IF YOU FINISH BEFORE TIME IS UP, YOU MAY CHECK YOUR WORK ON THIS SECTION ONLY. DO NOT TURN TO ANY OTHER SECTION IN THE TEST.

SECTION 3 READING COMPREHENSION

36 questions   *35 minutes*

Directions: Each passage is followed by questions based on its content. Answer the questions following the passage on the basis of what is **stated** or **implied** in that passage.

Passage for Questions 1–6

World War II involved so many people on such a large stage in so many military actions that no book exists large enough to tell the entire story. We learn about many sensational events, but more keep popping
Line up as we continue to study the event. Consider how long it took before
(5) the story of Oskar Schindler (popularized by the movie *Schindler's List*) was unearthed. Another sensational, but much less happy, story connected to the events of World War II concerns the unfortunate fate of the cruiser S.S. *Indianapolis*.

The S.S. *Indianapolis* was coming up on her 13th year of military
(10) service when she was commissioned to carry a secret cargo to the island of Tinian near Guam. Neither she nor her passengers knew that this May voyage would be her last.

The S.S. *Indianapolis* successfully delivered her cargo—the uranium-235 necessary for the atomic bomb about to be dropped on Hiroshima.
(15) But just days after leaving Tinian's port, she was torpedoed by a Japanese sub. Within twelve minutes she sank, still carrying 300 sailors.

Those "lucky" enough to abandon ship, approximately 900 men, thrashed about in oily, shark-infested water, clinging to life rafts and other pieces of flotsam. Many of the sailors did not survive the first
(20) night; these men, many burned, others lacking life jackets, grew weary of swimming and drowned. The others who died mainly either grew too dehydrated to resist drinking the salty ocean water or died of shark bite. Some died from heroism; they worked too hard to keep up the others' spirits and neglected to marshal their own energy reserves. And a few,
(25) driven mad by the ordeal, swam to their deaths, convinced by mirages that help, or food, or oases were nearby.

It took four days before help arrived; by then, only 316 men clung to life.

And the inexcusable thing is that they were found only by accident.
(30) Captain McVay, commander of the S.S. *Indianapolis* had requested an escort after leaving Guam but was refused. The port of Leyte, his next point of destination, failed to notice the ship's tardiness; no one thought to send out search parties. And none of the planes traveling along their shipping route noticed the huge oil slick or the ship wreckage. Pure luck
(35) allowed Lt. Wilbur C. Gwinn to catch sight of the survivors. All in all, historians call the sinking of the S.S. *Indianapolis* the Navy's greatest sea disaster.

1. The writer's main purpose is apparently
_____.

   (A) to tell about shark attacks in the sea
   near Guam
   (B) to tell about what happened to the
   S.S. *Indianapolis* in her first year of
   service
   (C) to tell about the sinking of the S.S.
   Indianapolis
   (D) to tell about how Oskar Schindler
   helped Jews escape World War II

2. The author's attitude about the sinking of
the S.S. *Indianapolis* can best be described
as _____.

   (A) bitter
   (B) pleased
   (C) hopeless
   (D) relieved

3. Why does the author use a single sentence
in paragraph five?

   (A) S/he ran out of things to say on that
   topic.
   (B) S/he accidentally hit enter while
   typing.
   (C) S/he thought that the information
   conveyed in that paragraph was
   unimportant.
   (D) S/he wants to call attention to the
   duration of time the survivors spent in
   the water.

4. According to the passage, what will happen
if one drinks seawater?

   (A) Nothing, it makes great kool-aid.
   (B) One will know the difference between
   good and evil.
   (C) One will die.
   (D) One will feel refreshed.

5. How many men died due to the sinking of
the S.S. *Indianapolis*?

   (A) 300
   (B) 316
   (C) 584
   (D) 884

6. Which of the following is an example of
flotsam as used in line 19?

   (A) fish
   (B) wreckage
   (C) seaweed
   (D) tides

Passage for Questions 7–11

Although you might hate to admit it, bugs and beetles, earthworms and maggots all play an intrinsic role in the cycle of life. Without decomposition, the world would soon become overpopulated with
Line people, animals, plants, insects, and environments to house them all.
(5) The engines of decomposition are run by bugs and beetles, earthworms and maggots. One man's poison is another man's meat, you might say.

Fungi aid these decomposers by secreting enzymes that digest material on which it grows. Scientists classify the fungi that feed on dead things as saprophytes. Saprophytes come in many varieties
(10) including downy mildew on grapes, onions, and tobacco; powdery mildew on grapes, apples, cherries, lilacs, peaches, and roses; <u>smut</u> on corn, wheat, and onions; rust on wheat, oats, beans, asparagus, and some flowers; brown rot on some fruits; and various spots, blights, and wilts on leaves.

(15) Because they attack only dead organic matter, saprophytes decompose much plant and animal residue. They also attack foodstuffs such as bread, processed meat and cheese, and picked fruits and vegetables. Some saprophytes are responsible for the destruction of timber, textiles, paper, and leather.

7. Saprophytes decompose all but which of the following, according to the article?

   (A) bread
   (B) leather
   (C) wheat
   (D) cantaloupes

8. A group of scientists visit the site of a village in 1993; the houses are entirely made of wood. A year later, these scientists revisit the village only to find the village has gone. What inference can we draw that explains this phenomenon?

   (A) The village has been overrun by surrounding villages.
   (B) Downy mildew has taken over the village trees.
   (C) Saprophytes have decomposed the wooden building materials.
   (D) The villagers have all moved away.

9. What is the author's primary intent in writing this passage?

   (A) to discuss poisons that grow naturally in the region
   (B) to give an overview of the fungi's role in the cycle of life
   (C) to give a lecture on common plant diseases
   (D) to address the difficulties in growing sound lumber

10. A disease strikes the world, destroying all the saprophytes. What will happen?

    (A) Nothing will decompose, and the living will die from overpopulation and exposure to disease.
    (B) Everything will decompose, even the living.
    (C) Timber and leather will disappear, drastically raising prices of such goods.
    (D) Animals will die, causing starvation around the world.

11. Which of the following is the best definition for the word *smut* as used in this passage?

    (A) a fit of anger
    (B) damage to plants
    (C) mucous in the nasal passages
    (D) trashy reading material

Passage for Questions 12–15

Human beings suffer many types of mental disorders and have done so since the dawn of civilization; Greek physician Hippocrates studied these diseases more than a millennia ago. He thought they came from
Line imbalances in the bodily fluids; unsurprisingly, he diagnosed rest,
(5) exercise, and dietary change as a way of restoring balance to the body. Conversely, Middle Age doctors concluded that mental illness came from demon possession; therefore, they prescribed exorcism, torture, and flogging to get rid of the possessing demons.

Modern psychologists attribute mental disorder to chemical reactions
(10) in the body. They have broken down the various types of mental afflictions into broad categories, grouping together the illnesses that have similar symptoms. The categories range from personality disorders (that affect one's ability to discern right from wrong) to affective disorders (that bring about severe bouts of depression) to somatoform
(15) disorders (that cause illness without any physical reason for being sick), just to name a few.

One of the most commonly known (but not necessarily commonly observed) disorders is schizophrenia. People with schizophrenia have trouble making contact with reality. Most commonly, schizophrenics
(20) suffer severe distortion of thoughts, perceptions, and feelings. Often these people will hear voices or even see people who really don't exist. One famous schizophrenic, whose life story was recently examined and popularized by the movie *A Beautiful Mind,* is physicist John Nash.

12. What emotion was the author feeling as s/he wrote this article?

    (A) intellectual curiosity
    (B) dread
    (C) surprise
    (D) confusion

13. The best title for this piece would be _____.

    (A) Under Pressure
    (B) A Splinter in the Mind's Eye
    (C) All Screwed Up
    (D) Mental Illness: How to Help

14. Which of the following accurately describes the organization of this passage?

    (A) three paragraphs discussing famous people who were mentally ill
    (B) two paragraphs talking about what causes depression
    (C) one paragraph talking about how our perception of mental illness has changed over time, followed by two paragraphs of examples
    (D) two paragraphs talking about how our perception of mental illness has changed over time, followed by one paragraph of examples

15. According to the passage, all but which of the following words describe John Nash?

    (A) victim of a personality disorder
    (B) Nobel Prize winner
    (C) physicist
    (D) diagnosed schizophrenic

Passage for Questions 16–20

What was once a mystery has now become the subject of routine memorization. Students learn as early as the seventh grade about twins, both fraternal (when two eggs get fertilized) and identical (when one
Line fertilized egg divides into two separate embryos). The United States
(5) currently contains two million sets of twins; about fifty million sets of twins exist worldwide. Of these, about fifteen percent are identical.

During the past decade, the rate at which twins are conceived has increased. This has taken place for two closely related reasons. First, women are delaying having children. Women have joined the work
(10) force, taking on careers that are just as important as their husbands. Often they put off having kids until they are sure they won't lose their jobs when they go on maternity leave. This means that women are not starting to have kids until their late thirties and sometimes forties. Unfortunately, this is a time during which the body starts naturally
(15) resisting conception. As women get older, their body becomes increasingly inefficient. They become more likely to release two eggs rather than one during the menstruation cycle; the release of two eggs naturally increases the chances that twins will be conceived.

The second reason why women are increasingly likely to have twins is
(20) closely related to the first. Because women are starting families later in life, they often experience poor conception rates. To compensate for this, women turn to fertility drugs. Using fertility drugs increases the chances that the women will release two eggs or that a single egg will split into two embryos.

(25) Whatever the reason that the chances of conceiving twins are increasing, the chances of these twins surviving have also improved. Medical technology has improved greatly; doctors now use stethoscopes so <u>perceptive</u> that they can detect multiple fetal heartbeats without confusing them with the mother's. Moreover, physicians use ultrasound
(30) technology, the use of sound waves to create a visual image of the developing embryo and to monitor fetal development. Finally, advances in nutrition research help ensure a healthy pregnancy from even before conception.

16. What is the purpose of paragraph three?

    (A) to take up space
    (B) to give a third reason why women are increasingly likely to conceive twins
    (C) to give an example of how medical technology has improved
    (D) to explain how fertility drugs affect the likelihood of conceiving twins

17. The author wrote this piece in order to inform people of _____.

    (A) the dangers of using fertility drugs.
    (B) factors that determine how often twins are conceived.
    (C) how bodily changes affect how often twins are conceived.
    (D) how many pairs of twins exist worldwide.

18. How many sets of twins are there in the world?

    (A) 2 million
    (B) 15 million
    (C) 50 million
    (D) 70 million

19. How would you define the word *perceptive* as used in the passage?

    (A) able to notice obvious things
    (B) able to notice subtle things
    (C) able to notice expensive things
    (D) able to notice sweet things

20. According to the article, how many twins are identical?

    (A) 200,000
    (B) 450,000
    (C) 650,000
    (D) 750,000

Passage for Questions 21–25

Cholera is an infection of the small intestine; its symptoms include watery diarrhea, vomiting, and, therefore, dehydration. It strikes as the result of consuming food or water that is contaminated with the bacterium *Line* *Vibrio cholerae.* Doctors nowadays can successfully treat cholera with
(5) antibiotics and intravenous fluid infusions, but the disease remains potent. Take, for example, the cholera outbreak in Rwanda in 1994; more than 23,000 people died, despite the <u>ministrations</u> of physicians.

One such cholera epidemic struck the small town of Lexington, Kentucky, in the 1820s. The disease devastated the town, frightening
(10) Lexingtonians so much that no one dared venture out of doors. Bodies lay unburied, rotting, and ignored all over town.

Finally, someone dared do something to combat the plague. Was it the governor? Was it one of the genteel, respected Lexington families? A principled young doctor willing to pay the final price to fulfill his Hippocratic
(15) oath? No. It was a drunkard who owed back taxes to the state named "King" Solomon. As one might assume, "King" Solomon eventually contracted cholera himself and died, but not before he buried enough bodies to beat back the disease.

Despite "King" Solomon's efforts, cholera killed hordes of people,
(20) leaving scores of orphans behind. Shamed into public service by the actions of "King" Solomon, William Morton donated $9,000 to provide a school for those orphaned by the epidemic.

21. From what source did "King" Solomon likely get his nickname?

   (A) from the Greek word, *solo*, which means alone, and *mon*, which means man
   (B) from the old movie, *King Solomon's Mines*
   (C) from the biblical story of wise King Solomon
   (D) from the famous saying, "rich as King Solomon"

22. When did cholera break out in Rwanda?

   (A) 1800
   (B) 1820
   (C) 1900
   (D) 1994

23. From what bacterium does cholera come?

   (A) *Vibrio pestis*
   (B) *Vibrio plagae*
   (C) *Vibrio pneumoniae*
   (D) *Vibrio cholerae*

24. What topic should the author discuss next, if s/he chooses to continue paragraph four?

   (A) more information about the symptoms of cholera
   (B) more information about "King" Solomon
   (C) more information about William Morton and his school
   (D) more information about the cholera outbreak in Rwanda

25. Which of the following is the best definition of *ministrations* as used in this passage?

   (A) religious attentions
   (B) musical therapy
   (C) medical techniques
   (D) holistic theory

Passage for Questions 26–31

When foul play takes place, it becomes necessary to determine the cause of death and other details that can lead to the guilty party. We call this type of investigation forensic investigation. People in the United States
Line find themselves increasingly interested in this topic—witness our tastes in
(5) entertainment. Increasing numbers of TV shows and movies developed since 1980 deal with forensic investigation. TV series like *The X Files*, *CSI*, and *ER* as well as movies like *The Fugitive* come to mind as examples that support this claim.

Although the first instance of forensic medicine occurred in 300 B.C.,
(10) when doctors in Greece performed autopsies to discover the origins of disease plaguing their city, people were initially too squeamish to allow routine dissections of human corpses. The Greeks, the Romans, the Chinese, and the Muslims all enforced cultural taboos that prevented people from opening dead bodies. Indeed, human dissections were strictly
(15) forbidden in the Middle Ages. However, autopsies lost their stigma during the Renaissance; Leonardo da Vinci dissected 30 corpses on his own. By the 1800s, the study of bodily pathologies came into full flower, culminating in the discovery and study of cells by the early 19th century.

The first methodical forensic investigators used the Bertillon system,
(20) also called "bertillonage," from about 1882 to 1905. Generally speaking, the method depended upon measuring parts of the adult body that resist change, for example, the skeleton, especially the skull, arm span, feet, forearm, and fingers. Even though forensic medicine has become increasingly refined over time, it nevertheless still pays its respects to the Bertillon
(25) system; often doctors will compare measurements taken during autopsies with X-rays taken prior to death.

Modern forensic doctors can perform magical feats. From merely a skull and some information about the victim's DNA, doctors can actually recreate the victim's appearance while alive. Such information is useful when
(30) the skeletons have been subjected to extreme temperatures or long periods of time exposed to the elements. Many a Jane Doe has been identified using these modern methods.

26. Why would investigators compare measurements of a body before death with measurements of the body after death?

    (A) to confirm that the body is indeed dead
    (B) to verify that the deceased had gained weight prior to death
    (C) to find out what level of high school the deceased had
    (D) to learn cause of death

27. When did autopsies become routine, according to the article?

    (A) the 1200s
    (B) the 1400s
    (C) the 1600s
    (D) the 1800s

28. When did doctors favor the Bertillon system?

    (A) 1980 A.D.
    (B) 1907 A.D.
    (C) 1890 A.D.
    (D) 300 B.C.

29. What is the purpose of paragraph one?

    (A) to engage the reader's attention
    (B) to disgust the reader
    (C) to have an excuse to mention TV shows
    (D) to conclude the passage

30. What did the author hope to accomplish by writing this article?

    (A) to explain a cultural phenomenon that took place after 1980
    (B) to give a brief overview of the history of forensic medicine
    (C) to encourage readers to support modern medical procedure
    (D) to convince readers that reinstating the ban on autopsies is a good idea

31. If a Roman doctor insisted on performing autopsies, under what conditions would he have worked?

    (A) in public
    (B) in Greece
    (C) in secret
    (D) on TV

Passage for Questions 32–36

The cat has existed almost as long as the dog. Scientists trace the cat back to a weasel-like animal called *Miacis* that originated about 50 million years ago. Cats were present, but undomesticated, by the end of the Stone

Line Age. Initially, people viewed cats in a positive light; they were seen as
(5) advantageous to society. The Egyptians certainly found cats useful; they trained their felines to hunt fish and birds, as well as to destroy mice and rats in their warehouses. In fact, Egyptians considered the cat so useful that they protected <u>them</u> by law. They even started a cat cult (worshiping the cat goddess Bast) that lasted more than 2,000 years.

(10) Unfortunately for the cat, its reputation suffered by the time of the Middle Ages. At that time, people treated cats much as they treated witches, fearing their evil influences. <u>Posses</u> of frightened villagers hunted down cats, beating and torturing them, often burning them, hoping to catch a witch in disguise. Luckily for cats, they are now enjoying a resur-
(15) gence of good will. Many people love cats, whether for personal use or profit.

Unsurprisingly, therefore, cats figure prominently in children's stories. Early tales tell of clever felines, like "Puss in Boots" and "Dick Whittington and His Cat," both of whom made their masters rich. However, other
(20) stories tell of evil cats who aid their evil mistresses in casting spells and making trouble. Interestingly, if you order the stories by the date of their composition, you will notice a trend: Early stories talk about good cats, whereas stories handed down from the Middle Ages and early colonial era talk about evil cats. In short, the time when the story was conceived shows
(25) how society feels about cats.

32. The main idea of this selection may be expressed as _____.

    (A) a brief history of the feline
    (B) a brief history of the canine
    (C) a brief history of the witch
    (D) a brief history of the *Miacis*

33. The cat(s) who helped his master as mentioned in this passage _____.

    (A) were the three little kittens who lost their mittens
    (B) were Tom and Jerry
    (C) was Puss in Boots
    (D) was Bast

34. If stories about cats reflect society's current opinion of them, we can expect 21st century tales, shows, and movies to _____.

    (A) give generally negative portrayals of cats
    (B) give generally neutral portrayals of cats
    (C) give generally positive portrayals of cats
    (D) experience no change at all

35. The word *posse* as used in line 12 is best defined as . . .

    (A) a group of acquaintances who happen to be going in the same direction
    (B) holding a position so that someone can take your picture
    (C) the Latin verb meaning to be able to
    (D) a band of people with a common purpose

36. In which time period would cats be experiencing negative social feedback?

    (A) 1990 A.D.
    (B) 1300 A.D.
    (C) 1000 B.C.
    (D) 2000 B.C.

STOP

IF YOU FINISH BEFORE TIME IS UP, YOU MAY CHECK YOUR WORK ON THIS SECTION ONLY. DO NOT TURN TO ANY OTHER SECTION IN THE TEST.

SECTION 4 MATHEMATICS ACHIEVEMENT

47 questions   *40 minutes*

Directions: At the end of each problem, you have a choice of four possible answers. Work out each problem and then choose the best possible answer.

Sample:
What number is 22 more than 6% of 450?
(A) 25
(B) 49
(C) 38
(D) 54

1. Change 4.05×10^{-3} to a decimal.

   (A) 0.405
   (B) 0.0405
   (C) 0.00405
   (D) 0.000405

2. Find side x in the diagram.

   (A) 6
   (B) 7
   (C) 5
   (D) 4

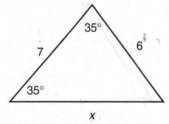

3. Find the closest two-place decimal approximation to two-sevenths.

   (A) 0.27
   (B) 0.28
   (C) 0.285
   (D) 0.29

4. Find the measure of $\angle e$ if angles f, a, and b, respectively, measure 88°, 63°, and 29°.

   (A) 33°
   (B) 29°
   (C) 88°
   (D) 62°

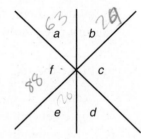

5. Maureen weighed 138 pounds on July first. If she lost $2\frac{1}{3}$ pounds per week, how much did she weigh at the end of six weeks?

   (A) 130 pounds
   (B) 134 pounds
   (C) 128 pounds
   (D) 124 pounds

6. If $9p - 7 > 12$, which of the following choices can be a possible value of p?

   (A) 0
   (B) 1
   (C) 2
   (D) 3

7. The sides of a pentagon-shaped area are 49.2 feet, 56.4 feet, 62.7 feet, 47.3 feet, and 65.4 feet. If a fence costs $3.74 per foot, find the cost of a fence for the entire perimeter and round off to the nearest dollar.

   (A) $1,532
   (B) $1,050
   (C) $1,051
   (D) $1,531

8. The sum of the first and second of four consecutive even integers is 8 more than the fourth. Find the smallest integer.

   (A) 12
   (B) 14
   (C) 16
   (D) 10

9. Examine the rectangle and the equilateral triangle and then select the best answer.

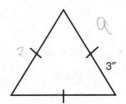

   (A) The perimeter of the rectangle is 10″ more than the perimeter of the equilateral triangle.
   (B) The perimeter of the equilateral triangle is 8″ less than the perimeter of the rectangle.
   (C) The perimeter of the rectangle is 11″ more than the perimeter of the equilateral triangle.
   (D) The perimeter of the equilateral triangle is 12″ less than the perimeter of the rectangle.

10. Given the inequality $3 \le 2x + 1 < 9$, select a possible value for x.

    (A) 0
    (B) 4
    (C) 3
    (D) 5

11. This rectangle is made up of small squares, each with an area of 16 square inches. Determine the perimeter of rectangle *ABCD*.

    (A) 30
    (B) 48
    (C) 34
    (D) 36

12. Given the equation $pq - r = s$, find the value of q.

    (A) $\dfrac{s+r}{p}$

    (B) $\dfrac{sr}{p}$

    (C) $\dfrac{s-p}{r}$

    (D) $\dfrac{p+r}{s}$

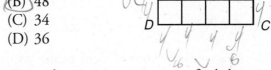

13. Six oranges and eight apples cost $5.66. If one orange costs $0.37, how much does one apple cost?

    (A) $0.28
    (B) $32
    (C) $0.37
    (D) $0.43

14. The sides of a triangle are represented by x, $x + 3$, and $2x + 1$. If the perimeter is 20, find the smallest side.

    (A) 9
    (B) 8
    (C) 4
    (D) 6

15. Find the sum of $(3r^2 - 2r - 7)$ and $(-4r + 8 - r^2)$.

    (A) $2r^2 + 5r - 1$
    (B) $7r^2 + 6r - 2$
    (C) $2r^2 - 6r + 1$
    (D) $5r^2 - 6r - 7$

16. What is the smallest number we can add to the quotient of 35 and 7 to produce an answer that is a multiple of 4?

    (A) 1
    (B) 2
    (C) 3
    (D) 4

17. In a study, five out of eight people are not left-handed. How many left-handed people would you expect in a population of 6,400?

    (A) 3,000
    (B) 2,400
    (C) 2,000
    (D) 1,800

18. Eloise works for 46 hours at a rate of $15.84 per hour for the first 40 hours and time-and-a-half for any hours above 40. What is her total salary?

    (A) $776.16
    (B) $633.60
    (C) $142.56
    (D) $728.64

19. Given the two following equations, find the value of p:

$$3p - 2q = 2$$
$$4p + 2q = 26$$

    (A) 4
    (B) 5
    (C) 3
    (D) 2

20. A bed of earth is to be planted around a rectangular pool. If the bed of earth is 45 feet long and 34 feet wide and the pool is 31 feet long and 26 feet wide, how many square feet of earth do we need?

    (A) 1,530 sq ft
    (B) 806 sq ft
    (C) 2,336 sq ft
    (D) 724 sq ft

21. Change $43\frac{1}{2}\%$ to a fraction.

    (A) $\frac{87}{100}$
    (B) $\frac{87}{200}$
    (C) $\frac{435}{200}$
    (D) $\frac{435}{100}$

22. The price of a suit is increased by 20% and then reduced by 10%. If the final selling price is $194.40, what was the original price of the suit?

    (A) $140
    (B) $150
    (C) $170
    (D) $180

23. Simplify $\dfrac{\frac{5}{8} + \frac{1}{4}}{\frac{5}{6} - \frac{2}{36}}$.

    (A) $3\frac{1}{4}$
    (B) $5\frac{1}{2}$
    (C) $5\frac{1}{4}$
    (D) $4\frac{2}{3}$

24. Determine the area of triangle *ABC*.

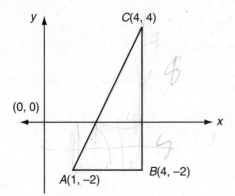

(A) 13
(B) 9
(C) 10
(D) 17

25. Vicky and Howard own a gasoline station. They agree to split the profits in the ratio 5 : 3, with Vicky getting the greater share. In one week, if they make a profit of $2,480, how much does Howard get?

(A) $310
(B) $1,550
(C) $930
(D) $750

26. If $r = \dfrac{2}{3}$, $s = \dfrac{3}{5}$, and $3r + 10s + t = 15$, find the value of *t*.

(A) 7
(B) 5
(C) 6
(D) 4

27. Change $\dfrac{5}{7}$ to a two-place decimal.

(A) .66
(B) .83
(C) .71
(D) .62

28. For all real numbers *r* and *s*, $r \# s = r^2 - 3s$. Find the value of 5 # 8.

(A) 1
(B) 3
(C) 5
(D) 2

29. If one screw weighs 2 grams, how many screws are there in a package weighing 78 kilograms? 1 kilogram = 1,000 grams.

(A) 14,000
(B) 20,000
(C) 28,000
(D) 39,000

30. Tanisha kept a record of the calories she consumed every day of the week.

Calories

4,000 ┤
3,400 ┤
2,800 ┤
2,200 ┤
1,600 ┤
      Mon Tues Wed Thurs Fri Sat Sun

On an average, how many calories did she consume per day for the seven days?

(A) 2,800
(B) 3,400
(C) 3,000
(D) 2,600

31. Change 150 minutes to hours.

(A) 3 hours
(B) $2\dfrac{1}{2}$ hours
(C) $3\dfrac{1}{2}$ hours
(D) $2\dfrac{3}{4}$ hours

32. *ABCD* is a parallelogram and *AB* = 12″, *BC* = 12″.

Find the measure of ∠1.

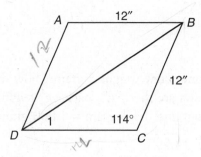

(A) 114°
(B) 66°
(C) 64°
(D) 33°

33. Find the price of 24 pens at the price of $\frac{1}{2}$ dozen for $6.52.

(A) $14.94
(B) $13.04
(C) $26.08
(D) $32.60

34. Find the quotient of $2\frac{5}{6}$ and $3\frac{2}{3}$.

(A) $\frac{19}{21}$

(B) $\frac{24}{25}$

(C) $\frac{17}{22}$

(D) $\frac{18}{19}$

35. If $4 < x < 9$ and $5 \geq x > 3$, which of the following choices is a possible value of *x*?

(A) 6
(B) 3
(C) 5
(D) 2

36. If $\frac{a}{b} = \frac{c}{d}$, find the value of a in terms of *b*, *c*, and *d*.

(A) $bc - d$

(B) $\frac{bc}{d}$

(C) $\frac{bd}{c}$

(D) $\frac{cd}{b}$

37. Two-thirds of what number is equal to 18 more than 60% of 40?

(A) 27
(B) 33
(C) 36
(D) 63

38. Find the missing number in the following expression: 6(? + 5) − 3 = 135.

(A) 6
(B) 12
(C) 20
(D) 18

39. If U is the universal set of all countries of South America, P = {Uruguay, Chile, Brazil} and Q = {Argentina, Colombia, Paraguay}, find the intersection of the two sets.

(A) Argentina
(B) Colombia, Paraguay
(C) empty set
(D) Chile, Argentina

40. A cylinder contains 8 kilograms of chemicals. If a manufacturer wants to package the chemicals in 20-gram containers, how many of these small containers can be packaged? 1 kilogram = 1,000 grams.

(A) 200
(B) 300
(C) 400
(D) 500

41. The difference of 24 and a number is equal to the product of six-sevenths and 21. Find the number.

    (A) 4
    (B) 6
    (C) 8
    (D) 9

42. Which of the following statements is true?

    (a) $4^2 + 5(9-3)$
    (b) $3 \times 17-5$
    (c) $2|-5| + 4|2|$
    (d) 6^2-2^3

    (A) $a > b$
    (B) $b < a$
    (C) $d \geq b$
    (D) $c < d$

43. If *ABCD* is a square, which statement is false?

    (A) Angle *B* is a right angle.
    (B) The measure of angle *B* equals the measure of angle *C*.
    (C) The measure of angle *B* plus the measure of angle *A* equals 180°.
    (D) *BC* is perpendicular to *AD*.

44. The base of a parallelogram is 4 more than its side. If its perimeter is 44 and its height is 7, find its area.

    (A) 88
    (B) 91
    (C) 76
    (D) 98

45. Find the sum of $\frac{2}{a} + \frac{3}{b}$.

    (A) $\dfrac{2ab}{a+b}$

    (B) $\dfrac{6}{ab}$

    (C) $\dfrac{3a}{2b+3a}$

    (D) $\dfrac{2b+3a}{ab}$

46. The library has a policy of ordering 5 fiction, 2 historical, 3 biographical, and 3 science books in that order. If 124 books were ordered, what subject was the last book?

    (A) fiction
    (B) historical
    (C) biographical
    (D) science

47. Express 7.002 as a fraction. *Reduce to lowest terms.*

    (A) $7\dfrac{2}{100}$

    (B) $7\dfrac{1}{500}$

    (C) $7\dfrac{2}{1,000}$

    (D) $7\dfrac{1}{50}$

STOP

IF YOU FINISH BEFORE TIME IS UP, YOU MAY CHECK YOUR WORK ON THIS SECTION ONLY. DO NOT TURN TO ANY OTHER SECTION IN THE TEST.

SECTION 5 ESSAY

1 question   *30 minutes*

Directions: Write an essay responding to the following topic. Please write legibly and use only blue or black ink.

Topic: *If you were on a deserted island, what things would you miss most? Why?*

— things: family & friends, books
family: close love em lots
friends: same
books: explore
TV:

If I were stranded on a deserted island, the things I would miss the most would be my family and friends, my phone, my books.

I would miss my family and friends the most because I love them more than anything in the world. I would feel lonely and lost without my friends and family.

I would miss my phone because if I had it and there was service (which is very improbable) I would be able to call for rescue. I could also play games on it if I got bored, but it would probably run out of battery and then I would be stuck with a dead phone, which is useless.

I would miss my books because if they were there I could read them and hopefully

35. **(A)** We're looking for a synonym for calm. The other choices have the opposite meaning. If you are unfamiliar with these words, it would be a good idea to look them up and make note cards.

36. **(A)** The word that would be **contrary** to opulent or wealthy would be frugal.

37. **(C)** This is the only choice that makes sense.

38. **(C)** "Contrasting" is the clue word, telling us that we are looking for the opposite of exterior for the first blank. We have two choices: C (interior) and D (inside). The opposite of tasteful for the second blank matches with B and C. Only choice C fits both blanks.

39. **(A)** Because the prosecution could not produce some sort of witness, the judge had to do something **negative**. The best choices are to dismiss or withdraw (A and B). The prosecution could not produce a **good** witness, so that would be A, credible or believable.

40. **(D)** The word "yet" tells us we're looking for **contrast**. The first half of the sentence describes his "off-putting" or **negative** appearance, so the second half must be **positive**.

Section 2 Quantitative Reasoning

1.

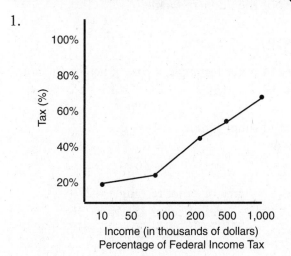

Tax (%) / Income (in thousands of dollars) / Percentage of Federal Income Tax

ANALYSIS

The horizontal axis represents income in thousands of dollars while the vertical axis represents the percentage of federal income tax. Approximate the percentage of federal income tax on $90,000, change the percent to a decimal, and multiply by $90,000.

WORK

According to the graph, it looks like the percent income tax on $90,000 is about 25%.

$$25\% = 0.25$$
$$0.25 \times \$90,000 = \$22,500 \approx \$23,000$$

ANSWER: (B)

2.
ANALYSIS

Add up all the ratios and divide into 124. Find the remainder and then check to see which is the last book in the remainder.

WORK

$$5 + 2 + 3 + 3 = 13$$
$$\frac{124}{13} = 9\frac{7}{13}$$

There is a remainder of 7. In order, we can purchase 5 fiction and 2 historical books. The historical book is the last book we can order.

ANSWER: (B)

3.
ANALYSIS

Use the Pythagorean Theorem $a^2 + b^2 = c^2$, where a and b are two legs of a right triangle and c is the hypotenuse.

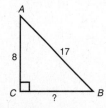

WORK

$$a^2 + b^2 = c^2$$

$b = 8$, $c = 17$: $\qquad a^2 + 8^2 = 17^2$

$$a^2 + 64 = 289$$

Subtract 64: $\qquad\qquad a^2 = 225$

Take the square root: $\qquad a = 15$

ANSWER: (D)

4.

ANALYSIS

First of all, change 6 inches to $\frac{1}{2}$ foot.

Determine how many $\frac{1}{2}$ foot tiles are needed

for one side of the pool and then multiply by 4, for all four sides.

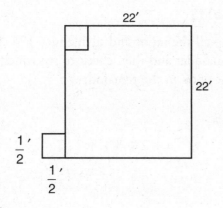

WORK

$$\frac{22}{1/2} = \frac{22}{0.5} = 44 \text{ tiles for one side}$$

$$44 \times 4 = 176 \text{ for all 4 sides}$$

ANSWER: (B)

5.

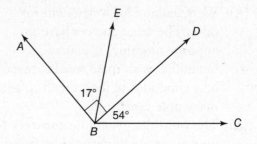

ANALYSIS

First, find the measure of angle *EBD*. Then add the result to 54° (measure of angle *DBC*) to find the measure of angle *EBC*.

WORK

$$m\angle DBE = 90° - 17° = 73°$$
$$m\angle EBC = 73° + 54° = 127°$$

ANSWER: (C)

6.

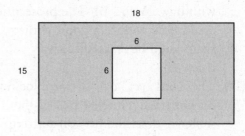

ANALYSIS

Subtract the area of the inner square from the area of the outer rectangle.

WORK

area of outer rectangle = base × height (or *bh*)

$b = 18$, $h = 15$: $\qquad = 18 \times 15$

$$= 270$$

area of inner square $\quad = s^2$

$s = 6$: $\qquad\qquad\qquad = 6^2$

$$= 36$$

area of outer rectangle = 270

$\underline{- \text{ area of inner square} = \quad 36}$

shaded area = 234

ANSWER: (A)

7.

ANALYSIS

We want to find a monomial that, when multiplied by itself three times, is equal to $64a^3b^9$.

WORK

$$\sqrt[3]{64a^3b^9} = 4ab^3$$

Check: $4ab^3 \cdot 4ab^3 \cdot 4ab^3 = 64a^3b^9$ ✔

ANSWER: (D)

8.

ANALYSIS

Find the area of the floor (20×32) and then divide the total weight (2,085) by the area.

WORK

$$20 \times 32 = 640$$
$$2,085/640 = 3.257 \approx 3.26$$

ANSWER: (D)

9.

ANALYSIS

Add the negative and positive numbers separately and then combine the two answers.

WORK

$$(-4) + (-6) = -10$$
$$(+9) + (+3) = \underline{+12}$$
$$+2$$

ANSWER: (B)

10.

ANALYSIS

Divide 5^8 by 5^6 and then simplify.

WORK

$$\frac{\overset{2}{4} \times \overset{5^2}{5^8}}{\underset{1}{2} \times \underset{1}{5^6}} = 2 \times 25 = 50$$

ANSWER: (A)

11.

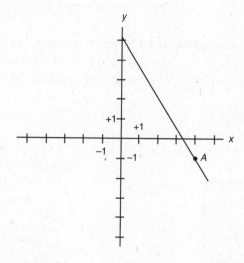

ANALYSIS

The x-coordinates of points to the right of the y-axis are positive. The y-coordinates of points below the x-axis are negative.

WORK

4 units to the right and 1 unit down: $(4, -1)$

ANSWER: (B)

12.

ANALYSIS

Multiply the expression inside the parentheses by 2 and simplify the resulting equation.

WORK

$$4(x + 2) - \quad + 1) = 12$$
$$4x + 8 - \quad - 3 = 12$$
$$+ 5 = 12$$
$$1x = 7$$
$$x = 7$$

ANSWER: (A)

13.

ANALYSIS

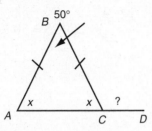

Draw a diagram of an isosceles triangle. Let x = each of the base angles. Then set the sum of the measures of all three angles equal to 180°.

WORK

$$(x) + (x) + (50) = 180$$
$$2x + 50 = 180$$

Subtract 50: $2x = 130$
Divide by 2: $x = 65$

$\angle BCD$ and
$\angle BCA$ are
supplementary: $m\angle BCA + m\angle BCD = 180$
$x = m\angle BCA = 65$: $65 + m\angle BCD = 180$
Subtract 65: $m\angle BCD = 115$

ANSWER: (C)

14.

ANALYSIS

Let w = width and $2w + 4$ = length and add all the sides.

WORK

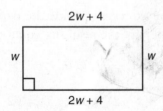

Perimeter $= (2w + 4) + (2w + 4) + w + w$
$= 2w + 4 + 2w + 4 + w + w$
$= 6w + 8$

ANSWER: (B)

15.

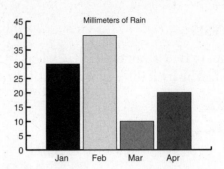

ANALYSIS

Construct a table and select the values for each month. Then substitute into each of the choices.

WORK

Jan	Feb	Mar	Apr
30	40	10	20

Jan − Mar = 20 millimeters
$30 - 10 = 20$ ✔

ANSWER: (B)

16.
ANALYSIS

$$5\frac{1}{4}\% = \frac{5\frac{1}{4}}{100}$$

WORK

$$\frac{5\frac{1}{4}}{100} = \frac{21/4}{100} = \frac{21}{4} \div \frac{100}{1} = \frac{21}{4} \cdot \frac{1}{100} = \frac{21}{400}$$

ANSWER: (A)

17.

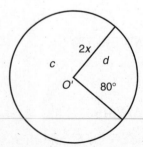

ANALYSIS

Since circle O' is larger than circle O and the central angles are congruent, area $d >$ area b and area $c >$ area a.

WORK

area $c >$ area a ✔

ANSWER: (A)

18.
ANALYSIS

Divide 212 by 1.06.

WORK

$$
\begin{array}{r}
200. \\
1{\scriptstyle\wedge}06.\overline{)212{\scriptstyle\wedge}00.} \\
212 \\ \hline
\end{array}
$$

ANSWER: (D)

19.

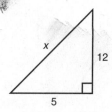

ANALYSIS

Use the Pythagorean Theorem to solve for x and then substitute into the given inequalities.

WORK

$a = 5$, $b = 12$, $c = x$.

$$
\begin{aligned}
a^2 + b^2 &= c^2 \\
5^2 + 12^2 &= x^2 \\
25 + 144 &= x^2 \\
169 &= x^2 \\
13 &= x \\
x &= 13 \\
5 + 12 &> x \\
17 &> 13 \ ✔
\end{aligned}
$$

ANSWER: (D)

20.

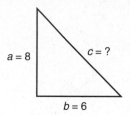

ANALYSIS

Use the Pythagorean Theorem to find the hypotenuse. Then add up all the sides of the triangle.

WORK

$$
\begin{aligned}
a^2 + b^2 &= c^2 \\
8^2 + 6^2 &= c^2 \\
64 + 36 &= c^2 \\
100 &= c^2 \\
c &= 10
\end{aligned}
$$

Perimeter $= a + b + c = 8 + 6 + 10 = 24$

ANSWER: (B)

21.
ANALYSIS

Let $x =$ the unknown number.

WORK

$$
\begin{aligned}
x &= \frac{2}{3} \times 30 + 15 \\
x &= 20 + 15 \\
x &= 35
\end{aligned}
$$

ANSWER: (A)

22.
ANALYSIS

Determine the values of a, b, c, and d and then substitute into (A), (B), (C), and (D).

WORK

$$a = 20$$
$$b = 60$$
$$c = 30$$
$$d = 90$$

$$b + c = d$$
$$60 + 30 = 90$$

ANSWER: (C)

23.

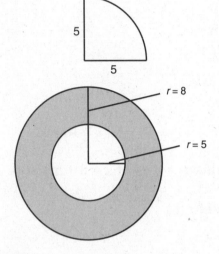

ANALYSIS

Area of circle, $A, = \pi r^2$, where $\pi = 3.14$ and r = radius.

WORK

A. area of quarter circle $= \dfrac{1}{4}$ area of whole circle.

$$A = \frac{1}{4} \times \pi r^2$$

$\pi = 3.14$, $r = 5$:
$$A = \frac{1}{4} \times 3.14 \times 5^2$$

$$A = \frac{1}{4} \times 3.14 \times 25$$

$$A = 19.625 \approx 19.6$$

B. radius of outer circle, $r_o = 8$
radius of inner circle, $r_i = 5$

shaded area = area of outer circle −
area of inner area
$$= \pi (r_o)^2 - \pi (r_i)^2$$

$\pi = 3.14$, $r_o = 8$,
$r_i = 5$:
$$= (3.14)(8)^2 - (3.14)(5)^2$$
$$= (3.14)(64) - (3.14)(25)$$
$$= 200.96 - 78.5$$
$$= 122.46$$

ANSWER: (B)

24.
ANALYSIS

The best way to determine which of the inequalities includes the larger numbers is to construct a diagram.

WORK

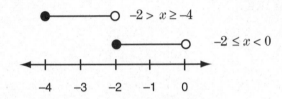

$-2 > x \geq -4$

$-2 \leq x < 0$

ANSWER: (A)

25.
WORK

A. $(3 \times 10^3) - (2 \times 10)^2 = 3 \times 1{,}000 - (20)^2$
$$= 3{,}000 - 400$$
$$= 2{,}600$$

B. 2,600

ANSWER: (C)

26.
WORK

A. Average $= \dfrac{43 + 56 + 62}{3} = \dfrac{161}{3} \approx 53.7$

B. $30\% \times 900 - 28\% \times 800 =$
$0.30 \times 900 - .28 \times 800 = 270 - 224 = 46$

ANSWER: (A)

27.

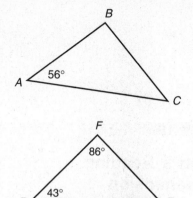

ANALYSIS

We can't determine the measure of $\angle C$ because we are only given the measure of one angle in the triangle.

ANSWER: (D)

28.

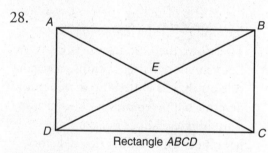

Rectangle *ABCD*

ANALYSIS

The diagonals of a rectangle are congruent and they also bisect each other.

WORK

Since the diagonals are congruent ($AC = BD$) and they bisect each other, all the pieces are equal ($AE = EC = DE = BE$).

$$AC = BE + EC$$

ANSWER: (C)

29.
WORK

A. $240 + 27\% \times 900 = 240 + 0.27 \times 900 =$
$240 + 243 = 483$

B. $\dfrac{3,000}{17-12} = \dfrac{3,000}{5} = 600$

ANSWER: (B)

30.
WORK

A. $\begin{aligned} \dfrac{2}{3} &= \dfrac{4}{6} \\ + \dfrac{5}{6} &= \dfrac{5}{6} \\ \hline \dfrac{9}{6} &= \dfrac{3}{2} \end{aligned}$

B. $\begin{aligned} \dfrac{8}{9} &= \dfrac{8}{9} \\ - \dfrac{1}{3} &= \dfrac{3}{9} \\ \hline &\dfrac{5}{9} \end{aligned}$

$\dfrac{3}{2} \div \dfrac{1}{2} = \dfrac{3}{2} \times \dfrac{2}{1} = 3$

$\dfrac{5}{9} \div \dfrac{2}{5} = \dfrac{5}{9} \times \dfrac{5}{2} =$
$\dfrac{25}{18} = 1\dfrac{7}{18}$

ANSWER: (A)

31.
WORK

A. $-2\,|-3| = -2(3) = -6$
B. $2\,|3| = 2(3) = 6$

ANSWER: (B)

32.
ANALYSIS

Using the given information, draw and label the line.

WORK

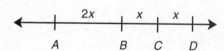

ANSWER: (C)

33.

ANALYSIS

We don't know the value of x, so we can't determine the values of the given expressions.

ANSWER: (D)

34.

ANALYSIS

Find the prime factors of 30 and 20, determine the greatest common factor, and then compare with 4.

WORK

A. Greatest common prime factor
$$30 = 2 \times \mathbf{\underline{5}} \times 3$$
$$20 = 2 \times 2 \times \mathbf{\underline{5}}$$

B. 4

ANSWER: (A)

35.

WORK

A. $\dfrac{21.6}{(0.8)(0.3)} = \dfrac{21.6}{0.24} = 90$

B. $120\% \times 75 = 1.20 \times 75 = 90$

ANSWER: (C)

36.

WORK

A. $168 = 4 \times 42 = 2 \times 2 \times 21 \times 2 =$
$2 \times 2 \times 7 \times 3 \times 2$: 5 distinct prime factors

B. 6

ANSWER: (B)

37.

ANALYSIS

Solve equation A for the positive square root.

WORK

A. $2x^2 = 242$
$x^2 = 121$
$x = \pm 11$
$x = 11$

B. $5x + 2 = 62$
$5x = 60$
$x = 12$

ANSWER: (B)

Section 3 Reading Comprehension

1. **(C)** The article only briefly mentions Oskar Schindler; therefore, we cannot say that the author intends to tell Schindler's story in detail. Omit choice D. The article does not discuss the S.S. *Indianapolis* in her first year of military service, so don't choose B. The article does discuss the shark attacks near Guam (A), but only in the course of telling the reader about the sinking of the *Indianapolis*. Therefore, the best answer is C.

2. **(A)** Look at your answer options. You can rule out B and D because these options describe happy emotions. The author, if nothing else, does not connote happiness while telling this sad story. You might be tempted by choice C because the story does deal with a very hopeless situation; however, the best answer is A. The author uses phrases (like the emphasis on luck and the word "inexcusable" in paragraph six) to show the author's bitterness toward the horrible circumstances that led to this great tragedy.

3. **(D)** Choices A and B are just silly. Choices C and D have opposite meanings; if one is true, then the other must necessarily be false. But setting off a single sentence as a full paragraph calls the reader's attention to the information in that sentence. After all, we don't normally treat a single sentence as a full paragraph, and

doing so sets off signals in our brains that something strange is going on. The best answer is D.

4. **(C)** The article states in paragraph four that men lost control and drank seawater; this information comes in a paragraph discussing the various ways in which these drifting men died. Therefore, we can conclude that drinking seawater will kill you. Choice C is the only answer that says that drinking seawater will kill the drinker.

5. **(D)** While the article gives the reader many figures, the second paragraph states clearly that 300 men went down with the ship. Nine hundred men flailed in the water at first, dwindling to only 300 four days later. To find the total number of men who died before being rescued, take 900 and subtract the 316 survivors; you get 584, the total number of men who died while in the water. Now add the 300 who went down with the ship, and you get 884.

6. **(B)** Flotsam is another word for trash that is formed by objects breaking up in water; most likely flotsam is the wreckage of the *Indianapolis*. But, even if you don't know the definition of flotsam, you can infer it. Paragraph two describes the condition under which the men who got off the ship before it sank were laboring. They are described as being in oily water that is littered with life rafts, men, and sharks; the ship has sunk. Imagine what that would look like—boxes, pieces of wood, pieces of sail, furniture—all of these would be floating in the water until they grew too heavy to stay afloat.

7. **(D)** While saprophytes, which decompose organic material, probably do decompose cantaloupes, the article does not state this. It does state that saprophytes decompose bread, leather, and wheat. Check out paragraph two for proof.

8. **(C)** Since we are given no information about surrounding villages, we cannot conclude that choice A is possible. Downy mildew (choice B) does not attack trees and therefore cannot be true. Naturally, the villagers have moved away, but their moving away does not cause buildings to decompose; their moving merely allows decomposition to progress unchecked. The best inference is C. Left to their own devices, the saprophytes have decomposed the wood that made up the villages.

9. **(B)** The author does not spend a great deal of time discussing poisons (A), a wide range of plant diseases (C), or tips on growing good timber (D). The author does, however, spend the entire passage discussing the fungi's role in the cycle of life.

10. **(A)** According to the article, if saprophytes disappeared, we would have nothing left to break down unneeded things like old buildings or dead organic matter; living things would then get squeezed out by the dead things. Choice A is correct.

11. **(B)** Choices A and C are trying to trick you into associating the word "smut" with a "snit" (fit of anger) or "snot" (mucous in the nasal passages); rule them out. A common definition for "smut" is indeed trashy reading material (D), but that definition does not fit the context of a passage discussing fungi and decomposition. The only definition that makes sense, therefore, is B. "Smut" is something that causes damage to plants.

12. **(A)** The article does not use words that connote dread (B), surprise (C), or confusion (D). It reads as an unbiased, fairly clinical discussion of a mental disorder. The best answer is A.

13. **(B)** Even though someone may be experiencing great pressure and stress, s/he does not necessarily fall victim to mental disorder. We cannot, therefore, assume that choice A is the answer. Choice C could work, but it is quite insensitive and offensive; rule it out. Choice D does not work because the article does not give tips on how to deal with mental illness; it gives only information on the symptoms schizophrenia brings. The best answer is B.

14. **(D)** Because the reader can find only one paragraph discussing a famous schizophrenic, you can omit choice A. The article discusses how to identify schizophrenia, not how to treat depression; rule out choice B. Choice C is simply wrong because as choice D states, the article discusses, over the course of two paragraphs, how doctors viewed and treated mental illness, and then gives one example of a famous schizophrenic, John Nash.

15. **(B)** People who have seen *A Beautiful Mind* may know that John Nash eventually received the Noble Prize, but the article does not state this fact. Remember, you must answer questions based on the information given you on the exam, not based on information you know from outside sources.

16. **(D)** Choice A is absurd, so forget about it. The author does not give three reasons for why women are more likely to conceive twins; rule out choice B. The article does discuss advances in medical technology, just not in paragraph three; so, choice C is incorrect. The correct answer is D.

17. **(B)** The author does not try to warn anyone about anything; leave aside choice A. Other than discussing the effect of aging on a woman trying to conceive, the author does not discuss other bodily factors that affect

conception; rule out C. The article does mention how many pairs of twins exist, but only as an aside—an interesting tidbit to throw into the mix. The article sets out to tell people general information about twins. The best answer, therefore, is B.

18. **(C)** According to the information in paragraph one, 50 million sets of twins exist in the world.

19. **(B)** Referring to your great vocabulary you recall that to be perceptive is to be able to notice subtle things. But, even if you don't remember that, you can infer it. Distinguishing among heartbeats must require some attention and skill; noticing obvious things, expensive things, or sweet things simply does not apply to that situation.

20. **(D)** The article states that 15% of twins are identical. So multiply 0.15 by 50 million. You get 750,000, or choice D.

21. **(C)** Much of American culture is affected by biblical information; King Solomon was a wise Hebrew ruler. He was rich, but was, more importantly, famous for his ability to solve sticky problems. You may know the story in which two women were fighting over a child, each claiming to be the child's mother. Solomon ordered the child to be cut in half so that both women could have a piece, knowing that the real mother of the child would not allow that to happen. Sure enough, he gave the child to the woman who protested the most. Since "King" Solomon was wise enough to know that burying the cholera-stricken bodies was crucial for general survival and brave enough to risk his life burying them, we can select choice C as the best answer.

22. **(D)** The article states in paragraph one that cholera broke out in Rwanda in 1994.

23. **(D)** Paragraph one states that cholera comes from the bacterium *Vibro cholerae.*

24. **(C)** The author has already given information about cholera symptoms (A), "King" Solomon (B), and the cholera outbreak in Rwanda (D). The article, as printed here, leaves off at the point when it is discussing William Morton and his school for orphans; we should conclude that, if the article continues, it will continue discussing William Morton and his school for orphans.

25. **(C)** The word *ministrations* might make you think of religious ministry, but that definition does not make sense here; omit choice A. Choices B and D also do not make sense; moreover they were not theories at the time being described in this passage. Leave them aside. The best answer is C. It makes sense given the sentence's context, and it existed during the time of the Lexington cholera outbreak.

26. **(D)** Measurements don't help a doctor determine whether someone is dead; checking pulses does. Omit choice A. Measurements might let a doctor notice that the victim indeed gained weight before death, but does this matter? Not really, unless obesity contributed to the death. Forget about choice B. Measurements apply to physical characteristics, not mental ones like whether one completed high school; omit choice C. Measurements, however, might indeed help doctors determine the cause of death.

27. **(C)** Paragraph two states that autopsies became routine during the Renaissance. The Renaissance took place during the 15th to 17th centuries (or the 1400–1600s).

28. **(C)** Paragraph three states that the Bertillon system was popular from 1882 through 1905. Therefore the best answer to choose is C, since 1890 falls within the range of that time period.

29. **(A)** Connecting current things to past ones is a great way to get people to pay attention. By mentioning current, popular TV shows and movies, the author is trying to hook his/her reader. Therefore, choice A is the best answer.

30. **(B)** The author intends to give a brief overview of forensic medicine. None of the other options are true. The article does not discuss cultural phenomena after 1980, although it briefly discusses an undated comment on modern abilities to use DNA to identify people after death; omit choice A. The author clearly approves of forensic medicine, so you can rule out choice D. Even though the author might want to encourage the study and practice of forensic medicine, s/he does not include propagandic details that would aggressively encourage us to do so. The best answer is B.

31. **(C)** Because autopsies did not become routine until the Renaissance, and because Rome fell long before then, we can assume that Roman doctors had to do their forensic study in secret. See paragraph one.

32. **(A)** The article discusses felines, canines, witches, and the *Miacis*, but it mainly discusses how people's reactions to cats changed over time. This, therefore, is a brief history on cats.

33. **(C)** Paragraph three states that Puss in Boots helped his master, as did Dick Whittington's cat.

34. **(C)** If a society likes cats, and also likes stories, then that society will create stories that tell good things about cats; if a society hates cats, it will tell stories that tell bad things about cats.

35. **(D)** As modern-day students will know from rap music, a posse is a group of people who band together for a

common purpose—be that for fighting, partying, or simply like-mindedness. Choice B tries to make you think of pose, while choice C tries to confuse you by mixing up your languages. Choice A is almost right because it refers to a group, but it relies on physical directions; therefore, choice A does not contain a broad enough definition.

36. **(B)** Anything that happened Before the coming of Christ (B.C.) refers, most likely, to Egyptian dynasties (given the purposes of our article), and the article states that Egyptians worshipped cats. Rule out choices C and D. Currently, post 1990, we love cats (see the final two lines of the second paragraph); rule out choice A. Choice B is left, by process of elimination. You should know that during the Middle Ages (500–1500) witch scares abounded, making it likely that people would fear witches.

Section 4 Mathematics Achievement

1.

ANALYSIS

To multiply a number by 10^{-3}, move the decimal place left three places.

WORK

$$4.05 \times 10^{-3} = 0.00405$$

ANSWER: (C)

2.

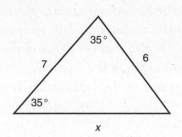

ANALYSIS

Since two angles are both 35°, the angles are congruent and the sides opposite these angles are also congruent.

WORK

The sides measuring x and 6 are congruent, so $x = 6$.

ANSWER: (A)

3.

ANALYSIS

Write two-sevenths as a fraction, divide the denominator into the numerator and then round off to two places.

WORK

$$\frac{2}{7} =$$

$$
\begin{array}{r}
0.285 \approx 0.29 \\
7\overline{)2.000} \\
1\ 4xx \\
\hline
60 \\
56 \\
\hline
40 \\
35 \\
\hline
\end{array}
$$

ANSWER: (D)

4.

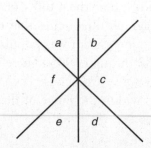

ANALYSIS

Angles *b* and *e* are vertical angles and are therefore congruent.

WORK

measure of $\angle b$ = measure of $\angle e = 29°$

ANSWER: (B)

5.
ANALYSIS

Maureen lost $2\frac{1}{3}$ pounds per week for six weeks, so multiply 6 by $2\frac{1}{3}$ and then subtract from 138 pounds.

WORK

$$6 \times 2\frac{1}{3} = \frac{\overset{2}{\cancel{6}}}{1} \times \frac{7}{\underset{1}{\cancel{3}}} = \frac{14}{1} = 14$$

$$138 - 14 = 124$$

ANSWER: (D)

6.
ANALYSIS

Solve for the inequality.

WORK

$$9p - 7 > 12$$

Add 7: $\qquad 9p > 21$

Divide by 9: $\qquad p > 2\frac{1}{3}$

Let $p = 3$: $\qquad 3 > 2\frac{1}{3}$ ✔

ANSWER: (D)

7.
ANALYSIS

Add up all five sides and multiply the cost per foot of fencing, $3.74.

WORK

$$49.2 + 56.4 + 62.7 + 47.3 + 65.4 = 281$$

$$
\begin{array}{r}
281 \\
\times \$3.74 \\
\hline
11\ 24 \\
196\ 7 \\
843 \\
\hline
1,050.94
\end{array}
$$

ANSWER: (C)

8.
ANALYSIS

Let x = the first even integer, $x + 2$ = the second even integer, $x + 4$ = the third even integer, $x + 6$ = the fourth even integer.

WORK

The sum of the first and second of four consecutive even integers is 8 more than the fourth.

$$(x) + (x + 2) = (x + 6) + 8$$
$$2x + 2 = x + 14$$

Subtract 2: $\qquad 2x = x + 12$

Subtract x: $\qquad x = 12$

ANSWER: (A)

9.

ANALYSIS

All the sides of the equilateral triangle are 3″. The opposite sides of the rectangle are congruent. Find both perimeters and substitute into the choices.

WORK

perimeter of the rectangle =	$6'' + 6'' + 4'' + 4'' = 20''$
perimeter of the triangle =	$3'' + 3'' + 3'' = 9''$

The perimeter of the rectangle is 11″ more than the perimeter of the equilateral triangle.

$$20'' = 9'' + 11'' ✔$$

ANSWER: (C)

10.

ANALYSIS

Split the inequality into two parts.

WORK

$3 \le 2x + 1$	$2x + 1 < 9$
$2 \le 2x$	$2x < 8$
$1 \le x$	$x < 4$

Our number, x, is larger than or equal to 1 and less than 4.

3:
$$3 \le 2x \quad + 1 < 9$$
$$3 \le 2(3) + 1 < 9$$
$$3 \le \quad 6 + 1 < 9$$
$$3 \le \quad\quad 7 \quad < 9 ✔$$

ANSWER: (C)

11.

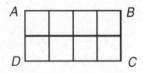

ANALYSIS

Find the sides of each square. Then, to determine the perimeter of rectangle *ABCD*, add up the outer sides of the squares.

WORK

If the area of the square equals 16, each side is 4.

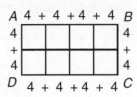

Perimeter = $12 \times 4 = 48$

ANSWER: (B)

12.

ANALYSIS

Rearrange the equation so as to list *q* alone.

WORK

	$pq - r = s$
Add *r*:	$pq = s + r$
Divide by *p*:	$q = \dfrac{s + r}{p}$

ANSWER: (A)

13.

ANALYSIS

Let R = 1 orange and A = 1 apple.

WORK

$$6R + 8A = 5.66$$
$$6(0.37) + 8A = 5.66$$
$$100 < 6(0.37) + 8A = 5.66 >$$
$$6(37) + 800A = 566$$
$$222 + 800A = 566$$
$$800A = 344$$
$$A = 0.43$$

ANSWER: (D)

14.

ANALYSIS

Add up all the sides and set the sum equal to 20. Then solve for *x*, the smallest side.

WORK

$$(x) + (x + 3) + (2x + 1) = 20$$
$$4x + 4 = 20$$

Subtract 4: $\quad 4x = 16$
Divide by 4: $\quad x = 4$
Check: $\quad (x) + (x + 3) + (2x + 1) = 20$
$$(4) + (7) + (9) = 20$$
$$20 = 20 \checkmark$$

ANSWER: (C)

15.

ANALYSIS

Rearrange the second polynomial in descending powers of *r* and then add both polynomials.

WORK

$$3r^2 - 2r - 7$$
$$+ \; -r^2 - 4r + 8$$
$$\overline{2r^2 - 6r + 1}$$

ANSWER: (C)

16.

ANALYSIS

The easiest way of finding the answer is to just substitute the possible answers and to then find the solution that is a multiple of 4.

WORK

3: $\qquad \dfrac{35}{7} + 3 = 5 + 3 = 8 = 2(4)$

ANSWER: (C)

17.

ANALYSIS

If five out of eight people are not left-handed, the remaining three are left-handed. Take 3/8 of 6,400.

WORK

$$\frac{3}{8} \cdot 6,400$$
$$= 2,400$$

ANSWER: (B)

18.

ANALYSIS

Multiply 40 hours by $15.84. Then multiply time-and-a-half hours, 6, by the product of 1.5 and $15.84. Add both results.

WORK

$$40 \times \$15.84 = \$633.60$$
$$+ \; 6 \times 1.5 \times \$15.84 = \underline{\;\;142.56}$$
$$\$776.16$$

ANSWER: (A)

19.

ANALYSIS

Add the simultaneous equations in order to eliminate the *q*s.

WORK

$$3p - 2q = 2$$
$$+ \; 4p + 2q = 26$$
$$\overline{7p \qquad = 28}$$

Divide by 7: $\qquad p = 4$

ANSWER: (A)

20.

ANALYSIS

Draw a diagram. The shaded area is the bed of earth surrounding the pool. Subtract the pool area, the inner area, from the entire area.

WORK

entire area: $\quad 45 \times 34 = 1,530$
$- \;$ pool area: $\quad 26 \times 31 = \underline{\;\;806}$
$$724$$

ANSWER: (D)

21.

ANALYSIS

Write $43\frac{1}{2}\%$ as $\dfrac{43\frac{1}{2}}{100}$ and then simplify.

WORK

$$\frac{43\frac{1}{2}}{100} = \frac{87}{2} \div \frac{100}{1} = \frac{87}{2} \times \frac{1}{100} = \frac{87}{200}$$

ANSWER: (B)

22.

ANALYSIS

Let x = the *original price* of the suit. Since the price is increased by 20%, let the *second price* = 120%x or 1.20x. The second price, 1.20x, is reduced by 10%, so the *final price* is 90% of the second price = 90%(1.20x) = 0.90(1.20x). Set the final price equal to $194.40.

WORK

$$0.90(1.20x) = 194.40$$
$$1.08x = 194.40$$

Divide by 1.08: $\quad\quad\quad\quad x = 180$

ANSWER: (D)

23.

ANALYSIS:

Add the two fractions in the numerator.
Subtract the two fractions in the denominator.
Then divide the results.

WORK

$$\begin{array}{cc} \dfrac{5}{8} = \dfrac{5}{8} & \dfrac{5}{6} = \dfrac{5}{6} \\[2mm] +\dfrac{1}{4} = \dfrac{2}{8} & -\dfrac{2}{3} = \dfrac{4}{6} \\[2mm] \hline \dfrac{7}{8} & \dfrac{1}{6} \end{array}$$

$$\frac{7}{8} \div \frac{1}{6} = \frac{7}{\cancel{8}_4} \times \frac{\cancel{6}^3}{1} = \frac{21}{4} = 5\frac{1}{4}$$

ANSWER: (C)

24.

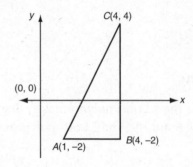

ANALYSIS

The formula of the area of a triangle is $A = \frac{1}{2}bh$,

where A = area, b = base, and h = height. Find the distance between points A and C and between points B and C.

WORK

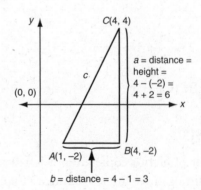

$$A = \frac{1}{2}bh$$

$b = 3,\ h = 6:$ $\quad\quad A = \frac{1}{2}(3)(6) = \frac{18}{2} = 9$

ANSWER: (B)

25.

ANALYSIS

Let $5x$ = Vicky's share and $3x$ = Howard's share. Add the two shares together and set the total equal to $2,480.

WORK

$$5x + 3x = 2,480$$
$$8x = 2,480$$

Divide by 8: $\quad\quad x = 310$

Vicky's share: $\quad 5x = 5(310) = 1,550$

Howard's share: $\quad 3x = 3(310) = 930$

ANSWER: (C)

26.

ANALYSIS

Substitute the given values for r and s.

WORK

$$3r + 10s + t = 15$$

$r = \dfrac{2}{3}, s = \dfrac{3}{5}:$ $\quad 3\left(\dfrac{2}{3}\right) + 10\left(\dfrac{3}{5}\right) + t = 15$

$$2 + 6 + t = 15$$
$$8 + t = 15$$

Subtract 8: $\quad\quad\quad\quad\quad\quad t = 7$

ANSWER: (A)

27.

ANALYSIS

Divide 5 by 7 and round off to 2 places.

WORK

$$
\begin{array}{r}
.714 \\
7\overline{)5.000} \\
\underline{4\ 9\text{xx}} \\
10 \\
\underline{7} \\
30 \\
\underline{28}
\end{array}
$$

ANSWER: (C)

28.

ANALYSIS

Substitute 5 and 8 for r and s.

WORK

$$r \# s = r^2 - 3s$$
$$r = 5, s = 8:\ 5 \# 8 = (5)^2 - 3(8) = 25 - 24 = 1$$

ANSWER: (A)

29.

ANALYSIS

Change 78 kilograms to grams and then divide by 2 grams. There are 1,000 grams in a kilogram.

WORK

$$78 \text{ kilograms} = 78 \times 1,000 \text{ grams} = 78,000 \text{ grams}$$

$$\frac{78,000}{2} = 39,000$$

ANSWER: (D)

30.

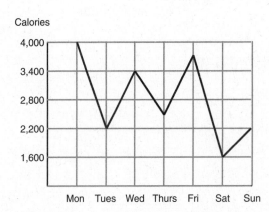

ANALYSIS

Find the number of calories she consumed each day for seven days and then determine the average. Each horizontal line between 1,600 and 4,000 represents 300 calories.

WORK

Day	Number of Calories
Monday	4,000
Tuesday	2,200
Wednesday	3,400
Thursday	2,500
Friday	3,700
Saturday	1,600
Sunday	2,200
Total	19,600

Divide 19,600 by the total number of days, 7:

$$
\begin{array}{r}
2800 \\
7\overline{)19,600} \\
14\ \text{xxx} \\
\hline
5\ 600 \\
5\ 600 \\
\hline
\end{array}
$$

ANSWER: (A)

31.

ANALYSIS

There are 60 minutes in an hour, so divide 150 by 60.

WORK

$$\frac{150}{60} = 2.5 = 2\frac{1}{2} \text{ hours}$$

ANSWER: (B)

32.

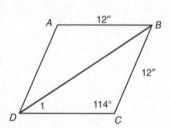

ANALYSIS

In a parallelogram, opposite sides are congruent, so $DC = 12$. If $DC = 12$ and $BC = 12$, we have isosceles triangle BCD, and the angles opposite congruent sides have the same measures.

Subtract 114° from 180° (the total of the measures of the angles in a triangle). The result represents the sum of the other two angles. Since *BCD* is an isosceles triangle, the base angles are congruent, and we just have to divide the result of subtraction by two.

WORK

$$180° - 114° = 66°$$
$$\frac{66°}{2} = 33°$$

ANSWER: (D)

33.

ANALYSIS

Determine how many $\frac{1}{2}$ dozens there are in 24.

Then multiply the answer by \$6.52.

WORK

$$\frac{1}{2} \text{ dozen} = 6$$

$$\frac{24}{6} = 4$$
$$4 \times \$6.52 = \$26.08$$

ANSWER: (C)

34.

ANALYSIS

Change both mixed numbers to fractions and then divide.

WORK

$$2\frac{5}{6} \div 3\frac{2}{3} = \frac{17}{6} \div \frac{11}{3} = \frac{17}{\cancel{6}_2} \times \frac{\cancel{3}^1}{11} = \frac{17}{22}$$

ANSWER: (C)

35.

ANALYSIS

The variable x must meet both conditions. That is to say, it must be between 4 and 9 and at the same time it also must be greater than 3 and less than or equal to 5.

WORK

$$4 < x < 9 \qquad 5 \geq x > 3$$

Try 5: $\qquad 4 < 5 < 9$ ✔ $\qquad 5 \geq 5 > 3$ ✔

ANSWER: (C)

36.

ANALYSIS

Multiply the means and extremes and solve for a.

WORK

$$\frac{a}{b} = \frac{c}{d}$$

$$\underbrace{a : b = c : d}_{\text{extremes}}^{\overbrace{\qquad}^{\text{means}}}$$

or:

$$ad = bc$$

Divide by d: $\qquad a = \dfrac{bc}{d}$

ANSWER: (B)

37.

ANALYSIS

Let x = the unknown number and change 60% to 0.60.

WORK

$$\frac{2}{3}x = 0.60 \cdot 40 + 18$$

$$\frac{2}{3}x = 24 + 18$$

Multiply by 3: $\qquad \dfrac{2}{3}x = 42$

Divide by 2: $\qquad 2x = 126$

$$x = 63$$

ANSWER: (D)

38.

ANALYSIS

The simplest way of finding the missing number is to substitute each of the choices into the given expression.

WORK

$$6(? + 5) - 3 = 135$$

Try 18: $\qquad 6(18 + 5) - 3 = 135$

$$6(23) - 3 = 135$$

$$138 - 3 = 135$$

$$135 = 135 ✔$$

ANSWER: (D)

39.

ANALYSIS

There are no elements in common.

ANSWER: (C)

40.

ANALYSIS

Change the kilograms to grams and then divide by 20, the weight of each container.

WORK

8 kilograms = 8 × 1,000 grams = 8,000 grams

$$\frac{8{,}000 \text{ grams}}{20 \text{ grams}} = 400$$

ANSWER: (C)

41.

ANALYSIS

Let x = the unknown number and translate the sentence into an algebraic expression.

WORK

$$24 - x = \frac{6}{7} \times 21$$
$$24 - x = 18$$
$$-x = -6$$
$$x = 6$$

ANSWER: (B)

42.

ANALYSIS

Determine the value of each expression in the given expressions and then substitute into the possible answers.

WORK

(a) $4^2 + 5(9-3) = 16 + 5(6) = 16 + 30 = 46$
(b) $3 \times 17 - 51 = 51 - 5 = 46$
(c) $2|-5| + 4|2| = 2(5) + 4(2) = 10 + 8 = 18$
(d) $6^2 - 2^3 = 36 - 8 = 28$

(A) $a > b$ or $46 > 46$
(B) $b < a$ or $46 < 46$
(C) $d \geq b$ or $28 \geq 46$
(D) $c < d$ or $18 < 28$ ✔

ANSWER: (D)

43.

ANALYSIS

Draw a diagram to help out and remember that all angles in a square are right angles.

WORK

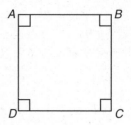

(A) Angle B is a right angle. ✔
(B) The measure of angle B equals the measure of angle C. ✔
(C) The measure of angle B plus the measure of angle A equals 180°. ✔
(D) BC is perpendicular to AD. ✗

ANSWER: (D)

44.

ANALYSIS

Add up all the sides and set the total equal to the perimeter, 44. Then determine the area of the parallelogram by multiplying base times height.

WORK

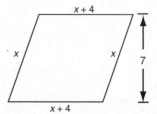

Let A = area of the parallelogram, P = perimeter of the parallelogram, x = the side, and $x + 4$ = the base.

$$P = x + x + (x + 4) + (x + 4)$$

$P = 44:$
$$44 = 4x + 8$$
$$36 = 4x$$
$$x = 9 \text{ (the side)}$$
$$x + 4 = 13 \text{ (the base)}$$

$$A = bh$$
$b = 13,\ h = 7:$ $\quad A = (13)(7) = 91$

ANSWER: (B)

45.

ANALYSIS

The least common denominator is ab.

WORK

$$\frac{2}{a} = \frac{2b}{ab}$$

$$+\ \frac{3}{b} = \frac{3a}{ab}$$
$$\overline{\phantom{+\ \frac{3}{b}}}$$
$$\frac{2b + 3a}{ab}$$

ANSWER: (D)

46.

ANALYSIS

Add up all the ratios and divide into 124. Find the remainder and then check to see which is the last book in the remainder.

WORK

$$5 + 2 + 3 + 3 = 13$$
$$\frac{124}{13} = 9\frac{7}{13}$$

There is a remainder of 7. In order, we can purchase 5 fiction and 2 historical books. The historical book is the last book we can order.

ANSWER: (B)

47.

ANALYSIS

Three decimal places represent thousandths.

WORK

$$7.002 = 7\frac{2}{1000} = 7\frac{1}{500}$$

ANSWER: (B)

Section 5 Writing Sample Checklist

☐ **Read the question and writing prompt again.** Did you answer the question? You won't have time to rewrite the essay during the actual exam, so read the question carefully the first time and keep it in mind. Underline keywords in the questions to help you remember.

☐ **Read your introduction.** Did you include all of the information necessary for a reader to understand your essay? Does it include a thesis statement?

☐ **Underline your thesis statement in the introduction.** Does it address the question and give your opinion on it?

☐ **Underline the thesis statement in the conclusion.** Does it agree with your original thesis?

☐ **Underline the topic sentences of your body paragraphs.** Now read all of the underlined sentences in your practice essay. Do these sentences focus on the same topic? Do they fit together? Do they flow?

☐ **TExAn.** To illustrate your <u>Topic</u> sentence in each body paragraph, check to make sure you have a *specific* <u>Ex</u>ample. Again, make sure it is specific, rather than another general statement. Then make sure you <u>An</u>alyze or explain *how* this example proves your point.

    This is an important step, so get used to including this information **as you write** your paragraphs.

☐ **Check your handwriting.** Is your text legible? Get used to forming your words clearly. Frustrated readers cannot score you highly if they cannot read your essay.

☐ **Proofread.** Correct the most glaring errors, especially run-ons, comma splices, and fragments. Make sure you capitalize when necessary and punctuate logically. Check your spelling, especially of easily confused words (to/too, their/there, etc.). Notice how you use transition words.

☐ **Have someone else read this essay.** Choose a good writer and reader to comment on your work.

Practice writing more essays, and you will improve each time. During the actual exam, you will only have time to proofread and check your examples, so most items on this list will have to become second nature to you.

Scoring Your Practice Tests

CHAPTER 7

HOW TO SCORE YOUR SSAT PRACTICE TEST

Now that you've finished your Practice Test, let's see how you did. Compare your answer sheet to the answer key provided, and correct your test. (Make sure you're using the Practice Test One Answer Key to check your Practice Test One Answers.)

Now, let's calculate your Raw Scores. Get out your SSAT Practice Test One Scoring Sheet (starting on page 472). Begin with the Verbal Skills section, go through the form, putting check marks (✔) in the appropriate boxes according to whether the answer is correct, incorrect, or skipped. Then, total the number of check marks at the bottom of the Verbal Skills column. Check out the sample below to make sure you're doing it right. (**Note:** for the purposes of this explanation, we're assuming that all answers that do not appear on this sample—i.e., from 14 through 40—are correct. Also, note that since skipped answers do not count against you, you do not need to tally up that figure.)

SSAT Upper-Level Practice Test One: Verbal (One Section)

	Correct Answers	Wrong Answers	Skipped Answers		Correct Answers	Wrong Answers	Skipped Answers
1.	✔			41.		✔	
2.	✔			42.		✔	
3.	✔			43.	✔		
4.		✔		44.	✔		
5.		✔		55.			✔
6.			✔	56.			✔
7.			✔	57.	✔		
8.			✔	58.	✔		
9.	✔			59.	✔		
10.	✔			60.	✔		
11.	✔						
12.	✔						
13.	✔						

Total # Correct	Total # Wrong / 4
41	4 / 4

First, we need to figure your Verbal Raw Score. You need to subtract the value of the incorrect answers from the value of the correct answers. To do this, you need to figure out the value of the incorrect answers, which, as you may recall, is a –1/4 for each incorrect answer. So, follow the instructions on the chart: total the number of incorrect answers, and then divide that number by 4. In our example above, we missed 4 questions; we would therefore divide the number of incorrect answers (4) by 4, which gives us 1. Now we simply fill in the rest of the chart as follows:

SSAT Practice Test One: Verbal (One Section)

	Correct Answers	Wrong Answers	Skipped Answers		Correct Answers	Wrong Answers	Skipped Answers
1.	✔			41.		✔	
2.	✔			42.		✔	
3.	✔			43.	✔		
4.		✔		44.	✔		
5.		✔		55.			✔
6.			✔	56.			✔
7.			✔	57.	✔		
8.			✔	58.	✔		
9.	✔			59.	✔		
10.	✔			60.	✔		
11.	✔						
12.	✔						
13.	✔						

Total # Correct	Total # Wrong / 4
41	4 / 4 = 1

Verbal Raw Score 41 – 1 = 40

And so, our Verbal Raw Score totals 40. At this time, you would repeat the process for each of the other skill sections (the Quantitative section and the Reading section). You should have three final Raw Scores when you finish.

You might be initially confused about computing the scores on the Quantitative Raw Score Form, but it's fundamentally no different from how you compute the Verbal Raw Score. Check out this example to make sure you're on track. (Again, we'll assume that all of the questions that don't appear on this chart—i.e., from 4 through 21—are correct.)

SSAT Practice Test One: Quantitative (Two Sections)
Section 1   Section 2

	Correct Answers	Wrong Answers	Skipped Answers		Correct Answers	Wrong Answers	Skipped Answers
1.		✔		1.	✔		
2.		✔		2.		✔	
3.			✔	3.		✔	
				⋮			
22.			✔	22.	✔		
23.		✔		23.			✔
24.			✔	24.			✔
25.			✔	25.		✔	

Total # Correct	Total # Wrong / 4		Total # Correct	Total # Wrong / 4
18	*3* / 4 = .75		*20*	*3* / 4 = .75

18   −   .75 = **17.25**   20   −   .75 = **19.25**

————————— Combine —————————

Quantitative Raw Score 17.25 + 19.25 = **36.50**

However, knowing your Raw Scores isn't enough. You need to know what those scores mean and in the language that the SSAT Board (and your school administrators) use. So, we convert your Raw Scores into Scaled Scores. Simply find the score nearest yours on the Scaled Score chart (on page 478), rounding up or down as appropriate. Using our sample, we see, therefore, that our Verbal Raw Score of 40 translates into a Verbal Scaled Score of 725. Similarly, our Quantitative Raw Score of 36.50 translates into a Quantitative Scaled Score of 725 (When in doubt, it is better to be conservative. Round down. So our Raw Score of 36.5 rounds to 35 rather than 40 on the Raw Score column.)

SSAT Upper-Level Scaled Score

Raw Score	Reading	Verbal	Quantitative
60		800	
55		800	
50		779	800
45		752	782
40	800	725	755
35	722	698	725
30	692	671	698
25	662	644	668
20	632	617	641
15	602	590	614
10	572	563	584
5	542	533	557
0	512	506	530
−5 and lower	500	500	500

THINKING ABOUT YOUR SCORES

Now that you have a sense of what your SSAT score would likely be, you might like to compare your performance to other students like you taking the exam. Look at the bottom of the SSAT Scaled Score chart to find the Percentiles section. We've reprinted this section below for your convenience.

Median 50th Percentile

	Reading	Verbal	Quantitative
Grade 8	647	660	676
Grade 9	653	667	699
Grade 10	659	670	705
Grade 11	647	656	704

According to this data, if you are a ninth grader who scored a 667 on the Verbal Skills Scaled Score, you will have performed better than 50 percent of the other students taking the SSAT. Keep in mind, however, that you are taking Practice Exams. While we have done our best to provide you with some great and effective study material, they are not, and cannot ever hope to be, actual SSATs. Therefore, keep in mind that variation in testing format, testing conditions, question type and frequency, and even your own physical and emotional status can cause some variation in results. The scores you earn on these Practice Exams are estimates of how you will do on an actual SSAT. Every test, SSAT or some other type, has to take into consideration a Standard Error of Measurement, which is to say that your scores can fluctuate in a small range depending on what's happening on your actual test date. A student who earns a score of 700 on the Verbal portion of the SSAT, for example, on one test date might test as high as 721 *or as low as 679* on another.

A FEW FINAL WORDS

As our time together is now drawing to a close, we would like to leave you with a bit of advice; advice that we've said earlier in this book but bears repeating at this stage of the game. Don't get discouraged by the testing experience. Your SSAT scores are only part of any school administration process. Many other factors, including that essay we talked about, affect your ability to get into the school of your choice.

All in all, if you're discouraged in any way regarding your scores on these Practice Exams, take heart. Review the study tips and advice back in the Introduction, and focus on doing your best on the actual exam day. Isn't that what practice is for? Identifying the weak spots so as to shore them up?

We wish you the best. Good luck and study hard!

SSAT Practice Test One: Verbal (One Section)

	Correct Answers	Wrong Answers	Skipped Answers
1.			
2.			
3.			
4.			
5.			
6.			
7.			
8.			
9.			
10.			
11.			
12.			
13.			
14.			
15.			
16.			
17.			
18.			
19.			
20.			
21.			
22.			
23.			
24.			
25.			
26.			
27.			
28.			
29.			
30.			
31.			
32.			
33.			
34.			
35.			
36.			
37.			
38.			
39.			
40.			

	Correct Answers	Wrong Answers	Skipped Answers
41.			
42.			
43.			
44.			
45.			
46.			
47.			
48.			
49.			
50.			
51.			
52.			
53.			
54.			
55.			
56.			
57.			
58.			
59.			
60.			

Total # Correct	Total # Wrong / 4
	/ 4 =

_____ − _____ =

Verbal Raw Score

Convert your SSAT Verbal Raw Score to the SSAT Verbal Scaled Score using the chart on page 480:

Verbal Scaled Score

SSAT Practice Test One: Quantitative (Two Sections)
Section 1   Section 2

	Correct Answers	Wrong Answers	Skipped Answers		Correct Answers	Wrong Answers	Skipped Answers
1.				1.			
2.				2.			
3.				3.			
4.				4.			
5.				5.			
6.				6.			
7.				7.			
8.				8.			
9.				9.			
10.				10.			
11.				11.			
12.				12.			
13.				13.			
14.				14.			
15.				15.			
16.				16.			
17.				17.			
18.				18.			
19.				19.			
20.				20.			
21.				21.			
22.				22.			
23.				23.			
24.				24.			
25.				25.			

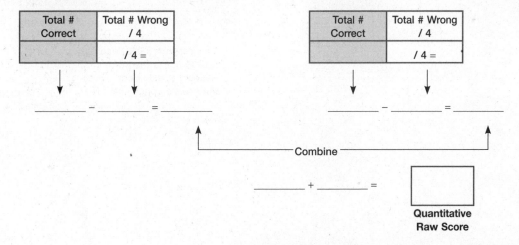

Total # Correct	Total # Wrong / 4
	/ 4 =

Total # Correct	Total # Wrong / 4
	/ 4 =

_____ − _____ = _____   _____ − _____ = _____

————————————— Combine —————————————

_____ + _____ =

Quantitative Raw Score

Convert your SSAT Quantitative Raw Score to the SSAT Quantitative Scaled Score using the chart on page 480:

Quantitative Scaled Score

SSAT Practice Test One: Reading (One Section)

	Correct Answers	Wrong Answers	Skipped Answers
1.			
2.			
3.			
4.			
5.			
6.			
7.			
8.			
9.			
10.			
11.			
12.			
13.			
14.			
15.			
16.			
17.			
18.			
19.			
20.			
21.			
22.			
23.			
24.			
25.			

	Correct Answers	Wrong Answers	Skipped Answers
26.			
27.			
28.			
29.			
30.			
31.			
32.			
33.			
34.			
35.			
36.			
37.			
38.			
39.			
40.			

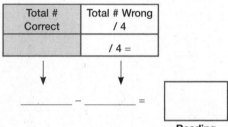

Total # Correct	Total # Wrong / 4
	/ 4 =

_____ – _____ =

Reading Raw Score

Convert your SSAT Reading Raw Score to the SSAT Reading Scaled Score using the chart on page 480:

Reading Scaled Score

SSAT Practice Test Two: Verbal (One Section)

	Correct Answers	Wrong Answers	Skipped Answers
1.			
2.			
3.			
4.			
5.			
6.			
7.			
8.			
9.			
10.			
11.			
12.			
13.			
14.			
15.			
16.			
17.			
18.			
19.			
20.			
21.			
22.			
23.			
24.			
25.			
26.			
27.			
28.			
29.			
30.			
31.			
32.			
33.			
34.			
35.			
36.			
37.			
38.			
39.			
40.			

	Correct Answers	Wrong Answers	Skipped Answers
41.			
42.			
43.			
44.			
45.			
46.			
47.			
48.			
49.			
50.			
51.			
52.			
53.			
54.			
55.			
56.			
57.			
58.			
59.			
60.			

Total # Correct	Total # Wrong / 4
	/ 4 =

_____ – _____ =

Verbal Raw Score

Convert your SSAT Verbal Raw Score to the SSAT Verbal Scaled Score using the chart on page 480:

Verbal Scaled Score

SSAT Practice Test Two: Quantitative (Two Sections)
Section 1   Section 2

Correct Answers	Wrong Answers	Skipped Answers		Correct Answers	Wrong Answers	Skipped Answers
1.				1.		
2.				2.		
3.				3.		
4.				4.		
5.				5.		
6.				6.		
7.				7.		
8.				8.		
9.				9.		
10.				10.		
11.				11.		
12.				12.		
13.				13.		
14.				14.		
15.				15.		
16.				16.		
17.				17.		
18.				18.		
19.				19.		
20.				20.		
21.				21.		
22.				22.		
23.				23.		
24.				24.		
25.				25.		

Total # Correct	Total # Wrong / 4		Total # Correct	Total # Wrong / 4
	/ 4 =			/ 4 =

_____ − _____ = _____   _____ − _____ = _____

Combine

_____ + _____ =   [Quantitative Raw Score]

Convert your SSAT Quantitative Raw Score to the SSAT Quantitative Scaled Score using the chart on page 480:   [Quantitative Scaled Score]

SSAT Practice Test Two: Reading (One Section)

	Correct Answers	Wrong Answers	Skipped Answers
1.			
2.			
3.			
4.			
5.			
6.			
7.			
8.			
9.			
10.			
11.			
12.			
13.			
14.			
15.			
16.			
17.			
18.			
19.			
20.			
21.			
22.			
23.			
24.			
25.			

	Correct Answers	Wrong Answers	Skipped Answers
26.			
27.			
28.			
29.			
30.			
31.			
32.			
33.			
34.			
35.			
36.			
37.			
38.			
39.			
40.			

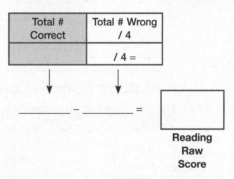

Total # Correct	Total # Wrong / 4
	/ 4 =

_____ − _____ =

Reading Raw Score

Convert your SSAT Reading Raw Score to the SSAT Reading Scaled Score using the chart on page 480:

Reading Scaled Score

SSAT Upper-Level Scaled Score

Raw Score	Reading	Verbal	Quantitative
60		800	
55		800	
50		779	800
45		752	782
40	800	725	755
35	722	698	725
30	692	671	698
25	662	644	668
20	632	617	641
15	602	590	614
10	572	563	584
5	542	533	557
0	512	506	530
−5 and lower	500	500	500

Median 50th Percentile

	Reading	Verbal	Quantitative
Grade 8	647	660	676
Grade 9	653	667	699
Grade 10	659	670	705
Grade 11	647	656	704

HOW TO SCORE YOUR ISEE PRACTICE TEST

Now that you've finished your Practice Test, let's see how you did. Compare your answer sheet to the answer key provided, and correct your test. (Make sure you're using the Practice Test One Answer sheet to check your Practice Test One Answers.)

Now, let's calculate your Raw Score. Get out your ISEE Practice Test One Answer Sheet (on page 484). Starting with the Verbal Reasoning section, go through the form, writing a "yes" next to each number of the questions you got correct; leave the boxes blank if you skipped or missed any questions. Then, total the number of "yes" indicators at the bottom of the Verbal Reasoning column. Repeat the process for each of the other columns. You should end up with four final Raw Scores at the bottom of your Scoring Sheet. Check out the sample below to make sure you're doing it right. (**Note:** we're assuming that all answers on this sample not shown on this chart due to condensing it are correct.)

Verbal Reasoning		Quantitative Reasoning		Reading Comprehension		Mathematics Achievement	
	Correct?		Correct?		Correct?		Correct?
1.	Yes	1.	Yes	1.	Yes	1.	
2.		2.	Yes	2.	Yes	2.	Yes
3.	Yes	3.	Yes	3.	Yes	3.	
4.	Yes	4.		4.	Yes	4.	Yes
5.	Yes	5.	Yes	5.	Yes	5.	Yes
6.		6.	Yes	6.	Yes	6.	Yes
7.	Yes	7.	Yes	7.	Yes	7.	Yes
8.	Yes	8.	Yes	8.	Yes	8.	Yes
...		...		...		...	
34.	Yes	34.	Yes	34.	Yes	34.	
35.		35.	Yes	35.	Yes	35.	
36.		36.		36.	Yes	36.	Yes
37.	Yes	37.				37.	Yes
38.	Yes					38.	Yes
39.	Yes					39.	
40.	Yes					40.	Yes
						41.	Yes
						42.	
						43.	Yes
						44.	Yes
						45.	Yes
						46.	
						47.	

Total Correct: (Raw Score) 36   Total Correct: (Raw Score) 34   Total Correct: (Raw Score) 36   Total Correct: (Raw Score) 39

Knowing your Raw Score isn't enough however; you need to know how these Raw Scores translate into the Scaled Scores that the ERB sends out to your prospective schools. Go to page 486, where you will find a chart of scaled scores. Locate the number on the Verbal Reasoning Scaled Scores chart that matches the number of correct answers you got on the Verbal Reasoning section of the Practice Test (i.e., your Verbal Reasoning Raw Score). Repeat this process for each of the remaining sections of the Practice Exam.

Using our sample Scoring Sheet above, you would locate the number 36 on the Verbal Reasoning Scaled Score chart, the number 34 on the Quantitative Reasoning Scaled Score chart, the number 36 on the Reading Comprehension Scaled Score chart, and the number 39 on the Mathematic Achievement Scaled Score chart. Check out the following chart for how this plays out:

Practice Test	Raw Score		ISEE Scaled Score Range
Verbal Reasoning	36	. . . is	913–928
Quantitative Reasoning	34	equivalent	922–937
Reading Comprehension	38	to . . .	919–934
Mathematics Achievement	39		915–930

At this point, you might be wondering why we are presenting your final ISEE Scaled Score as a range rather than a single number. Good question! The reason is that, despite the fact that we have presented you with an outstanding set of Practice Tests with which to prepare for the ISEE, they are not, after all, and cannot ever be, *actual* ISEE exams. Small variations take place in testing format and frequency of question type that make it impossible for us to state without doubt what your likely score would be. And so, we have provided the best approximation of the score you would likely get when taking an actual ISEE. In any case, you can rest assured that the more answers you get right, the higher your score will be. Aim for perfection and do your best in the process!

Now you try. Figure your scores and record the results here.

Practice Test	Raw Score		ISEE Scaled Score Range
Verbal Reasoning		. . . is	
Quantitative Reasoning		equivalent	
Reading Comprehension		to . . .	
Mathematics Achievement			

THINKING ABOUT YOUR SCORES

Now that you have a sense of what your ISEE score would likely be, you might like to compare your performance to other students like you taking the exam. Look at the bottom of the ISEE Scaled Score chart to find the Percentiles section. We've reprinted this section on the next page for your convenience.

Verbal Reasoning				Quantitative Reasoning		
	Percentiles				Percentiles	
	75th	50th	25th		75th	50th	25th
8th grade	889	876	861		891	877	862
9th grade	894	880	865		894	880	864
10th grade	897	886	869		901	884	867
Reading Comprehension				**Mathematics Achievement**		
	Percentiles				Percentiles	
	75th	50th	25th		75th	50th	25th
	897	883	869		894	879	865
	901	888	872		899	884	869
	906	891	875		905	889	871

According to this data, if you are a ninth grader who scored an 880 on the Verbal Reasoning Scaled Score, you will have performed better than 50 percent of other students taking the ISEE. If you are a ninth grader who earned a 916 on the Verbal Reasoning Scaled Score, you will have performed better than 75 percent of other students taking the ISEE.

A FEW FINAL WORDS

As our time together is now drawing to a close, we would like to leave you with a bit of advice; advice that we've said earlier in this book but bears repeating at this stage of the game. First, don't get discouraged by the testing experience. A wide range of students take the ISEE, and so the ISEE asks questions that cross over a wide range of skills and topics. However, your scores will only be compared to the scores of students in your grade who are likely learning these skills at the same rate you are. In other words, the scores of an eighth grader will not be compared to those of a ninth grader. Second, your ISEE scores are only part of any school administration process. Many other factors, including that essay we talked about, affect your ability to get into the school of your choice.

All in all, if you're discouraged in any way regarding your scores on these Practice Exams, take heart. Review the study tips and advice back in the Introduction, and focus on doing your best on the actual exam day. Isn't that what practice is for? Identifying the weak spots so as to shore them up?

We wish you the best. Good luck and study hard!

ISEE Practice Test One Scoring Sheet (Raw Score)

Verbal Reasoning	Correct?	Quantitative Reasoning	Correct?	Reading Comprehension	Correct?	Mathematics Achievement	Correct?
1.		1.		1.		1.	
2.		2.		2.		2.	
3.		3.		3.		3.	
4.		4.		4.		4.	
5.		5.		5.		5.	
6.		6.		6.		6.	
7.		7.		7.		7.	
8.		8.		8.		8.	
9.		9.		9.		9.	
10.		10.		10.		10.	
11.		11.		11.		11.	
12.		12.		12.		12.	
13.		13.		13.		13.	
14.		14.		14.		14.	
15.		15.		15.		15.	
16.		16.		16.		16.	
17.		17.		17.		17.	
18.		18.		18.		18.	
19.		19.		19.		19.	
20.		20.		20.		20.	
21.		21.		21.		21.	
22.		22.		22.		22.	
23.		23.		23.		23.	
24.		24.		24.		24.	
25.		25.		25.		25.	
26.		26.		26.		26.	
27.		27.		27.		27.	
28.		28.		28.		28.	
29.		29.		29.		29.	
30.		30.		30.		30.	
31.		31.		31.		31.	
32.		32.		32.		32.	
33.		33.		33.		33.	
34.		34.		34.		34.	
35.		35.		35.		35.	
36.		36.		36.		36.	
37.		37.				37.	
38.						38.	
39.						39.	
40.						40.	
						41.	
						42.	
						43.	
						44.	
						45.	
						46.	
						47.	

Total Correct:
(Raw Score) ☐

Total Correct:
(Raw Score) ☐

Total Correct:
(Raw Score) ☐

Total Correct:
(Raw Score) ☐

ISEE Practice Test Two Scoring Sheet (Raw Score)

Verbal Reasoning	Quantitative Reasoning	Reading Comprehension	Mathematics Achievement
Correct?	Correct?	Correct?	Correct?
1.	1.	1.	1.
2.	2.	2.	2.
3.	3.	3.	3.
4.	4.	4.	4.
5.	5.	5.	5.
6.	6.	6.	6.
7.	7.	7.	7.
8.	8.	8.	8.
9.	9.	9.	9.
10.	10.	10.	10.
11.	11.	11.	11.
12.	12.	12.	12.
13.	13.	13.	13.
14.	14.	14.	14.
15.	15.	15.	15.
16.	16.	16.	16.
17.	17.	17.	17.
18.	18.	18.	18.
19.	19.	19.	19.
20.	20.	20.	20.
21.	21.	21.	21.
22.	22.	22.	22.
23.	23.	23.	23.
24.	24.	24.	24.
25.	25.	25.	25.
26.	26.	26.	26.
27.	27.	27.	27.
28.	28.	28.	28.
29.	29.	29.	29.
30.	30.	30.	30.
31.	31.	31.	31.
32.	32.	32.	32.
33.	33.	33.	33.
34.	34.	34.	34.
35.	35.	35.	35.
36.	36.	36.	36.
37.	37.		37.
38.			38.
39.			39.
40.			40.
			41.
			42.
			43.
			44.
			45.
			46.
			47.

Total Correct: (Raw Score)	Total Correct: (Raw Score)	Total Correct: (Raw Score)	Total Correct: (Raw Score)

1999 ISEE Practice Test Upper-Level Scaled Scores (MIN = 760 and MAX = 940)

Verbal Reasoning		Quantitative Reasoning		Reading Comprehension		Mathematics Achievement	
Raw Score	Range*	Raw Score	Range*	Raw Score	Range*	Raw Score	Range*
40	940	35–37	940	36	940	45–47	940
39	922–937	34	922–937	35	923–938	44	925–940
38	919–934	33	919–934	34	922–937	43	924–939
37	916–931	32	916–931	33	920–935	42	924–939
36	913–928	31	912–927	32	919–934	41	921–936
35	910–925	30	909–924	31	917–932	40	918–933
34	907–922	29	906–921	30	916–931	39	915–930
33	904–919	28	903–918	29	914–929	38	913–928
32	901–916	27	899–914	28	913–928	37	910–925
31	898–913	26	896–911	27	911–926	36	908–923
30	895–910	25	893–908	26	910–925	35	905–920
29	892–907	24	890–905	25	908–923	34	903–918
28	889–904	23	886–901	24	907–922	33	900–915
27	886–901	22	883–898	23	905–920	32	898–913
26	883–898	21	880–895	22	914–919	31	895–910
25	880–895	20	877–892	21	912–917	30	892–907
24	877–892	19	873–888	20	899–914	29	889–904
23	874–889	18	870–885	19	896–911	28	887–902
22	871–886	17	867–882	18	904–909	27	884–899
21	868–883	16	864–879	17	890–905	26	882–897
20	865–880	15	860–875	16	887–902	25	879–894
19	862–877	14	857–872	15	882–897	24	877–892
18	859–874	13	854–869	14	878–893	23	874–889
17	856–871	12	851–866	13	872–887	22	872–887
16	853–868	11	847–862	12	867–882	21	869–884
15	850–865	10	844–859	11	861–876	20	867–882
14	847–862	9	841–856	10	856–871	19	864–879
13	844–859	8	838–853	9	850–865	18	861–876
12	841–856	7	834–849	8	844–859	17	858–873
11	838–853	6	831–846	7	835–850	16	856–871
10	835–850	5	828–843	6	827–842	15	883–868
9	832–847	4	825–840	5	821–836	14	851–866
8	829–844	3	821–836	4	815–830	13	847–863
7	826–841	2	818–833	3	811–826	12	846–861
6	823–838	1	815–830	2	807–822	11	843–858
5	820–835	0	812–827	1	804–819	10	841–856
4	817–832			0	801–816	9	838–853
3	814–829					8	835–850
2	811–826					7	832–847
1	808–823					6	830–845
0	805–820					5	827–842
						4	825–840
						3	822–837
						2	820–835
						1	817–832
						0	815–830

Range is 15 points wide; range can be wider at some point. The results of taking an actual ISEE exam may vary slightly.

	Percentiles			Percentiles		
	75th	50th	25th	75th	50th	25th
8th grade	889	876	861	891	877	862
9th grade	894	880	865	894	880	864
10th grade	897	886	869	901	884	867
	Percentiles			Percentiles		
	75th	50th	25th	75th	50th	25th
8th grade	897	883	869	894	879	865
9th grade	901	888	872	899	884	869
10th grade	906	891	875	905	889	871

Index